UNDERSTANDING HOUSING POLICY

Also available in the series

Understanding the environment and social policy
Tony Fitzpatrick

"The intersection of social policy and environmental policy is strategically and morally vital yet has remained a strangely neglected area. No longer. This comprehensive book covers real world challenges, sustainable ethics, a host of applied policy issues, and some bigger questions about the possibility of a green welfare state." Ian Gough, Emeritus Professor, University of Bath

PB £21.99 (US$36.95) **ISBN** 978 1 84742 379 5 **HB** £65.00 (US$85.00) **ISBN** 978 1 84742 380 1
384 pages February 2011
INSPECTION COPY AVAILABLE

Understanding community
Politics, policy and practice
Peter Somerville

"In developing his conception of beloved community, Peter Somerville brings a fresh and radical perspective to communitarian theory and practice. This book will inspire and provoke readers in equal measure." Jonathan Davies, University of Warwick

PB £19.99 (US$34.95) **ISBN** 978 1 84742 392 4 **HB** £65.00 (US$85.00) **ISBN** 978 1 84742 393 1
304 pages February 2011
INSPECTION COPY AVAILABLE

Understanding social citizenship (second edition)
Themes and perspectives for policy and practice
Peter Dwyer

"A second edition of this excellent book is most welcome. Dwyer's understanding of social citizenship is second to none and this new edition provides an updated discussion and assessment of all the practical and theoretical issues that students need to know about this important area of study." Nick Ellison, University of Leeds

PB £19.99 (US$32.95) **ISBN** 978 1 84742 328 3 **HB** £65.00 (US$85.00) **ISBN** 978 1 84742 329 0
280 pages June 2010
INSPECTION COPY AVAILABLE

Understanding theories and concepts in social policy
Ruth Lister

"This is an admirably clear and comprehensive account of the theories and concepts of contemporary social policy. Excellent and essential for undergraduate and postgraduate social policy and social theory courses." Fiona Williams, Professor of Social Policy, University of Leeds

PB £19.99 (US$34.95) **ISBN** 978 1 86134 793 0 **HB** £60.00 (US$80.00) **ISBN** 978 1 86134 794 7
328 pages June 2010
INSPECTION COPY AVAILABLE

For a full listing of all titles in the series visit www.policypress.co.uk

www.policypress.co.uk

INSPECTION COPIES AND ORDERS AVAILABLE FROM:
Marston Book Services • PO Box 269 • Abingdon • Oxon OX14 4YN UK
INSPECTION COPIES
Tel: +44 (0) 1235 465500 • Fax: +44 (0) 1235 465556 • Email: inspections@marston.co.uk
ORDERS
Tel: +44 (0) 1235 465500 • Fax: +44 (0) 1235 465556 • Email: direct.orders@marston.co.uk

UNDERSTANDING HOUSING POLICY

Second Edition

Brian Lund

First published published in Great Britain in 2011 by
The Policy Press
University of Bristol
Fourth Floor, Beacon House
Queen's Road
Bristol BS8 1QU
UK

t: +44 (0)117 331 4054
f: +44 (0)117 331 4093
tpp-info@bristol.ac.uk
www.policypress.org.uk

North American office:
The Policy Press
c/o International Specialized Books Services
920 NE 58th Avenue, Suite 300
Portland, OR 97213-3786, USA
t: +1 503 287 3093
f: +1 503 280 8832
info@isbs.com

British Library Cataloguing in Publication Data
A catalogue record for this book is available from the British Library.

Library of Congress Cataloging-in-Publication Data
A catalog record for this book has been requested.

ISBN 978 1 84742 631 4 paperback
ISBN 978 1 84742 632 1 hardcover

Cover design by Qube Design Associates, Bristol
Front cover: photograph kindly supplied by www.alamy.com
Printed and bound in Great Britain by Hobbs, Southampton
The Policy Press uses environmentally responsible print partners

Contents

Detailed contents

List of boxes, figures and tables

Boxes

Figures

Tables

Preface to second edition

The first edition of this book was well received by both reviewers and students but a second edition was essential. When the first edition was published the housing market was buoyant, housing construction was accelerating and New Labour was making progress in upgrading the housing stock. Gordon Brown's elevation to the Labour Party leadership promised further improvement as he placed housing alongside health and education as a government priority and endorsed a target to increase new housing construction in England to 240,000 by 2016. Expansion plans were also set out for Scotland, Wales and Northern Ireland. Then came the 'credit crunch' and everything changed, not least the possibility that New Labour might win a fourth term in office. It did not. The 2010 general election produced a Conservative–Liberal Democrat Coalition government.

Housing policy is about why the state has intervened in the housing market, the forms this involvement has taken and the impact it has made. Chapter One sets out various theoretical approaches to understanding housing policy indicating how each approach carries assumptions about the nature of housing problems and how they ought to be tackled. Chapter Two is new and concerned with the political – often ignored in the housing literature – and the processes involved in constructing housing policy. Chapter Three explores housing policy development since the 19th century and Chapter Four sets out the contemporary institutional context within which housing policy is generated and delivered (students may prefer to read Chapters Three and Four first). A comparative dimension is added in Chapter Five with the accounts of housing policy in selected countries aimed at highlighting the impact of the specific national contexts in which housing policy has developed. Chapter Six explores the 'affordability' idea and the various ways the state has attempted to reduce housing consumption costs to below market prices. Homelessness is discussed in Chapter Seven in the context of the different meanings attributed to the term and the ways these meanings have been reflected in policy.

In the 2000s, only 1% was added to the housing pool each year, demonstrating the salience of ensuring that new construction meets future requirements and the importance of keeping the existing stock in good condition. This is the subject of Chapter Eight on 'decent and sustainable homes'. Overcrowding and single dwellings in multiple occupation are also analysed in this chapter, with overcrowding identified as a neglected social condition. Chapter Nine explores 'low demand', a term applied in the mid-2000s to an issue that has also been labelled 'problem estates', 'unpopular housing' and 'deprived neighbourhoods'.

In the past, housing problems have tended to be identified as pathological conditions that can be remedied without too much disruption to the existing social and economic order. Chapter Ten, using the notions of class, gender, ethnicity and disability, offers a different standpoint and examines what is problematic from a social justice perspective. The conclusion is a personal and, at times, polemical reflection on the lessons – drawn from the past – that might be applied to the future.

Housing policy changes quickly as governments respond to the rollercoaster housing market, but the numerous websites and other references cited in the book should enable students to keep up to date. In common with most textbook authors, I have left out far more than I have put in. Nonetheless, responsibility for any errors and omissions remains mine.

Acknowledgements

Thanks are due to a number of people who have contributed to the publication of this book. I am grateful to staff at The Policy Press for their help and I would like to thank all the people in the housing policy community whose work has made this publication possible. My more personal gratitude is to Sukey, Daniel, Rachel, Milligan and Stanley for their continual support and encouragement.

one

Understanding housing policy

Summary

- Housing policy is concerned with the processes involved in state intervention in the housing market.
- There are a number of approaches to studying housing policy each containing:
  - a normative order against which housing problems are identified;
  - explanations of the causes of housing problems; and
  - accounts of why and how the state has intervened in the housing market.
- This chapter examines five approaches to understanding housing policy:
  - laissez-faire economics;
  - social reformism;
  - Marxist political economy;
  - behavioural approaches; and
  - social constructionism.

What is housing policy?

Housing was once described as 'the wobbly pillar under the welfare state' (Torgersen, 1987, p 116) because, unlike health and education, the state has not seen its role as the main provider. Indeed, housing is intrinsically different to education and health care in that it represents a 'home' rather than a locale for a temporary activity such as 'going to school' or 'entering hospital'. Nevertheless, although housing in the UK has not had the status of a 'universal' social service to be distributed primarily according to 'need', the state has intervened extensively in the housing market. Thus, housing policy is best understood as attempts by governments to modify the housing market or, perhaps more accurately, housing markets (there being marked regional and local variations in supply and demand) to achieve social objectives. The Conservative–Liberal Democrat Coalition government stated that it wanted to:

- increase the number of houses available to buy and rent, including affordable housing;
- improve the flexibility of social housing (increasing mobility and choice) and promote homeownership;
- protect the vulnerable and disadvantaged by tackling homelessness and supporting people to stay in their homes; and
- make sure that homes are of high quality and sustainable (DCL, 2010a).

The Scottish Government has declared its mission as 'Everyone should have a safe, warm home which they can afford' (Scottish Government, 2010a, p 1).

This book adopts a broad view of housing policy as involving:

- financial policies designed to increase or reduce the costs of house purchase – often related to national economic management, for example, setting interest rates;
- taxation measures aimed at encouraging or discouraging housing investment and consumption, for example, Stamp Duty Tax, payable on purchasing a house, which can be changed either to stimulate or depress the housing market;
- the basis on which people have rights and obligations in a dwelling – sometimes called 'tenure' (see **Box 1.1**);
- direct subsidies to producers and consumers;
- infrastructure support for housing construction such as the roads and schools necessary to make developments sustainable;
- community care policy, for example, 'supported' housing and home improvement agencies;
- physical planning constraints and incentives;
- supply, allocation and management policies in the social housing sector;
- security for the 'quiet enjoyment' of a 'home' and the lifestyle choices that such security promotes;
- 'social capital', that is, the value of the social networks people can draw on that may accrue from living in a neighbourhood; and
- housing-related policies aimed at reducing 'social exclusion'.

Box 1.1: Tenure

In the past 'tenure' was related to privileges and duties involved in land possession, but today it is usually used to refer to the rights and obligations involved in occupying a dwelling. In the UK it is conventional to identify four main types of tenure although these do not correspond to precise legal formats.

- **Owner-occupation:** where the occupier owns the land freehold or, as a leaseholder, rents land for a specified period after which the land and the dwelling revert to the freeholder.
- **Renting from a local authority as a 'secure' tenant:** where the tenant has a right to buy the property and protection from eviction if the tenancy agreement is kept. However, under Coalition government proposals, new tenants of local authorities will have more limited security of tenure.
- **Renting from a private landlord:** usually as an 'assured shorthold' tenant with the presumption that the landlord has the right to possession at the end of an agreement.
- **Renting from a not-for-profit landlord:** often called a 'housing association' or, when subject to regulation, a 'registered social landlord'. Housing association tenancies are often 'assured' tenancies that give tenants greater security than 'assured shorthold' tenancies, but, under Coalition government proposals, the security offered will change (see chapter 11).

Understanding housing policy

Any taxonomy of the perspectives applied to understanding housing policy is open to dissent and many classifications are available (e.g. Lister, 2010). The perspectives identified later contain normative orders against which housing problems are recognised, including notions of what causes housing problems and accounts of why and how the state has intervened to overcome the acknowledged problems (see Chapter Two). Today, various 'think tanks' work within the perspectives, converting the underlying ideas into policies to offer political parties and promoting 'epistemic communities' – networks of knowledge-based experts who claim authority via relevant knowledge and who share common causal notions and evaluative criteria.

Laissez-faire economics

Being a revival of 18th-century classical economic theories, this approach is sometimes called 'neoclassical economics', 'neoliberalism' or the 'New Right'. Following the basic premises set out by Adam Smith in his treatise on *An Inquiry into the Nature and Causes of the Wealth of Nations* (Smith, 1970 [1776]), laissez-faire economists assert that:

- free exchange promotes the division and specialisation of labour allowing individuals to concentrate on producing the goods they are most suited to create;
- the state should confine itself to doing what only the state can do – the maintenance of law and order, the policing of contracts and the production of large infrastructure projects, which it can never be in the interest of any individual to construct; and
- because individuals are rational maximisers of their self-interest, if the state obeys these rules, then the market's 'hidden hand' will promote everyone's welfare.

Laissez-faire economics dominated housing policy for most of the 19th century. State involvement in the housing market embraced removing 'nuisances' to protect public health and promote social order, but not stimulating housing production by direct state provision or state subsidies. During the 20th century, economic liberalism was on the defensive as the state assumed a larger role in shaping and partially replacing the housing market through subsidised local authority housing, improvement grants, rent control and creating a favourable tax regime to support homeownership. Friedrich Von Hayek was the most important figure in restoring 'free market' ideas. He embraced Adam Smith's 'laissez-faire' ideas, added lessons drawn from the experience of state intervention and set out proposals for renewing the application of market principles. The Institute of Economic Affairs, a 'think tank' established in 1957, converted Hayek's beliefs into concrete policy proposals and, by the mid-1970s, a developed philosophical critique of 'unjustified' state activities in the housing market plus a set of remedies was available.

Market efficiency

Laissez-faire theorists believe that housing is a commodity with no intrinsic merit: a dwelling's value is its exchange price as determined by the interaction between supply and demand. Consumers have different views about how much to spend on housing and different preferences about style, location and amenities. The price of a house reflects its value according to consumer preferences and the alternative uses of the resources deployed in its construction, that is, the other ways the site, labour and materials could be exploited. Laissez-faire economics asserts that 'asset prices are *always and everywhere* at the correct price' (Cooper, 2008, p 9; emphasis original). There is no such thing as an irrational price 'bubble' – a sudden price increase is simply the market responding to changing fundamentals. Markets benefit low-income groups via 'filtering'. If higher-income groups purchase new homes this leaves vacancies that are filled by lower-income households, and so on down the chain until the least well-housed households improve their circumstances. Filtering theory was popular in the 19th century and has been recently revived with, for example, the Policy Exchange – a right-wing 'think tank' – claiming that subsidised social housing matters far less than total new housing production (Morton, 2010).

The New Right allows only two exceptions to the rule that the state should 'leave to be'. First, the state can eliminate externalities. An externality is a side impact of an activity that affects other parties without being reflected in the price of the good or service involved. Slum dwellings, for example, generate externalities because they affect the health of people living *outside* the slum and thus they can be demolished at public expense. Writing in 1841, Nassau Senior, a prominent free market advocate, put the matter plainly when he said:

> With all our reverence for the principle of non-interference, we cannot doubt that in this matter [slums] it has been pushed too far. We believe that both the ground landlord and the speculating builder ought to be compelled by law ... to take measures which will prevent the towns which they create from being the centre of disease. (quoted in Holmans, 1987, p 25)

Second, some market economic theorists permit an income subsidy to the poor to enable them to afford a minimum housing standard supplied by the market.

Market distortions

The laissez-faire economic approach claims that state intervention in the housing market has caused more problems than it has solved. Rent control and subsidised council housing are the primary culprits. Rent control was introduced in 1915 but, after 1989, was gradually phased out. According to the New Right, rent control had the following undesirable consequences:

- it prevented private savers investing in new houses to let;
- it limited labour mobility because workers benefiting from rent control were reluctant to move and thereby lose their protected status; and
- it produced underinvestment by landlords in their properties.

Subsidised council housing is also regarded as part of the housing problem rather than part of its solution (see **Box 1.2**), and some neoclassical economists condemn the physical planning system for restricting land supply and thereby pushing up house prices and increasing overcrowding and homelessness (Evans, 1988).

Box 1.2: Hayek on subsidised council housing

Hayek presents the most polished exposition of the case against state provision of subsidised dwellings. He argues that:

> The old buildings which at most stages of the growth of a city will exist at the centre ... will often provide for those of low productivity an opportunity to benefit from what the city offers at the price of very congested living. (Hayek 1960, pp 346–7)

So, says Hayek:

> If we want to abolish the slums we must choose between two alternatives. We must either prevent these people from taking advantage of what to them is part of their opportunity, by removing the cheap but squalid dwellings from where their earning opportunities lie, and effectively squeeze them out of the cities by insisting on certain minimum standards for all town dwellings; or we must provide them with better facilities at a price which does not cover costs and thus subsidise both their staying in the city and the movement of more people into the city of the same kind. (Hayek, 1960, p 348)

Hence, according to Hayek, subsidised council housing promotes the movement of poor people into areas where they cannot afford to live without subsidy. Once subsidised council housing has been provided more people move to an area to try to take advantage of the new, low-cost housing opportunities thereby promoting further urban growth and pressures for yet more subsidised council housing.

Government failure

The New Right believe that state intervention in the housing market not only generates problems, but that state housing supply is likely to be inefficient. Only competition can supply the incentives necessary for efficiency and, if the state becomes a monopoly accommodation supplier, as it did for family rented housing in the 1970s, then it is bound to be inefficient.

Social reformism

Social reformism is a sweeping term but it serves to connect strands of thought that have combined, fragmented and coalesced at various times during the 19th and 20th centuries. There were two main elements in the development of social reformism. Social liberalism and Fabian socialism emerged at the end of the 19th century and both claimed that capitalist economies produce unjust outcomes. During the 20th century, Fabian socialism and social liberalism fused into a broad social–democratic, reformist approach that emphasised the gradual improvement achievable by tackling specific social problems through state action. Today, social reformists maintain that housing has special characteristics which, taken together, mean that markets will not operate efficiently (see *Box 1.3*).

Box 1.3: Why is housing 'special'?

- Housing is expensive relative to incomes and the requirement for independent accommodation comes at an inconvenient time in the lifespan before people have been able to accumulate wealth. Thus, purchasing a home usually involves borrowing from institutional lenders who may have the power to influence market operations, for example, in the 1970s some building societies 'red-lined' certain districts where they were unwilling to lend because they perceived such areas as bad risks. Borrowing also means that homeowners' outgoings are strongly influenced by interest rates especially if variable rate loans are used.
- Houses are durable and therefore have a value for future generations. Anticipating the future may involve building to high standards that existing consumers cannot afford. House durability also means that a house is both a 'consumer' good, with a flow of services involved in living in a house, and an 'investment' good with potential gains achievable from price increases.
- Housing supply is inelastic. The best year for UK house-building (1968) added only about 2% to the housing stock. Hence, the housing market is 'made' by the existing supply of dwellings. Moreover, the house-building process takes a long time and, therefore, supply may not respond quickly to changes in demand.
- The housing stock is immobile (well, almost – 8% of homes in the USA are 'mobile'). This means that it offers solid security for lenders – you cannot run away with it. However, there is limited opportunity to switch existing

---

> supply to areas of new demand, reflected, in part, in wide variations in house prices in different parts of the country.
> * Houses are built on land, which is an absolute scare resource, made scarcer by planning controls. Thus land supply is not automatically responsive to demand. In the UK 1995–2007 housing boom, the real price of residential land rose by 260%, but its supply fell by 19% (Aldred, 2010).
> * Housing is a necessity. People cannot opt out of consumption and, unlike other goods, it is difficult to vary consumption on a day-by-day basis.

In addition, social reformists argue that the market is incapable of resolving certain housing issues. Glennerster (2009), for example, extends the 'externalities' idea to cover the following:

* Clustering of poor accommodation in an area making it imprudent for individual owners to improve their property. Property values do not increase because shoddy property sends bad 'signals' about an area. Whole area improvement by collective action can spark a 'virtuous circle' of revival, but this can lead to undeserved 'betterment' gain.
* Unfettered building may produce urban sprawl, leaving city centres without populations and prone to crime. Existing urban infrastructure assets are wasted and journeys to work are long.
* The unregulated market can polarise communities. It excludes the poor from areas where the middle class or the rich wish to live. This produces ghettos – possible breeding grounds for crime and disorder.

Some social reformists go further and claim that housing, good enough to be called a 'home', is so fundamental to forming personal integrity that it should be regarded as a 'merit' good. Housing consumption should be encouraged by the state because income levels generated by market transactions will be insufficient for many to afford the 'decent' housing necessary for character development. Moreover, many consumers may be unwilling to purchase appropriate quantities of housing.

Marxist political economy

Marxist political economy maintains that relationships between individuals and social institutions are determined by the production mode used in a particular society. Capitalism is a form of production based on two classes: a capitalist class (bourgeoisie) owning the means of production and a proletariat or working class that, because it does not own capital, is forced to work for the bourgeoisie in order to subsist. Whereas Fabian socialists and social liberals believe that capitalist exploitation is partial, to Marxists it is total. This exploitative economic relationship is the real foundation of all other legal, political and ideological 'superstructures', including the state.

When applied to housing this approach generates a number of propositions:

- The real exploitation of the worker takes place at the point of production when building workers are paid less for their labour than the exchange (market) value of the houses they create. In addition, since housing has particular characteristics as a commodity – it is expensive to produce relative to worker earnings – then special institutions are necessary to *realise* the value of the house. These institutions – banks, private landlords and so on – spread the housing costs over the worker's lifetime. By demanding a share of the surplus value created when houses are constructed 'exchange institutions' add to working-class exploitation.
- There are factions of housing capital with different shortterm interests but the same longterm interest in ensuring that the capitalist system continues. Industrial capital wants to ensure that its workers can be housed at minimal cost; land capital wants to maintain high land values; and development capital wants to secure access to cheap land. Unrestricted competition between the various capital factions may undermine the overall system, so it is the state's business to ensure that the activities of the factions of capital are complementary rather than contradictory. Thus, the state uses its power to assist the development process in an attempt to ensure maximum profitability for all.
- Capitalism needs a contented, efficient labour force and a 'reserve army of labour' that can be injected into the economy when required and ejected when superfluous. State housing policy aims at providing such a flexible, efficient workforce – to 'reproduce labour power' in ways that reflect capitalist values. Homeownership – designed to convince working people that they have an investment stake in capitalism, to promote an ethic of 'possessive individualism' and to provide the 'psychic' benefits of security, independence and respectability – will be encouraged. Only standardised, cheap housing, linked to producing a physically efficient labour force, will be available to those unable to pay the market price.
- Housing has an 'exchange' value to capitalists – its efficiency in generating profits – but a 'use' value in meeting human needs to the working class. Therefore, in a market capitalist economy, housing will be affected by its investment value as well as by the 'need' for accommodation.
- 'Capitalist rule cannot allow itself the pleasure of creating epidemic diseases among the working class with importunity; the consequences fall back on it and the angel of death rages in its ranks as ruthlessly as

in the ranks of the workers' (Engels, 1872). Thus, attempts will be made to eradicate 'plague spots' to protect the bourgeoisie but, given that the housing conditions of the poorest members of the working class are determined by the wages paid in the capitalist system, such action merely displaces the problem elsewhere.

Marx abandoned systematic thinking about the nature of society under communism at an early stage of his intellectual development arguing that 'it is not the consciousness of men that determines their being, but on the contrary, their social being that determines their consciousness' (Marx, 1859, p 5). New organisations would emerge only from the new economic relationships created by ending capitalism. He predicted that, after capitalism's demise, there would be a transitional stage based on working-class domination of the state, but that eventually the state would 'wither away' and communism – the organisation of production and distribution by self-managing 'communes' – would emerge.

Behavioural approaches

The approaches to understanding housing policy examined so far have been 'structural' in that the causes of housing problems are located in the ways the economic and social systems operate. In contrast, there is long tradition in thinking about housing issues that places the blame for housing problems on how some of its occupants behave. This approach can be traced to the theories of Malthus who, in his *An Essay on the Principle of Population* (1803), argued that, because population increases in geometrical ratio whereas agricultural production grows only arithmetically, the consequences of unrestrained population growth would be famine and disease. Malthus advocated 'moral restraint' – delayed marriage – as the check on population growth and, to the extent that the labouring classes did not practise such restraint, then they were to blame for famine, disease and destitution. Towards the end of the 19th century, behavioural approaches to explaining housing problems became very influential as attempts to mitigate the housing conditions of the urban working class were linked to improving 'character'.

During the 20th century, behavioural approaches became subservient to structural approaches in explaining housing problems. In the 1980s, however, they returned to prominence as 'underclass' theories. In *Losing Ground* (Murray, 1984), Charles Murray asserted that an 'underclass' had developed in the United States characterised by young females reliant on state welfare to maintain their children and young males, separated from the necessity to support their offspring, adopting a lifestyle of crime and irresponsibility. He applied the 'underclass' idea to Britain claiming to have recognised similar trends – escalating illegitimacy, rising crime and a growing aversion to work (Murray, 1992). Other authors have identified a tendency for the 'underclass' to become concentrated in certain areas, thereby compounding the impact of their behaviour (Anderson, 1992; Hill, 2003).

Although often associated with the New Right and labelled 'neo-conservatism', the behavioural approach also featured in Marxism and has been a strong undercurrent in social reformism. Marx referred to the 'lumpen-proletariat' as a 'passive putrefaction of the lowest strata of the old society' (Marx, 1948, cited in Bovenkirk, 1984) and the 'New Liberals' and Fabian socialists identified a 'residuum' requiring 'over-parenting' to improve their conduct. Tony Blair adopted the behavioural approach. In 1997 he said:

> I have chosen this housing estate to deliver my first speech as Prime Minister….There is a case not just in moral terms but in enlightened self-interest to act, to tackle what we all know exists – an underclass of people cut off from society's mainstream, without any sense of shared purpose. The basis of this modern civic society is an ethic of mutual responsibility or duty….You only take out if you put in. (Blair, 1997a)

New Labour quickly dropped the term 'underclass' from its lexicon, but the notion that rights had to be accompanied by obligations – if necessary by enforced fulfilment – was a recurring theme in housing policy during New Labour's term in office, and David Cameron's notion of a 'broken society' contains 'underclass' elements.

Social constructionism

The dominant approaches to understanding housing policy have tended to assume that the problems it addresses are objective and self-evident and that different governments respond to these problems according to their ideological tendencies (Jacobs et al, 2003a). In contrast, social constructionism focuses on 'What's the problem?' and asserts that housing problems are not obvious, and 'out there' waiting to be exposed. Rather they are constructed through the social processes of claims-making via problem definition and attaching causal notions to a problem. Thus, when used as a noun, 'housing' simply means 'houses', but when used as a verb, 'housing' refers to a process or activity, to quote one dictionary definition, 'to take or put into a house' (Wordnet, 2004). This 'taking and putting' process involves a number of stages whereby housing conditions *become* housing problems and policy develops from the causative notions *attributed* to these problems.

Social constructionism is a dimension of the postmodernist thinking that came to prominence in the 1980s. Social constructionism challenges 'modern' thinking by questioning global, all-encompassing, rational views that claim to capture objective knowledge of reality. In its most zealous form – sometimes called the 'strong' version – social constructionism rejects the notion of 'essentialism' – the idea that the external world exists independently of our representations of it. Its objective is to supply an account of the processes by which phenomena are socially constructed and thereby expose the ways in which certain understandings have become privileged and regarded as 'the truth'. Social constructionism's key concepts are 'meaning' and 'power'. According to the approach, language, codified into 'discourses', is the key to meaning. These 'discourses' – systems of knowledge – classify and order events and persons and give some groups power over others because 'dominant discourses' frame the image and often the self-perception of the 'subjects' of the discourses (see ***Box 1.4***). Social constructionism provides a vehicle for examining what Foucault has called 'governmentality' – the ways in which governing takes place without seeming to govern. Power is exercised by the creation of 'technologies of the self' whereby people absorb socially constructed norms of 'responsible' conduct (Foucault, 1991).

Box 1.4: The social construction of homelessness

In *Citizen Hobo: How a Century of Homelessness Shaped America* (2003), Todd Depastino explores how different labels are applied to homeless people at different times creating changing 'welfare subjects' – 'tramp', 'hobohemian', 'transient', 'skid row bum' – which reflect the shifting concerns of American society. All the terms applied were 'discourses' on a lifestyle rather than descriptions of the condition of lacking shelter. These dominant 'discourses' were not always shared by their 'subjects'. For many hobos an 'unsettled way of living' was an acceptable, even attractive, way of life – 'a civilisation without a home' – to quote a title chapter in Depastino's book. It took a significant expansion of the American welfare state after the Second World War in the form of subsidised mortgages, unemployment compensation and grants for higher and vocational education to ensure that many of the returning GIs did not go back to their former hobo way of life. Dominant discourses on homelessness as an unnatural, pathological way of life triumphed when the 'hobohemians' accepted this representation of their condition.

The social constructionists' claim that we cannot know reality apart from our interpretation of it has led to accusations of moral relativism and a lack of political purchase. However, 'weaker' versions of social constructionism do not deny the reality of the housing conditions experienced by people but wish to draw attention to the ways these conditions have been construed as 'problematic'. There is also a political agenda implicit in the social constructionist approach. Nozick (2001) argues that social constructionists desire to change society and, by portraying reality as contingent, societal transformation becomes more plausible. In 'deconstructing' dominant 'grand narratives', social constructionists have helped to release the 'subjects' of these constructions and enabled them to interpret their own circumstances with an equal claim to legitimacy as those promoted in 'grand narratives'. This has produced an interest in 'identity' politics, that is, the personal liberation of groups marginalised from mainstream politics.

Normative orders and housing: Discourses at the end of the 19th century

The approaches to understanding housing policy outlined earlier can be illustrated by reference to discourses on 'the housing issue' at the turn of the 19th century that were to form the contexts for housing policy throughout the 20th century. The laissez-faire approach was still dominant at the time but under challenge from Marxist political economy and varieties of social reformism. The behavioural approach was an underlying theme in all the approaches and the social constructionist perspective can be applied retrospectively to augment understanding of how housing 'subjects' were created.

Laissez-faire

The entitlement notion was at the heart of the laissez-faire approach as applied in the 19th century. Adam Smith's account of how the market *should* operate was interpreted as an account of how the market *was* operating and it followed that those successful in markets were fully entitled to their rewards. Any interference with legitimately acquired property infringed liberty. Numerous books and pamphlets endorsing 'self-help' promoted the entitlement idea with Samuel Smiles becoming the most famous self-improvement advocate. He was President of the National Provident Association and his two books, *Self Help* (1859) and *Character* (1871), sold in large numbers. Full of individualist mottos such as 'the spirit of self-help is the root of all genuine growth in the individual' they became manuals for the belief that hard work promoted property-ownership.

By the end of the 19th century the laissez-faire approach had conceded the case for state intervention when 'externalities' could be clearly demonstrated. However, it drew a line under any attempt to improve housing conditions that involved redistributing income and wealth. Subsidised housing was regarded as illegitimate because, as one Member of Parliament said, 'If such a principle were admitted he did not know where it could stop. The next demand made on them [Parliament] might be to provide clothing if not carriages and horses' (quoted in Wohl, 1983, p 314).

If, as laissez-faire interpretations suggest, wealth is the product of character, then it follows that economic failure results from character deficiency. During the 19th century 'destitution', meaning extreme want of the means of subsistence including shelter, was prevented by the 'offer of the house', that is, accommodation in a workhouse. According to the *Poor Law Report of 1834*, workhouse conditions 'should be not really or apparently so eligible as the situation of the independent labourer of the lowest class' (Checkland and Checkland, 1974, p 375). Accepting 'the house' involved 'pauper' status, a recognition of personal failure in a market economy that was marked by indignities such as incarceration and separation from one's spouse and children. Redemption came from finding a job and departure from the workhouse. At the start of the 20th century, workhouses accommodated over 500,000 people in their 'permanent wards' and between 7000 and 17,000, depending on the season, in 'casual wards' (Royal Commission on the Poor Laws and Relief of Poverty, 1909).

Social reformism

Social reformists maintained that laissez-faire capitalism was incapable of overcoming the 'housing famine' without state intervention. The 'land issue' was at the heart of the critique. In *Progress and Poverty* (George, 1979 [1879]), Henry George argued that land values were created by the community. He advocated a single land tax that would reclaim for the community any rise in value not due to the landlord's efforts. Many 'New Liberals', adopting George's approach, argued that the housing shortage was caused by landowners who were hoarding in anticipation of future higher values. Moreover, in urban areas, where landowners leased their land to developers, they were avoiding local taxation in the form of rates and hence were paying no tax on their 'unearned' capital appreciation. Winston Churchill put the issue bluntly in 1909:

> Roads are made, streets are made, railway services are improved, electric lights turn night into day ... water is brought from reservoirs a hundred miles off in the mountains – and all the

while the landlord sits still….To not one of those improvements does the land monopolist … contribute and yet by every one of them the value of his land is enhanced … he contributes nothing even to the process from which his own enrichment is derived. (Churchill, 1909)

Taxing land at its potential use value would persuade landowners to release land and make them pay their fair share of local taxation.

Land values also formed an important element in Ebenezer Howard's 'garden city' idea. In *Garden Cities of Tomorrow* (Howard, 1902), he argued that the 'magnets' of living in the city or the country could be combined by residence in a planned garden city surrounded by a rural 'green belt' and organised through a not-for-profit trust. A vital component of Howard's scheme was the retention of enhanced land values by the community. As the city grew land values within its boundaries would increase and this 'betterment gain' could be used by the non-profit trust to provide community facilities and stimulate cooperative housing ventures. Fabian socialism shared many of the New Liberals' basic tenets but was more willing to advocate land nationalisation rather than taxing development gain and to support municipal housing with the arguments that building by direct labour organisations would eliminate the developer's profits and that local authority housing would retain enhanced land values for community use.

Marxist political economy

Marxist political economy underpinned a number of political movements formed towards the end of the 19th century: the Social Democratic Federation, the Socialist League and the Independent Labour Party. They adopted Marx's basic premise that the 'housing famine' was caused by capitalist exploitation of the working class and concentrated their efforts on debunking the idea that social reform within capitalism was an answer to working-class housing problems. They promoted land nationalisation plus higher wages to be achieved by working-class action as potential solutions. It is also possible to detect Marxist political economy influence in the growth of *independent* working-class organisations concerned with housing supply such as cooperatives and building societies.

Behavioural approaches

Laissez-faire economics maintained labour discipline by making the consequences for failure in a market economy unpalatable. However, by the turn of the 19th century, this overt disciplinary approach to social control was being supplemented by more subtle mechanisms. Employer-provided housing was one such device. Joyce (1980) has estimated that housing provided by employers contributed about 10% to the Victorian dwelling stock. Some estates were built as 'model villages' linked to factories and provided high-quality accommodation. However, the paternalism and social control involved in their management made them unacceptable to the independently minded working class. As Ravetz (2001, p 37) comments:

> We are told that when Lever toured his village it was, among other things, to confirm that any worker off sick had placed his boots in the window, as proof that he really was indoors and not truanting in the big city ... as a trade unionist wrote to Lever in 1919, 'No man of an independent turn of mind can breathe long in the atmosphere of Port Sunlight'.

Octavia Hill (1838–1912) adopted a similar paternalistic approach. She believed in refurbishing both people and places and was against subsidies to tenants because she thought state support would produce a 'pauper mentality'. According to Hill, slum dwellings were the product of two influences, both linked to 'character'. Uneducated slum landlords tried to make a quick profit from dilapidated dwellings – Hill was fond of quoting a slum landlord and undertaker who claimed to be in the private landlord business for 'the bodies it produced'! Such private landlords had to be replaced by 'fit and proper' housing managers. She also believed that tenants contributed to their housing conditions by ill-disciplined behaviour. Her housing management philosophy was 'tough love', combining efficient administration of reconditioned older property with character reformation. Such reformation was to be achieved through the personal influence of a housing worker sustained by a home visit for the weekly collection of rent and sanctions plus incentives to promote good conduct. Drunk and disorderly behaviour and rent arrears were punished by summary eviction whereas speedy repairs and extra rooms rewarded good conduct.

Social constructionism

Although this approach was not available to apply to the housing issue at the end of the 19th century it can be applied retrospectively to enhance understanding of how housing 'subjects' were constructed. According to the social constructionist approach, creating 'subjects' involves a process of fashioning an 'ideal type' citizen by contrasts with those not conforming to the ideal.

In the 18th and early part of the 19th centuries the inhabitants of the British Isles were thought to be 'a mad, bad and dangerous people' (Hilton, 2006) and much 19th-century legislation can be interpreted as an attempt to construct an 'ideal type' national-citizen and embody this construction in social norms to produce a more stable society. The 'ideal citizen' was constructed as property-owning, male, English and, at least in the early part of the 19th century, Protestant.

Political rights were related to property-ownership on the grounds – established by Cromwell in his defeat of the Levellers – that property marked a 'permanent interest' in the affairs of the realm. Thus, the 1832 Reform Act extended the right to vote on the basis of a £10 annual property qualification and redistributed seats from 'rotten' boroughs (where the MP was nominated by a wealthy patron). A distinction was made between 'the people' and the 'populace' with 'the people' to be involved in government and 'the populace' to be governed. Property rights were regarded as essential for full membership of the 'body politic' because proper government depended on a property-stake to anchor citizens to responsibility. A writer to *The Times* put the matter succinctly in stating:

> Property, which bespeaks, first the means of obtaining education; next, a stake in the maintenance of law and order; and lastly independence of ordinary temptations, may be far from a universal or unvarying test of character; but as a test at once general and tangible there is none so good. (*The Times*, 17 August 1835, cited in Mitchell, 2007, p 137)

In the post-Chartism years – after the working man had demonstrated his appetite for work and his acceptance of the existing social order – the franchise was gradually extended. In 1867, when Disraeli unexpectedly made voters out of hundreds of thousands of working-class householders in urban areas whose rates were 'compounded' in the rents they paid to landlords, he announced:

> England is safe in the race of men who inhabit her, safe in something much more precious than her accumulated capital, her accumulated experience. She is safe in her national character, in her fame and in that glorious future which I believe awaits her. (Disraeli, 1867)

Granting the vote to the working-class urban *householder* – not his wife or daughters; not his sons who remained at home; not his 'lodger'; not the inhabitants of common lodging houses or the workhouse – enabled the

Tories to form potential alliances with the 'respectable' working man. It was 'household' suffrage and he was head of the household. The exclusion of the rural working-class householder remained an anomaly until the 1884 Reform Act enfranchised 1.76 million new voters, mainly agricultural workers, by extending voting rights to rural areas on the same terms as applied to urban districts.

The role ascribed to women cemented the working-class man's developing social inclusion. The arguments presented to deny women the vote were numerous, but most were based on the idea that men and women occupied separate domains that, when united in matrimony, made a whole. Helen Bosanquet (1906) cogently expressed this view in *The Family*. She defined the 'Family' (always with a capital) as a 'practical syllogism' of 'two premises and their conclusion' with its purpose being 'the mutual convenience and protection of all the members belonging to it' (Bosanquet, 1906, p 16). The father was the source of authority, an authority derived 'not only by natural disposition ... but mainly by the natural and necessary division of labour between the two chief members of the partnership' (Bosanquet, 1906, p 272). The wife was assigned the functions of domestic manager and carer of home and children, while the husband and adult children assumed the responsibility to provide income. Men, according to Bosanquet, were 'incapable of the more domestic duties incident upon the rearing of children' and it was 'largely this incapacity which gives him the power both of concentration and width of view' (Bosanquet, 1906, pp 272–3) that enabled him to participate in politics. 'If the husband is the head of the Family', she continued:

> the wife is the centre. It is she who is primarily responsible for the care of the children; to the utmost extent of which the family means will allow, it is her duty to see they are well cared for, both physically and morally; and it is generally agreed that this duty can be properly fulfilled only by personal attention. (Bosanquet, 1906, p 279)

Bosanquet recognised that women sometimes worked outside the home, but she claimed that 'nothing could so well emphasize the importance of the woman in the Family as the miserable condition of home and children when she is not in the Family but in the mill' (1906, p 294).

Disraeli's reference to England being 'safe in the race of men who inhabit her' reflected England's dominance in the notion of a 'United Kingdom'. The construction of 'Englishness', via contrasts with the 'other', especially 'the Irish', gave the English working man a sense of identity. The ideal-type Englishman aspired to property and a wife for his comfort in the domestic sphere – to become the independent 'John Bull yeoman'. He was not Irish but could be contaminated by adopting 'Irish' ways. Engels' depiction of the Irish in England reflected attitudes that would persist well into the 20th century:

> The majority of the families who live in cellars are almost everywhere of Irish origin…. In short, the Irish have, as Dr Kay says, discovered the minimum of the necessities of life, and are now making the English workers acquainted with it. The Irishman loves his pig as the Arab his horse, with the difference that he sells it when it is fat enough to kill. Otherwise, he eats and sleeps with it, his children play with it, ride upon it, roll in the dirt with it, as anyone may see a thousand times repeated in all the great towns of England. The southern facile character of the Irishman, his crudity, which places him but little above the savage, his contempt for all humane enjoyments, in which his very crudeness makes him incapable of sharing, his filth and poverty, all favour drunkenness. (Engels, 1845, p 32)

As Poovey (1995, p 8) has stated: 'The phrase social body promised full membership in a whole (and held out the image of that whole) to a part identified as needing both discipline and care'. 'Difference' constructions, consolidated in the 19th century, when underpinned with the behavioural approach, generated a hierarchy of 'subjects'. As a person moved up the hierarchy then – by contrast with those below – inclusion in the 'body politic' or 'social body' was enhanced. Lowest of the low in these 'housing classes' was the 'vagrant', especially the Irish vagrant, without settlement rights and constantly being 'moved on'. Next came the residents in the workhouse 'permanent wards' with men often deprived of the right to live with their children and unmarried mothers likely to be placed in the workhouse 'canary ward' – marked by its yellow uniforms designed to remind the mother of her fall from grace. Then there were the common lodging houses where people could buy a communal shelter for a night. More self-contained accommodation might be found in a single room let on a weekly basis or in a cellar dwelling – common in Liverpool. One step upwards on the housing ladder was to rent rooms in a tenement or in a 'two-up, two down' terraced house. A house with a 'parlour', semi-detached if possible and in the developing suburbia, was a clear sign of respectability. As Giles (2004, p 18) comments 'Any household with social pretensions had its "best" parlour and a small room that acted as a study for the *paterfamilias*'.

Overview

- Housing policy is about the state attempting to make corrections to the housing market.
- Each approach to understanding housing policy is linked to a political agenda and contains, explicitly or implicitly, a normative theory used to establish the nature and causation of housing problems. The debates on housing policy at the end of the 19th century illustrate perspectives that were to influence policy throughout the 20th century.

Questions for discussion

1. Examine the websites of the 'think tanks' listed below. On which approach to the study of housing policy are they based?
2. Should a local authority tenancy depend on signing a work contract?
3. Compare and contrast Marxist political economy and laissez-faire economics on the state's role in housing.

Further reading

Theorising Welfare by **Martin O'Brien** and **Sue Penna** (1998) is a good introduction to normative and explanatory theories of welfare. **Todd Depastino's** (2003) *Citizen Hobo: How a Century of Homelessness Shaped America* is an excellent example of the application of the social constructionist approach to understanding housing problems although Depastino may not recognise it as such.

Websites

Various 'think tanks' reflect the diversity of approaches to understanding housing policy and the development of policy prescriptions. See, as examples, the websites of the following think tanks by typing their names into a search engine:

- The Policy Exchange
- The Centre for Policy Studies
- The Fabian Society
- Civitas
- The Centre for Social Justice
- The Institute for Public Policy Research

two

Housing: The political/policy process

Summary

- 'Politics' is about the struggle over power. The term embraces disputes about the legitimacy of political institutions; the authority to determine the issues admitted into the political system; and the policy formation and implementation processes occurring within established political structures.
- Each approach to understanding housing policy, except the behavioural approach, is linked to explanations of continuity and change in housing policy.
- The idea of 'governance' – associated with the 'new public sector managerialism' – has become influential in explaining the nature of the contemporary policy process.

What is politics?

Politics is a contested concept, but has been crisply defined as 'the struggle over power' (Marsh and Stoker, 2002, p 7). 'Struggle' indicates an active, ongoing process involving conflict, whereas 'power' points to the struggle's aim – to take charge and make decisions backed by the state's authority. Political parties are major contestants in the power struggle (see **Box 2.1**).

Box 2.1: Political parties and housing

A political party has been defined as:

> an autonomous group of citizens having the purpose of making nominations and contesting elections in hope of gaining control over governmental power through the capture of public offices and the organization of the government. (Huckshorn, 1984, p 10)

Parties organise antagonism and their focus is on the struggle to secure authority over the formal state structure.

In the early 19th century, the Conservatives (the successors of the Tories) and the Liberals (a mixture of 'Whigs' and 'Radicals'), aware of the need for popular support lest reputations be broken by the press and heads be fractured by the 'mob', developed mechanisms to make connections to the people. Mass political appeal became more important following franchise extension for, as Sidney Webb noted, 'if you allow the tramway conductor to vote he will not forever be satisfied with exercising that vote over such matters as the Ambassador to Paris ... he will ... seek ... to obtain some kind of control over which he lives' (quoted in Hay, 1983, p 25). Disraeli is usually associated with the first attempt to stir popular support with his 'one-nation Toryism', but this was expressed in novels such as *Sybil* or *The Two Nations* [Refs X2?] and franchise reform rather than in social change. In the 1880s the Liberal Party, observant of the mounting power of the 'respectable working man', promoted housing construction via land reform as part of its 'social liberalism' agenda.

Whereas the Conservative and Liberal Parties cultivated links from Parliament to the people, the Labour Party developed via links from the people to Parliament. In 1900, the Labour Representation Committee – a coalition of Trade Unions, the Independent Labour Party, the Fabian Society and the Social Democratic Federation – was formed to secure direct 'labour interest' representation in Parliament. When, in 1906, 30 'Labour' members were elected to Parliament they formed their own parliamentary organisation under the name 'The Labour Party' and, partially through the pivotal roles of the Party Conference and National Executive, developed a housing policy with the following characteristics:

- The belief that local authority housing, unlike 'speculative building' was a 'plannable instrument' and could be allocated according to criteria other than the ability to pay.
- State housing would promote good design.
- Community gains would arise from state involvement in development.

- New housing should meet future standards and hence current subsidies were necessary.
- City congestion could only be reduced by planned movement to 'garden suburbs' and new towns.
- Private landlordism embodied an exploitative relationship and should be discouraged.

The Conservative response to the Liberal and Labour challenges was to defend property-ownership as the mark of full inclusion in the 'social body', but to downplay the salience of landownership (Readman, 2010). Under the developing belief that 'property-owners are conservative' (Barker, 1909, p 566), the Conservatives started to promote homeownership as the essence of a 'property-owning democracy' and to portray social housing as a response appropriate only to the inner-city 'slum' problem.

By the 1950s the UK was a two-party nation: in the 1955 general election the Conservatives obtained 49.7% of the popular vote, Labour 46.4% and the Liberals only 2.7%. The close contests between the two main parties in the 1950s, 1960s and 1970s contributed to the notion that this was a period of 'consensus' politics and, although housing was on the periphery of this alleged consensus, the Conservatives were willing to allow council housing a role when supply and demand was seriously unbalanced, whereas, when in government, Labour began to endorse homeownership with more enthusiasm. Margaret Thatcher, determined to apply market forces to rented accommodation and reduce the role of council housing to as near to zero as possible, fractured this consensus, although her use of state support to promote homeownership (contrary to pure market principles) might be construed as continuing the 'one-nation' Tory tradition.

Following its crushing defeat in the 1979 general election, its 'lurch to the Left' in the early 1980s and the establishment of the Social Democratic Party in 1981 (later to merge with the Liberals to form the Liberal Democrats), the Labour Party gradually moved towards the centre ground culminating in the formation of 'New Labour' in the mid-1990s and a marked reduction in the influence of the Party Conference and the National Executive in policy development. New Labour promoted 'third way' politics, manifest in the housing domain by enthusiasm for homeownership, a friendly attitude to private landlordism and the use of housing associations rather than local authorities to supply and manage social housing.

By the 1980s the two-party politics in the UK had started to fray and, after the 2005 general election, New Labour held 55% of the parliamentary seats, the Conservatives 31% and the Liberal Democrats 10% with other parties such as the Democratic Unionists and Scottish Nationalists holding the remainder.

Following heavy defeats in the 1997, 2001 and 2005 general elections, the Conservative Party, under David Cameron's leadership, moved closer to the political centre. There was talk of 'Red Toryism' – respecting time-honoured values, valuing local communities and allowing the 'little man' to participate in the economy (Blond, 2010); or 'compassionate conservatism', with a concern about poverty and the 'big society' based on Edmund Burke's idea that 'to be attached to the subdivision, to love the little platoon we belong to in society is ... the first link in the series by which we proceed towards a love of our country, and to mankind' (Burke, 1790, quoted in Norman, 2010, p 106). Anxious to detach its 'nasty' and 'neoliberal' labels, the Conservatives showed an interest in homelessness by setting up the Conservative Homelessness Foundation and establishing the Commission on Social Justice with Ian Duncan Smith, a former Tory leader, as its Chair. This Commission promoted the notion of a 'broken Britain' in need of repair and, although some of its recommendations suggested an endorsement of 'underclass' ideas, their tone emphasised help rather than coercion. The Conservative Party's 2010 manifesto highlighted New Labour's failure to reduce poverty and inequality and attributed this failure to a reliance on 'top-down government and bureaucratic micro-management'. It declared:

> So we need a new approach: social responsibility, not state control; the Big Society, not big government.... So we need to redistribute power from the central state to individuals, families and local communities. We will give public sector workers back their professional autonomy. They will be accountable to the people they serve and the results they achieve will be made transparent. If people don't like the service they receive they will be able to choose better alternatives.... We will use the state to help stimulate social action, helping social enterprise to deliver public services and training new community organisers to help achieve our ambition of every adult citizen being a member of an active neighbourhood group. (Conservative Party, 2010a, pp 35–6)

Initially the Conservatives under Cameron had backed the notion that local resistance to building proposals was at the heart of the housing supply problem. In early 2006 Cameron claimed that:

> the failure to provide an adequate number of new homes in Britain has contributed to the affordability problem. This situation is bananas. I say it's bananas because one of the problems we've faced is a system that encourages people to believe we should Build Absolutely Nothing Anywhere Near Anyone. (Cameron, 2006)

In June 2007, the Conservative Shadow Housing Minister, Michael Gove, condemned Gordon Brown's housing target as 'displaying a poverty of ambition' (Gove, 2007, quoted in *Inside Housing*, 2007a) and declared that a huge increase in the supply of new homes was needed. However, as the depth of 'Middle England' resistance to new construction became evident, the Conservatives backed away from state-directed house construction in favour of what they called 'open source', 'collaborative planning'. Although there would be 'a presumption in favour of sustainable development' (Conservative Party, 2010b), neighbourhoods would be able to produce a neighbourhood plan which, if endorsed by 50% of the inhabitants, would have to be accepted by the local authority.

The specific housing policies in the Conservative 2010 manifesto included proposals to abolish New Labour's 'top-down' approach to housing supply and management, with its emphasis on targets and performance indicators, in favour of local authority discretion in establishing local housing needs. This was backed by Local Housing Trusts and incentives to build in the form of payments to local authorities for allowing housing construction and developers having to pay a tariff to compensate the community for loss of amenities and additional infrastructure costs. Part of this tariff would be kept by the neighbourhoods in which a development took place.

People would have a 'right to bid to run any community service instead of the state' (Conservative Party, 2010a, p 75), Home Information Packs would be abolished and home energy efficiency would be promoted by a Green Deal 'giving every home up to 6,500 worth of energy improvement – with more for hard-to-treat homes – paid for out of savings made on the fuel bills over 25 years' (2010a, p 93). Good social tenants would be given equity stakes and there would be a right to move. Although earlier Conservative Party policy documents had proposed the abolition of secure tenancies for social tenants, the 2010 manifesto stated that there would be 'respect for tenures and rents of social housing tenants' (2010a, p 75).

New Labour secured 258 seats in the 2010 general election and was forced back into its traditional heartlands in Scotland, Wales and the English conurbations. Its manifesto was mainly a reprise of proposals announced towards the end of its term in office, for example, a renewed role for local authorities in house-building, a two-year suspension of Stamp Duty Tax for first-time buyers of houses valued at less than £250,000 and a commitment to 'work with Housing Associations to develop a new form of affordable housing targeted at working families on modest incomes who struggle in the private sector and rarely qualify for social housing' (Labour Party, 2010, p 31).

The Liberal Democrats won 57 seats. The party's manifesto contained a potpourri of proposals related to housing including a 'mansion' tax of 1% on the value of houses above £1 million; taxing capital gains at 40% rather than 18% (with implications for private landlords); scaling back HomeBuy schemes; a £400 cashback payment for installing energy-saving devices in homes; cheap loans to bring empty properties back into use; returning 'decision-making, including housing targets, to local people' (Liberal Democrats, 2010, p 81); reviewing the 'unfair' Housing Revenue Account system (2010, p 80); promoting 'Home on the Farm' schemes to encourage farmers to use underutilised building for affordable housing; and equalising VAT on new-build with VAT on repairs.

The 2010 election campaign focused on New Labour's economic record and housing was not a significant issue. Although the merits and limitations of public spending cuts in the current financial year were debated, the UK's accumulated public sector net debt of £903 billion, 62.2% of GDP (Office for National Statistics, 2010a), was largely ignored. With the 307 seats secured in the 2010 general election the Conservatives fell short of an overall majority and entered into a coalition with the Liberal Democrats.

Power contests are observable in a variety of settings, not just in the specific processes and institutions deemed 'government'. In the housing domain 'the "latent" power over how people think' (Prokhovnik, 2005, p 13) – establishing what is 'common sense' and thereby setting boundaries to ideas about what is possible – is particularly important. The miner's response – 'when we were told about it' – to George Orwell's query about when housing become a problem in his area (Orwell, 1937) illustrates how perceptions of the possible limit aspirations for change. The authority to determine the issues adopted into the governmental process is also significant (Bachrach and Baratz, 1962): to become a social issue a housing situation has to be recognised as problematic by those with authority. This chapter explains how the perspectives applied to understanding housing policy examined in Chapter One – with the exception of the behavioural approach – are linked to particular approaches to *explaining* what goes on in the political/policy process.

Laissez-faire and public choice theory

The 'laissez-faire' economic approach has adopted public choice theory as its principal explanation of why state intervention in the housing market accelerated in the first 80 years of the 20th century. Public choice theorists divide the democratic process into three elements: the voting system, interest group activity and how state officials behave when organised into bureaucracies. All participants in the political process are thought about in terms of neoclassical economics' basic premise: they act rationally to promote their selfinterest. There is no quest for 'the common good' in political activity – politicians are motivated by securing election to pursue power, prestige and material advantage. In order to attain such advantages they must win more votes than their rivals and will adopt strategies to obtain these votes. They will try, for example, to attract the median voter – the additional voter necessary to secure a majority – and thus will pursue policies that redistribute income from the rich to middle-income groups and the poor who form the majority of the electorate (Tullock, 1976). In their hunt for power politicians rely on public apathy, such apathy being 'rational' because each voter has only a tiny impact on an election result.

In seeking power politicians are susceptible to interest group influence. These 'pressure groups' exist to take a 'free ride' on their fellow citizens: they seek to persuade politicians to give special privileges to the domain in which they have a vested interest. Politicians may rely on interest groups to secure a 'winning coalition' at elections and, when in power, they may respond to interest group demands to ensure cooperation in regulating a complex policy domain. Interest groups will engage in a variety of tactics to enhance their influence over politicians, for example, 'log-rolling', where a variety of interest groups may act together against unorganised groups. Thus, for example, the construction industry, estate agents, landowners and the financial institutions may combine to demand government intervention to 'kick-start' the housing market in a period when house prices are declining. They will make their demands in 'the public interest', but there will be losers – new entrants to the housing market who would benefit from falling prices – if the government agrees to such demands. Thus, when prices started to fall in 2008, there was a clamour from those with interests in high house prices to stop this decline. New Labour, also with an interest in high house prices because of its promotion of 'asset-based welfare' and the tax income from Stamp Duty, responded in a number of ways (see Chapter Three). The result was a return to house price inflation with prices increasing by 10.2% in 2009/10 before entering a downward trend in the second half of 2010. The more cynical public choice theorists might add that the political neglect of housing market inflation up to 2007 might be associated with the capital gains made by certain MPs via their tax-supported second homes!

Bureaucratic self-interest is the third influence identified by public choice theorists. State officials are portrayed as motivated by 'salary, prerequisites of the office, public reputation, power, patronage and the ease of managing the bureau' (Niskanen, 1973, pp 22–3): they may act as 'knaves' by promoting their self-interest, and not 'knights' by upholding the 'public good' (Le Grand, 2003). Their welfare is served by maximising the agency's budget. Niskanen (1973) asserts that in public services there is a single buyer (the politician) and a single seller (the bureaucrat). The bureaucrat has a virtual monopoly on information about the costs of the organisation and will offer the politician only a single package to accept or reject so there will always be a degree of inefficiency – labelled X-inefficiency by public choice theorists – in service delivery. Public choice theory was important in influencing the development of 'quasi-markets'.

Quasi-markets

Margaret Thatcher embraced the market as the means to ensure efficiency and consumer satisfaction in service delivery but, in acknowledgement that certain services had characteristics that make it difficult to apply full market principles, her market endorsement was modified into a pursuit of 'quasi-markets' (see **Box 2.2**).

Box 2.2: What is a quasi-market?

A quasi-market has been defined as:

> A market in the sense of independent agents competing with one another for the custom of purchasers, but a quasi-market in that, unlike in a normal market, purchasing power came not directly from the consumer but from the state. (Le Grand, 2001)

After 1986 the quasi-market in rented accommodation took the form of:

- rented housing suppliers – local authorities, housing associations and private landlords – competing for 'customers' on the common basis that market rents would be charged.
- low-income households would have their housing costs subsidised by Housing Benefit available on equal terms to tenants of all types of landlord.

Nicholas Ridley, Secretary of State for the Environment with responsibility for housing in the middle 1980s, had a vision of local government not as a service supplier, but as 'enabling' the market to provide. A flat-rate poll tax (community charge) would inhibit the ability of local government to supply free services and Ridley looked forward to a time when the council would 'meet once a year to award contracts, have lunch, and go away again for another year' (Ridley, 1986). Ridley's scenario would have involved expanding private welfare, a 'contract' culture and 'residual' public services. However John Major, with his 'Citizens' Charters', adjusted this market orientation towards a notion of citizenship (Lund, 2008) and the Conservative's initial emphasis on free markets was tailored towards the 'new public sector managerialism'. Local authorities were labelled 'strategic enablers' rather than mere 'enablers' suggesting that there was a 'public interest', greater than the sum total of individual interests as reflected in market outcomes, that a strategy could promote. The quasi-market in rented accommodation was modified by restraining the push towards market rents so that 'rents in the social sector remain affordable for tenants in low paid work' and funding was promised 'to support the creation of mixed communities' (Department of the Environment and Welsh Office, 1995, p 2).

Governance and the new public sector managerialism

New Labour elevated the 'strategic enabling' idea. Its gurus were sociologists identifying trends – Giddens (1998) with his 'third way' and Etzioni (1993) with his 'communitarianism' – rather than normative political theorists. Going 'with the grain', rather than 'grand narratives' for change motivated by ideology, became New Labour's lodestone. Words and phrases such as 'partnerships', 'joined-up government', 'policy networks', 'the big tent', 'choice', 'channel management', 'modernisation', 'personalisation' and 'third sector' entered New Labour's lexicon.

In an attempt to encapsulate these organisational changes the term 'governance' – with its origins in the Greek verb kubernáo meaning 'to steer' – began to permeate academic discourse on policy analysis. There was talk of 'the hollowing out of the state' (Rhodes, 1994) and a 'new institutionalism' in policy analysis emerged with an emphasis on the salience of networks, policy communities and partnerships in generating and managing change. Rather than 'governing' to achieve a specified end via direct state power – 'command and control' – 'governance' was seen as steering a course via cooperation with external and internal agencies through turbulent global forces. 'Governance' became linked to what became labelled the 'new public sector managerialism', which established its credentials by what it was *not* – via comparison between the 'old ways' and the 'modern'. It identified itself through a series of contrasts (see ***Figure 2.1***).

Housing was in the vanguard of this managerialism as applied to the public sector. In the 1950s and 1960s, central government adopted a 'leave to be' approach to local government's role in housing supply: it set 'cost yardsticks' to control the level of central subsidies, but left local authorities

Figure 2.1: The 'new public sector managerialism'

What it is *not*	What it *claims* to be
Rule-bound (bureaucratic)	Focused on objectives measured by performance indicators/targets
Paternalist	Customer-centred
Centrally directed: 'top-down' with a single authority structure and planned and managed by a 'system controller'	Operating through 'networks': 'network management' emphasised a divided authority structure with managers acting as 'mediators' guiding interactions and providing opportunities
Ossified	Joined-up
Ideological	Pragmatic and dynamic: policy is 'evidence-based' with 'what works counts'
Directed to universal standards	Results-oriented and market-tested

to decide on quantity, design and management (Griffiths, 1966) – not quite the central control depicted by governance theorists. However, in the 1980s, local authority housing was represented as bureaucratic and paternalist – an embodiment of the ossified 'old ways'. Housing strategies, first made mandatory for local authorities in the late 1970s, assumed a new importance in the early 1990s when central resources were distributed according to the strategy's perceived 'quality' – 'quality' being assessed according to the willingness of the local authority to reduce its stock in accordance with the 'enabling' role. Business plans were required and, in 1996, local authorities had to make a clear separation between those who represented the 'client' function and those who supplied the service with the service role subject to market-testing via Compulsory Competitive Tendering (CCT).

New Labour replaced CCT by a requirement to seek 'best value' in service delivery. 'Best value' promoted competition on a voluntary basis, but Blair declared 'There can be no monopoly of services delivery by councils; the 1970s will not be re-visited. But there will be zero tolerance of failure: there is no room for poor performance' (Blair, 1997b). Thus, despite its emphasis on measured change emerging from network interaction, New Labour maintained a degree of central direction via targets and performance indicators. It believed that a combination of top-down performance targets plus greater choice and 'personalisation' would lead to 'a self-improving system because incentives for improvement and innovation are embedded within it' (Cabinet Office, 2006, p 4).

At its zenith the 'target culture' included numerous targets and performance indicators such as:

- the average time to re-let council dwellings;
- the proportion of households accepted as statutorily homeless who were accepted as statutorily homeless by the same authority or another authority within the last two years; and
- the percentage of responsive repairs for which the local authority made and kept an appointment.

Most New Labour targets and performance indicators emphasised efficient delivery to the consumer, but some 'equality' benchmarks were set, for example, 'narrowing the gap between the most deprived areas and the rest of the country' (HM Treasury, 2000, p 1). Nevertheless, although New Labour asserted that its objective was to combine efficiency and social justice, the former dominated the latter. The Coalition government, as part of its 'new localism' agenda, quickly announced the abandonment of central performance targets, yet New Labour's 'performance culture' achieved some worthwhile results. Pawson and Jacobs (2010) assessed change between 2001/02 and 2007/08 against a number of indicators such as average vacancy levels and urgent repairs delivered on time and found that good progress had been made on most of the indictors.

Social reformism

Sometimes labelled 'understanding paternalism' (Lux, 2009), social reformism merged analysis *of* policy (from outside the system) with analysis *for* policy (inside the system).

Organic theory was at the heart of both Fabian socialism and social liberalism at the turn of the 19th century and beyond. It used the body as a metaphor for society and did not make a clear distinction between normative theory (what ought to be) and explanatory theory (what is) because it regarded society as undergoing a natural evolutionary process leading to a 'higher' and better social order. According to Lloyd (1901, p 577) 'the organic theory of society is entertained by nearly every serious thinker at the present time.' Leading Fabians, Sidney and Beatrice Webb, 'saw society as an evolving organism, in which collectivist rationality was inexorably replacing individualistic chaos' (Marquand, 2008, p 63). This evolution was inevitable, but it could be stimulated by experts with knowledge of the 'facts'. Equipped with the 'facts' and inductive reasoning the 'new samurai' (as H.G. Wells described them[1905, p 310]) would lead society through an 'irresistible glide' (Webb and Webb, 1913, p 56) into a new social order dominated by an efficient state directed towards meeting individual needs that were at one with society's needs. Each individual was to be equipped to fulfil 'his humble function in the great social machine' (Webb, 1890, p 115).

Although democrats in desiring a universal franchise, the Webbs viewed the democratic process simply as a means to choose the 'modern efficients' needed to run the state. Social reform must come from above with state affairs 'more and more the business of elaborately trained experts, and less the immediate outcome of popular feeling' (Webb, 1908, pp 57, 71). Beatrice confided to her diary:

> We have little faith in the 'average sensual man', we do not believe that he can do much more than describe his grievances, we do not think that he can prescribe the remedies….We wish to introduce into politics the professional expert and through him extend the sphere of government. (Webb, 1948, p 120)

Organic theory developed a sociological arm. Associated with Emile Durkheim (1858–1917) and Talcott Parsons (1902–79) functionalist sociological theory adopted the notion that society was 'a social system of interrelated parts [and] survived because it evolved institutional structures to fulfil the basic needs of the system, its "functional prerequisites"' (Kilminster, 1998, p 154). However, a dimension of this functionalism later stressed certain 'dysfunctional' elements in society (Merton, 1949), with, for example, the 'slum' viewed as disruptive to a harmonious society due to its 'disorganisation' and association with crime, immorality and disease. From this modified functionalist perspective the natural order of adjustment would, in time, eradicate the slum, but this process could be accelerated by the attentions of 'rational' planners gathering the 'facts' on an issue and acting 'with the grain' of functional adaptation. For social reformers the evolutionary process of social amelioration would inevitably lead to large-scale state involvement in housing supply because the state embodied the 'rational' common good. This 'understanding paternalism' dominated the housing of the working class until the late 1970s and underpinned the design of many council house estates.

Rational policy analysis

The 'universal rationalism' associated Fabian socialism and social liberalism permeated much of the early 'policy analysis' literature. Harold Lasswell, often regarded as the inventor of the 'policy orientation' in political science (Hudson and Lowe, 2009, p 5), claimed that the 'policy process' was 'a suitable object of study in its own right primarily in the hope of improving the rationality of the flow of decisions' (Lasswell, 1951, p 3). Thus, Lasswell combined analysis *for* and *in* policy with analysis *of* policy. He suggested that a rational approach to policy development would divide the process into a series of stages – a cycle – albeit that these stages might not unfold in a linear manner. The stages involved: gathering 'intelligence'; 'promotion' of the issue; prescription concerning what should be done; 'innovation' of a policy; practical policy 'application'; 'termination' when the problem had been solved; followed by impact 'appraisal' (Lasswell, 1951). New Labour, under its belief in 'evidence-based', 'what works counts', social policy, attempted to apply this 'rational' approach to certain dimensions of housing policy (see ***Box 2.3***).

Box 2.3: The policy cycle and rough sleeping

New Labour's 1997 manifesto declared that 'there is no more powerful symbol of Tory neglect in our society today than young people without homes living rough on the streets' (Labour Party, 1997). On gaining office, New Labour gathered 'intelligence' on the issue via the Social Exclusion Unit, set up in the Prime Minister's Office. Having examined the available evidence (Social Exclusion Unit, 1998a), the government reached the conclusion that sleeping rough was not primarily a housing shortage issue but a matter of the rough sleepers' disturbed personal biographies and their 'lifestyle culture'. Thus, the policy response to rough sleeping should be to persuade rough sleepers to come in 'out of the cold' to places where they were less prone to develop a rough-sleeping culture and where they would receive help and eventually be allocated independent accommodation with 'support' if necessary. The Supported Housing Programme (see Chapter Ten) was to play an important role in delivering help when people had 'moved on' into independent accommodation. A 'Rough Sleeping Unit', under a 'Czar', was established to coordinate a new rough-sleeping 'initiative' (DETR, 1999a) and a target for reducing rough sleeping was announced to be monitored through an annual rough-sleeper count. In accordance with the 'what works is what counts' mantra at the heart of rational policy analysis, the initiative was subject to periodic reviews with the policy being 'tweaked' according to their conclusions. The 2008 review, *No One Left Out: Communities Ending Rough Sleeping* (DCL, 2008a) proclaimed policy success – the target of reducing rough sleeping by two thirds had been met and sustained with rough sleeping down from 1850 in 1998 to 483 in 2008. It was now time to announce a new goal to be met by year of the Olympics:

> We want to see real and sustainable reductions in rough sleeping year on year, so that no one in England has to sleep rough by 2012. Our vision is to end rough sleeping once and for all. (DCL, 2008a, p 7)

Lasswell's 'rational' approach was criticised as an inaccurate representation of the real policy process, with Lindblom (1959), for example, arguing that policymaking was a matter of 'muddling through', not planned action. 'Path dependence' – a propensity for initiatives to be incremental because they are locked into existing policy frameworks – was identified. Hall (1993) made distinctions between 'first-order' changes in 'settings', for example, modification in the distribution of the annual budget; 'second-order' changes in 'techniques', for example, a gradual move to a greater reliance on means-testing; and third-order changes in 'goals'. 'Goal' changes were rare and involved major changes in 'settings' and 'techniques'. New Labour's shift in 2003 towards stimulating housing supply might be regarded as a 'goal change', at least in intent, and the Coalition government's reaction to the UK's public-sector deficit also represents a major paradigm change.

Pluralism

In their formative years, social liberalism and Fabian socialism had an elitist tone: the working class would be guided into a new order by an intellectual 'samurai'. However, following the 1918 Representation of the People Act, which tripled the size of the electorate from 7.7 million in 1912 to 21.4 million in 1918, social reformism began to develop more democratic models of the political/policy process. Social liberalism and elements of Fabian socialism began to fuse into the 'social democratic' approach, with pluralism forming an element in its explanatory framework. At the heart of pluralism was the notion that society consists of a range of social groups and that 'there are multiple centres of power, none of which is wholly sovereign' (Dahl, 1961, p 4). The state was seen as a neutral arbiter between various sections of society, all of which were perceived as having roughly equal access to the political process. However, Bachrach and Baratz (1962) questioned Dahl's notion of equal access to power by describing a second power dimension – covert exclusion of people and ideas from decision-making with 'covertness' used as a tactic to conceal power concentrations. They describe such a system as 'bounded pluralism' (see **Box 2.4**).

Box 2.4: 'Bounded pluralism' and housing policy: High-rise housing

Reflecting on the mass housing era starting in the early 1950s, Dunleavy (1981, p 1) comments:

> Contrary to the implicit assumptions of most of the sociological literature on slum clearance, probably a majority of the three million people displaced

by redevelopment between 1955 and 1975 did not move out to houses in the suburbs but were rehoused on mass housing estates in inner and core city areas. Over this period nearly 440,000 high-rise flats were built, with around nine-tenths of this total in inner urban areas.

A number of interests in the 'policy community' promoted this mass high-rise housing: the major construction firms and their architects; planners; local councillors; and the Ministry of Housing and Local Government. They were brought together by an 'extensive network of advisory committees' (Dunleavy, 1981, p 18).

The intended beneficiaries of the clearance process – inner-city slum dwellers – were absent from this 'bounded' policy development and implementation system (Dennis, 1972; Gower Davis, 1974). Dunleavy (1981, p 94) notes that the nature of local authority procedures created 'a fundamental and massive imbalance of power resources and constraints on their use between councils and clearance area residents'. People living in 'slums' experienced 'housing' as a verb – 'understanding paternalism', with its 'top-down' approach to policy development meant that they were 'taken or put into accommodation'. Hollow (2010) records the process in a Sheffield clearance scheme. The old Park Hill area was characterised as 'a worn out area adjacent to the city centre, and with a reputation derived from a crime wave centred there in the 1920s' (Hollow, 2010, p 121). In the early 1950s it was to be replaced by a development that would meet the new inhabitants' physical requirements – and hence their economic capabilities – in an efficient manner so 'dimensions, light and layout were all measured … to ensure that each resident received a regulation flat to provide for their basic needs' (Hollow, 2010, p 123). Moreover, 'inspired by the work of sociologists such as Michael Young and Karen Stephen, who praised the social cohesion found in working class slums' (Hollow, 2010, p 124), its deck access design would encourage the 'social citizen'. 'Streets in the sky', symbolised by access to all the flats for a milk float, would stimulate the street interaction of the area it replaced. To foster such interaction the city council employed a sociologist who became the first resident on the new estate. What the potential inhabitants thought of the new scheme is unknown: they were never asked and subsequent surveys of in situ tenants were 'only valued if they were expressed in terms suitable to the surveyor' (Hollow, 2010, p 131).

Policy implementation and policy failure

The 'rational', analysis *for*, policy model tends to stop at Lasswell's 'termination' phase on the assumption that, once a policy had been determined, then the state's power will ensure successful implementation with 'failed intelligence' responsible for any glitches in the implementation process. But implementation is not a mere administration/managerial process involving pulling the right levers in the state machine: policy execution depends on acquiescence from the agencies involved in delivery: officials, down to the 'street level', can interpret a policy and the policy's 'subjects' can resist and modify its impact, thereby producing policy failure (see *Box 2.5*).

Box 2.5: The 1988 Housing Act (Tenants' Choice)

The 1988 Housing Act allowed local authority tenants to choose to transfer their homes to a different 'approved' landlord either individually or collectively. It was influenced by public choice theory and aimed at opening up 'the closed world of the local authority estates to competition and to the influence of the best housing management practices of other landlords' (DoE, 1987, para 1.16). Despite rigged ballots (non-voters in a transfer ballot were counted as 'yes' votes), and the high consultancy costs for tenants' advice and support, only 1470 homes in five schemes were transferred (ODPM, 2005a). The number of individual transfers is unknown (probably zero). The 1996 Housing Act repealed the 'tenants' choice' provisions in the 1988 Act. Its failure was the consequence of resistance from local government – the policy was presented as an attack on local authority managerial incompetence (see Ridley, 1991) – plus tenants' trust in their local authority, rather than 'alternative' landlords who might be private landlords intent on pushing up rents.

Moran et al (2008, p v) offer a timely reminder that:

> all our talk of 'making' public policy, of 'choosing' and 'deciding' loses track of the home truth, taught to President Kennedy by Richard Neustadt, that politics and policy making is mostly a matter of persuasion. Decide, choose, legislate as they will, policy makers must carry people with them, if their determinations are to have the full force of policy.

'Persuasion' takes place at all stages in the political process and, according to some authors (Jones, 2002; Osborne, 2005), 'spin' – presenting a policy to maximise public support – became a hallmark of New Labour governance. 'Persuasion' has a particular salience at the policy-execution stage (see *Box 2.6*).

Box 2.6: From policy failure to policy success: Stock transfer

Although the tenants' choice provisions in the 1988 Housing Act were a failure, the seeds of later success, in the form of 'voluntary' stock transfer, sprang from this policy breakdown. 'Voluntary' transfer reflected earlier initiatives: in the early 1980s, Knowsley Council transferred 3000 homes to Stockbridge Village Trust and Glasgow City Council set up a number of community-based associations to receive some of its stock. In the late 1980s, noting government hostility to council housing, but conscious of the need to retain some low-cost social housing in their areas, some local authorities – mainly small, based in the South and Conservative-controlled – started to transfer their stock to specially created housing associations. In England, a tenant ballot was not legally necessary for transfer, but approval from the central government was unlikely without a ballot. Local voluntary stock transfer (LVST), with its local authority endorsement, plus the nature of the new landlords, seemed to make stock transfer a smoother process than under the tenants' choice mechanism.

Blair was not an admirer of local government as a service supplier. Soon after becoming Prime Minister he declared:

> The days of the all-purpose local authority that planned and delivered everything are gone. They are finished. Local authorities will still deliver some services but their distinctive leadership role will be to weave and knit together the contribution of the various local stakeholders. (Blair, 1998, p 13)

New Labour regarded council housing as 'a "redundant project", characterised by falling demand, poor quality stock, unresponsive services and poor management and requiring significant rebranding' (Pawson and Mullins, 2010, p 16). In addition to this failure of council housing to match New Labour's 'modern' image, stock transfer offered the opportunity to upgrade council housing with private-sector finance. New Labour promoted LVST by:

*   offering tenants the carrot of a 'decent home' by setting a national target that all social-sector homes should be 'decent' by 2010 (see Chapter Eight);
*   supplying extra resources to promote transfer in the form of debt write-off and capital grants;
*   involving tenants in the early stages of stock transfer when the various options on how to achieve the decent homes standard had to be discussed;
*   restricting local government access to the finance needed to achieve the decent homes standard if the housing stock continued to be managed under local authority ownership;

- creating the option to transfer management to an Arm's Length Management Organisation (ALMO) set up to achieve the decent homes standard (see Chapter Eight), a device regarded by some commentators as a halfway stage to full stock transfer (Murie and Nevin, 2001);
- announcing that, irrespective of ownership, all social-sector rents would be determined by a common formula; and
- promoting the 'community ownership' and 'community housing mutual' models in Scotland and Wales (Pawson, 2009a).

Despite sustained opposition, some from within the Labour Party and organised by 'Defend Council Housing', stock transfer gained momentum. Between 1997 and 2009, almost a million dwellings were removed from local authority ownership via LVST. By 2010, almost half the local authorities in England and Wales had no 'council' houses. New Labour's various 'persuasion' techniques had produced dividends.

Marxist political economy

Interpretations of Marx's writings have identified two major models of the state's role in capitalist development – the 'instrumental' and the 'arbiter'. In the 1970s, 'instrumental Marxism' claimed that the state is a straightforward instrument used by the ruling class to dominate society and ensure the continuation of the capitalist system. Taking their cue from the dictum that 'the state is but a committee for managing the common affairs of the whole bourgeoisie' (Marx and Engels, 1848), instrumental Marxists asserts that the capitalist class uses the state for a variety of purposes:

- to take the steam out of radical movements by means of temporary concessions at times of social unrest;
- to maintain profits in times of surplus production;
- to sustain capitalist ideology through the nature of the institutions supported by the state;
- to keep workers fit to work in a capitalist economy; and
- to maintain the 'reserve army of labour' that capitalism needs in order to be able to respond to its boom–bust cycle of production.

The 'arbiter' model is grounded on Marx's earlier works in which – whilst disputing the notion, as propagated by social reformists, that the capitalist state could act in accordance with the 'common good' – he recognised that the state may obtain a degree of neutrality from capitalism and that it may act in the interests of the proletariat at certain moments in history.

This model allows the organised working class some influence in the historical construction of state housing policy via its involvement in social movements and offers a degree of optimism on the outcomes of struggles within and against the state. By placing its emphasis on class power as the mechanism for viable change the 'arbiter' model promises the possible erosion of capitalism by the ceaseless pressure from the working class arising from its everyday experience as welfare producers and recipients. It also allows Marxists to provide a more convincing account of why and how housing policy evolved with real improvements being made in working-class housing provision at times when the labour movement was strong (eg 1914–21 and 1945–51). However, although ascribing 'relative autonomy' to the state and allowing 'grassroots', 'rank-and-file' social movements a potential role in social change makes the Marxist account more plausible, it reduces its distinctness when compared to the social reformist perspective.

Social constructionism

Social constructionism is more of an epistemological position, a view on the nature of knowledge, than an explanatory theory. Social constructionists claim that all 'discourses' are situated historically and, because value and significance are culturally and historically specific, they are best understood when located in the detailed circumstances of their development. In explaining their passage into the social construction paradigm, Rose and Miller (2008, p 6) state:

> Perhaps the first move was from 'why' to 'how'. Theorists of the state addressed 'why-type' questions.... Why did a new institution appear, or why did an existing one change – a question often answered by gesturing to global processes such as modernization and individualization. We asked a different question, not 'why' but 'how', thereby lightening the weight of causality, or at least multiplying it and enabling us to abstain from the problems of 'explaining' such indigestible phenomena as state, class and so on.... Instead why not be content to trace small histories and their interesting trajectories? Why not study events and practices in terms of their singularity, the interrelations they define and the conditions that make them possible?

According to social constructionism, power influences the extent to which a particular discourse becomes 'realised', that is, widely regarded as an objective account of the real world. Thus, when applied to housing policy development, social constructionism adopts a systematically sceptical approach. It asks a series of questions about all *claims* that a given housing situation constitutes a housing problem (see Saraga, 1998, p 192):

- Who says so?
- What interests do they represent?
- Why do they say this? (What assumptions are they making?)
- How do they justify their views?
- What are the implications of their assumptions?

Answers to these questions are found via a detailed examination of the *specific* contexts of a condition *becoming* a social problem and the responses made to the problem in accordance with dominant discourses (see Box 2.7). Social constructionism has also embraced Foucault's idea of 'governmentality' (see Chapter One) – whereby 'conduct' meaning 'to guide', meets 'conduct' as self-regulating behaviour. His insight has been developed within the social constructionist perspective by a focus on the 'othering' process. People are separated from the mainstream via their assignment to a category or grouping characterised by what they are not: mainstream society–underclass; hard-working families–the unemployed; natives–immigrants; included–excluded; families–lone mothers; respectable–disreputable; owner–social tenant. 'Othering' has two benefits for the interests involved in the 'othering' process. Through a calculated administration of shame – stigmatising 'the other' –an enhanced feeling of self-worth and belonging is given to those outside the category. Moreover, those in the 'other' category may be encouraged to change their situation by the promise of inclusion (see ***Box 2.7***).

Box 2.7: Constructing *the* 'council' tenant

From the 1920s to the early 1970s being a council tenant carried a mark of respectability. Whilst it did not have the kudos attached to owner-occupation and, in some areas, there was a stigma attached to living in estates that housed former slum inhabitants (Rogaly and Taylor, 2009), being a council tenant was desired above the private landlord alternative. The sector was regarded as a 'core working-class' domain (Harloe, 1995, p 292) and 'a prize hard to come by' (Crossman, 1966, quoted in Jacobs et al, 2003b). The 'othering' process was present in the 1930s – with one local newspaper commenting on a characteristic smell in a housing estate (Jones B., 2010) – but the first post-war strike at the council tenant's character came from Peter Walker who, when Shadow Secretary of State for the Environment, contrasted the dependency of the council tenant with the homeowner's responsibility (Walker, 1977). In the countdown to the 1979 general election, Margaret Thatcher stepped up the stigma when, in response to a council tenant who had complained about the condition of her council home, she said:

> I hope you will not think me too blunt if I say that it may well be that your council accommodation is unsatisfactory but considering the fact you have been unable to buy your own accommodation you are lucky to have been given something which the rest of us are paying for out of our taxes. (Thatcher, 1979)

By the 2000s, academics had been talking about the 'residualisation' of local authority housing for many years – implying that a 'residue' remained – local authority housing had been rebranded as 'social' housing and a popular book on public housing – Lynsey Hanley's *(2007) Estates: An Intimate History* – stated:

> Play word association with the term 'council estate'. Estates mean alcoholism, drug addition, relentless petty stupidity, a kind of stir-craziness induced by chronic poverty and the human mind caged by the rigid bars of class and learned incuriosity. (Hanley, 2007, p 20)

Some New Labour politicians began to endorse this 'shameless' image of council tenants. In a speech to the Fabian Society on 5 February 2008, Caroline Flint, then Minister for Housing with a seat in the cabinet, asked 'Could new tenants who can work sign commitment contracts when getting a tenancy, agreeing to actively seek work alongside better support?' She claimed that the proposal was a way of overcoming a culture of 'no one works around here' (Flint, 2008, quoted in Wintour, 2008). Thus, as Gregory (2009, p ix) states, 'public housing is tainted by association with the imagery and stigma of the sink estate and this undermines popular support for all social housing'.

Overview

- With the exception of the behavioural approach each perspective on understanding housing policy has links to explanations of change and continuity:
  - laissez-faire (public choice theory);
  - social reformism (functionalism/rational policy analysis/organic theory);
  - Marxist political economy (class conflict); and
  - social constructionism (specific discourses/'governmentality').
- In response to perceptions of change in policy-formation procedures, 'governance' has become a fashionable term to apply to the political/policy process.

Questions for discussion

1. What connects the laissez-faire perspective to public choice theory?
2. Is the distinction between analysis *for* policy and analysis *of* policy useful?
3. In what ways does the new public sector managerialism claim to be 'new'?
4. Why was New Labour's stock transfer to registered social landlords more successful than 'tenants' choice'?

Websites

Introduction to public choice theory. Available at:
http://perspicuity.net/sd/pub-choice.html
Pluralism theory: A glossary of political terms. Available at:
http://www.auburn.edu/~johnspm/gloss/pluralist_theory
What is social constructionism? Available at:
http://www.psy.dmu.ac.uk/michael/soc_con_disc.htm

Further reading

Understanding the Policy Process: Analysing Welfare Policy and Practice (2009) by **John Hudson** and **Stuart Lowe** is a sound introduction to policy analysis; *Regulating Social Housing: Governing Decline* (2006) by **David Cowan** and **Morag McDermont** makes good use of the 'governmentality' idea to explore social housing and its regulation; and *Where the Other Half Lives: Lower Income Housing in a Neoliberal World* (2009) edited by **Sarah Glynn** is grounded in Marxist theory.

three

Housing policy: Continuity and change

Summary

- Poor housing conditions became problematical because they were regarded as a threat to social order and the nation's moral and physical health.
- At the end of the 19th century, a housing shortage was identified and many ideas were in circulation about how to overcome this scarcity (see Chapter One).
- Homeownership and council housing developed rapidly in the interwar period.
- Between 1945 and 1977, housing policy was dominated by 'the numbers game' with the political parties attempting to outbid each other on the quantity of houses they would produce.
- Labour governments attempted to tackle the housing problem by promoting subsidised local authority housing for 'general needs' in planned new towns and local authority estates.
- Initially, the Conservative Party maintained a robust council house-building programme but then switched emphasis from building for 'general needs' to building to meet the requirements arising from slum clearance. It promoted owner-occupation and attempted to revive private landlordism by relaxing rent controls.
- Both the major political parties encouraged the improvement of older homes and, from the early 1960s, started to promote housing associations.
- In the 1980s and 1990s, the Conservatives attempted to apply market forces to housing supply and consumption.
- In its first term, New Labour adopted the same policy orientation as the Conservatives but, after 2003, an attempt was made to stimulate housing supply – a project derailed by the 2008 'credit crunch'.

- The Coalition government rejected New Labour's centrally directed attempt to stimulate supply.

Housing becomes a social problem

It was the identification of the 'externalities' involved in concentrated poor housing that transformed housing into a social problem. Urban growth developed through short-distance moves of less than 30 miles by young people in search of work and freedom from village norms supplemented by migration from Ireland and the Scottish highlands. The migrants were of child-bearing age and those born in towns and cities soon provided the main source of population growth. Dwelling supply, drainage and sewerage could not keep pace with this billowing urban population with the result that many people were crammed into insanitary accommodation. However, poor housing conditions are not necessarily problematic: housing had to be constructed as a social problem. This was accomplished by a new group of experts in the 'public good' who thought it necessary to centralise administration to control 'externalities' and so secure a more wholesome nation.

Housing, health and the public good

Edwin Chadwick (1800–90) was the most formidable exponent of sanitary reform to advance the 'public good'. His *Report on the Sanitary Condition of the Labouring Population of Great Britain* (Chadwick, 1842) assembled a variety of statistics and opinions to demonstrate that existing sanitary arrangements generated a variety of 'externalities' (see *Box 3.1*).

> **Box 3.1:** Extracts from the *Report on the Sanitary Condition of the Labouring Population of Great Britain* (Chadwick, 1842, pp 369–72)
>
> - That of the 43,000 cases of widowhood, and 112,000 cases of destitute orphanage relieved from the poor rates in England and Wales alone, it appears that the greatest proportion of deaths of the heads of families occurred from [insanitary conditions] and other removable causes.
> - That the ravages of epidemics and other diseases do not diminish but tend to increase the pressure of population.
> - That the younger population, bred up under noxious physical agencies, is inferior in physical organization and general health.

- That the population so exposed is less susceptible of moral influences, and the effects of education are more transient than with a healthy population.
- That these adverse circumstances tend to produce an adult population short-lived, improvident, reckless, and intemperate, and with habitual avidity for sensual gratifications.
- That these habits lead to the abandonment of all the conveniences and decencies of life, and especially lead to the overcrowding of their homes, which is destructive to the morality as well as the health of large classes of both sexes.

Chadwick was so anxious to ensure that his findings produced action that he consulted Charles Dickens on how to present his report for maximum impact. He also ignored alternative analyses circulating at the time that stressed 'work, wages and food' as causing poor health in favour of the politically less controversial notion of a polluted atmosphere (Hamlin, 1998). Nevertheless, his report did not produce immediate results and it required pressure group activity from the 'Health of Towns Association' to promote the measures. Ever helpful to the cause, Charles Dickens included references to Chadwick's thesis in *Dombey and Son*, first published in monthly parts between 1846 and 1848:

> Those who study the physical sciences ... tell us that if the noxious particles that rise from vitiated air were palpable to the sight ... we would see them rolling on to corrupt the better portions of the town. But if the moral pestilence that rises with them ... could be made discernible too, how terrible the revelation. Then should we see depravity, impiety, drunkenness, theft, murder and a long train of nameless sins against the natural affections and repulsions of mankind. (Dickens, 1953 [1846–48], p 625)

The 1848 Public Health Act set up a Central Board of Health with powers to establish local boards to regulate offensive trades, provide parks and public baths, remove nuisances and manage sewers wherever the death rate exceeded 23 per 1000 population.

Public health and local governance

The attempts of Chadwick, the Secretary to the Central Board of Health, to use its powers to cajole the localities into action were firmly resisted on the grounds that he was interfering with property rights and local governance.

In 1858 such opposition led to the abolition of the Board in a climate of opinion well captured by *The Lancet* (12 February 1858):

> a few doctrinaires nursed in the narrow conceits of bureaucracy, scornful alike of popular knowledge and of popular government, seized upon the sanitary theory as a means of exercising central power of domiciliary inspection and irresponsible interference with the conduct and property of Englishmen….The truth is we do not like paternal governments.

Despite Chadwick's demise there was sporadic progress towards improving public health through better understanding of the causes of ill health, middle-class panic during periodic cholera outbreaks and the work of 'ad hoc' health authorities set up by some localities under private legislation.

The 1875 Public Health Act, which consolidated and enhanced earlier legislation, was a major progressive step. It set out the duties of the sanitary authorities, to be established in every locality, as securing an adequate sewage disposal system, a water supply and a method of drainage. The Act also allowed local authorities to supervise street widths and building heights. Using the Act's authority, the Local Government Board, established in 1871, issued a new code of model by-laws that, although not compulsory, was adopted by many local authorities. Tens of thousands of terraced dwellings were built under these by-laws, each with an indoor water supply and a walled yard containing a privy and perhaps a coalhouse, laid out in such a way as to facilitate sewage removal and provide ventilation. Sir John Simon, who framed the Act, described it as 'the end of a great argument'. So it was. Commenting on the application of the model by-laws in Preston, Morgan (1993, p 59) asked 'Was Preston's housing revolutionised?' and concluded that 'the short answer is that most new housing was, and that it was good enough to have survived to the present day, still mostly in good condition'. However, not all authorities adopted the model by-laws and, when adopted, they were not always enforced. In Leeds, for example, building back-to-back houses continued until 1937, justified by the arguments that they were warmer and that their lower building cost brought rents within the range of poor people (Wohl, 1983).

The slum

The 1875 Public Health Act ensured that new dwellings were built to sanitary standards and water and sewerage municipalisation, paid collectively through the rates, made basic hygienic standards more affordable to the working class. Nevertheless, the problem of unwholesome dwellings, built before sanitary regulations were adopted, remained. These dwellings became known as slums, a term referring to individual houses deemed 'unfit for human habitation' and entire districts – *the* slum – regarded as an area of social pathology, the breeding ground for disease, crime and immorality. The slum 'nuisance' was to be eradicated by forcing landlords to repair or demolish individual unfit dwellings or by removing entire slum areas. Local government's role was not to build, except in exceptional circumstances and with special permission, but to flatten slums and assemble a site for rebuilding by private enterprise and philanthropic organisations.

In 1885 the Royal Commission on the Housing of the Working Classes investigated the impact of this 'nuisance removal' and concluded that, in many areas, the situation had deteriorated since the 1850s. It recommended that local authorities should be allowed to build outside clearance areas and the Treasury should charge the lowest possible interest rate for housing schemes without making a loss. In addition, the 1883 Cheap Trains Act, requiring railway companies to operate cheap workman's trains, should be enforced and railway companies should be compelled to build houses to replace those demolished to make way for new railroads. In 1890, the Housing of the Working Classes Act permitted local authorities to erect houses outside clearance areas provided that no scheme made a loss. As Morton (1991, p 2) has pointed out: 'There was no question at this point of any agency operating on other than commercial terms. Authorities were expected to act like commercial companies and seek a return not exceeding 5 per cent'. Although some authorities ignored the 'no loss' requirement, only 20,000 local authority houses had been built by 1914.

Housing policy: 1900–39

The Liberal reforms: 1906–14

Despite the numerous solutions to the 'housing issue' in circulation at the turn of the century (see Chapter One), the legislation passed by the Liberal Party between 1906 and 1914 had little impact. In his 1909 'People's Budget', Lloyd George, influenced by Henry George's ideas, introduced land taxation at 20% on 'unearned increments' arising from land sales and an annual tax on the capital value of undeveloped land. However, problems with land valuation and adverse court judgements meant that, by 1914, only £612,787 had been collected and the tax was abandoned. Despite some experimental schemes in new town planning, the garden city idea failed to gain momentum and its advocates turned their attention to controlling suburban development. Between 1893 and 1908, cheap public transport had allowed half a million acres of land to be used for suburban building and it was argued that this new suburbia had to be planned to avoid past mistakes. The 1909 Housing and Planning Act was a diluted version of an attempt to allow local government to shape the emerging suburbs by permitting them to acquire land by compulsory purchase. Rather than grant such a power, the Act gave local authorities the permissive authority to control new estate development after a lengthy exercise in public consultation (Packer, 2001). Few local authorities used the Act.

Rent control

In 1914, private landlordism was a 'cottage industry', but a big one with possibly 90% of households renting from private landlords. Most landlords owned only a few houses and financed their purchases from personal savings plus borrowing from insurance companies, building clubs and building societies. In the early 20th century, the residential property market experienced a slump, but, contrary to market theory, vacant properties existed close to overcrowded and unfit dwellings. This was because the private landlord sector was divided into sub-markets and many landlords were reluctant to move 'downmarket' to house a 'lower class' who may not be able to pay rent on a regular basis. Landlord–tenant relationships at the lower levels of the market were strained, it being a constant battle to extract rent from poor families prone to 'moonlight flits' and aggressive behaviour.

House-building stopped on the outbreak of the First World War and worker movement into the munitions factories led to rent increases. Faced with working-class unrest, notably the rent strikes in Glasgow led by Mary Barbour, the government introduced rent control and restricted interest rates on the associated mortgages. Rent control was buttressed by giving tenants tenure security to prevent landlords from evicting sitting tenants to extract a higher rent. Although rent control was due to be revoked six months after the end of hostilities, fear of social unrest prevented such a move and the Conservatives, in power for most of the interwar period, attempted to back out of rent control gradually. Their general approach was to classify dwellings according to their markets and decontrol those sectors where they thought supply and demand were in balance. New building for rent was decontrolled soon after the end of the war and, by 1939, dwellings with a high rateable value had been decontrolled and houses with mid-range rateable values became decontrolled on vacant possession. Only low-value houses, about 44% of the total rented stock, remained controlled and the Conservatives declared their intention to abolish all rent control as soon as possible. Private landlordism experienced a modest revival in the mid-1930s prompted by the political dominance of the Conservative Party making a return to rent control unlikely, the favourable economic conditions for residential construction (Kemp, 2004) and the 1933 Housing (Financial Provisions) Act that allowed local authorities to guarantee loans made by building societies for building rented accommodation.

Council housing for the working class

The genesis of mass council housing can be found in the requirement to accommodate the munitions workers needed to produce the weapons required for the First World War. The requirement to attract skilled labour in a climate of worker militancy produced a 'welfare' approach to housing. After 1915, subsidised permanent dwellings were sponsored by the Ministry of Munitions and, by 1918, 10,284 homes on 38 estates had been constructed. Gretna, with the largest concentration of munitions workers, became a 'mini welfare state' with state public houses, canteens and community buildings, as well as state housing.

The Fabian Society, whose members occupied influential positions on the various wartime reconstruction committees, played a significant role in framing the 1919 Housing and Town Planning Act. This Act made it mandatory for each authority to compile a plan to meet its housing needs and granted 'open-ended' central subsidies to local authorities to offset building costs above a set rate contribution. The Fabians received valuable support from garden city advocates who, although maintaining that building 100 garden cities was the best way to create a 'land fit for heroes to live in', endorsed the view that community provision, not profit-motivated private enterprise, was the right path. Treasury opposition to subsidised local authority housing was overcome by fear of social strife. Lloyd George put the issue bluntly; 'Even at the cost of £100,000,000', he said, 'what was that compared with the stability of the State' (quoted in Johnson, 1968, p 346). Although subsidised local authority housing was regarded as a temporary expedient, scheduled to end in 1927, the new homes were to be built to high standards. The Tudor Walters Committee Report (Tudor Walters, 1918), mainly written by the Fabian Socialist, Raymond Unwin, recommended that the houses should be built at low densities and have bathrooms, gardens and, in some cases, 'parlours'. As Burnett (1986, p 255) has stated, 'every Englishman was, or felt he was, a disinherited country gentleman and social stability would be created by mimicking the "manor" in suburban estates'.

Central subsidies to local government acted as a 'butterfly valve' in the interwar period serving to direct local authorities towards central priorities. The 1919 Housing and Town Planning Act ran into difficulties because too many local authorities, competing for the limited capacity of the construction industry, overheated the market. In 1921 the Conservatives, aware that working-class power was being eroded by rising unemployment (Swenarton, 2009), used escalating house prices as a reason to end 'open-ended' central subsidies . The 1923 Housing Act introduced lower, fixed subsidies to assist local authorities to build houses, but councils were able to build only when they had demonstrated that the private sector could not build sufficient new dwellings. The contrast between the Conservatives' 'residual' view of council housing and Labour's more comprehensive 'suburban solution' was revealed in the 1924 Housing (Financial Provisions) Act passed by a minority Labour government. This Act, part of a long-term agreement between the government, unions and the building industry, removed the restrictions on house-building by local authorities and, in return for meeting targets for new building, granted higher subsidies. The 1930 Housing Act, another minority Labour government measure, introduced special subsidies to encourage local authorities to tackle the unfitness problem.

Replacing the overcrowded slums

During the interwar period, homeownership developed at a rapid rate (see **Box 3.2** and *Figure 3.1*) and its growth influenced the Conservative Party's attitude to council housing. In the late 1920s, the Conservatives continued subsidies to local authorities under both the 1923 and 1924 Acts – albeit at reducing levels – but, in the early 1930s, leading Conservatives expressed anxiety about 'the trend of recent events, which tend to turn our local authorities into owners and still more managers of small house properties' (quoted in Yelling, 1992, p 90). The 1933 Housing (Financial Provisions) Act ended general subsidies for local authority housing retaining only the 1930 subsidy related to the buildings required for rehousing people displaced from the slums. The 1935 Housing Act granted extra subsidies to reduce overcrowding by building flats. It is clear that, in the 1930s, Conservative housing strategy was to confine the state to removing 'pathological' conditions in the cities by building new flats leaving private enterprise to build new dwellings for homeowners on suburban sites. In England and Wales, council housing as a proportion of total building declined from 44.4% (in 1919–24) to 21.5% in the late 1930s, but in Scotland, council housing dominated the private sector by a ratio of about three to one (Holmans, 2008).

Figure 3.1: *Housing tenure in the UK, 1919–2010*

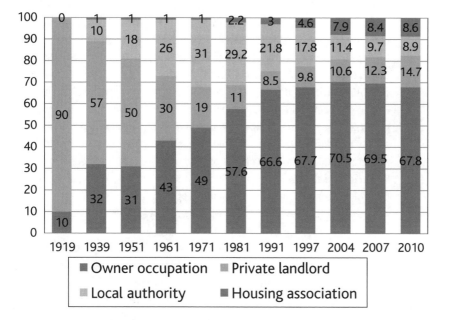

Sources: Adapted from Holmans (2008), DCL (2010b, Table 101) and Office for National Statistics (2010b)

Box 3.2: The growth of homeownership

The proportion of homeowners in 1918 has been estimated at 10% but, as Holmans (2008, p 130) states, this estimate 'has no firm basis.... It appears to have gained credence through repetition'. Nonetheless, even if, as seems likely, the percentage of homeowners in 1918 was more than 10%, the expansion of the tenure to 34% in 1939 was significant. A variety of factors influenced this growth:

- State assistance in the form of:
    - direct subsidies for inexpensive, private-sector houses under the 1919 Housing (Additional Powers) Act and the 1923 Housing Act;
    - tax relief on mortgage interest although the impact of such relief was modest because Schedule A tax (see *Box 3.4*) had to be paid;
    - mortgage guarantees from local authorities;
    - loans from local authorities to the owner-occupiers under the 1899 Small Dwellings Acquisitions Act and the 1925 Housing Act under which loans worth £55 million were made between 1919 and 1928.

- Suburban railway and road extension (at least until the 1935 Restriction of Ribbon Development Act) made it possible for more people to live at a distance from their place of work. This trend, together with the dearth of planning controls, enabled builders to erect dwellings on 'greenfield' sites. In the interwar period, building land was only 10% in real terms of its price in the 2000s (Aldred, 2010). Cheap land helped to keep prices stable at an average of £590, worth about £27,500 in 2009 after allowing for general inflation.

- Finance for house purchase became more accessible because savings invested with building societies, helped by tax concessions to investors, increased rapidly and some developers offered guarantees on part of a mortgage. The numerous building society offices offered a convenient and generally safe haven for the savings of the middle class and the skilled working class. Rent control had made a traditional repository of such savings, direct investment in houses to let, less attractive. In the 1930s, real interest rates declined making homeownership more affordable.

- Many landlords, concerned about rent control, sold their properties. By 1938 1.4 million former private landlord houses had become owner-occupied. New investment in private renting declined due to rent control and competition from homeownership with its more favourable tax regime (Merrett, 1979).

- Throughout the interwar period, owner-occupation was sustained by what has been called 'the ideology of homeownership' (Ronald, 2008). The Conservative MP Noel Skelton, who endorsed property-ownership as a means to foster individualism and self-reliance, coined the term 'property-owning democracy' (Skelton, 1924) – a term indicating that those without property were excluded from democracy. As Scott (2003) has demonstrated, middle-class movement into owner-occupied suburbia was accompanied by the development of a suburban identity. This was characterised by the idealised married women's role as expert housewife, providing a happy and clean home for her family via labour-saving devices and efficient household management practices plus the stable, respectable, male citizen spending his leisure time in home-related activities. Homeownership was distinguished from council housing by a bay window, greater embellishment and especially by a name such as 'Chez Nous' or 'Dunroamin'. As one aspiring homeowner noted, 'the working class, generally, does not inhabit places worthy of a name' (quoted in Gardiner, 2010, p 296). The success of homeownership 'normalisation' and the related council tenant 'othering' was revealed in the 'Cutteslowe Wall', first built in 1934 by owner-occupiers across a road to divide the homeowners from the adjoining council estate and not finally pulled down until 1959 (Collison, 1963).

Labour, 1945–51: A planned solution

At the outbreak of the Second World War, the government did not wait for social unrest before putting rent controls in place. In 1939 rents were frozen except for very high-value properties.

Although progress was made between the wars, a serious housing shortage remained that was intensified by the war. Some 458,000 houses were destroyed with 250,000 badly damaged and, when hostilities ceased, household formation accelerated and the birth rate increased. Housing became *the* political issue and a squatting movement developed with homeless people, sometimes led by the Communist Party, taking over disused army camps and empty luxury flats. Despite these problems, there was no housing equivalent of the Beveridge report on social security, perhaps a reflection that an obvious remedy – state-directed production, which had been so successful in meeting the needs of the war economy – was available. In 1945, the *Daily Mirror* declared that 'Housing will have to be tackled like a problem of war. We make, as if by miracle, tanks, aircraft, battleships, pipelines, harbours! Are we then incapable of building houses?' (14 June).

Aneurin Bevan, who became responsible for the housing programme in 1945, favoured local authorities as house-builders because they were, in his words, 'plannable instruments' and could meet, in a direct manner, the needs of poor people for homes to rent. The government offered local authorities a new flat-rate subsidy for 'general needs' houses, which tripled the subsidies on offer in the late 1930s and made them available for 60 rather than 40 years. Bevan made it mandatory for local authorities to make a rate contribution to house-building, allowed local authorities to borrow from the Public Works Loans Board at an interest rate below the market rate and introduced a strict building licence system to control the use of materials by the private sector. The supply of local authority houses would form part of a planned physical environment (see *Box 3.3*).

Box 3.3: Post-war planning

The 1947 Town and Country Planning Act:

- imposed taxes of between 40% and 100% on the 'betterment' value of development land;
- set up a Central Land Board with powers to purchase land compulsorily;
- placed a duty on local authorities to prepare development plans;
- allowed local authorities to acquire land by compulsion; and

> • required most developments to have planning permission, which meant that housing supply, unlike any other privately supplied good, was controlled and regulated by the local democratic process.
>
> The 1946 New Towns Act made provision to:
>
> • establish new towns to relieve congestion in the major cities;
> • revive the fortunes of interwar 'depressed areas'; and
> • create balanced communities.

Mixed communities

Bevan wanted to ensure that all new housing schemes promoted mixed communities and demanded that three out of four new houses should be owned by local authorities and built to high standards. He asserted 'We don't want a country of East Ends and West Ends, with all the petty snobberies this involves' (quoted in Foot, 1975, p 78). His vision was that local authority housing should replicate the social mix of the Welsh village with its 'living tapestry of a mixed community' (quoted in Foot, 1975, p 78). The 1949 Housing Act removed the requirement, present in all previous housing legislation, that local authority housing was to be supplied only to 'the working class' and, although opposed by other cabinet members, Bevan insisted on higher standards than had been provided in the interwar period. Space in each house was increased by 134 square feet, an outbuilding was added and there were water closets, both upstairs and downstairs, in each family dwelling. Such improvements increased the cost of a council house by 35% compared to pre-war levels. In 1948, Bevan ended the prefabricated bungalows programme, started in 1944, arguing that such homes were 'rabbit hutches' of low quality with limited space. Labour was not opposed to homeownership – it was a matter of priorities – but 80% of the houses built between 1945 and 1951 were local authority houses. Labour's 1951 manifesto stated that, in future, 'Most of these houses will as now be built for rent and not for sale, and for the benefit of those whose housing need is greatest' (Labour Party, 1951, p 4).

The Conservatives and housing policy, 1951–64

The 'people's house'

Housing construction was sluggish between 1945 and 1951 and actually declined between 1950 and 1951. In the late 1940s, the Conservatives blamed the slow progress on state involvement, arguing that restrictions on the private sector and land value taxation were impeding the housing drive. At the 1950 Conservative Party Conference the delegates passed a resolution, against the wishes of the leadership, calling for a target of 300,000 houses per year and started a political numbers auction that lasted until the 1970s (see *Figure 3.2*). The 1951 Census revealed the dire housing situation – 48% of households did not have access to all four basic amenities: a cooking stove, piped water, a water closet and a fixed bath (Addison, 2010, p 34). There were marked area differences in housing conditions with, as examples, 66% of households in the South Wales valleys not having a fixed bath, 27% of households in South Yorkshire without exclusive use of a lavatory and 51% of dwellings in Glasgow with only one or two rooms compared to 5.5% in Greater London (Kynaston, 2007).

In its 1951 manifesto, the Conservative Party declared that 'In a property-owning democracy, the more people who own their homes the better' (Conservative Party, 1951, p 3). Initially, Harold Macmillan, the minister responsible for meeting the 300,000 per annum target, contemplated an

Figure 3.2: *Housing construction in the UK, 1919–2009 (000s)*

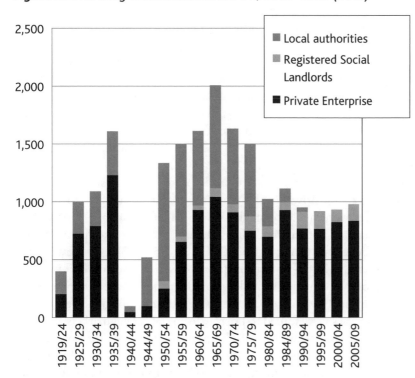

Sources: Adapted from DCL (2010b, Table 241) and Holmans (2008)

enhanced role for the private sector, stating in his memoirs 'I introduced, in answer to several arranged questions, my new policy, on [the] ratio between council and private building, 1 for 1 instead of 1 for 5' (Macmillan, 2004, p 119). However, he soon realised that he had no hope of meeting his target through private enterprise as the private sector had built only 26,000 dwellings in the previous year. Thus, for a time, the Conservatives relied on local government and continued the system of private-sector building licences. By reducing standards (the so-called 'people's house' was 15% smaller than those built in the 1940s), encouraging terrace building and increasing subsidies, 300,000 new dwellings were built in 1953, with 245,000 by local authorities.

Stimulating the private sector

A committee, set up in 1951 to discuss ways to restore the free market in housing, set out the long-term objectives of Conservative housing policy as:

• the encouragement of homeownership;
• the limitation of subsidies to slum clearance; and
• the majority of people – tenants and owner-occupiers – should pay the full cost of the accommodation they occupy (Weiler, 2003, pp 362–3).

Macmillan was highly successful in organising the mass production of local authority housing, and, at first, he resisted both party demands to promote homeownership and Treasury insistence on reducing subsidies. However, sensitive to Conservative concerns about the growth of state housing and the fear that the new towns were a device to help Labour move its supporters into the Tory heartlands (Seldon, 1981), he started to prepare for a return to the 1930s' policy.

Initiatives introduced in the mid-1950s marked some tentative Conservative steps towards applying free-market principles to housing. The policies were heralded in the White Paper, *Housing: The Next Step*, which acclaimed homeownership as 'the most satisfying to the individual and most beneficial to the nation' (MHLG, 1953, p 3). Homeownership was encouraged by abolishing licences for private-sector building and allowing local authorities to make more loans for house purchase; loans increased from 21,000 in 1951/52 to 77,000 in 1964 (Merrett, 1982). Local authorities were forced to borrow from the capital markets at higher interest rates than had been available from the Public Works Loan Board, 'general needs' subsidies were withdrawn and available central resources were concentrated on slum clearance. The statutory contribution from the rates to council housing was ended and an attempt was made to persuade local authorities to charge more 'realistic' rents with local rent rebate schemes to cushion the impact on low-income households. Private-sector solutions to the substandard housing problem were encouraged by introducing mandatory improvement grants for basic amenity installation.

Worries that large urban authorities were intent on extending into the counties by purchasing land for new estates, prompted housing policy to become a matter of containing 'urban England' (Shapely, 2007). In 1955, the extension of green belts to areas other than London was promoted through a circular to local planning authorities. The Minister for Housing, Duncan Sandys, stated:

> I am convinced that for the well-being of our people and for the preservation of our countryside the unrestricted sprawl of the great cities must be contained.... But I regret that nowhere [outside London] has any formal green belt as yet been posed. I am accordingly asking all planning authorities concerned to give this matter further consideration, with a view to submitting to me proposals for the creation of clearly defined green belts, wherever this is appropriate. (Sandys, 1955, quoted in Elson, 1986, pp 13–14)

'Rachmanism'

In the early 1950s, the Conservatives attempted to revive the private landlord sector by abolishing rent control on new property and allowing rent increases in return for better maintenance. The strategy culminated in the 1957 Rent Act. Rents above a specified rateable value were decontrolled and 'creeping decontrol' was introduced by ending rent control when a house became vacant. This experiment in free-market economics was a political disaster. It did not halt the decline in private landlordism – in 1957 there were 4.5 million privately rented homes, but by 1965 the total had fallen to 3.5 million – but it generated a political storm as the vicious tactics of a small number of slum landlords to secure vacant possession added a new term to the English language – 'Rachmanism' – named after Perec Rachman, the most notorious practitioner of the abuses. Private landlordism's already tarnished reputation was blemished again and, in an attempt to cool the political controversy, 'general needs' subsidies were restored to local authorities in 1961 and, in 1963, homeownership was stimulated by the abolition of Schedule A tax (see ***Box 3.4***).

> ## Box 3.4: Taxation and homeownership
>
> Schedule A was a tax levied on the rental income all homeowners were assumed to have paid to themselves. It ensured that a homeowner was treated in the same way as a private landlord who had to pay tax on rental income. As part of Schedule A payment, both owner-occupiers and private landlords were allowed to deduct their mortgage interest payments from their income tax liability. Schedule A tax had a diminishing impact in the years after the Second World War because the house values on which it was based were fixed at 1936 levels. Thus, as the real impact of Schedule A tax abated, tax relief on mortgage interest became more valuable to homeowners. When Schedule A tax was abolished for resident owners in 1963, mortgage interest tax relief continued and thereby the subsidy to homeowners was enhanced. The tax concession was important to people paying the standard rate of taxation and very valuable to those people paying the higher rates of tax, especially when interest and taxation rates were high.

Labour and housing, 1964–70

Despite the heated housing debate during the 1964 election campaign, the two principal parties adopted similar policies. The Conservative Party, although lukewarm on local authority housing, had to give it a role. Private landlordism had been totally discredited by the publicity given to Rachman's abuses and an attempt, started in 1962, to create a 'third sector' of non-profit landlords renting at cost through 'cost rent societies', a form of housing association, needed time to make an impact. A ten-year plan (MHLG, 1963) promised 400,000 houses each year, a substantial portion being local authority homes. Labour outbid the Conservatives by setting a target of 500,000 houses per year. The party had a stronger commitment to public housing than its adversary, but thought it necessary to declare its support for homeownership by a promise to reduce the mortgage interest rate to 4%.

The Labour government of 1964–70 attempted to adopt an even-handed approach to local authority tenants and homeowners. Its five-year housing programme promised to split new building 50/50 between the two sectors. Homeownership was stimulated by an 'option mortgage' scheme allowing low-income households, not benefiting from mortgage interest tax relief, to receive a low-interest loan. Gradually, Labour began to restore the balance between public- and private-sector building that had tipped in favour of homeownership in the late 1950s and early 1960s but, as Dunleavy (1981, p 24) has commented, 'if Labour's strategy was successful in terms of the number of public housing completions, it contained the seeds of its own demise in the type of housing being completed'. Some low-rise estates were designed on 'Radburn' principles – separating vehicle and pedestrian access – but the most significant policy failure was high-rise (see **Box 3.5**).

Box 3.5: Cities in the sky

Flats were never popular with the people they were designed to house. Their form was alien to the ground-level terraced property familiar to the English working class and flats 'were the products of monolithic and large-scale design which gave little scope for the users to modify through their ordinary domestic behaviour' (Ravetz and Turkington, 1995, p 57). Yet, although survey after survey demonstrated that people did not want flats, flats were what they got (Kynaston, 2007). Until the mid-1950s, technological limitations restricted block heights, but advances in construction techniques allowed high-rise building. By 1966–67, 25% of the dwellings constructed were high-rise and, in the major cities, the proportion was far higher – up to 70% in Greater London. Over 60% of tower blocks were built by industrialised systems.

High-rise was the product of a number of influences. Le Corbusier (1927) had asserted that houses should be 'machines for living in'. Well-spaced tower blocks, providing homes with equal access to daylight, should be linked by 'streets in the air' to encourage social interaction and allow the areas around the blocks to be used as parkland. By the early 1950s the architectural profession was in thrall to Le Corbusier's 'high modernism' with Peter and Alison Smithson, leading architects and fervent believers in 'streets in the sky', declaring that 'Folk-build is dead in England' (quoted in Kynaston, 2009, p 280). The major building firms, who possessed the techniques for systems building, regarded high-rise as a source of profit and used their influence on the National Building Agency and senior politicians to promote tower blocks. Central government wanted housing 'units' to be built quickly and regarded system building as a way of achieving this objective. Many city authorities demanded more homes within their boundaries in order to retain rateable value and preserve civic status (Glendinning and Muthesius, 1994), whereas suburban authorities, abetted by the green belt policy, resisted most attempts to move 'overspill' from clearance areas to the counties. High-rise building was also assisted by an influential 'anti-suburban' movement that developed in the 1930s and was at its zenith in the 1950s. It objected to 'the march of bricks and mortar'. Its flavour was captured by the urban historian Lewis Munford when he declared:

> The suburban movement from the centre carries no hope or promise of life at a higher level. Just as our expanding technological universe pushes our daily existence further from its human centre, so the expanding urban

---

universe carries its separate fragments even farther from the city, leaving individuals more dissociated, lonely and helpless than he probably ever was. (Munford, 1961, quoted in Barker, 2009, p 23)

Private landlords and improving older dwellings

In the 1950s, the Labour Party's attitude to private landlordism was aggressively negative and it developed proposals for local authorities to take over the sector. However, in office, and influenced by the Milner Holland Report on London housing (Milner Holland, 1965), which demonstrated that, despite rogue landlords, the majority of landlord–tenant relationships were satisfactory, Labour replaced municipalisation with regulation. New mechanisms were set up to regulate rents, giving tenants and landlords the opportunity to ask rent assessment committees to determine a 'fair' rent – one that ignored scarcity value – for a property. Labour also promoted a switch away from clearance towards home improvement on an area basis, justifying the change as a positive measure aimed at reducing the disruption of established communities via clearance. However, the policy was also a response to the financial crisis of 1967; rehabilitation was cheaper than demolition and new-build.

Conservative housing policy, 1970–74

'Fair' rents and rent rebates

The 1972 Housing Finance Act made provision for local authority rents to move towards the 'fair' rents charged in the private sector with poorer tenants protected from rent increases by a national rent rebate scheme for council tenants. If, having charged 'fair' rents, a particular local authority housing revenue account made a surplus – the 'fair rents' producing more than the costs involved in providing council houses – this surplus had to be paid to the government.

It is possible to construe the 1972 Housing Finance Act in two ways. It can interpreted as a move towards restoring a free market in rented accommodation especially if one accepts that there was a potential link to be made between 'fair' rents and future 'market' rents. Alternatively, the Act can be seen as a rational/technical measure designed to make use of available resources more effectively. It was presented in this way in the White Paper *Fair Deal for Housing* (DoE, 1971, p 4), which condemned the existing system of distributing housing subsidies based on the historical entitlements of earlier legislation as providing 'subsidy for housing authorities which do not need it' and 'giving too little to authorities with the worst problems of slum clearance and overcrowding'. The Act also introduced a national rent allowance scheme for tenants in the private landlord and housing association sectors.

Labour, 1974–79: The party's over

Labour recast the policy contained in the 1972 Housing Finance Act. The national system of rent rebates and allowances was retained but local authorities were instructed to charge only 'reasonable' rents. The 1975 Housing Rents and Subsidies Act consolidated all existing assistance and granted a subsidy worth 66% of loan charges on new capital investment. The ideas on neighbourhood renewal contained in the Conservatives' White Paper *Better Homes: The Next Priorities* (DoE, 1973) were adopted and incorporated into the 1974 Housing Act. Housing associations were given a major role by the legislation. If registered with the Housing Corporation they became entitled to the Housing Association Grant (HAG) designed to pay, as a capital sum, the difference between a project's cost and the amount that could be raised by charging 'fair' rents. Between 1974 and 1976 local authorities and housing associations were provided with resources to purchase and refurbish properties owned by private landlords in 'stress' areas – partly meeting the long-standing demand from Labour Party activists to 'socialise' the private landlord sector. In addition, housing associations were encouraged by the HAG to build new homes. These measures, combined with the impact of a more generous improvement grant regime and the subsidies needed to boost council house construction because of high interest rates, meant that housing expenditure almost doubled between 1971/72 and 1975/76.

The 1976 sterling crisis and the agreements made with the International Monetary Fund produced big cuts in capital expenditure. Anthony Crosland, Secretary of State for the Environment, declared that 'the party's over' and a housing review concluded:

> We should no longer think about [housing] only in terms of national totals; we must try to secure a better balance between investment in new houses and the improvement and repair of older houses … and we must make it easier for people to obtain the tenure they want. (DoE, 1977, p 7)

Economic circumstances and the growing popularity of owner-occupation, described in the housing review as a 'basic and natural desire of all people', had combined to modify Labour's faith in public housing. The council building programme was cut back and local authority autonomy to decide how many new houses to build, subject only to meeting 'cost yardsticks', was ended. The Environmental Secretary, Peter Shore, declared that Britain was 'pensioning off the bulldozer' (Shore, 1976, quoted in Harrison, 2010, p 80). Improvement grants were scaled back and the policy of bringing private landlords into the 'social' sector was curtailed.

The New Right and housing policy

In 1975 the Conservative party acquired a leader with firm anti-collectivist beliefs as was demonstrated in Ranelagh's record of Margaret Thatcher's first and only visit to the Conservative Research Department:

> Another colleague had also prepared a paper arguing that the 'middle way' was the pragmatic path for the Conservative Party to take.... Before he had finished speaking to his paper, the new Party leader reached into her briefcase and took out a book. It was Friedrich von Hayek's *The Constitution of Liberty*. Interrupting our pragmatist, she held the book up for all of us to see. 'This,' she said sternly, 'is what we believe' and banged Hayek down on the table. (Ranelagh, 1991, p ix)

By 1975 there were years of experience of state intervention in housing against which the ideas of laissez-faire economists could be tested. It was the predictions made by such theorists as Hayek that made their arguments so powerful. In 1960, Hayek had warned that subsidised state housing would result in uncontrollable expenditure and the large increase in state subsidies to council housing in the late 1970s could be interpreted as confirmation of Hayek's prediction. The experience of state housing also created concern about the lack of consumer influence in the local authority sector. It was alleged that architects working for local authorities had ignored the views of potential tenants in designing their 'urban utopias'. State housing's negative features were contrasted with the positive aspects of homeownership, which, so it was argued, encouraged personal responsibility and gave people a capital stake in society.

The Right to Buy

Selling council houses was not a new idea – it had started in the late 19th century – but, although some Conservative-controlled authorities were enthusiastic about sales (Jones B., 2010), its national impact was limited despite the government granting local authorities a general consent to sell in 1952. During the 1974 election campaign, the Conservatives promised to allow council tenants to buy their homes at 33% less than the market value. In 1975, a member of the shadow cabinet suggested that council tenants who had occupied their houses for 20 years should be given their homes. According to Gilmour (1992, p 142) 'Mrs Thatcher feared that those on the Wates estates, the least well-off owner occupiers, whom she regarded as "our people" would have resented council house occupiers being given something for nothing' and hence the outright gift suggestion was changed to the discount system of 1974, but on more generous terms. This proposal caused great concern amongst Harold Wilson's advisors and a scheme to sell council homes was prepared in secret by Labour but never published (Haines, 1977; see also ***Box 3.6***).

Box 3.6: The 1980 Housing Act

Council house privatisation was linked to the notion of tenants' rights in the 1980 Housing Act. Local authority tenants became 'secure tenants' with a clearer set of rights regarding possession. People who had been 'secure tenants' for three years (later reduced to two) were given an additional individual right to purchase their homes at a substantial discount on its market value: 33% for three years' tenancy rising by 1% per year to a 50% maximum, later extended to 60% on houses and 70% on flats, subject to a 'cost floor' based on the capital expenditure on the house made by the local authority in the last eight years. Tenants of non-charitable housing associations were given similar rights. The push of higher rents was added to the pull of discounts by introducing a new system that withdrew subsidy from local authorities on the assumption that they would increase their rents according to ministerial guidelines. Later, eligibility for Housing Benefit was restricted so that, by 1988, only households on less than 50% of average male gross earnings were able to claim, compared to 110% of average male gross earnings in 1983.

Liberalising the private sector

In the early 1980s some circumspect moves aimed at reviving private landlordism were introduced and a number of innovative but limited schemes to promote low-cost homeownership were set up. In 1986, the Building Societies Act completed a process of allowing building societies and banks to compete in a deregulated mortgage market. Mortgage deregulation made it possible to expand homeownership with deregulation shifting 'the market to one where consumers could obtain the funding they wanted at the market price rather than being subject to market restrictions' (ODPM, 2005a, para 3.34).

Changing housing associations

From the early 1960s both the major political parties showed an increasing interest in housing associations as housing's 'third arm', but for different reasons. Mullins and Murie (2006, p 187) pose the question: are housing associations 'state, market or third sector?' and their legal status as 'public' or 'private' has been legally contested. Their political appeal resided in this ambiguity: Labour regarding them as a vehicle to 'socialise' private landlordism and the Conservatives as an alternative to local authority housing. Until the late 1980s, housing associations obtained their capital finance from public funds and their borrowing, therefore, counted as part of the Public Sector Borrowing Requirement. The 1988 Housing Act transformed housing association governance and paved the way for their expansion as part of a 'special regime', regulated, 'independent' sector. Their borrowing did not count in calculating the public debt and their activities were usually not subject to public-sector obligations relating to civil rights, but their status as 'regulated social landlords' gave them access to private credit at good interest rates (Purkis, 2010). Under the 1988 Act, as McDermont (2010, p 2) has stated, a once 'voluntary housing movement' was able to transform itself 'into a sector of entrepreneurial private businesses now seen as the (principal) solution to present day problems in social housing provision'. The Act placed all new housing association tenants under the formal legal regime governing tenant–landlord relationships in the private landlord sector but still subject to Housing Corporation regulation. The Right to Buy was abolished for new housing association tenants making private-sector investment in housing association stock more attractive. Housing associations had to rely on private finance for an increasing proportion of their investment and had to compete to secure the HAG – now named the Social Housing Grant (SHG) – according to which association could meet the Housing Corporation's objectives at the lowest cost. Rents were expected to move towards 'market rents' with Housing Benefit mitigating the impact on low-income households.

The 1987 Conservative Party manifesto was aimed at reducing the role of local authorities as housing suppliers and at using market forces, underpinned by a more selective system of housing assistance, to promote the private rented sector. Homeownership retained its dominant position in the party's ideology but its new policy initiatives were directed mainly at the rented sector. This switch in attention from homeownership to renting may have been caused by the consequences of homeownership expansion becoming more apparent. Council house sales had made a substantial contribution to increasing homeownership – up from 57% in 1979 to 66% in 1987 – but recorded homelessness was increasing rapidly.

Moreover, the cost of homeownership to the Treasury in the form of tax relief on mortgage interest more than doubled in the early 1980s. A White Paper was published stating the policy objectives:

> First to reverse the decline of private rented housing and improve its quality; second to give council tenants the right to transfer to other landlords if they choose to do so; third to target money more accurately on the most acute problems; and fourth to continue to promote the growth of owner occupation. (DoE, 1987, p 3)

The Conservatives had mixed success in achieving these objectives.

Private landlords

Private landlordism was promoted by:

- removing rent controls on new private-sector lettings with Housing Benefit 'taking the strain' for low-income households;
- ending security of tenure: under the 1988 Housing Act all tenancies entered into after 15 January 1989 were 'assured' tenancies with 'assured shorthold' – lasting for a minimum of six months and ended by serving a two-month notice – as the norm;
- allowing investors in private landlordism to claim up to 40% of their investment against their tax liability for five years through the Business Expansion Scheme; and
- enabling housing associations to manage property on behalf of private landlords.

These measures helped to halt the decline of the private landlord sector and its share of the housing stock increased by 1% between 1987 and 1997. However, the cost was high in terms of additional expenditure on Housing Benefit and the tax income forgone under the Business Expansion Scheme (estimated at £40,000 per property). Housing Investment Trusts, designed to encourage investment by financial institutions in private landlordism, had little impact.

Council housing

Under the 1988 Housing Act a statutory procedure was established to enable local authority tenants to change landlords via individual action or a 'tenants' choice' ballot (see Chapter Two). In addition, Housing Action

Trusts (HATs) were to be set up to take over local authority estates, improve them and then sell the stock into a variety of tenures. However, implementing this policy proved troublesome. Despite extensive publicity, tenants showed little interest in leaving their local authority via 'tenants' choice' and few alternative landlords came forward to buy council estates. HATs encountered local opposition and Margaret Thatcher (1993, p 601) expressed her disappointment in saying 'one would never have guessed that we were offering huge sums of taxpayers' money – it would probably have worked out at £100 million a HAT – to improve the conditions of some of the worst housing in the country'. HATS gained modest momentum only when tenants were given assurances that they could return to their local authority when the improvements had been made. Between 1988 and 1995, moves towards ending the provider role of local government came more from local authorities using large-scale *voluntary* transfer than from tenants concerned about the quality of local authority management (see Chapter Two).

Selectivity

Targeting money more accurately on the most acute problems was achieved by means testing improvement grants and limiting their application to the 'fitness' standard. The more selective Housing Benefit eligibility criteria and increases in rents (see **Figure 3.3**) continued the trend towards reliance on means-tested consumer subsidies. Between 1978/79 and 1996/97, government housing expenditure declined from 5.8% to 1.5% of total expenditure, whereas spending on Housing Benefit increased from 1.2% to 3.8% (Hills, 2004).

Homeownership

Promoting homeownership was knocked off course by the crisis in the late 1980s and early 1990s. The removal of restrictions on borrowing in the mid-1980s and the announcement by the Chancellor that tax relief on mortgage interest would be limited to one person per house produced steep increases in house prices as potential buyers entered the market before the relief was ended (Lawson 2010). Feeling confident and affluent, many homeowners began to spend on consumer durables and a large equity slice was taken out of housing by remortgaging. The subsequent rise in consumer spending followed by the use of interest rates to dampen the boom – the mortgage interest rate reached 15.4% in February 1990 – led to a slump in house prices. Mortgage arrears increased, repossessions escalated and 'negative equity' – homes worth less than the amount

Figure 3.3: *Trends in rents, England, 1980–2009 (£s per week)*

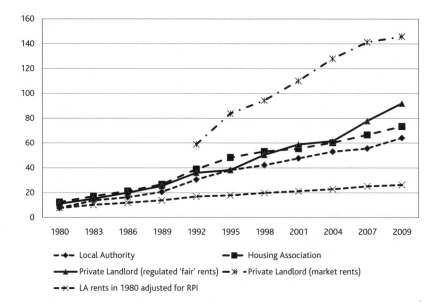

Note: After 1989, new lets in the private rented sector were deregulated. By 2007, only 5% of private tenant rents remained regulated. LA = local authority; RPI = Retail Price Index.
Sources: Adapted from DCL (2010b, Tables 702, 703, 731) and DoE (1994a)

borrowed – emerged as a significant problem especially in the South. In order to prevent a further downward house price spiral the government introduced a 'housing market package', which provided finance to housing associations to purchase unsold homes built for owner-occupation. The decline in house prices dampened tenant enthusiasm for the Right to Buy and a 'rent into mortgage' scheme had few takers. To reduce the Public Sector Borrowing Requirement, Major's government started to phase out tax relief on mortgage interest.

Limitations on capital finance to local authorities significantly reduced council house building and, by the early 1990s, housing policy had 'come to be seen increasingly as an arm of regeneration policy for low-income inner cities and marginal estates, rather than an end in itself' (Hills, 1998, p 124). However, by 1995, Major's government was backing away from the 'laissez-faire' ideas promoted by Thatcher. The White Paper *Our Future Homes: Opportunity, Choice, Responsibility* (Department of the Environment and Welsh Office, 1995) stressed strategic enabling, mixed communities and 'social' rather than 'market' rents.

New Labour and housing

As Kemp (1999, p 134) noted, 'Apart from a few specific manifesto commitments on housing, it was not clear what Labour's housing policy objectives would be, nor what instruments it would use to pursue them'. Indeed, for two years, New Labour accepted the spending programme set out by the Conservative government, which had included substantial cuts to public support for social housing because anticipated spending had been brought forward to counter the early 1990s' housing recession. Consequently, housing policy marked time and Conservative policies on homeownership, private landlords and the social housing sector were continued. New Labour extended the Conservative target for new building on brownfield (previously developed land including gardens) and set a minimum density guideline of 30 dwellings per hectare. Innovation, such as it was, occurred in the role ascribed to housing in the social exclusion agenda; in starting a programme aimed at ensuring that all social-sector homes were 'decent'; and in extending choice in the social sector. However, between 1997 and 2003, house prices accelerated (see *Figure 3.4*) and new house construction stagnated. As Chancellor, Gordon Brown started to take control of the housing agenda intervening directly in 2003 when the Treasury identified volatility in the United Kingdom housing market as a barrier to joining the eurozone (HM Treasury, 2003).

Figure 3.4: House Prices, UK, 1980–2010 (cash and real terms)

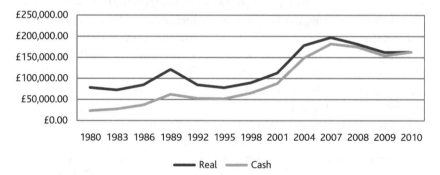

Note: A number of house price statistics are available, for example, Halifax, Land Registry, Nationwide. They vary because the methodologies used in their compilation are different. However, although absolute values vary, they all indicate similar trends.
Source: Nationwide (2010)

Sustainable Communities: Building for the Future (ODPM, 2003a) announced infrastructure investment to support housing construction in four 'growth areas' – the Thames Gateway, Ashford, Milton Keynes/South Midlands and the London–Stansted–Cambridge corridor – additional grants to housing associations and an initiative to tackle low demand in certain parts of the North. The Treasury appointed Kate Barker to examine ways to deliver stability in the housing market to meet future housing needs. Her final report (Barker, 2004) recommended a step-change in housing supply to be achieved by setting national and regional affordability targets that, if unmet, would trigger land release. This new emphasis on supply culminated in *Homes for the Future: More Affordable, More Sustainable* (DCL, 2007a). Housing supply would be ratcheted to 240,000 per year by 2016 and 70,000 affordable homes a year would be provided by 2010/11, with 45,000 in the social housing sector.

Unfortunately within months of publication the plans in *Homes for the Future: More Affordable, More Sustainable* were derailed by the 'credit crunch'. House prices started to decline as did new housing starts, mortgage foreclosures increased and the number of homeowners with 'negative equity' started to climb. The government's response was to introduce new mortgage rescue schemes and to bring forward resources allocated to future social housing to 'kick-start' the market. Finance was injected into the banking system, and the Bank of England reduced its base rate from 5.75% in July 2007 to 0.5% in August 2009 and increased the money supply. An attempt was also made to stabilise the financial institutions by outright nationalisation or state acquisition of shares.

The Conservative–Liberal Democrat Coalition

Although reductions in public expenditure in 2010/11 had been opposed by the Liberal Democrats in the 2010 election campaign, Conservative views on the need for immediate cuts prevailed. Capital spending on housing was reduced by £450 million for 2010/11 and the 2010 Budget (HM Treasury, 2010a) and Spending Review (HM Treasury, 2010b) announced substantial cuts in producer and consumer incentives to be implemented before 2014/15.

Given the similarity between the Conservative and Liberal Democratic manifestos on New Labour's 'top-down' approach to stimulating supply, it is not surprising that *The Coalition: Our Programme for Government* included proposals to 'rapidly abolish Regional Spatial Strategies' and 'in the longer term' to 'radically reform the planning system ... based on the principles set out in the Conservative Party publication *Open Source Planning*' (HM Government, 2010, p 11). Conservative Party 'Green Deal' and housing trusts proposals were endorsed, 'the creation and expansion of mutuals, co-operatives, charities and social enterprises' (2010, p 29) was supported and the Liberal Democrat commitment to review the 'unfair Housing Revenue Account' was included as was the 'Home on the Farm' proposal (2010, p 12). However the Liberal Democrats' plan to levy VAT on new properties and repair costs at an equal rate was rejected and the party's more radical proposals were watered down. A mansion tax would not be levied and the proposal to increase capital gains tax to 40% – with implications for private landlords – was replaced by a proposition to 'seek ways of taxing non-business capital gains at rates similar or close to those applied to income' (2010, p 30). In the event, the Coalition's budget increased capital gains tax from 18% to 28% for higher earners.

Overview

- In the 19th century the 'housing issue' was constructed as a sanitary problem related to 'externalities' of order, health and morality.
- The Labour Party adopted council housing as its principal means of delivering affordable housing in planned suburban environments.
- The Conservative Party, although prepared to support council housing to overcome extreme housing shortages, preferred homeownership and private landlordism.
- From the 1960s, both the major political parties showed an interest in housing associations – Labour to replace the private landlord and the Conservatives to replace council housing.
- Between 1979 and 1997, the Conservative Party applied market principles to the supply and distribution of housing, but with a bias towards owner-occupation.
- New Labour initially followed the direction of Conservative policy but, after 2003, attempted to influence housing supply. This policy was disrupted by the 2008 'credit crunch'.
- The Coalition government has backed away from direct central involvement to promote overall housing supply.

Questions for discussion

1. What were the arguments for and against sanitary reform in the 19th century?
2. Why was private landlordism in decline for most of the 20th century?
3. Labour was the party of council housing, the Conservatives were the homeownership party. Discuss this statement.
4. Why did homeownership expand in the 20th century?

Further reading

Christopher Hamlin's *Public Health and Social Justice in the Age of Chadwick: Britain, 1800–54* (1998) is a perceptive account of sanitary reform. *The Politics of Housing: Power, Consumers and Urban Culture* (2007) by **Peter Shapely** examines local responses to national policy.

Websites

The Victorian Web contains many original documents on housing in the 19th century. It is available at www.victorianweb.org/history/sochistov.html

Statistics from the latest edition of *UK Housing Review* by Steve Wilcox are available at: http://www.cih.org/publications/downloads/ukhr.htm

four

The governance of housing

Summary

- In England, the 'core executive' works through a variety of semi-autonomous and private agencies to meet its housing objectives.
- In recent years direct responsibility for housing policy in England has been located in a department with a remit also covering such functions as planning and local government.
- The Department for Work and Pensions has a key role in housing policy in the UK because it is responsible for Housing Benefit.
- Local authorities have a 'strategic enabling' role in meeting local housing need but their provider role in rented accommodation is being supplanted by housing associations.
- New Labour maintained control over social housing agencies through financial levers and regulatory regimes.
- Private-sector regulation has been 'light-touch'.
- The Coalition government is committed to greater local autonomy in determining and meeting housing requirements.
- Since 1999, various degrees of devolved power have been granted to the Scottish Parliament, the National Assembly of Wales and the Northern Ireland Assembly.

The central state owns very few dwellings and, to meet its objectives, it has to operate via a range of housing supply agents. This chapter sets out the roles of the various participants in the housing system.

The core executive

The cabinet

Although the notion requires qualification because many decisions are made outside formal decision-making structures (for examples, see Powell, 2010; Rawnsley, 2010), the official UK government website states that the 'Cabinet is the committee at the centre of the British political system and is the supreme decision-making body in government' (Directgov, 2010).

Cabinet membership is regarded as symbolic that the policy domain represented by a departmental minister has high priority in the government's objectives. Under Blair, housing was represented by a secretary of state with housing as only part of the minister's responsibilities but, when Brown became Prime Minister, he invited the Minister for Housing to attend the cabinet whenever housing matters were considered – a symbol that housing would join health and education as government priorities. Following the formation of the Coalition government the Housing Minister was no longer invited to cabinet meetings.

The cabinet is served by the Cabinet Office, which portrays its role as sitting 'at the very centre of government' and, together with the Treasury, providing the 'head office of government'. It describes its core functions (Cabinet Office, 2010) as:

- Supporting the Prime Minister to define and deliver the Government's objectives; thus the Cabinet Office includes the Prime Minister's Office with its Policy Implementation Unit.
- Supporting the Cabinet to drive the coherence, quality and delivery of policy and operations across departments.
- Strengthening the Civil Service to ensure the civil service is organised effectively and has the capability in terms of skills, values and leadership to deliver the Government's objectives.

HM Treasury

The inclusion of the Treasury by the Cabinet Office as part of the 'head office of government' reflects its importance. It controls the lion's share of the public resources necessary to stimulate housing supply, maintain the existing housing stock and ensure that housing is affordable.

Department for Communities and Local Government (DCL)

After 1919, the Ministry of Health was in charge of housing policy but, in 1951, responsibility was transferred to the Ministry of Housing and Local Government. Subsequently housing became part of the domain of other departments such as the Department for the Environment. The Office of the Deputy Prime Minister (ODPM) was created in 2002 from the portfolio of the former Department of Transport, Local Government and the Regions – its title reflecting the political position and interests of the then Deputy Prime Minister, John Prescott. The Department for Communities and Local Government was created in 2006 as the successor department to the ODPM. The 2010 Spending Review (HM Treasury, 2010b) projected a 51% real-term reduction in the DCL's resource budget by 2014/15 and, in the context of the 'new localism', it will become 'more enabling and less intervening' (Kerslake, 2010a).

Department for Work and Pensions (DWP)

This department is responsible for a range of benefits and services aimed at reducing poverty and encouraging work. After 1979, housing subsidies were switched from 'producer' subsidies towards means-tested 'consumer' subsidies in the form of Housing Benefit, administered by local authorities under rules set by the DWP.

Homes and Communities Agency (HCA)

Set up in 2008, the HCA joined up the delivery of housing and regeneration under one agency, bringing together the functions of English Partnerships, the investment functions of the Housing Corporation and key housing and regeneration programmes previously delivered by the DCL such as housing market renewal and the 'decent homes' programme. According to the DCL, this integrated approach would enable the HCA 'to hold a "single conversation" with local authorities and other partners on the specific housing and regeneration needs of their individual areas' (DCL, 2009a).

English Partnerships had been formed in 1999 as the national regeneration agency charged with identifying and assembling land, especially brownfield and other publicly owned land, for development. The Housing Corporation was a non-departmental public body set up in 1964 to distribute resources to housing associations and to monitor their activities.

The Cave Review (Cave, 2007, p 9) on social housing regulation concluded that because social housing is rented at below market price:

this creates a system in which tenants cannot switch and are put at risk of poor treatment by providers....This is not a standard market failure but a consequence of the objective of delivering housing at affordable rather than market prices. It does, however, make a strong case for regulation to protect tenants.

Accordingly Cave recommended that 'regulation is best accomplished by an independent regulatory body, created by Statute' (Cave, 2007, p 12). New Labour accepted this recommendation and the Housing Corporation's regulatory powers relating to housing associations were passed to the Tenant Services Authority (TSA), which, in 2010, also started to regulate all social housing providers, including local authority landlords and Arm's Length Management Organisations (ALMOs). The Coalition government declared its intention to abolish the TSA and transfer some of its functions to the HCA, effectively recreating the Housing Corporation, albeit that an independent regulatory committee within the HCA would take over regulation of the 'economic' functions of social landlords 'in order to maintain lender confidence' and promote 'value for money for the taxpayer' (DCL, 2010c, p 2). However, in relationship to the TSA's role in protecting the social tenant as 'consumer', greater reliance would be placed on local tenant panels and the HCA would only be involved in setting broad standards and in cases of a 'breach of standard(s) resulting in serious detriment to tenants' (DCL, 2010c, p 13).

The rise and fall of the regional dimension

In its earlier departmental forms, the DCL maintained a regional structure of civil servants who played an important role in distributing housing resources to local government. They could adjust the distribution produced by the General Needs Index, a calculation of the housing needs in each authority, according to their perceptions of the quality of each local authority's Housing Strategy. In 1994, these civil servants were merged with regional officials from other departments to form 'Single Regional Government Offices'. The Housing Corporation also had regional offices to help distribute its resources. Regional Development Agencies (RDAs), with substantial business representation, were established in 1999 to develop and coordinate regional economic development and Regional Assemblies, with nominated local councillors, were also set up. A complex system of Regional Planning Bodies and Regional Housing Boards, with representatives from the various regional organisations, was created to help determine the scale of housing provision over a 15-year period and to allocate land release targets for housing to local authorities. In 2008, the regional dimensions of housing and regeneration resource allocation were transferred to the HCA.

Regional spatial strategies

In 2005, Regional Housing Boards and Regional Planning Boards were merged and Regional Assemblies were given the formal authority to approve regional spatial strategies, which established building targets that had to be incorporated into each local authority Local Development Framework (LDF) that set out plans for local development. However, the 2004 Planning and Compulsory Purchase Act made it clear that the Secretary of State could direct changes in the regional spatial strategies and, because some Regional Assemblies proved troublesome in their opposition to expanding housing supply, they were abolished in April 2010 and their responsibilities transferred to RDAs. One of the first acts of the Coalition government was to abolish regional spatial strategies and this was followed by an announcement that RDAs would be closed down with Local Enterprise Partnerships, aimed at promoting the economic development of 'natural economic areas' below regional level, established to fill part of the gap. A Regional Growth Fund was set up to sustain projects in England offering economic growth, especially in areas heavily reliant on public-sector employment, but the resources available to this fund were lower than the finance available to RDAs and would be distributed through a competitive bidding process.

Local government

In England the 36 metropolitan district councils in urban areas are responsible for all local authority functions, although the fire service, police and public transport responsibilities are exercised through Joint Boards. Until 1995, local government powers outside the urban areas were divided between County Councils and District Councils (see Table 4.2), but a process of local consultation led to the unitary model being introduced in some areas but rejected in others. Parish and Town Councils cover areas up to 30,000 people – but usually far less – and have limited responsibilities for local services and environmental improvements. In London, 33 boroughs have housing powers. The elected Mayor of London is responsible for setting out and delivering a long-term strategy for London, assisted by the Greater London Authority (GLA). The elected London Assembly scrutinises the policies of the Mayor and GLA.

In Scotland, 32 unitary councils were set up in 1986 to replace the nine regional councils and 53 district councils. In Wales, there are now

24 unitary councils. The Northern Ireland Housing Executive assumed the housing responsibilities of local authorities under the 1971 Housing Executive (Northern Ireland) Act.

Table 4.1: The distribution of functions in County Council/ District Council areas

County Councils	District Councils	Shared
Education	Local planning	Recreation
Social services	Housing	Cultural matters
Transport	Local highways	
Strategic planning	Building regulation	
Fire services	Environmental health	
Consumer protection	Refuse collection	
Refuse disposal	Leisure services and parks	
Smallholdings		
Libraries		

Capital expenditure

Although the difference is somewhat blurred, it has become conventional in local government finance to distinguish between capital expenditure (investment for the future to be financed by borrowing) and revenue (current) expenditure to be consumed and paid for in a particular year. Under New Labour local authorities obtained capital finance through a number of channels:

• 'Prudential borrowing', that is, raising loans from capital markets according to a code set by the Chartered Institute for Public Finance and Accountancy.

- Asset sales: local authorities kept all the receipts from selling land but only 25% of Right to Buy receipts.
- The 'single capital pot': usually distributed over a three-year cycle and composed of central estimates, with a regional input, of the need to spend compiled for each service but available for use by local authorities according to local priorities.
- Ring-fenced capital support available only for a use specified by central government, a restriction on local autonomy that the Coalition government is committed to change.
- Under the Private Finance Initiative (PFI) 'credits' became available to local authorities if they entered into an agreement with the private sector under which capital and management is provided by a private contractor in return for performance-related payments by the local authority across a long-term contract, typically 25–30 years. PFI has been used extensively to finance schools and hospitals but its housing use has been limited.

The provider role

In 1981, local authorities in England owned 4.5 million dwellings. By 2009, the Right to Buy, stock transfer and restricted new building had reduced the stock to 1.8 million with over half managed by Arm's Length Management Organisations (see Chapter Eight). Revenue finance is governed by the Housing Revenue Account (HRA), which must be balanced every year according to complex and constantly changing rules in relationship to the local authority 'General Fund' that pays for services other than the direct 'landlord' function. In 1989, the HRA was 'ring-fenced' (rents could not be supported by other local government income steams) and central government set 'guideline' rents for each local authority. In 2002, central government took control not only of the general level of rents set by local authorities, but also the specific rent of each dwelling. Although social rents would remain 'affordable', it was declared that there should be a closer link between the qualities tenants value in a dwelling across the local authority and housing association sectors – now firmly labelled 'the social sector'. A 'target' rent for each dwelling was set according to a formula taking into account the average manual worker's earnings in an area plus dwelling size and capital. Over time rents would converge to the target rent, adjusted for inflation, according to a complex transitional mechanism. The impact of these 'target' rents has varied according to place – some local authorities having a surplus on their HRA and others a deficit – with the surpluses centrally redistributed to meet the deficits. In 2009/10, the system was in *overall* surplus by £100 million and, as rents move closer to targets, council tenants will be producing resources for the

Treasury – a 'tenant tax' – estimated to rise to £894 million per annum by 2022/23 (Local Government Association, 2008). Rent restructuring was justified with the argument that consistency in social rents was fairer (DETR, 2000a), but rent convergence between the local authority and housing association sectors had the bonus of reducing resistance from local authority tenants to stock transfer.

Between 1979 and 2006, both the Conservatives and New Labour were intent on reducing local government's role as a home provider but, from 2007, New Labour's attitude started to change. The 2007 Green Paper *Homes for the Future: More Affordable, More Sustainable* (DCL, 2007a) was cautious in expanding local government's provider function but, as the 2008/09 recession began to bite, a share of the HCA's resources was allocated to a special local authority new-build programme. In addition, New Labour entered into discussions with local government on ways to allow the revenue resulting from new building by local authorities to escape absorption into the complex system of local government finance and ways to allow local authorities to use any surplus arising from renting the existing stock and Right to Buy receipts. This new freedom was expected to contribute to a revival in building council houses and, in its 2010 manifesto, New Labour claimed that 'councils would build up to 10,000 council houses a year by the end of the next Parliament' (Labour Party, 2010, p 25). In their 2010 manifesto, the Liberal Democrats stated that they would relax Treasury control of local authority borrowing related to building new council houses. The 2010 Conservative Manifesto was silent on the matter, but the Coalition's *Our Programme for Government* (HM Government, 2010, p 12) stated that the 'unfair Housing Revenue Account' would be reviewed. *Implementing self-financing for council housing* (DCL, 2011) set out the basis of the Coalition government's reform of the Housing Revenue Account. The debt levels of each local authority would be readjusted in accordance with a valuation of its housing business. Some local authorities would then pay a sum to the government and others would receive a payment from the government. Thereafter local authorities would be free to manage their income and debt but subject to borrowing controls and central directives on rent levels. Unlike New Labour's proposals, only 25% of Right to Buy receipts would be retained by local government.

The 'strategic enabling' role

The '*strategic* enabling' role John Major designated for local housing authorities was maintained by New Labour. However the statutory guidance contained in *Creating Strong, Safe and Prosperous Communities* (DCL, 2008b) gave local authorities more discretion in constructing their housing strategies and suggested that they should be integrated into broader Sustainable Community Strategies. The 2002 Homelessness Act required every housing authority in England to adopt and publish a specific homelessness strategy aimed at preventing homelessness and ensuring that accommodation and support are available for people who are homeless or at risk of becoming homeless.

Performance indicators and targets

Monitoring 'delivery agent' performance was an essential component of New Labour's adoption of the 'new public sector managerialism'. Section 3.1 of the 1999 Local Government Act substituted competitive tendering with the requirement that every 'best value authority must make arrangements to secure continuous improvement in the way in which its functions are exercised, having regard to a combination of economy, efficiency and effectiveness'. Local authorities were required to publish best value reviews of their housing service according to nationally determined performance indicators. The indicators were numerous (see Chapter Two) but, in 2008, a new single set of 198 national indicators covering all aspects of local authority service provision – the National Indicator Set (NIS) – was introduced. The new indicators directly related to housing were reduced from 35 to 11 and most were supply-related. The revamped indicators were accompanied by a new performance regime centred on broad 'comprehensive area assessments', and 'Total Place' pilots in 13 areas were introduced aimed at identifying how collaboration and prioritisation could lead to greater value for money and innovation in service delivery. The pilots included local authorities, Primary Care Trusts, police authorities and other public-sector partners.

One of the first acts of the Coalition government was to abolish New Labour's performance evaluation framework, but it enthusiastically embraced the 'Total Place' idea. In 2010, as part of the 'localism' agenda, it was announced that the Audit Commission – set up in 1983 and responsible for auditing and inspecting public services plus overseeing performance – would be abolished.

Urban regeneration

The term 'regeneration' was adopted in the 1990s and its interpretation as being 'born again', in contrast to earlier terms such as 'renewal' and 'reconstruction', indicated its flavour and its fervour. The renaissance was to be 'holistic' and to achieve the desired change new urban governance mechanisms were established. Perhaps the most significant were the Urban

Development Corporations (UDCs), which acquired powers from local authorities in 12 urban areas in order to promote regeneration steered by business leaders and led by property development.

Although New Labour switched the urban regeneration emphasis in deprived neighbourhoods from property to people (see Chapter Nine) the stress on joint ventures continued with local authorities exhorted to set up Local Strategic Partnerships (LSPs). The DCL (2009b, p 1) defined an LSP as a single body that 'brings together at a local level the different parts of the public sector as well as the private, business, community and voluntary sectors so that different initiatives and services support each other and work together'.

Housing associations

A housing association is a not-for-profit organisation set up to supply accommodation. They are run by management boards made up of volunteers who, since 2003, can be paid. Unlike local councillors, management boards are not elected. When registered, housing associations become 'registered social landlords' and are entitled to apply for state financial assistance. **Box 4.2** sets out some of characteristics of the registered social landlord sector.

By providing land, finance and facilitating Section 106 agreements (see Chapter Six) local authorities have been able to secure 75–100% nomination rights on first lets, but subsequent re-lets and accommodation built without direct local authority assistance usually involve lower percentages. Some housing associations operate common registers and waiting lists with their local authorities, but despite the importance of nomination agreements and common registers/waiting lists – local authorities have significant duties with regard to those in housing need and a diminishing housing stock – there has been little research into the outcomes of nomination agreements. The limited evidence reveals 'tension' points between local authorities and housing associations related to whether associations are independent or vehicles of the council, the absence of realistic sanctions, and conflicting objectives, such as meeting needs versus financial viability and creating 'sustainable', balanced communities (Economic and Social Research Council, 2009). In 2008/09, 56% of 'general needs' housing association properties were let via nominations from local authorities (CORE, 2010). In Scotland, housing associations have a statutory obligation to accept local authority nominations within six weeks unless they can demonstrate good reasons for refusal.

Box 4.2: Registered social landlords (housing associations)

In 2010, there were 1578 registered social landlords in England owning 2,437,005 dwellings. Most of the stock is for 'general needs', but there were 101,000 units of supported housing and over 316,000 homes for older people. The sector's assets have been valued at £205 billion (market value) and, according to Elphicke (2010, p 5), 'housing associations are strong, successful and complex businesses, which play a significant role in our economy'. They vary considerably in size with the largest, Sanctuary, Guinness Trust and London and Quadrant, owning more than 50,000 dwellings, but with the smallest 30% owning less than 25 properties. The bulk of the stock is held by associations with between 2500 and 10,000 properties. Stock transfer associations (see Chapter Two) own almost the same number of properties as 'traditional' associations.

In 2008/09, 25.2% of general needs lettings by registered social landlords were to single parents, 16.5% to statutory homeless households, 15% to black and minority ethnic (BME) households, and 17.9% to households containing a person with a disability (3.5% to households with a person using a wheelchair). In 2010, the average rent for a housing association property was £77.90, about 13% above the local authority mean although this comparison ignores differences in size, location and quality. Tenants had 12% more income than local authority tenants. Housing associations are also involved in the government's low-cost homeownership schemes.

Scotland had 259 registered housing associations in 2008 many developed by transfers to community-based associations from the Scottish Special Housing Association set up after the Second World War to develop homes in parallel with local authorities. They own 279,144 homes (about 11% of the total stock) and are regulated by the Scottish Housing Regulator. The Welsh Assembly regulates the 75 Welsh associations and the 36 associations in Northern Ireland are registered with the Department for Social Development.

Data sources: CORE (2010), Tang (2010) and TSA (2010).

Central control and local autonomy

Despite its rhetoric on 'partnerships' and the 'big tent' embracing 'policy communities', under New Labour central government had considerable control over the activities of local authorities and housing associations. Local government was declared a 'policy-free zone' with its role being 'to deliver centrally determined policies in a strategic way' (Maile and

Hoggett, 2004, p 512). Rents were set by a national formula; resource allocation was determined by central views on the quality of housing strategies and business plans; the regional dimension to resource distribution lacked an elected element; and the everyday activities of local government were subject to performance targets and inspection. Housing association autonomy was also in question. State financial assistance was subject to a bidding process and accompanied by detailed regulation, inspection and performance indicators. Moreover, housing association rents were set by central government according to targets based on a formula similar to the one applied to local authorities. As Malpass (2000, p 259) has argued, housing associations had become 'little more than agents of the state and the voluntary element has been reduced to marginal and largely symbolic importance, providing a fig-leaf for those who really hold the power'.

The Coalition government has attempted to reverse the tendency, manifest well before New Labour gained office, for central government to take increasing control over local government. The requirements to meet targets and performance indicators have been substantially reduced, many ring-fenced capital and revenue streams have been absorbed into mainstream allocations, and local authorities have been given new powers to borrow against the revenue stream arising from business rates. Reform of Housing Revenue Accounts also has the potential to enhance local authority autonomy. However in the context of substantial cuts in central support to local authorities and housing associations – the 2010 Spending Review (HM Treasury, 2010b) projected a 7.1% per year reduction in central support over the four years 2011/12 to 2014/15 – such autonomy might be interpreted as an attempt by central government to deflect responsibility for substantial cutbacks in services.

Tenant empowerment: Exit and voice politics

Exit politics

Between 1979 and 1996, the Conservatives attempted to break up local government's rented accommodation monopoly for families through 'tenants' choice' and produce a system whereby, by developing a range of 'independent' landlords, tenants could take part in 'exit' politics. Although 'tenants' choice' was a failure, finally abandoned in 1996 (see Chapter Two), stock transfer has increased the number of 'independent' social landlords from which tenants can choose.

New Labour also promoted choice via 'choice-based lettings' (CBL). The dominant method of allocating 'social housing', especially after the Cullingworth Report (Cullingworth, 1969), was for housing officers to match applicants on the waiting list to suitable homes based on a 'needs' assessment. In contrast, CBL, in the words of the DCL:

> allow applicants for social housing (and existing tenants seeking a move) to apply for available vacancies which are advertised widely (e.g. in the local newspaper or on a website).

> Applicants can see the full range of available properties and can bid (i.e. apply) for any home to which they are matched (e.g. a single person would not be eligible for a three-bedroom house). The successful bidder is the one with the highest priority under the scheme with priority assessed by a 'banding' or a points scheme. Authorities provide feedback that helps applicants to assess their chances of success in subsequent applications. (DCL, 2010d)

Sustainable Communities: Homes for All (ODPM, 2005b) set out the government's expectation that all local authorities should have a CBL scheme in place by 2010 and its intention to extend CBL to cover not only local authority and registered social landlord properties, but also low-cost homeownership and properties to rent from private landlords. Moreover, in recognition that housing markets do not follow local authority boundaries, it promised to develop CBL schemes on a regional and/or sub-regional basis.

Research on CBL schemes has demonstrated mixed outcomes. Pawson et al (2006, p 14) concluded:

> Typically, CBL generates improved tenancy sustainment and this is testament to its effectiveness in better matching people to properties and improving service user satisfaction with letting outcomes. Similarly, the evidence of consumer responsiveness to variations in demand illustrates growing comprehension of CBL mechanisms on the part of some housing applicants.

This research also found that concerns that homeless families would have more limited choices than other applicants and would be placed in the least desirable properties were unfounded. It stated:

> In practice, however, the evidence suggests that landlords have been able to configure their policies and procedures so that members of this group [the homeless] are somewhat less likely to be housed in such areas than under pre-CBL arrangements.

> This might have been achieved simply by increasing the chances of homeless applicant households being housed in 'average popularity' areas. In fact, CBL has increased the propensity for formerly homeless households to be accommodated in high demand estates. (Pawson et al, 2006, p 11)

However, there are constraints on the impact of CBL:

- To exercise choice prospective tenants must not be too constrained by supply restrictions otherwise, rather than tenants choosing landlords, landlords choose tenants. Social housing supply became more restricted under New Labour perhaps explaining why, despite CBL, the percentage of tenants stating that they had enough choice when obtaining their new home had remained stubbornly static since 1999, at 39% (DCL, 2010e).
- Choice depends on information about the track record of potential landlords, but existing information is limited for the social housing sector and very restricted on the quality of private landlords.
- There is a conflict between 'need' and 'choice' in allocating social housing especially if supply is limited. As Pawson et al (2006, p 14) state: 'There was a feeling that "ordinary" people, that is, those not eligible for priority, were losing out in the system.... People felt there was not enough social housing.'

Voice politics

Social housing supply constraints means that social housing tenants are, at best, 'captive consumers', hence 'voice' rather than 'exit' politics may be a more productive path towards 'tenant empowerment'. 'Voice' politics involves giving tenants more influence in shaping the pattern of social housing by enabling their opinions to be heard and acted on. To enhance 'voice' politics in the local authority domain New Labour introduced Tenant Participation Compacts (TPCs). Beginning in April 2000, local councils had to start a process of agreeing a framework for tenant involvement directed towards the attainment of 'best value' in housing services delivery. The declared objective of the compacts was to 'help to bring the quality of participation across all councils up to the best and to ensure that all tenants have equal opportunity to participate' (DETR, 1999b, p 6). However, after an initial flurry of interest, TPCs faded into the background.

Tenant Management Organisations

The Conservatives' desire to fragment local authority housing management produced some fruitful initiatives in tenant involvement in the form of Tenant Management Organisations (TMOs), now regarded as the 'gold standard' in tenant participation because formal powers are delegated to tenant organisations. In 1994, TMOs were encouraged by the introduction of a 'right to manage' giving all local authority tenant groups representing 25 or more households the right to assume a variety of management and maintenance responsibilities subject to training and a ballot in favour of the change. Housing associations' tenants were granted no such rights, which meant that, as stock transfer developed, the opportunities for tenant involvement in direct management diminished.

There are two broad types of TMO – tenant management cooperatives and estate management boards – although, in practice, the distinction is rather blurred. TMOs do not own the housing stock, but tenant management cooperatives are usually composed of residents and directly control their own staff whereas estate management boards often have councillor representatives and frequently use local authority officials. TMOs enter into agreements with their local authorities specifying the responsibilities delegated to them and the resources they will be allocated. In 2001, there were 202 TMOs covering about 84,000 properties. Research into TMO activities has produced favourable results. Price Waterhouse (1995, p 120) concluded that tenant management cooperatives were 'very effective mechanisms for securing improved housing services, higher levels of tenant satisfaction and more economical running costs' and estate management boards had shown that they could deliver 'a tenant-oriented service ... in the most difficult operational contexts'. Given this TMO success and their fit with Blair's promotion of 'social capital', it is surprising that they were not encouraged when Blair was Prime Minister – the number of TMOs in 2008 remained broadly constant at the 2001 figure. Perhaps the Conservative Party's enthusiasm for empowering the 'little platoons' of neighbourhood groups (Conservative Party, 2010, p 38), to be backed by the proposed creation of a 'Big Society' bank funded from unclaimed bank assets, may stimulate TMOs.

Housing cooperatives

This special form of housing association has been 'largely forgotten by UK housing policy makers since the 1990s' (Independent Commission for Co-operative and Mutual Housing, 2009a, p 1). In its purest form, a cooperative involves shared ownership and democratic management by the people who live in the houses. However – despite the absence of asset-ownership – other associations incorporating an element of mutuality such as TMOs (see earlier), community gateways (enabling small-scale community and cooperative activity within large-scale housing organisations) and community land trusts have also been included as cooperatives (Independent Commission for Co-operative and Mutual Housing, 2009b). Gulliver and Morris (2009) identified 836 cooperative and mutual housing organisations in the UK, managing about 169,000 homes (0.6% of all the UK housing stock), of which 54% were owned by the cooperative and 46% were management organisations and hence lacking the mutual ownership characteristic of the cooperative movement.

In the past, tenant participation has been a neglected dimension in the operations of registered social landlords. The Audit Commission (2004, p 4) noted that involvement 'is still often sidelined or done grudgingly'. As a remedy, the Audit Commission incorporated 'involvement reviews' into the regulatory and inspection procedures governing housing associations. However, progress in tenant involvement appears to have been limited by the 'business orientation' of housing associations, and local authority ALMOs have a better record in promoting 'voice' politics (Purkis, 2010).

In 2007, New Labour started to take a new interest in tenant involvement marked by the publication of *Tenant Empowerment: A Consultation Paper* (DCL, 2007b). It endorsed the Cave Review's recommendation that 'a national tenant voice should be established to give tenants both a voice and expertise at national level'. Tenant empowerment was a theme of *Communities in Control: Real People, Real Power* (DCL, 2008c), and in *Citizens of Equal Worth* (DCL, 2009c) a project group put forward specific proposals on how to create a 'National Tenants' Voice'. Its report stated:

> It is rare these days to hear anyone argue against the proposition that tenants should play a far greater role in shaping how their housing and community services are provided. But the practical reality is that tenant empowerment is often paid lip service, more spoken about than achieved. (DCL, 2009c, p 14)

In 2010, New Labour set up a National Tenants' Voice to give tenants a bigger say in the national politics of social housing, but the Coalition government ended its £1.5 million state funding, instead placing emphasis on local-level involvement via 'tenant panels'.

The financial institutions

Until the 1980s, building societies provided most of the finance for house purchases. They differed from commercial banks in being 'mutual'

– there were no shareholders – and their aim was to meet the reciprocal requirements of lenders and borrowers. Building societies had their origins in the 17th century, but expanded in the 19th century when working-class people agreed to pay into a fund to build houses. Having raised sufficient finance to acquire a house, lots were drawn to determine which member of the society should move into the new dwelling. Payments into the fund continued until every society member was able to own a house and then the society was terminated. To speed up the housing of its members some societies allowed people who did not require homes to join the association and paid interest on the investment. By the start of the 20th century, these 'permanent' societies dominated the sector.

In the 1970s, building societies were major financial institutions. Governments worked with them, offering loans in times when savings were low to stabilise the housing market, but their activities provoked criticism. It was alleged that their conservatism produced mortgage queues, their mutuality had become a myth and that unaccountable directors, not savers and mortgage-holders, controlled the movement (Boddy, 1980). They were accused of proliferating branch offices, being reluctant to lend in certain geographical areas and operating a cartel in fixing the mortgage interest rate. In the 1980s, the Conservative government attempted to deal with these criticisms by exposing the societies to more competition from banks, specialist mortgage companies and other financial institutions.

The movement of the banks into the mortgage market led to the breakdown of the building society cartel; by 1987 building societies were responsible for only 51% of net mortgage lending compared to 79% in 1980. The societies argued that, if the banks were allowed to compete in their business, then societies should be granted more scope to diversify. The 1986 Building Societies Act enabled such diversification: societies could raise more funds from wholesale markets, that is, to borrow from institutions as well as individuals; purchase land; act as developers; set up estate agencies; and offer cheque-clearing facilities. In the 1990s, the distinction between building societies and banks became opaque as many building societies converted to banks by abandoning their mutual status and offering dividends to shareholders. The societies converted to banks were more aggressive in their expansion plans and one such society, Northern Rock, became the first major 'credit crunch' casualty.

Shortly after becoming a bank, Northern Rock started its quest to increase its mortgage market share. It promoted its project not by the traditional mutual method of raising retail deposits, but by borrowing on wholesale markets with 'securitisation' (selling on the loans) as collateral. Northern Rock was not alone in its use of 'securitisation' – by 2006, over two thirds of all mortgages were financed in this way. However, Northern

Rock also attracted new mortgage business through such deals as its 'Together' loan – lending up to 125% of a house's value and up to six times the borrower's annual income (Brummer, 2008, p 100).

Referring to the 'sub-prime crisis in the USA (see Chapter Five), Smith et al (2010, p 2) comment: 'Somehow, the failure of a niche market in a single jurisdiction ... generated a shock sufficient to tip the global economy from growth to decline'. Northern Rock was the first UK casualty of the economic chill. In late 2007, suspicion in the wholesale market about 'sub-prime', 'toxic' or 'ninja' (no income, no job and no assets) loans, financed by 'securitisation', led to a lending standstill. Inability to borrow as old loans became due produced a liquidity crisis for Northern Rock, a run on the bank and its nationalisation in February 2008. Other banks encountered similar problems. Now that 'securitisation' was drying up, where were the funding sources? As house prices declined, had some of their UK loans turned toxic? Did they hold 'toxic' loans from the United States? Subsequently, it emerged that they did. The Royal Bank of Scotland, for example, had purchased a package of US sub-prime loans for $840 million put together by Goldman Sachs with the aid of a hedge fund that was betting on a collapse in the housing market. In 2010, the Royal Bank of Scotland, by then 84% owned by the UK taxpayer, received $100 million compensation because Goldman Sachs had supplied 'incomplete information' when selling the package (BBC News, 2010).

Concerns about bank losses produced a confidence crisis in the UK financial sector that provoked extensive additional state intervention: mortgage protection schemes were introduced; mergers were brokered; the government guaranteed deposits up to £50,000; capital was injected into the banking system; and interest rates were slashed. This action helped to stop the decline in house prices and, in 2009, the total number of home possessions was 46,000, significantly fewer than the 75,000 forecast at the start of the year.

The construction industry

Until the 2008/09 recession, the construction industry employed more than 2.8 million people and contributed 8.7% of the UK's GDP. 'Construction' encompasses a variety of activities including mining, house-building, repair and maintenance, large-scale civil engineering, architecture, design, and project management. It is highly fragmented with over 90% of construction companies employing fewer than 10 workers and with fewer than 130 companies with a workforce of 600 or more. 'Self-build' (both the individual owner who lays bricks and mortar and the owner of an individual plot who produces his or her own house by contracting with architects and builders) accounted for about 10% of total production in 2006 (Callcutt, 2007).

Despite there being 18,000 house-builders registered with the National House Building Council, a small number of major companies dominate residential construction: in 2006, about one third of total output was produced by the three largest firms (Jones and Watkins, 2009). It was argued that, until the 'credit crunch', builders could 'sell anything' (Barker, 2004, p 106) once they had acquired land and, hence, they concentrated on land acquisition, being unconcerned about expanding production in case extra supply undermined the price they could obtain for their product (House of Commons Office of the Deputy Prime Minister Select Committee, 2006).

Various attempts have been made to reform the construction industry with reports by both Latham (1994) and Egan (1998) stressing the need for team-working – led by the client – in project delivery and a requirement to recruit far more-qualified workers. However, despite the impact of building workers from Eastern Europe, the construction industry lacks sufficient qualified workers to meet the UK's assessed housing requirement and the shedding of workers in the recession has possibly increased the shortfall. In 2007, the Construction Industry Council Strategic Forum set a target of a net increase of 260,000 qualified people recruited and trained in the industry compared to the 2006 numbers and an increase in apprenticeship completions of 18,700 (House of Commons Business and Enterprise Committee, 2008). Despite this skill shortage, the Callcutt review of house-building delivery confidently stated that 'our Review shows clearly that the housebuilding industry and its supply chain have the potential to deliver 240,000 new good quality homes a year by 2016 and to achieve the zero carbon targets' (Callcutt, 2007, p 6). However, the credit crunch had a deep impact on the capacity of the house-building industry, which will take time to recover its 2007 potential.

Private landlords

The Labour Party's traditional hostility to private landlords reached its zenith in the mid-1970s when Labour started to use housing associations to buy out private landlords operating in the major cities – an initiative that foundered on the public expenditure restraints imposed in the late 1970s. Even the Conservatives appeared to have given up on the sector with the Conservative Political Centre stating that 'the private landlord, as he exists now and has existed, will, within a generation, be as extinct as the dinosaur. There is nothing that can be done about this' (Conservative Political Centre, 1974, quoted in Rugg and Rhodes, 2008, p 3). Only in the late 1980s did the Conservatives make a robust attempt to revive private landlordism via the abolition of rent control for new tenants.

In its opposition years, Labour's attitude towards private landlords gradually changed and, as New Labour, the party embraced landlords as an integral part of the housing system. The Housing Green Paper (DETR, 2000a, sections 5:1 and 5:2) stated:

> A healthy private rented sector provides additional housing choices for people who do not want to, or are not ready to, buy their own homes…. Through its flexibility and speed of access, it can also help to oil the wheels of the housing and labour markets…. Landlords can be assured that we intend no change in the present structure of assured and assured shorthold tenancies, which is working well. Nor is there any question of our re-introducing rent controls in the deregulated market.

New Labour promoted responsible private landlordism by encouraging 'landlord forums' and voluntary accreditation schemes whereby landlords were brought into the 'big tent' of mainstream provision in return for adopting acceptable standards. In England, the sector expanded from 10.1% of the housing stock in 1997 to 14% in 2008/09, an increase of over one million units, but larger institutional landlords were in relative decline, being replaced by landlords acquiring a few properties under buy-to-let schemes (Rugg and Rhodes, 2008). 'Buy to let' had been started in 1996 when some mortgage lenders agreed to offer loans to private landlords on terms close to those available to owner-occupiers. Its growth was rapid, stimulated by available credit (some of the banks in trouble in 2008 had substantial buy-to-let portfolios); poor returns from stocks and shares; lack of faith in the future of final salary pensions; a favourable tax regime (landlords could offset mortgage payments against tax); capital growth; the expansion of higher education; and the political consensus on landlordism. Although about 40% of this increase resulted from existing landlords transferring to the more favourable buy-to-let mortgage rates (Rugg and Rhodes, 2008), by 2007, there were 991,600 buy-to-let mortgages, valued at over £116 billion, compared to only 7713 valued at £575 million in 1997. However, this expansion was not without controversy. Except in large city centres, landlords added few new properties to the stock (Rugg and Rhodes, 2008) and they compete in the same market sector as first-time buyers.

The private landlord sector operates in a series of 'niche' markets such as the housing benefit market, young professionals, students, immigrants and asylum seekers, housing tied to jobs, and corporate lettings to high-income renters. This diversity and the 'cottage industry' nature of the sector

– 58% of landlords own four or less properties (Rugg and Rhodes, 2008, p 130) – makes it difficult to regulate without harming its flexibility. On average, private tenants stay for only 1.7 years in the private landlord sector compared to eight years for social tenants and 12 years for homeowners.

New Labour adopted a 'light touch' to regulating the private landlord sector, but a more proactive approach to two sub-sectors: low-demand areas and houses in multiple occupation (see Chapter Eight). In its 2000 Green Paper, New Labour stated:

> There are, however, areas of declining housing demand, particularly in parts of our northern cities, where the large-scale operations of some unscrupulous landlords, often inked to criminal activities such as Housing Benefit fraud, drug-dealing and prostitution, are destabilising local communities.... This unholy alliance of bad landlords and bad tenants creates a complex and intractable set of problems. (DETR, 2000a, sections 5:32 and 5:33)

The 2004 Housing Act granted powers to local authorities to license private landlords in low-demand areas, but strictly limited their use. Licensing powers could be introduced only with the permission of the 'appropriate national authority' and only in conjunction with other measures likely to contribute to the improvement of the social and economic conditions in the area.

The private landlordism review, commissioned by the DCL (Rugg and Rhodes, 2008), suggested a number of 'directions of travel' for the private landlord sector. These included the accumulation of better evidence on how the sector functions; initiatives to encourage smaller, good landlords to expand their portfolios and move into the business of letting full time, and helping larger corporate landlords to increase their lettings and so attract higher levels of institutional investment. In addition 'equalising rental choice so that low income tenants could regard a private landlord tenancy as equal to a social tenancy' (Rugg and Rhodes, 2008, p xxiii) and a 'light-touch' licensing system for all landlords, but with encouragement to local authorities to concentrate on the very worst landlords, were recommended.

In its response to the review New Labour noted its finding that, overall, there was a high level of satisfaction with the private landlord sector, but stated:

> the Government has been conscious of concerns about the way in which some parts of the sector operate. This was particularly true for that part of the sector catering for more vulnerable households and those on low incomes with less ability to pay. (DCL, 2009d, p 9)

Its principal remedies were to endorse a compulsory private landlord register (compulsory registration had been introduced in Scotland in 2006) with a registration number required for landlords involved in tenancy agreements, court repossession proceedings and Housing Benefit claims. Landlords guilty of persistent abuses and failure to comply with the regulatory regime would lose the licence. In addition, the mandatory regulation of private-sector letting and management agents was proposed and local authorities were encouraged to develop local lettings agencies. One of the first announcements of the Coalition government was that there would be no compulsory private landlord register or mandatory regulation of private-sector letting and management agents. As the private rented sector was being deregulated there were recurrent attempts to attract finance from pension and insurance funds into investment in large-scale private landlord companies via tax concession packages: the Business Expansion Scheme (1988), Housing Investment Trusts (1996) and Real Estate Investment Trusts (2007). All these initiatives failed and a review of the private landlord sector by Crook and Kemp (2010, p 180) concluded that 'The sector also failed to attract City funding except at the margin, and for niche markets .... The specific initiatives to attract more corporate landlords did not work as intended.'

In 2010 the Treasury returned to the policy initiative on investment in the private landlord sector. It noted that in the UK 'while banks and building societies have been active in lending to private landlords (mostly individuals), institutional investment, e.g. by pension and insurance funds, has been virtually absent from the PRS [Private Rented Sector]' (HM Treasury, 2010c, p 25). It explored the possible reasons for this low investment level including low yields (compared to commercial lettings), private landlordism's poor reputation and high management costs (individual landlords often manage their own properties), and explored possible tax concessions to stimulate institutional investment. In an attempt to lever more institutional finance into the sector, the HCA launched a Private Rented Sector Initiative to give institutions the opportunity to invest in private renting on a large-scale, long-term basis supported by HCA resources. However, under the Coalition government, the Treasury ruled out giving financial support to increase the delivery of homes to rent, claiming that institutional investment would remain only a 'niche' part of the sector.

Devolution

Scotland

In the past, there have been differences between the housing policies pursued in England and Scotland related to legal variations in landlord/tenant law, political affiliations and the relative autonomy granted to the Scottish Office that, until 1999, held responsibility for Scotland's housing programmes. By the mid-1970s, social housing accommodated two thirds of Scotland's population compared to about one third in England. This social-sector dominance reflected a response to the extreme housing conditions in Scotland's cities – the 1951 Census revealed Glasgow's population density to be 163 per acre compared to 77 in Manchester. By 2010, the Right to Buy, stock transfer and restrictions on new building by local authorities had reduced the council housing stock to 13.2%. Housing associations held 10.9%.

Housing was included in the areas of responsibility devolved to the Scottish Parliament in 1999. The Scottish Parliament has primary legislation powers and limited tax-raising capacity, but Housing Benefit is reserved for Westminster and the main fiscal and economic levers, so important to housing outcomes, reside in the UK Treasury. Its executive arm, the Scottish Executive – renamed the Scottish Government in 2007 by the Scottish Nationalist Party – receives finance from Westminster as 'the Scottish Block' based on the 'Barnett formula' – also used to distribute finance to Wales and Northern Ireland. Within the 'block' finance allocated, the devolved administrations can switch across budget headings at will and are not tied to delivering UK-wide policy objectives.

Given New Labour's dominance in the Scottish Parliament until 2007, it is not surprising that housing policy in Scotland, with the notable exception of homelessness policy (see Chapter Seven), has reflected policy in England, despite overall public expenditure being 15% per capita above the English level (Birrell, 2009). However, the terminology has been different. Thus, as examples, the 2006 Housing (Scotland) Act introduced 'Home Reports', analogous to the English 'home information packs', plus a tenancy deposit scheme for the private landlord sector, similar to the system in England. Scotland's LIFT (Low-cost Initiative for First Time Buyers) mirrored England's low-cost homeownership scheme and the Scottish Executive promoted stock transfer but with different procedures, using the Scottish Housing Quality Standard – a more demanding yardstick than the 'decent homes' one used in England – to assess investment requirements. The Right to Buy was first modified in Scotland with all new social tenants being subject to the same restrictions. However, existing tenants retained their established rights, which were more generous than in England because they were not subject to maximum limits. Despite the transfer of Glasgow's 81,000 council houses to the Glasgow Housing Association Ltd (GHA), local authorities and tenants in Scotland have been less enthusiastic about stock transfer than their counterparts in England, partly because, in Scotland, local authorities retain Right to Buy receipts thereby producing more 'in-house' resources for refurbishment. There has been a tendency to emphasise the 'community ownership' model, for example, the Glasgow transfer to the GHA was to be followed by delegation to smaller, community-based housing organisations. Scotland has had its own version of the New Deal for Communities (see Chapter Nine) in the form of the Community Regeneration Fund established in 2004. Although the language used to describe the fund's purposes was different to the rhetoric surrounding the New Deal for Communities – with an emphasis on social inclusion rather than social exclusion – Matthews (2010) has detected a similar tendency to 'pathologise' the communities chosen to receive extra resources.

Wales

The National Assembly of Wales, established in 1999, was granted neither the right to vary taxation nor primary legislative powers, but it could change secondary legislation. The 2006 Government of Wales Act made provision for a Legislative Competence Order (LCO) to be initiated by the Welsh Assembly, thereby reducing dependence on finding an appropriate Westminster bill to which a Welsh dimension could be attached (Birrell, 2009). In 2010, the Welsh Assembly requested legislative competence in the housing domain including power to abolish the Right to Buy, but the necessary legislation was not passed before the general election. The Coalition government expressed concern that the LCO included the power to abolish the Right to Buy, but Parliament passed the LCO giving the Welsh Assembly the ability to suspend the Right to Buy under certain conditions and allowing it to look at the regulation of social landlords, homelessness provision, bringing empty homes back into use and security of tenure.

The housing policies adopted in Wales have been similar in England with 'Welsh' incorporated into the title of each initiative. However, as in Scotland, voluntary stock transfer has had less appeal to local government even after the policy was made more palatable by an emphasis on community control.

Northern Ireland

Prior to 1971, the housing function in Northern Ireland was discharged by 66 local authorities, three new town commissioners and the Northern Ireland Housing Trust, set up after the Second World War to supplement the house-building activities of local government. Following the civil rights marches and the subsequent intensification of violence in 1968/69, the government set up the Cameron Commission to inquire into the disturbances. It concluded that a major cause of the Troubles was 'a rising sense of continuing injustice and grievance among large sections of the population' centred around the 'unfair methods of allocation of houses built and let by such authorities, in particular refusals and omissions to adopt a points system' (Cameron, 1969, p 140). The Cameron Commission's findings led to the establishment of an appointed Northern Ireland Housing Executive in 1971 that became Northern Ireland's single comprehensive housing authority under direct Westminster political control until the establishment of the 'modern' Northern Ireland Assembly in 1998 as part of the Belfast Agreement. The Northern Ireland Assembly was allowed legislative competence in housing, but was suspended in October 2002 when its powers reverted to the Secretary of State for Northern Ireland. It remained suspended until May 2007. The Northern Ireland Housing Executive is accountable to the Northern Ireland Assembly via a division of the Northern Ireland Executive – the Department for Social Development.

Housing policy in Northern Ireland has reflected English policy modified in relation to Northern Ireland politics. Thus, for example, stock transfer from the Northern Ireland Housing Executive has not been promoted in part because of 'the potential problems of community ownership in the context of communal conflict' (Birrell, 2009, p 67). This has contributed to housing associations owning only 3.3% of the stock compared to 8.5% in England.

The specifics of the housing market in Northern Ireland were highlighted when, partially because of the 'peace dividend', house prices more than doubled between 2004 and late 2007 compared to a 31% increase in England. Historically, house prices in Northern Ireland had been lower than in England, but in 2007 only London and South West England had higher prices. This boom was followed by a corresponding bust: prices had declined by 30% at the end of 2009 with only a modest recovery in 2010. One impact of the price boom was an increase in private landlordism, a tendency that continued into the bust as buy-to-let landlords snapped up 'bargains'. In 2001, 7.6% of the stock was rented privately, in 2009, the figure was 16.8%. This growth prompted the Department for Social Development to launch *Building Sound Foundations: A Strategy for the Private Rented Sector*

(2010) with its emphasis on improving management in the sector and improving accessibility with, for example, the use of rent deposit schemes.

The report of the Independent Commission on the Future for Housing in Northern Ireland, chaired by Lord Best (Best, 2010), made a number of recommendations, many drawn from policy initiatives in England, but with some of proposals related specifically to the situation in Northern Ireland. Thus, for example, noting that 'Northern Ireland has the highest proportion of children living in fuel poverty anywhere in the UK; lone parents are spending 56% of their income on fuel (compared with well under half of this figure in Britain)', it emphasised the special salience of a 'National Home Insulation Programme to retro-fit existing homes' (Best, 2010, pp 27, 7). Noting also that 'over 90% of public housing is segregated on religious grounds', it recommended 'that the Northern Ireland Housing Executive and housing associations continue to undertake shared housing projects when development opportunities arise, not least on "neutral" sites' (Best, 2010, pp 29, 8).

The impact of devolution

Birrell (2009) places housing policy under devolution in his 'incremental change and low-level differences' category as opposed to his 'innovations, flagship policies and distinctiveness' category. Indeed, there have been no 'headline' policy differences in the housing domain comparable to the phasing out of prescription charges in Wales and free personal and social care in Scotland. Relative spending levels on housing as a proportion of total spending have reflected pre-devolution trends, except that Wales had dropped below England (Wilcox, 2009a). Moreover, the 'low-level differences' in Scotland and Wales, have tended to reflect internal 'Old' and 'New' Labour divisions within the Labour Party on issues related to 'privatisation' (stock transfer and the Right to Buy). Even the Scottish National Party, despite abolishing the Right to Buy for new social tenants, has not diverted far from the mainstream policy path. Mullins and Murie (2006, p 10) conclude their discussion of the 1998 devolution measures by stating:

> It seems unlikely that devolution will exert a sufficiently strong influence to overwhelm the nationalizing, unifying and converging forces of national economic management, global markets and 'housing developers' approaches to design and marketing.

However, the influence of politics on housing policy has yet to be tested as, for most of the devolution period, New Labour was dominant in all the devolved administrations (in Northern Ireland via periods of direct rule) and, in Scotland, the Scottish Nationalist Party has formed only a minority administration. Devolution politics may become more intense in a climate of public spending cuts. The 2010 Spending Review (HM Treasury, 2010b) set out a cumulative real-terms reduction of 7% to revenue budgets across the devolved governments.

Overview

- Over the past 20 years, the general policy direction has been towards central and local government 'steering' the housing market with greater emphasis on choice and supply diversity. However, despite New Labour's pluralist rhetoric, central government managed the detailed implementation of its social housing policy through targets and performance indictors.
- Elected representatives now have more autonomy in determining housing policy in Scotland, Wales and Northern Ireland but, as yet, the exercise of this autonomy has been limited.

Questions for discussion

1. What is meant by 'the core executive'?
2. Examine the main differences between housing associations and: a) private landlords; and b) local authorities.
3. In what ways has central government controlled the housing activities of local government and housing associations?
4. How can tenants become more involved in the policy and management decisions made by local authorities and housing associations?

Further reading

Introducing Affordable Housing (2009) by **Stephen Harriott** and **Lesley Matthews** offers a sound description of social housing and its regulation. **Derek Birrell's** *The Impact of Devolution on Social Policy* (2009) is a good account of devolution and its impact. *Transforming Private Landlords: Housing, markets and public policy (2010)* by **Tony Crook** and **Peter Kemp** is a good overview of private landlordism.

Websites

Reviews of government policy in England can be found at the website of the Select Committee for the Department for Communities and Local Government, accessible via the House of Commons home page at: http://www.parliament.uk/commons/index.cfm. This site also contains research papers and answers to written questions on housing policy.

The websites of the National Housing Federation, the Chartered Institute of Housing and Shelter have commentaries on housing policy and links to other sites.

Inside Housing (http://www.insidehousing.co.uk) is a weekly commentary on housing policy and the site gives access to a range of policy/research papers via 'Housemark'. *Social Policy Digest* is a valuable gateway to a range of housing policy sources. It is available at: http://journals.cambridge.org/spd/action/home

Policy documents and statistics relating to the devolved governments can be found at the following sites. For Wales:

http://cymru.gov.uk/topics/housingandcommunity/housing/?lang=en
http://wales.gov.uk/topics/statistics/theme/housing/?lang=en

For Scotland:

www.scotland.gov.uk/Topics/Built-Environment/Housing
www.scotland.gov.uk/Topics/Statistics/Browse/Housing-Regeneration/HSfS

For Northern Ireland:

www.dsdni.gov.uk/index/hsdiv-housing.htm
www.dsdni.gov.uk/index/stats_and_research.htm

five

Comparative housing policy

Summary

- Cross-national comparisons contribute to understanding the global and national factors influencing housing policy and allow the array of potential national housing strategies to be appreciated. However, there are obstacles to forming robust conclusions due to limited comparable data on policy inputs and outcomes.
- Since the 1980s, housing policies appear to have been converging towards a greater reliance on market forces underpinned by selective consumer subsidies.
- Policy transfer is difficult to identify, but there is evidence that some policies have been transmitted between countries.

Housing: The global context

This chapter is mainly concerned with housing in member states of the Organisation for Economic Co-operation and Development (OECD), but it is necessary to place its contents within a global perspective. UN-HABITAT, an agency of the United Nations, has attempted to summarise global housing conditions by estimating the 'slum' population. In 2003, it defined a 'slum' as 'a heavily populated urban area characterised by substandard housing and squalor' and, in 2007, it gave a more precise definition relating to 'slum' households rather than 'slum' areas. A 'slum' was defined as:

> a group of individuals living under the same roof in an urban area who lack one or more of the following:

- durable housing of a permanent nature that protects against extreme climate conditions;
- sufficient living space which means not more than three people sharing the same room;
- easy access to safe water in sufficient amounts at an affordable price; access to adequate sanitation in the form of a private or public toilet shared by a reasonable number of people;
- security of tenure that prevents forced evictions. (UN-HABITAT, 2007a, p 1)

The Challenge of Slums: Global Report on Human Settlements (UN-HABITAT, 2003, p 63) noted the negative undertones of the term 'slum' when used in developed countries, but claimed that 'in developing countries, the word lacks the pejorative and divisive original connotation, and simply refers to lower quality or informal housing'. However, this allegedly neutral interpretation has been attacked by academics and many 'informal urban settlement' inhabitants who argue that the pathological undertones of the term 'slum' has facilitated evictions as part of the process of creating new 'cosmopolitan' cities with the associated loss of vibrant informal economies (Angotti, 2006).

According to UN-HABITAT (2007b) nearly one billion people, one in every six, live in slums and, at the prevailing rate of increase, there would be about two billion in 2030. The United Nations' target – to halve by 2015 the number of people without sustainable access to safe drinking water and basic sanitation (currently 2.6 billion) – gives a global context to the following account of housing in selected OECD countries.

Why compare?

There are four principal reasons for engaging in comparative studies:

- Cross-national comparison offers the opportunity to identify possible global factors in housing policy development and thereby highlight the specific determinants of national policies. As Doling (1997, p 23) says, 'Simply put, it can aid the better understanding of the social world'. Part of this understanding involves exploring broad structural trends, the role of 'policy transfer' between countries and the contribution of the relationships between the state, the market and civil society in particular countries. Nonetheless, identifying cross-national policy trends is bedevilled by the variability and complexity of potential policy interventions. Policy inputs are diverse, ranging across intricate and constantly changing direct subsidies, cheap loans and tax breaks to producers, often applied at regional and local level, to the state's regulatory activities and complicated consumer assistance systems in the form of tax concessions and means-tested allowances. These policy interventions are embedded in the pathways established in the specific historical contexts of particular countries.

- Examining housing policies in other countries can supply ideas to apply to the UK by identifying what policies are in operation elsewhere and, perhaps, assessing their effectiveness. As examples:
  - Bradshaw and Finch (2004) examined the impact in 22 countries of consumer housing subsidies – equivalent to Housing Benefit in the UK – on family income. They found that, compared to other countries, Housing Benefit made only a modest contribution to mitigating housing costs and, allowing for housing expenses, the UK 'child support package' ranking moved from third to eighth in the list of counties studied when Housing Benefit was taken into account.
  - Scanlon and Whitehead (2004) identified major differences in the cost of private renting in the UK compared to Sweden and Germany indicating the possible impact of a UK supply shortage.
  - Given the UK's poor performance in mitigating child poverty, Bradshaw et al (2008, p 9) attempted to answer the question: 'do these poor families have the saving grace of good quality housing?' They reached the conclusion that 'the hypothesis that the UK has a saving grace in the quality of its housing can only be upheld with some reservations' (Bradshaw et al, 2008, p 23).

- However, comparing policy effectiveness across countries is problematic because governments hold divergent views about what constitutes a 'successful' housing policy and this is reflected in available policy outcome measures. Thus, for example, the indicators of poor housing standards in the USA such as 'on at least three occasions during the past 3 months, all flush toilet broken at the same time for 6 hours or more' and 'having unvented gas, oil or kerosene heaters as primary heating equipment' (Schwartz, 2010, p 24) are very different to the Housing Health and Safety Rating System (HHSRS) operating in England. Indeed, in the UK, each of the devolved governments now has its own aspirational housing standard and, as Sir Bob Kerslake, when Chief Executive of the Homes and Communities Agency, has pointed out, 'Bizarrely, Britain, unlike most of Europe and the US, uses a home's bedroom count rather than overall footprint, to indicate the size – and therefore the desirability – of the property' (Kerslake, 2010b).

- This lack of comparability between the standards used to measure housing outcomes results in the use of somewhat rudimentary indicators of between-country differences simply because they are available. The shortage of comparable information on housing costs led Bradshaw and Finch to use 20% of average income as a crude proxy for 'necessary' household housing expenditure and Scanlon and Whitehead had no quality indicator. Bradshaw et al located useful comparative data on space standards, perceived safety in the local area and the alleged incidence of rot, damp and leaks, but they recognised that 'There aren't very many, or particularly good sources of comparative data on housing' (Bradshaw et al, 2008, p 9).

- Even when comparable information is available, its interpretation presents problems and there is a danger of imposing ethnocentric criteria when 'evaluating' housing outcomes. For example, an attempt may be made to compare housing standards between countries in terms of the number of rooms per person, but such an indicator ignores extended family values and the climate opportunities for a 'street culture' that reduces requirements for living space. In the study by Bradshaw et al (2008, pp 12–14), Spain had a poor relative position in the league table for average rooms per person for families with children, but performed much better on *perceptions* of space availability. Tenure differences, frequently used in comparative studies, are also difficult to interpret due to the widespread variations in housing conditions *within* tenures and the different meanings attributed to tenure. As Ronald (2008, p 6) states 'tenure is a slippery concept and the meanings, rights and obligations of "owning" a home vary radically from society to society'. 'Social housing' is a particularly flexible notion with Haffner et al (2009, p 4) noting that 'it is something defined in terms of who owns it or how rents are set' but claiming that its essential defining characteristic 'is how accommodated is allocated' with 'social housing ... allocated according to need rather than demand or price'.

- Comparative studies can undercut what we take for granted by demonstrating that a particular housing system is not 'natural' and hence inevitable. For instance, although homeownership is often seen in the UK as a 'natural' tenure that will expand with affluence (Saunders, 1990), there is no clear relationship between a country's wealth and its proportion of homeowners.

- Housing is not a mandate of the European Union, but the common elements of the EU's financial system and the requirement to remove obstacles to the free movement of persons have implications for housing policy in the UK, as does the use of other mandates to pursue housing objectives. Doling (2006, p 338) has detected the European Union developing 'a sort of housing policy by stealth'. Thus, for example, in 2008 the European Commission allowed member states to redirect up to 4% of their European regional development fund allocation towards energy efficiency in existing social housing stock.

Housing policies: Five national case studies

In 1990 and 1999, Esping-Andersen identified three 'worlds of welfare capitalism' – Liberal, Conservative/Corporate and Social Democratic. This classification was based on levels of labour decommodification; use of market mechanisms; universal or selective social rights; the role of the family; and the linkage between the different political institutions, actors and policies (ie corporate political structures).

Other authors (eg Ferrera, 1996; Allen et al, 2004) have identified a fourth category – South European welfare states. Spain, Portugal, Greece and Italy are characterised by polarisation between well-protected workers and those with minimal entitlements, a strong reliance on family networks to provide welfare and fragmented welfare delivery systems. These states have a high proportion of homeowners and, hence, a large share of total personal wealth is held in the form of housing equity.

Housing was not a factor in the initial construction of Esping-Andersen's typology, which ignores considerable variations over time within welfare regimes. Schwartz and Seabrooke (2009) developed a housing classification system based on the percentage of homeowners and the levels of mortgage debt (an indication, they claim, of reliance on liberal 'commodified markets' in housing provision). High homeownership plus high levels of mortgage debt was labelled 'Liberal Market'; low homeownership plus high mortgage debt was called 'Corporatist Market'; low homeownership plus low mortgage debt was branded 'Statist Developmental'; and high homeownership plus low mortgage debt was characterised as 'Catholic Familial' (see *Table 5.1*).

A study by the European Commission on *Housing Exclusion: Welfare Policies Housing Provision and Labour Markets* (2010) used a classification of 'Social Democratic';'Corporatist';'Liberal';'Mediterranean/Rudimentary'; and 'Transition'.

Such a classification will be used in this chapter with specific countries taken as examples of particular housing regime types: USA (Liberal); Sweden (Social Democratic), Germany (Corporatist), Spain (Mediterranean/Rudimentary); and Czech Republic (Transition). Housing statistics for the selected countries are set out in *Table 5.2*.

Table 5.1: *A classification of housing regimes*

Liberal Market	Corporatist Market	Statist Developmental	Catholic Familial
UK	DENMARK	FINLAND	PORTUGAL
USA	NETHERLANDS	FRANCE	BELGIUM
CANADA	GERMANY	AUSTRIA	IRELAND
NEW ZEALAND		JAPAN	SPAIN
AUSTRALIA			ITALY
NORWAY			

Source: Adapted from Schwartz and Seabrooke (2009, p 9).

United States of America

Federal intervention in the housing system started in the 1930s when the economic depression severely impeded the functioning of the housing market: in 1931, 50% of all mortgages were in default and residential construction had declined by 95% since 1928. To deal with this situation the Federal Housing Administration (FHA) was set up to insure private mortgages and thereby stimulate private construction. The Federal National Mortgage Association (FNMA) was also established to purchase mortgages from lenders thereby freeing funds for new mortgages. In 1968, the FNMA was privatised and, quaintly known as Fannie Mae, it bought mortgages on the secondary market and pooled them to sell on to investors as mortgage-backed securities. Later the Federal Home Loan Mortgage Corporation – Freddy Mac – and the Government National Mortgage Association – Ginnie Mae – were set up to provide competition to Fannie Mae.

Under the 1937 National Housing Act, part of President Roosevelt's New Deal, federally funded public housing could be built and managed by local housing authorities. However, in response to complaints from the private sector about unfair competition, 'public' housing had to be linked to slum clearance schemes so that additional stock was not produced and occupancy was restricted to households with low incomes. The 1949 Housing Act extended the scope of the 1937 Act and set a target of 135,000 low-income units per year for six years. However, by the end of the 1950s, only 250,000 public housing dwellings had been constructed.

Public housing continued to be built as part of urban renewal programmes in the 1960s and early 1970s but, from the mid-1970s, new public housing projects were gradually replaced by producer subsidies aimed at stimulating private-sector housing construction for particular groups such as elderly people and low-income families. Most of these producer subsidies were consolidated in the 1986 Tax Reform Act that authorised a Low Income Housing Tax Credit, distributed by the states to companies and investors

Table 5.2: Housing statistics: Selected countries

	United Kingdom	Germany	Sweden	Czech Republic	United States	Spain
Population (millions)	60.9	82.3	9.0	10.2	303.8	40.5
GDP per inhabitant (US dollars)	35728	39442	43147	18194	46443	31142
Persons per dwelling	2.3	2.1	2.1	2.8	2.5	3.2
Poverty rate (50% of median income)	12.4	8.3	6.5	4.3	17	14.3
Gini coefficient[1]	36	28.3	25	25.4	40.8	34.7
Tenure (%)						
Owner-occupied	68	42	40	48	68	85
Private renting	12	58[2]	23	7	30	14
Social rented	20	6[2]	18	20	1	2
Cooperatives/co-ownership	0.3	4	16[3]	18	1	0
Social housing as a % of new dwellings	11	9	16	20	n/a	10.3
No bath/shower	0.2	0.6	0.6	0.8	n/a	0.3
Crime a problem in the neighbourhood as reported by poor people (%)	28.2	18.3	13	17.8	n/a	18.1
Noise a problem in the neighbourhood as reported by all people	19.8	27.1	12.7	18.4	n/a	26
% of dwellings built pre-1919	20	16	11	n/a	8	13
% of dwellings built pre-1945	41	29	32	32	24[4]	34
Dwellings per 1000 people	452	434	483	427	428	528
% of population spending more than 40% of disposable income on housing	17	24	8	10	n/a	7
New dwellings per 1000 people	3.2	3.4	3.3	3.2	6.8	12.6

Notes: All data relates to 2004–09.

[1] The Gini coefficient is a measure of inequality: 0 = total equality, 100 = total inequality.

[2] The 'private' sector in Germany is owned by a diversity of agencies and some operate as 'non-profit' organisations and cooperatives. Of the total stock, 6% has been estimated as 'social', that is, subsidised and subject to allocation rules, but is not defined as a specific sector.

[3] If the co-ownership sector is classified at homeownership, the owner-occupied sector increases to 55%.

[4] The figure is for pre-1949 dwellings.

Sources: Adapted from Ball (2009, 2010a), Lelkes and Zólyomi (2010), Ministry of Regional Development of the Czech Republic (2005), Eurostat (2010), Schwartz (2010) and Statistics Bundesamt, Deutschland (2010).

in housing, and redeemable against Federal tax liability. It was targeted at the acquisition, rehabilitation or new construction of rented housing for lower-income households. In the 1980s and 1990s, Federal government intervention in the housing market was significantly reduced, but many states entered the housing domain by sponsoring Community Development Corporations and promoting the use of Low Income Housing Tax Credit to stimulate housing production, often in conjunction with programmes for revitalising 'distressed' public housing.

Consumer subsidies in the United States have taken two main forms. Homeowners have been able to offset their mortgage interest payments against their tax liability. Such 'tax expenditure' amounted to over $100 billion in 2009 compared to $40.2 billion spent on direct housing subsidies (Schwartz, 2010). Under Section 8 of the 1974 Housing and Community Development Act, housing allowances were made available to low-income households renting at 'fair market rents'. In the 1980s, housing allowances were replaced by 'Section 8' housing vouchers based not on an individually determined 'fair market rent', but on 'payment standards' set for each area similar to the 'reference rents' adopted in the UK. In 2010, housing vouchers were the major form of Federal rental assistance for low-income families, helping over two million households. Prospective tenants are issued a voucher stating that they are covered by the scheme and, when accepted by a landlord offering accommodation, which, unlike the UK Housing Benefit system, has to meet set quality standards, they pay 30% of their income in rent. The remainder, up to the 'payment standard', is paid by the local housing authority, subsidised by the Federal government. The 1998 Quality Housing and Work Responsibility Act stated that extremely low-income households (with an income of less than 30% of an area's median family income) must receive at least 75% of all vouchers. Housing vouchers are not an entitlement – there is limited funding and a long waiting list. Only 1.7% of households use housing vouchers and, in August 2010, when Atlanta issued a new set of Section 8 vouchers, 30,000 people queued for about 450 vouchers. The riot police had to be called in to control the crowd.

Homeownership and the 'credit crunch'

In 1981, 65.3% of households in the United States were homeowners. This percentage declined in the 1980s and early 1990s but, by 2004, the percentage had increased to 68.8% before falling back to 67% after the 'credit crunch' (Schwartz, 2010).

Alan Greenspan, head of the US Central Bank from 1987 to 2006, dealt with financial shocks such as the economic impact of the 9/11 attacks by lowering interest rates. Low interest rates boosted the appeal of property-ownership and the excess demand oversupply led to house price inflation with the average price rising from $119,000 in 2000 to $192,000 in 2006. A new mortgage market, known as 'sub-prime', fuelled this house price boom. 'Sub-prime' mortgages were the outcome of two main influences. President Clinton wanted to increase homeownership amongst low-income households especially those headed by black people who were under-represented in the tenure: in 1996, only 45% of black households were homeowners compared to 65% for all households. Banks were encouraged to lower their requirements for property-backed loans and, in 1996, the United States Department of Housing and Urban Development (HUD) set a goal for Fannie Mae and Freddie Mac that at least 42% of the mortgages they purchased should be to borrowers whose household income was below the area median. President Bush shared Clinton's housing goals and issued a challenge to mortgage lenders to extend credit to low-income households backed by the 2003 American Dream Downpayment Act that granted Federal assistance to finance mortgage deposits for first-time buyers. In 2005, the target set for Fannie Mae and Freddie Mac was increased to 52%.

Despite this Federal intervention, the main 'sub-prime' driver was the profit anticipated by those involved in the mortgage chain. Mortgage suppliers identified commissions, bonuses and profits to be obtained by selling mortgages at high interest rates to sub-prime borrowers. These 'affordability products', sold to low-income households – 'African American borrowers were almost four times more likely than Whites to take on subprime credit' (Wyly, 2010, p 401) – typically offered a 'teaser' introductory interest rate, usually 2%, to be followed by a sharp increase of up to 10%. Interest-only 100% mortgages, often more, were offered and some borrowers were allowed to estimate their incomes on the mortgage application form – so-called 'liar' loans. The 'initiate and distribute' mantra resulted in mortgage brokers selling these mortgages to banks who then resold them in packages, often bundled with 'prime' mortgages, on the global financial market – a process known as 'securitisation'. 'Securitisation' meant that mortgage brokers had little incentive to check the credit history of borrowers. As Lanchester (2010, p 99) comments:

> If the borrower defaulted, so what? The lender no longer owned the risk anyway: it had been securitized and sold on. The initial lender was free to quote Bart Simpson: 'Sayonara, sucker'.

By 2007, this housing bubble had burst. The sustained house price inflation had increased supply and the Federal interest rate, which had reached a 1% low-point in 2004, started to creep upwards. Many sub-prime mortgage holders could not afford to pay the higher interest rates charged when the 'teaser' rates ended and repossessed or abandoned houses added to supply. The average house price was declining fast and the fall in sub-prime loan values caused an international financial crisis. 'Securitised', now 'toxic', mortgage loans had been sold throughout the world and several major banks still owned 'toxic' loans yet to be 'sliced and diced' as 'securitised' debts. As banks did not know who owned the bad debt they refused to lend to each other producing the 'credit crunch'. Gradually, the owners of 'toxic' loans started to become known and the Federal Housing Finance Agency placed Fannie Mae and Freddie Mac under 'conservatorship' effectively making the Federal government responsible for their debts. Bear Sterns was sold to J.P. Morgan for a fraction of its value a year earlier, Lehman Brothers went bankrupt, other banks merged and many required substantial Federal assistance to stay in business.

The Obama administration attempted to stall the mounting number of mortgage foreclosures – up from 1.2 million in 2007 to 3.2 million in 2008 (Squires, 2010) and with 25% of all homeowners in negative equity in 2009. Fannie Mae and Freddie Mac were authorised to refinance – on more favourable terms – mortgages that exceeded their value by up to 125% and the 'Home Affordable Modification Program' was aimed at reducing mortgages in immediate danger of foreclosure.

Private renting

Most Americans pay the market rent for their privately rented accommodation with means-tested vouchers helping those with the lowest incomes. Approximately 1.7 million households – half being elderly or disabled people – occupy privately owned dwellings subsidised by the government.

Public housing

As Schwartz (2010, p 125) has said, despite its diversity, 'public housing evokes many, mostly negative images in the popular imagination: extreme poverty, grim architecture, neglected grounds and, not least, crime'. In the 1990s, public housing was subject to a process of erosion. Under the Hope V1 programme, introduced in 1992, 'distressed' public housing complexes were upgraded or demolished and replaced, in part, by new units of 'mixed-income housing'. Public housing tenants whose homes were to be upgraded or demolished were given four options (see Schwartz, 2010):

- pass the screening test for the restricted number of public housing units in the new development;
- use a housing rental voucher to find a home in the private market;
- move to an empty unit, if available, in another public housing development; or
- find unsupported accommodation.

After 1992, more than 165,000 public housing units were demolished, but far less 'mixed-income' units were built and only about 24% of the original residents moved into the new properties. The 1.3 million remaining public-sector houses now represent just over 1% of the dwellings in the United States. President Clinton's 1998 Quality Housing and Work Responsibility Act devolved Federal responsibility for public housing to 3400 quasi-autonomous local public housing agencies and encouraged them to create 'balanced communities' with added social discipline. Such agencies were allowed to consider a prospective tenant's employment history when making allocation decisions and were required to set standards prohibiting people involved in 'anti-social behaviour' from acquiring a tenancy. One offence makes a public housing tenant liable to eviction. Adult residents of public housing have to contribute no less than eight hours of work per month within the community in which the adult resides, or participate on an ongoing basis in an economic self-sufficiency or job-training programme. Recipients of housing benefits can lose them if they do not fulfil work requirements.

Obama's administration has been described as 'the first "Metro Presidency"' (Katz, 2010). Early action lived up to the tag. An Urban Affairs Department was created, the 2009 American Recovery and Reinvestment Act contained substantial extra resources for public housing and HUD's 2010 budget was increased by 10.8%.

Germany

The reunification of Germany in 1990 brought together two very different housing systems. East German housing policy followed the basic tenets of communist ideology aiming at a sufficient home supply for those in need plus an equitable distribution of housing. In East Germany, 41% of the housing stock was owned by the state. It was let at very low rents and allocated according to need, requirements for key workers and as a reward for party loyalty. The cooperative sector (18%) and the private landlord sector were subject to rent control. Homeownership, mainly a residue of former regimes, constituted about 25% of the housing stock.

Housing was awarded only low priority in the first national plans of the German Democratic Republic and many pre-war dwellings fell into disrepair. Later plans gave housing a higher priority but the attempt to rectify the earlier neglect as quickly as possible produced small and somewhat austere dwellings in prefabricated, high- density units. Prior to reunification, housing was a source of discontent with long waiting lists for a small flat. Furthermore, 18% of dwellings had no shower or bath, 24% of households did not have sole use of a lavatory and 53% had no modern heating system.

In contrast, constituted as the Federal Republic in 1949, West Germany implemented a 'social market' in housing. The state was to be involved in rectifying imbalances between supply and demand but with the ultimate aim of applying market principles whenever the supply and demand were in balance. Thus, in West Germany, state involvement in the housing market has fluctuated according to perceptions of the supply–demand equilibrium. Moreover, the political system's federal structure gave considerable scope for variation between the Länder and between local authorities in the specifics of housing policy. In 2007 responsibility for bricks and mortar subsidies was transferred to the Länder with the federal government providing compensation until 2013.

The serious housing shortage at the end of the Second World War – only 9.5 million habitable dwellings for 15.3 million households – prompted the government to fund housing construction and impose rent controls. Subsidies for rented accommodation were made available, albeit in different forms, to all kinds of suppliers in return for compliance on the rent, size and quality of the dwellings, tenant incomes, and accepting nominations from local government. This form of subsidy produced a range of 'social' rented housing suppliers and good-quality houses. Non-profit organisations, some sponsored by trade unions, locally elected authorities and cooperatives offered accommodation at 'cost' or subsidised rents. Commercial organisations, anticipating long-term profits from 'social' letting with government subsidies, also entered the 'social' market, but were allowed to operate as full commercial landlords when the low-cost loans – paid in return for the acceptance of regulations akin to the non-profit sector – had been repaid. In West Germany, the term 'social housing' came to describe a method of housing finance accompanied by regulations on use rather than, as in the UK until the 1980s, housing owned by local government.

These arrangements plus the generous tax treatment of the 'pure' private landlord sector prompted a healthy new dwelling supply and, in accordance with the 'social market' philosophy, moves towards cementing market principles were made whenever supply and demand seemed to be in balance. In the mid–1960s, rent controls were gradually phased out by allowing decontrol wherever the local housing shortage was estimated to be below 3%. In order to protect the poorest from the full impact of higher rents, a comprehensive means-tested housing benefit (*Wohngeld*) was introduced, which applied to both the owner-occupation and the rented sector. Rent control was reintroduced in the early 1980s, but not on new dwellings and, over time, the rents of existing properties were allowed to increase towards new property rental values. In 1986, subsidies were withdrawn from organisations involved in 'social' renting and, although these subsidies were reintroduced a few years later in response to pressure from the flow of immigrants and census evidence of a housing shortage, the new subsidies were more selective and at a lower rate.

Before reunification the housing system in West Germany consisted of:

• *Owner-occupation:* At 43%, homeownership was low in comparison to the UK. This can be explained, in part, by West Germany's initial concentration on building flats in the cities to overcome the acute housing shortage. Later, the availability of a large, diverse private rented sector, and a less visible system of 'social housing' that did not stigmatise its residents, limited homeownership growth despite state encouragement through a favourable tax regime. In addition, the economy supplied low inflation and housing was not subject to the speculative booms characteristic of the UK. In West Germany, owner-occupation came to be regarded as the tenure for the long-term 'home': expensive, built in the suburbs to high standards on land subject to tight planning restraints and occupied in later life after a long period of saving.
• *Non-profit housing enterprises:* Cooperatives and companies owned by local authorities, the regional states, churches, trade unions or industrial companies owned about 22% of the stock. However, in accordance with the philosophy of the 'social market' with 'social housing' determined by subsidy, as the low interest loans received from the state were repaid, there was a tendency for such non-profit organisations to opt out of taking nominations from local authorities and for the municipal companies to become private.
• *Private landlords:* In 1990, about 36% of the housing stock belonged to the private landlord sector, which supplied a diverse range of dwellings catering for a variety of mainstream housing requirements.

Following German reunification in 1990, the East German housing system was subject to the 'big bang' of market forces. The state-owned housing stock was transferred to local authorities who, in return for debt reduction, were supposed to sell them, via communal housing companies, to private investors and tenants. The cooperatives retained their properties but, as an incentive to sell, they were allowed to write off debt provided they sold a proportion of their stock. Rents were to be increased in steps to match West German levels with *Wohngeld* helping poorer families to afford the increase. Tenants were given incentives to buy in the form of discounts on market prices and the Federal government allocated resources to improve older dwellings and for new building. This attempt to rebuild the East German housing system on West German principles was hampered by ownership claims on property built before the formation of the German Democratic Republic and by the movement of over two million East Germans to the West. By the early 2000s, the former East Germany had a large housing surplus with one in seven properties unoccupied. To cope with this surplus an extensive programme of demolition and improvement, with Federal subsidies, was implemented.

Population movement to the former West Germany prompted the government to stimulate housing supply by a combination of generous tax incentives and direct subsidies. There was a rise in house prices and housing investment peaked at 8% of national income in the late 1990s before going into steep decline as incentives were withdrawn in accordance with indicators that supply and demand were in balance.

In 2010, only 42% of the housing stock in Germany was owner-occupied although it was 11% higher in the old Federal Republic than in the East. This low rate of homeownership has been attributed to the cautious lending policies of the financial institutions, the good supply of rented accommodation accumulated after 1945 and the less generous subsidies to homeowners (Voigtländer, 2009). There was no house price boom that many countries experienced between 2000 and 2007 and this tendency to price stability has also been a factor in restricting homeownership. Renting from 'private' landlords, including the 'non-profit' sector, is about 58%. Rents are not controlled at the start of a tenancy but, when established, the Länder and municipalities regulate rents with the result that they have tended to lag behind inflation (Ball, 2009, p 45). In comparison to the UK, since 1989, private landlord tenants have good security of tenure and landlords benefit more from depreciation allowances and reductions in capital gains tax if dwellings are owned for a long period (Oxley et al, 2010). The share rented as 'social housing' has been in decline because the conditions attached to subsidies are time-limited (Kirchner, 2007). As low-cost loans are paid off, landlords have become free from state restrictions on allocations. Some of the stock has been sold to private investment trusts. In 2008, *Wohngeld* was received by 569,000 households, about 1.4% of all households.

Sweden

During its long period of Social Democrat government Sweden developed a comprehensive housing policy aimed at promoting a general improvement in living conditions for all its citizens, not just the poor. To stimulate overall supply, the government offered long-term, low-interest loans for the portion of the capital requirement most difficult to finance on the normal credit market. These state housing loans were an important dimension of the government's control of housing production with preferred suppliers, 'not-for-profit' housing corporations, often linked to municipal government, receiving higher loans than homeowners and private landlords. State loans to private landlords were accompanied by rent control, which, whilst ensuring that the rent of a new property was sufficient to meet capital and maintenance costs, aimed at preventing the rents for older property, built at lower cost, rising to market levels. Between 1968 and 1978, specific rent control was gradually relaxed in the expectation that accommodation available from 'cost-rent' housing corporations would dampen rent levels in the private landlord sector. Rents in the housing corporation sector were subject to negotiation between the National Tenants' Union and the National Federation of Cost-rental Housing Corporations mediated by a Rental Market Committee. The rents for dwellings owned by the municipal non-profit housing companies were then used as a yardstick for privately owned rental housing.

The Conservative government, elected to office in 1991, phased out interest rate subsidies and 'not-for-profit' suppliers were subject to the same tax regime as for-profit rental suppliers. This raised housing costs with rents absorbing about 30% of average incomes. Means-tested housing allowances were increased to mitigate the impact of higher rents on low-income households. In addition, access to mortgage finance was liberalised as a stimulus to homeownership. On regaining office, the Social Democrats continued the same broad policies as the Conservatives but, after 2000, a developing housing shortage in some areas, plus a low-demand problem in other districts, led to renewed state involvement in housing albeit on a more selective basis. Between 1997 and 2007, there was a boom in house prices interrupted only between 2000 and 2002 by the aftermath of the collapse of the 'dot.com' bubble. House-building in the owner-occupied sector responded to the boom but did not reach the levels attained before the early 1990s' recession.

Today there are four principal elements in the Swedish housing system:

- *Homeownership:* This accounts for about 40% of the housing stock. Owner-occupiers can deduct their mortgage interest costs from their tax liability at a rate of 30%, but are subject to tax on the imputed rental income and a capital gains tax.

• *Tenant-ownership cooperatives:* Members of tenant-ownership cooperatives own an individual share in the collective value of the properties. Usually members are responsible for the maintenance of their individual dwellings and can sell the 'right to occupy' their property at the market price although some cooperatives reserve the right to determine the sale price. In essence tenant-ownership, which accounts for about 19% of the housing stock, is a form of homeownership with the cooperative element used to manage a blocks of flats. Individual members of a cooperative can claim the same tax relief as single-family owner-occupiers.

• *Cost-rental housing corporations:* Many of these have strong connections with locally elected authorities. They own about 21% of the housing stock and charge rents that, in aggregate, cover historic costs. These costs are low because the stock was mainly built before the mid-1970s. Housing corporations do not only let their properties to low-income households.

• *Private renting:* Private renting accounts for 23% of the housing stock. The private rented sector in Sweden has been in decline as its profitability has been reduced because the general rent level in the private sector is set in relationship to the general rent level in the housing corporation sector. In many areas, rent levels in the private rented sector are well below the market-clearing rate.

Housing consumption is also subsidised by a mean-tested housing allowance system that has grown in importance as universal producer subsidies have been curtailed.

Spain

Housing supply in Spain is characterised by a high proportion of owner-occupiers (85%), a small private landlord sector (12%) and a very small public sector (2%).

Homeownership in Spain is one of the highest in the world and about 20% of Spain's urban population own a second home in the countryside or on the coast. Allowing for the second homes owned by people with a residence outside Spain, it has been estimated that around a third of the stock is not held as a main residence (Ball, 2009).

The high proportion of Spanish homeowners has been attributed to a cultural tradition of 'patrimony' – a specific stock of housing and land conserved within the extended family (Allen et al, 2004) – which was reflected in significant producer subsidies under the Franco regime and consumer subsidies under subsequent governments. Between 1997 and

2007, despite high levels of construction, house prices in Spain more than doubled and, although interest rates declined, home affordability became more problematic. In Spain, a high percentage of people aged 30 and over live in the parental home. This indicates that access to independent accommodation is problematic, but it also reflects the different social meaning attributed to young people leaving home. As Allen et al (2004, p 44) comment:

> Throughout a large part of Europe, the period between leaving the parental home and forming one's own family has come to be considered as a normal stage in the life process, facilitated by the availability of rented accommodation. In southern Europe, leaving the parental home has a definitive character. More than half of those who leave their parental home in Spain start with owning their own home. These young people skip the stage of living alone or in cohabiting couples in rented housing prior to marriage and having children.

Between 1998 and 2007, the house-building rate in Spain was very high with the housing stock growing by 5.7 million, nearly 30%. This house-building rate was a consequence of rising demand, especially from foreign buyers, the heavy use mortgage 'securitisation' (Ball, 2009) and the considerable incentives to local government to release land – in the form of taxes on land sales, requirements to give between 5% and 15% of development land to local government and the enhanced value of publically owned land. However, the 'credit crunch' had a major impact with prices declining by 10% in both 2008 and 2009 and housing starts plummeting to half the 2006 peak (Ball, 2010a).

In the past, the private rented sector was subject to rent control. The 1964 Ley de Arrendamientos Urbanos – imposing strict rent regulation and allowing transfer of leases to family members – prevented investment in the private landlord sector. In 1985, in an attempt to revive the private landlord sector, the Boyer Decree ended rigid rent control in by linking five-year rental contracts to increases in the retail price index at the end of the contract. However, the rent increases were insufficient to attract new investment and the rental market – concentrated in the main cities – continued to stagnate. In 2005, a Ministry of Housing was established and its 2005 Housing Plan aimed at stimulating private renting by subsidies to firms and public bodies purchasing property for letting and private individuals letting accommodation for a minimum period of 10 years to cover their insurance costs against unpaid rents and the repair costs.

Landlords also receive significant tax breaks. A limited scheme exists to help low-income families to pay their rent.

'Social housing' in Spain, in the sense of subsidised, not-for profit accommodation for rent, is very limited, being the product of autonomous municipal and charitable initiatives. However, there is long tradition of low-cost homeownership initiatives. Some newly built owner-occupied housing, known as 'publicly protected housing' and offered by a variety of suppliers, has been given subsidies in the form of reduced-interest loans and has been allocated via means-testing schemes.

The Czech Republic

Between 1948 and 1989, when part of Czechoslovakia, housing policy in the Czech Republic reflected communist thinking. Housing was provided and distributed not by the market, but in response to 'needs', economic requirements and political affiliations. There were four main tenure types:

- *State:* State housing – consisting of apartments nationalised in 1948–49 and dwellings constructed under the state-directed Complex Housing Construction Programme – accounted for 45% of dwellings in 1991. These estates were heavily subsidised and contained a large percentage of prefabricated ('panelak') flats. Management was provided by housing services companies acting on behalf of the state.
- *'Enterprise':* In this tenure form, particular state enterprises held the right to allocate dwellings built with finance from the state, state enterprises and bank loans. The tenure's purpose was to attract labour to preferred regions and industries.
- *Cooperative:* This tenure consisted of Building Housing Cooperatives set up under state supervision in the 1950s and pre-war cooperatives that were later merged into 'giant' associations (Lux, 2009, p 96). Most of the cost was financed by the state but, in return for individual contributions, prospective tenants could have quicker access to housing and, in some cases, better-quality homes.
- *Private:* Individually self-built houses were supported by state loans at low interest rates and were directed to workers in preferred industries.

Following the removal of the communist regime and the formation of the Czech Republic as a separate state from Slovakia, housing was subject to a 'transition' process of eliminating administrative allocation and establishing a more market-oriented system. Subsidies for both new and existing state-rented dwellings were substantially reduced (Lux and Sunega, 2007), cooperative members were allowed to purchase their properties and houses nationalised under the communist regime were returned to their original owners. State stock was transferred to the municipalities and some municipalities embarked on a selling programme to individual tenants, tenants who formed cooperatives and real-estate development companies. However, there was no general 'right to buy', as occurred in some other 'transition' states, it being argued that a good supply of rented accommodation promoted labour mobility. Rents became deregulated on vacant possession but the law provided reasonable protection from eviction. Rents for sitting tenants remained regulated (based on size, not location) and, despite substantial increases after 1991, they remained at below market rents. Thus, two segments exist in the rental market – market and regulated – with rent levels depended on when the dwelling was let rather than income. In 2006, a rent deregulation law aimed at gradually deregulating all rented housing by 2011 was passed.

In 1993, to protect lower-income households from the impact of rent increases, the government introduced a system of housing allowances. Initially, the allowances were given to households in the rental sector for a maximum of two years with the household expected to move to cheaper accommodation within this period. In 1996, a new system of housing allowances was introduced for households with a total income of less than 1.4 times (later 1.6 times) the subsistence level. The support was available to households in all tenures, but only about 7% of households receive the allowance (Lux and Sunega, 2007) and, because it is based on notional rather than actual rents, it covers only about 20% of costs.

The belief in market efficiency led to the virtual ending of state subsidies for house-building. This subsidy removal resulted in a sharp decline in dwelling construction from 44,594 in 1990 to only 12,662 in 1995 (Lux, 2009, p 99). This failure of the market to boost housing supply produced a move towards greater state intervention. Subsidised savings schemes were introduced to support homeownership and the shortage of accommodation for low-income families was to be overcome by new subsidies for municipal house-building targeted on people with special needs, on single-member households with an income below 80% of average monthly income, and on multiple-member households with an income of less than 150% of average monthly income. Renovation of older dwellings was stimulated by low-interest loans to municipalities and, under the 'panel programme' started in 2001, bank guarantees and subsidies were made available to modernise the 'panelak' estates.

There are now four sectors in the housing market:

- *Private rented:* At about 7% of the housing stock, this sector has been created mainly by the restitution of property nationalised in 1948 to the 'rightful' owners.
- *Municipal rented:* This accounts for 24% of occupied dwellings but is decreasing as a consequence of sales to cooperatives and tenants.
- *Co-operative sector:* This sector, at about 18% of the stock, is decreasing as sales to individuals outstrip acquisitions from the municipal sector.
- *Homeownership:* At 50% this sector is expanding from new-build (encouraged by tax breaks and low-interest loans for first-time buyers) plus transfers from the municipal and cooperative sectors.

Although new housing construction has not reached 1990 levels, there is not a critical housing shortage in the Czech Republic, but there are problems of dwelling size, maintenance, uneven distribution of dwellings relative to demand and a shortage of inexpensive housing for families. House prices increased from 2000 to 2003, then, after a period of decline, started to increase rapidly until 2007 when the rate of increase started to wane.

The 'convergence' thesis

Comparative housing research has been strongly influenced by 'structural' approaches. The social reformist approach has identified the 'logic of industrialisation' as the principal driver of housing change and a strong element of organic functionalism has permeated the approach. Donnison (1967), for example, identified 'developmental stages' in housing policy from 'haphazard' to 'comprehensive', implying that housing systems evolve towards a 'higher' order. According to Marxist theory, it is capitalism's requirements that determine housing policy, with the state intervening in the market to restore profitability when capitalism is in crisis (Harloe, 1995). Both variations of the 'structural' approach predict 'convergence' in housing systems. Schmidt (1989) attempted to test the convergence thesis by examining housing markets and housing policy in advanced industrialising countries from the 1970s to the mid-1980s. He found that:

> contrary to convergence theory, and its associated thesis of a particular 'logic of industrialism', institutional factors loom large. Analysing the structure of the market, ideological factors are found to be of the greatest importance. At the same time, housing market processes and the character of housing policy are primarily determined by institutional factors. (Schmidt, 1989, p 83)

However, an examination of the five national case studies outlined earlier, plus the UK experience, indicates a tendency towards convergence from the 1980s with 'recommodification' – a return to market principles in housing distribution – being the common factor. Such 'recommodification', although mediated through dissimilar housing regimes in different countries, has been reflected in the demise of public housing and rent control; more selective producer subsidies; an increase in the use of means-tested rent allowances; and the growth of homeownership. This stripped-down, more selective approach to housing policy, with the market dictating overall outcomes, was produced by a number of interacting factors. The abatement of mass housing shortages through the sustained house-building programmes in the 1960s and 1970s had an impact, as did the hegemony of neo-classical economic thinking within international financial organisations such as the World Bank and the impact of 'globalisation'. According to the 'globalisation' thesis, 'we are now entering a new phase in which cross-border flows in goods and services, investment, finance and technology are creating a seamless world market where the law of one price will prevail' (Weiss, 1998, p 167). Although housing immobility limits the impact of globalisation, its influence on financial and labour markets magnifies regional and local variations in economic conditions within countries through internal and international migration. This may have prompted a more 'selective' response from national governments. Globalisation also magnifies 'risk' and prompts governments to deflect this 'risk' onto homeowners in the context of greater volatility in the housing market. The 'credit crunch' illustrates the global context of housing policy, but its differential impact also demonstrates the salience of historically established national pathways in influencing housing outcomes. Thus, as examples, in the boom housing market of 2000–06, real prices fell in Germany and Japan compared to annual increases of 5.4% in the United States, 8.8% in the UK and 11.2% in Spain, and the credit crunch did not depress prices in Germany significantly below the trend (Ball, 2010a). The USA, UK and Spain made extensive use of 'securitisation', Germany and Sweden did not (Springler and Wagner, 2010).

Policy transfer

It is difficult to assess the extent of policy transfer between countries; few politicians, public officials or 'think tanks' are willing to admit to policy plagiarism. Nonetheless, it is possible to identify examples of how the experience of other countries has influenced UK policy and vice versa:

- In the 1960s the Conservative Party was attracted to the idea of a 'social market' economy that had produced an 'economic miracle' in West Germany. The means-tested rent rebate and rent allowances introduced under the 1972 Housing Finance Act had a marked similarity to West Germany's 1965 rent allowances scheme. Both were designed to cushion a move towards market rents across all sectors of the rented sector.
- The policy of 'stock transfer' from local government to 'registered social landlords' reflects a move towards the long-established models of 'social housing' in Sweden and Germany. Nevertheless, the 'unitary rental market', identified by Kemeny (1994) as characteristic of Germany and Sweden, whereby a variety of landlords have been directed towards 'social' purposes in return for state assistance and linking their rents to historic costs, has not been a characteristic of UK housing policy. In the UK, the incomes of tenants in the 'social' sector are lower in relationship to owner-occupiers than in either Germany or Sweden: 42% in the UK, 64% in Germany and 57% in Sweden (Stephens, 2005).
- The UK's scheme of choice-based lettings (see Chapter Seven) was based on the Delft lettings model developed in the Netherlands during the late 1980s.
- New Labour's proposals to link the payment of Housing Benefit to behaviour is similar to clauses in President Clinton's 1998 Quality Housing and Work Responsibility Act although no New Labour politician has acknowledged the connection.
- The Right to Buy scheme in the UK provided a model for the privatisation of state housing in some countries in their transition from state socialism.

Overview

- Although comparative studies of housing policy can contribute to an understanding of policy development and can supply ideas for new housing policies, they are limited by the availability of data suitable for comparative analysis.
- Case studies of housing policy in different countries supply evidence on the relative contributions of structural economic and social factors and specific national politics in explaining housing policy.
- Up to the mid-1980s, the specific 'national politics' of housing policy appear to have been more important than 'global' factors in explaining policy development. However, since the mid-1980s, there is some evidence of convergence in housing policies and the 'credit crunch' has illustrated a degree of interdependence between national housing systems.

Questions for discussion

1. Examine **Table 5.2**. What are the major differences between the countries included in the table?
2. What are the principal problems involved in comparative studies of housing policy?
3. On the basis of the information provided in **Table 5.2** can any country be regarded as having the 'best' housing policy?
4. Suggest possible cross-national indicators for comparative studies of the outcomes of housing policy.

Further reading

Richard Ronald's (2008) *The Ideology of Home Ownership: Homeowner Societies and the Role of Housing* is an interesting attempt to compare Anglo-Saxon and East Asian homeownership models. A comprehensive account of Spanish housing policy is available in **Allen et al** (2004) *Housing and Welfare in Southern Europe*. **Martin Lux's** (2009) *Housing Policy and Housing Finance in the Czech Republic during Transition* explores housing policy in a former communist state. An informed account of housing policy in the United States can be found in **Alex Schwartz's** (2010) *Housing Policy in the United States. Housing Allowances in Comparative Perspective* (2007) edited by **Peter Kemp** examines the role of means-tested consumer subsidies in the context of housing policies in 10 countries.

Websites

The United Nations Economic Commission for Europe provides current figures on housing outcomes (http://www.unece.org/stats/data.htm), and data on housing policy in the member states of the European Union is available at: http://www.iut.nu/Statistiques%20logement%20UE%202002.doc

The latest edition of the *European Housing Market Review* is available at: http://www.rics.org/site/scripts/download_info.aspx?fileID=2150&categoryID

The Joint Centre for Housing Studies, based at Harvard University, (http://www.jchs.harvard.edu) supplies comprehensive information on housing policy and its outcomes in the United States. The website 'global property' provides information on house prices throughout the world and is available at: http://www.globalpropertyguide.com/real-estate-house-prices/S

six

Affordable housing

Summary

- Rented accommodation has been made more affordable by producer subsidies and means-tested housing allowances.
- In the past, homeownership support was provided via tax concessions and grants for improvement but, in recent years, state support has become limited and income selective.
- Since the early 1990s, the physical planning system has been used to secure more affordable housing.
- After 2003, New Labour started to intervene more actively in the housing market to increase housing supply with the long-term objective of making housing more affordable.
- The Coalition government jettisoned New Labour's 'top-down' approach to stimulating housing supply in favour of offering council tax incentives to local government to deliver more homes.

What is meant by affordable housing?

Affordable housing is an elusive concept. It has been construed in a number of ways:

- The 'safety–net' version is connected to the perception that housing is a necessity and with the concern that, if a high proportion of income has to be devoted to housing costs, which are difficult to change in the short term, then insufficient resources will be available for other essentials. Sometimes called 'the residual income approach', this interpretation forms the rationale for Housing Benefit (HB) now directed towards preventing post–rent incomes falling below the basic social assistance level. Given that HB pays all rent up to a prescribed maximum if income is very low, then any rent unaffordable on the 'safety–net' definition is due to the ways that HB operates. Indeed, on this approach, if the safety net functions efficiently, there is no 'safety–net' reason why social housing rents should not rise to market levels (see DCL, 2009e). The Chancellor's statement that, in future, social-sector rents for new tenants should be set at a higher level reflects such reasoning (Chancellor of the Exchequer, 2010). The new tenure will be called 'affordable' and tenants will have limited security. Initially, the Chancellor announced that the 'affordable' rents would be 80% of market rents, but this was later modified to 80% of the Local Housing Allowance (see later). In London, for example, the average social rent for a two–bedroom house was £95 in 2010 compared with £310 for a private rented home. A rent of 80% of the LHA would be £232. Clearly 'affordable' is a very flexible term.

- Because HB is means–tested with a steep 65% taper, there is concern that reliance on the 'safety–net' objective discourages work both in the sense of entering the paid workforce (the 'unemployment trap') or, if in paid employment, working harder and longer (the 'poverty trap'). Thus, a different way to interpret affordability is to maintain that the rent paid should leave sufficient resources available for other requirements without the need to claim a housing cost-related and means-tested benefit if a household member is working. Rent affordability was an element in the rationale for rent control applied to the private rented sector until 1989 and is part of the justification for social housing. In 1989, the Housing Corporation declared 'Associations are ... expected to set and maintain their rent at levels that are within the reach of those in low paid employment' (Housing Corporation, 1989, p 1) and the Scottish Federation of Housing Associations (2010, pp 7–8) has stated:

> It is the SFHA's view that, for a rent (including service charges) to be deemed to be 'affordable', households with one partner in full time work should only exceptionally be dependent on Housing Benefit.

In 1995, the National Federation of Housing Associations (now the National Housing Federation) set an 'affordability test'. This stated that 'rents are affordable if the majority of working households taking up new tenancies are not caught in the poverty trap (because of dependency on Housing Benefit) or paying more than 25% of their income in rent' (National Federation of Housing Associations, 1995, p 4). This benchmark reflected a convention, widely applied in housing studies, of measuring 'affordability' in terms of a rent-to-income ratio. Although the 25%

yardstick has a long history – 'one week's pay for one month's rent' was a common rule of thumb at the end of the 19th century – it is arbitrary and other countries use different benchmarks with 30% often applied. Eurostat (2010) applies 40% or more of equivalised disposable household income after benefits as its 'housing cost overburden' threshold.

In 2008 average council rents were £86.1 and average housing association rents were £77.66 below the levels in the private landlord sector (Pawson and Wilcox, 2011 p 188). Nonetheless, 'of the new tenancies identified as belonging to working households 34% of housing association and 32% of local authority were dependent on Housing Benefit' (DCL, 2009e, p 5). These figures will increase as more social tenants are expected to pay rents closer to market levels.

Although rent regulation only started to be phased out in 1989, today the affordability notion is rarely applied to the private rented sector, it being assumed that market rents ought to be the norm with Housing Benefit 'taking the strain' for those on low incomes. The National Housing and Planning Advice Unit (NHPAU) concluded that 'at the 15th percentile house price, in the least affordable southern regions it is cheaper to rent than buy, whereas in the more affordable regions there is little difference between renting and buying' (NHPAU, 2010, p 26). Nevertheless, private-sector rents are high in the least-affordable regions – more than double in London compared to the North West (DCL, 2010b, Table 734). Walker and Niner (2010, p 2) found that in a sample of low-income working households (LIWH) – defined as less than median income – renting from private landlords:

> After excluding some extremely high outlying values from the survey, the rents paid are around 35 per cent of LIWH incomes, rising to about 39 per cent in London/Brighton and Hove…. The in-depth interviews with families with dependent children revealed that two-thirds spent more (often considerably more) than 30 per cent of their gross income on rent, and nearly a third experienced problems meeting their rent payments.

• A third way to test social rent affordability is to compare social rents with homeownership housing costs, taking into account that homeowners are acquiring an asset. Such a comparison indicates that social tenants should pay between 16% and 20% of income (DCL, 2009e) but, on average, council rents absorb 26.2% of a tenant's income before HB and housing association rents 30.9% (Kemp, 2008).

New Labour did not set out a specific affordable housing yardstick, but regarded social housing as affordable by definition. Responding to a parliamentary question, Baroness Andrews, Housing Minister in 2005, said:

> The Government define affordable housing as including social-rented housing and other forms of sub-market housing (known as intermediate housing)....Other forms of sub-market housing include forms of low-cost home ownership such as shared ownership and Homebuy and housing available at intermediate rents (above social rent but below market rent). Affordable housing can generally be accessed only by existing social housing tenants or people on waiting lists, or others groups specifically identified, such as key workers. (Baroness Andrews, 2005, quoted in Wilson, 2006, p 9)

The delivery of 'affordable' housing since 1991/92 is set out in *Figure 6.1*. As can be seen from *Figure 6.1*, 'intermediate' rental housing has had a low profile compared to social-rented housing and low-cost homeownership schemes but, according to a Charted Institute of Housing paper (Davies and Lupton, 2010), there were 7.2 million 'in-betweeners' – not likely to

Figure 6.1: Additional 'affordable' homes: 1991/92 to 2009/10 (England)

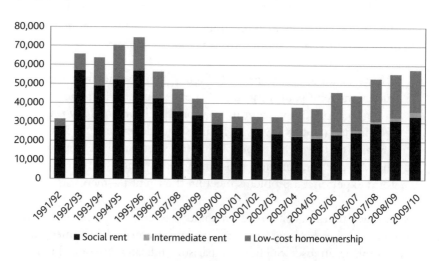

Note: Figures include conversions and acquisitions as well as new-build.
Source: Adapted from DCL (2010b, Table 1000).

be able to obtain social housing and not eligible for Housing Benefit, but finding it difficult to pay their housing costs.

In the past, housing has been made more affordable through a range of producer and consumer subsidies (see *Box 6.1*).

Box 6.1: Producer and consumer subsidies

Direct subsidies can be awarded to housing producers or consumers and can be means-tested or not means-tested (universal). When not subject to a direct income test the subsidy has often been linked to other selective criteria (see *Table 6.1*).

Table 6.1: Producer and consumer subsidies

	Means-tested	Not means-tested
Consumer	• Housing Benefit • Improvement grants after 1989 • Disabled Facilities Grant (Households without children under 19) • Energy Efficiency Grants • Mortgage Benefit (Income Support)	• Improvement grants before 1989 (subject to dwelling value) • Low-cost homeownership schemes (subject to area and job criteria plus a maximum income condition) • Right to Buy discount • Tax relief on mortgage interest (until 2000) • Disabled Facilities Grant (households with children under 19)
Producer	• Improvement grants for private landlords at certain times in the past	• Central government allowances to local authority revenue accounts, eg Major Repairs Allowance. • Social Housing Grant

Affordability in the 19th century

To the neoliberal economist, affordability is not an issue provided the market is allowed to operate. Supply and demand will balance over time with overcrowding and homelessness either short–term problems, manifest while supply catches up with demand, or a reflection of consumer preferences to spend household income on other goods and services. Laissez–faire thinking was influential in the 19th century, but the externalities of poor housing gradually pushed affordability towards social problem status.

Payment of water and sewerage costs through the rates eased the affordability problem, but there remained the issue of how to pay for the higher housing standards thought to be necessary for civilised living and character improvement. Lord Shaftesbury's 1851 Labouring Classes Lodging Houses Act gave local authorities the power to erect lodging houses but, according to the Act, the rents had not to be 'so low as to be an indirect means of giving relief to the poor' and certain clauses allowed local ratepayers to delay any proposed scheme. Only Huddersfield and Birmingham used Lord Shaftesbury's law. In eradicating slums, the government relied on voluntary organisations whose benevolent investors limited their return on capital investment to 5%. Unfortunately, the rents necessary to supply a 5% return were beyond the means of many working-class households. The charitable Peabody Trust, for example, offered austere but sanitary accommodation absorbing about 50% of low-paid workers' wages. This meant that unskilled labourers did not move into the properties – an outcome defended by 'filtering theory', with James Hole declaring in 1866 that 'by increasing the number of first class houses for mechanics the vacated tenements increase the supply for the second and third classes and thus all classes are befitted' (quoted in Boddy and Gray, 1979, p 43). Octavia Hill adopted a different approach. She recognised that 'trickle down' did not work because new demand was created by migration into cities and population increase, so she bought dilapidated properties, carried out urgent repairs and then rented the dwellings to tenants able to pay on a regular basis for a reconditioned dwelling. Although her tenants were the poor – not the better-paid artisans housed by the model dwellings companies – 'her flats could not be easily afforded by those earning less than a regular 16s to 18s' (Wohl, 1977, p 182). Hence the 'very poor' – about 16.5% of London's population – could not afford to live in her properties.

Standards and affordability

The Tudor Walters Committee (Tudor Walters, 1918), established to make recommendations on the standard of working-class dwellings to be constructed after the First World War, highlighted the affordability issue. It recommended far higher future benchmarks: bathrooms, gardens and, in some cases, a second living room – the 'parlour'. It accepted that state subsidies were necessary to achieve these standards, but argued that the ultimate level of subsidy would depend on the relationship between the initial cost of the dwelling and the rental income derived from it over a 60-year period indicating that, in time, the dwellings would require no subsidy.

The houses built under the 1919 Housing and Town Planning Act were of a high standard but, despite the subsidy, expensive to rent. They were occupied mainly by skilled workers or by the middle class (Jones, B, 2010): indeed, some local authorities used a means test to select only high-income tenants! Speaking about one of the first council estates built in Liverpool, a former tenant remarked:

> It was posh, our next-door neighbour used to have tea on the grass, the lawn she used to call it. Some of them even had cars, even in them days, and yes, a number used to have cleaning ladies to do for them. (Quoted in McKenna, 1991, p 182)

Attempts were made to overcome the affordability quandary in the 1920s by reducing the quality of council housing but, even with lower standards, many tenants still found it difficult to pay the rent and resorted to 'strategies that had served them in the old areas: the pawnshop, hire purchase, reducing expenditure on food, or taking in lodgers' (Olecnowicz, 1997, p 7). The problem was compounded in the 1930s when local authorities, directed towards meeting the housing needs arising from slum clearance, were confronted by the slum dwellers' very low incomes. Further reductions in quality were made with the average council house cost declining from 77% of an owner-occupied house in 1934 to 50% in 1939. Branson and Heinemann (1973, p 211) state that 'For the most part the blocks built at this time were severely utilitarian in character.... Some of these blocks seemed to emphasise that they were rough places for rough people'. Yet, even with lower standards, the affordability question remained. The 1930 Housing Act contained a provision to allow local authorities to operate 'differential' rent schemes, but few authorities adopted them either in the form of individual rent rebates or variable rents for 'compulsory' (rehoused from clearance areas) compared to 'voluntary' (rehoused from the waiting list) tenants. Council tenants with reasonable incomes strongly opposed such schemes. Moreover, many local authorities believed that means–tested subsidies were a step towards housing support becoming a major ratepayer responsibility because 'poor relief' could be interpreted as a public assistance matter, a traditional responsibility of local government.

From producer to consumer subsidies

Between 1945 and 1972, housing was made more affordable by rent control in the private landlord sector and continued central and local rate subsidies in the council sector. Rent pooling, with local authorities using the low build and loan costs of older houses to reduce the rents charged on new properties, helped to keep rents down. Only a few local authorities ran rent rebate schemes.

The 1972 Housing Finance Act marked the first serious attempt to move from producer to consumer subsidies with the White Paper heralding the

Act stating that the government's policy was 'subsidising people, not bricks and mortar' (DoE, 1971, p 42). It introduced a national rent rebate scheme for council tenants and a rent allowance scheme targeted on the tenants of other landlords. Rebates and allowances offered the opportunity for some low-income households to be able to afford to live in the better-quality local authority dwellings and for the tenants of private landlords to pay a rent sufficient to keep their houses in reasonable repair. The Act met resistance from council house tenants with decent incomes who objected to paying 'fair rents' – above the historic costs of providing their dwellings – and giving any surplus to the Treasury. Labour, on return to government in 1974, did not implement the 'fair rent' element of the 1972 Act, but retained the national rent rebate and rent allowance schemes.

Housing Benefit (HB)

Between 1983 and 1990, rent rebates, rent allowances and the rent payments made through Supplementary Benefit (now called Income Support) were united in a Housing Benefit scheme administered by local government and directed by the Department of Social Security (now the Department of Work and Pensions). Tighter eligibility criteria, excluding students from claiming and a steeper cut-out rate meant that, after 1988, the scheme became more of a safety net than a measure to enhance general rent affordability. Nonetheless, the possibility that if a household's income was low enough, they could pay a low or zero rent in the private landlord sector, prompted some tenants to move away from stigmatised, run-down council estates. The extent of this exodus is unknown, but it was restrained by changes in the HB regulations. As private-sector rents moved from 'fair' to market levels, the cost of HB escalated and measures such as 'reference rents' and the 'single room restriction' were introduced to contain expenditure. In 1996, 'pre-tenancy determinations' were introduced whereby prospective tenants could apply for a determination of a property's 'eligible rent' for HB purposes before the tenancy was agreed. It was argued that 'pre-tenancy determinations' made it easier for prospective tenants to 'shop around' for a property they could afford. The features of HB for social housing tenants are outlined in **Box 6.2**. In 2010 HB and Local Housing Allowance (LHA) (see later) were claimed by 4.8 million households in the UK: 1.3 million aged over 65; 1.1 million single-parent households; 1.14 million in the private landlord sector; and 279,000 tenants who were working. In 2009, the average HB award was £68 to local authority tenants, £87 to tenants of registered social landlords and £109 to LHA recipients in the private landlord sector. In 1988/89 expenditure on HB was £3.77 billion increasing to £11 billion in 1998/99 and to £19.7 billion in 2009/10 (DWP, 2010a).

> **Box 6.2:** Housing Benefit
>
> HB is means-tested with entitlement based on the difference between 'eligible rent' and a number of needs allowances equivalent to those used for Income Support. If income is at or below the needs allowances, HB will pay 100% of the 'eligible rent' but, for every £1 of income above the 'needs' allowances, HB is reduced by 65 pence – the 'taper'. People with capital above a set threshold are not eligible for HB and there are entitlement deductions for non-dependants living in a household.

New Labour's 2000 Housing Green Paper listed a number of problems in the ways HB operated (DETR, 2000a, para 11.4). It was 'complex, confusing and time consuming'; 'only 56% of local authorities in England and Wales administer benefits efficiently'; tenants worried about rent arrears or, worse, risk of eviction; landlords had cash-flow problems and concerns about renting to HB claimants; and there was a 'reluctance to risk taking up work – particularly where it is temporary or casual – because of the potential wait involved in re-claiming if the job ends'. Moreover:

> HB takes away responsibility from claimants. HB gives tenants little interest in the rent – provided it does not exceed local limits it can be reimbursed in full, often directly to the landlord. This means that some tenants are not even aware of how much rent is being paid.

Other points might have been added to this catalogue of troubles:

- HB makes a significant contribution to the 'poverty trap' for those *in* work, for example, in 2009, with a rent of £100 per week, a single parent with one child escapes the HB 'poverty trap' at gross earnings of £298 per week (Wilcox, 2009b, p 237). The DWP (2010b) calculated that the combined impact of the withdrawal of mean-tested benefits plus taxation and national insurance contributions meant that, in 2011/12, marginal deduction rates for working heads of families would be over 70% for 1,710,000 households.
- In 2007/08, the take-up level of HB was in the range of 80–87% by caseload (DWP, 2009). This is high relative to other means-tested benefits, but the aggregate figure masks important variations – the take-up rate for working people has been estimated at only 50% (DCL, 2009e).

New Labour's reaction to the problems identified in 2000 was to try to improve the efficiency of HB administration via the Audit Commission's performance indicator regime and to smooth out the uncertainties involved in claiming HB when moving in to and out of work. Local authority efficiency in processing benefit claims improved, but fraud and error was at the same level as in 2001/02 and the work incentive problem continued (DWP, 2009). HB remains a very complicated scheme – in the words of one commentator 'There are 66 words in the Lord's Prayer; 42 laws of cricket; but Housing Benefit regulations runs to 967 pages, five parts, six schedules and 40 statutory instruments' (quoted in Barbour, 2008, p 7). Thus, despite the administrative improvements, the scheme 'does not yet provide a secure pillar for tenants on the margins of the labour market' (Kemp, 2008, p 61).

Local Housing Allowance (LHA)

New Labour's flagship response to the problems identified in 2000 was to replace HB in the private landlord sector with a scheme called Local Housing Allowance (LHA). This scheme was rolled out for new and repeat claimants after April 2008, following trials in 18 pathfinder authorities. The essential features of LHA in its pathfinder stage were:

- Establishing a 'standard local rent' for Broad Rental Market Areas (BRMAs) by the Valuation Office Agency, based on:
  1. the number of rooms needed for a family of a particular size with, as under the former system, those under 25 only entitled to the single shared room rate, typically lower than for a one-bedroom property; and
  2. the 50th percentile of what private landlords charged for similar properties in an area.
- A set of eligibility criteria based on income similar to Housing Benefit.
- Paying the allowance to the tenant rather than the landlord.
- If the tenant found accommodation at a rent lower than the standard local rent then he or she could retain the difference.

New Labour justified the scheme with the arguments that it would promote choice – tenants 'could choose to rent a larger property and pay the excess, or spend less on housing and increase their available income'; enhance personal responsibility – 'wherever possible, LHA should be paid to tenants, so empowering people to budget for and to pay their rent themselves rather than have it paid for them'; and reduce barriers to work through the transparency of the scheme (DWP, 2007, p 1).

The pathfinders were useful in developing procedures to deal with 'vulnerable' tenants who found difficulty in paying the landlord. However, the salience of the pathfinder experience was limited by changes made to the scheme when it started to operate on a national basis, especially the limitation on the payment of the difference between the rent paid and allowance entitlement to £15. This nullified part of the choice argument and New Labour also proposed not to allow tenants to retain any of the difference between rent paid and the allowance.

As LHA was applied nationwide, landlord associations complained vociferously that too many tenants were claiming their allowance but not paying their rent and the National Landlords Association asserted that this was producing a decline in the number of landlords willing to let to benefit claimants (Build.co.uk, 2009). In response to these allegations, the DWP stated:

> we would like to consider returning an element of choice to customers that would enable them to decide to have their benefit paid directly to the landlord. We could consider requiring landlords to improve the quality or energy efficiency of their property in return for direct payments. (DWP, 2009, p 32)

However, the House of Commons Work and Pensions Committee (2010a, p 3) rejected this suggestion with the argument:

> Managing one's own finances is an important step towards personal responsibility and financial inclusion and, through this, readiness for work. There is evidence that giving tenants the choice of having rent either paid to them or the landlord would defeat this important objective of the scheme and help perpetuate benefit dependency.

When first announced, the LHA was to be extended to social tenants following the trials in the private landlord sector, but New Labour gradually backed away from such an extension arguing that because social housing is allocated and rents are determined by non-market factors, choice is limited.

The Coalition government and Housing Benefit

In a climate of public opinion influenced by press revelations of large HB claims – for example, 'a family of former asylum seekers have moved into a £2.1 million home in one of the smartest areas of London at a cost to the taxpayer of £8,000 a month after complaining about living in a poor area' (*Daily Telegraph*, 2010) – George Osborne, the Coalition government's Chancellor, adopted more radical measures aimed at reducing expenditure on HB and LHA by £4.2 billion by 2014/15 in relationship to its projected cost. These measures included:

- Future increases in HB would be linked to the Consumer Price Index (that excludes housing costs) rather than the Retail Price Index.
- New Labour's proposal to limit LHA to the actual rent paid was endorsed.
- From April 2011, LHA would be restricted to a maximum of four bedrooms and weekly rates would be capped at £250 for one bedroom, £290 for two, £340 for three and £400 for four.
- After October 2011, LHA rates would to be calculated on the 30th percentile of rents in a local area rather than the 50th percentile as under New Labour. These changes would have a significant impact especially in London with, for example, the maximum benefit for a three-bedroom house in South West London being reduced by £36 per week (Wilson and Cracknell, 2010).
- Reductions in HB for non-dependants would be increased, 'working-age' social tenants would only be able to claim benefit in accordance with household size and, from 2013, people who have been on Jobseeker's Allowance for more than 12 months will have their HB cut by 10% (a proposal later rescinded).
- There would be national cap on welfare benefits of £500.
- The 'single room restriction' would be extended to those aged under 35.

Although phased in over a number of years and accompanied by an increase in the 'discretionary' resources available to local authorities to mitigate hardship, these changes encountered opposition especially related to their impact in London. Using a definition of affordable as 25% or more of private rented properties let at rents below the maximum LHA entitlement, Shelter (2010) estimated that by 2016 only 36% of London boroughs would have affordable housing. It was predicted that the changes would lead to a mass exodus of poorer people from Inner London where rents are very high, an increase in homelessness and local authorities in London using cheaper accommodation, away from the capital, to accommodate homeless people (*Daily Mail*, 2010). Wilcox (2011) has calculated that the overall reform package would produce 963,980 losers with an average loss of £12 per week. Families in five bedroom houses would experience the largest loss at £57 per week.

Estimating affordable housing requirements

New Labour assumed that social housing was affordable because rents were subsidised and pooled whereas the market may not deliver affordable homes for low-income groups. In line with this affordability notion, when estimating the need for social housing, sometimes called the 'sub-market' sector, academics have adopted methods that attempt to calculate the requirements that the housing market cannot meet based on affordability assumptions, existing needs such as homelessness and overcrowding plus future household formation rates. The task is fraught with uncertainties, not least because social housing requirements depend on changes in access to other tenures and household formation is influenced by housing conditions with, for example, possible delays in marriage and children due to inability to afford a decent home. Estimates prepared for the Barker Report (Barker, 2004) indicated that 48,000 social houses per annum were required, but other projections (Holmans et al, 2004) placed the requirement considerably higher – at up to 87,000. Whatever the guesstimates, trends in local authority waiting lists indicate a growing demand in relationship to a declining supply (see ***Figures 6.2*** and ***6.3***). Demand for social housing varies by local authority. On average, 8.2% of households were on local authority waiting lists but, in Inner London, this was 13.6% and, in Newham, 30.2% (DCL, 2010b, Table 600).

Figure 6.2: *Local authority waiting lists (England)*

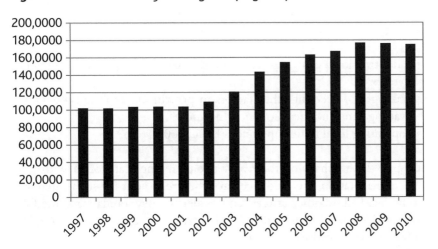

Source: Adapted from DCL (2010b, Table 600).

Allocating social housing

High demand and limited supply focused attention on the rationing process involved in social housing allocation. The British National Party attempted to secure votes by alleging that immigrants were obtaining a disproportionate share of the social housing stock and Margaret Hodge, MP for Barking, suggested changes in allocation procedures to favour established residents. The Equality and Human Rights Commission ordered research on the issue that examined allocation procedures, outcome statistics and public perceptions of the allocation processes as revealed in focus groups. The research concluded that 'Analysis of social housing allocation policies showed no evidence that social housing allocation favours foreign migrants over UK citizens' (Rutter and Latorre, 2009, p ix). The researchers found that 'new migrants to the UK over the last five years make up less than two per cent of the total in social housing'. Moreover, 'of the foreign born people who have arrived in the UK in the past five years about 17% are owner-occupiers, 11% live in social housing and 64% are private tenants' (Rutter and Latorre, 2009, p viii). Public perceptions, revealed in focus groups, that high proportions of migrants were living in social housing were attributed to council house transfer to the private-rented sector via the Right to Buy.

The methodology of this research has been questioned (Stone, 2009) and, in response to the notion that 'the system of allocating housing is complex and poorly understood' (Healey, 2009, p 4), New Labour issued allocation guidance stressing the importance of local authorities' responsibilities to involve, inform and consult local people in devising their allocation systems. It also directed attention to the 'flexibilities' local authorities have within allocation policies to meet local pressures by:

- 'adopting local priorities alongside the statutory reasonable preference categories';
- 'taking into account other factors in prioritising applicants, including waiting time and local connection'; and
- 'operating local lettings policies' (DCL, 2009f, p 5).

Despite the emphasis on the reasonable preference categories, with their 'need' orientation, the guidance gave the green light for such categories to be overlaid by other criteria and, under the new guidance, some local authorities started to include 'local contribution' criteria, for example, a job, in their allocation regulations.

In discussing the idea of affordable housing, Stone (2006) raises the question 'How long?' Although in 'need' at the time of allocation, circumstances change and the accelerating waiting lists have led to the idea of 'social tenancies for life' being questioned. The 2010 Spending Review (HM Treasury, 2010b) indicated that time-limited tenancies would be introduced. If implemented, this policy would accelerate the 'turnover' of social tenancies and help to reduce waiting lists, but at a potential cost of destabilising estates.

Promoting homeownership

'Home ownership has become so culturally embedded in most societies that it seems odd, for most, to question it' (Ronald, 2008, p 52). Indeed, in the UK, Howker and Makik (2010, p 18) claim that 'It's no longer something people aspire to – they view owning their own bricks and mortar as a right'. In the past, this honoured position has produced many schemes to make homeownership more affordable than its market price.

Tax relief on mortgage interest

Tax relief on mortgage interest was a major instrument of housing policy in the 1960s, 1970s and 1980s. Relief was given on the interest on the full amount of a loan of any size but, in 1975, when the average house price in the UK was £11,767, it was limited to the interest on £25,000 – raised to £30,000 in 1983. Until 1983, the allowable interest was deducted directly from taxable income, but under the mortgage interest relief at source (MIRAS) scheme the borrower paid the lender the interest less the standard rate tax relief. This scheme was also available to low-income households who did not pay tax. Failure to raise the threshold at which MIRAS ceased meant that its real value declined and, in the late 1990s, taking advantage of the general fall in interest rates, it was phased out prior to its ending in April 2000. The demise of MIRAS was justified on the arguments that the tax concession was unfair because it gave more assistance to high-rate taxpayers and those with the largest mortgages and that it artificially stimulated house prices by encouraging people to consume more accommodation than they required. Despite the end of MIRAS, tax advantages for homeowners still remain. Although Stamp Duty Tax cancels out the value of exemptions from Capital Gains Tax, no tax is paid on the imputed rental value of a home and this, when offset by potential mortgage interest tax relief as granted to private landlords, was worth £12 billion per annum in 2007/08, about £12.50 per week for each homeowner (DCL, 2009e).

After 2000, fiscal policy was used to dampen rather than stimulate the housing market. New Labour increased the Stamp Duty Tax rate to 1% on properties worth between £60,000 (£150,000 in deprived areas) and

£250,000, 3% on properties worth between £250,000 and £500,000, and 4% on those properties worth more than £500,000. These increases had little impact on house price inflation but produced substantial revenue for the Treasury with a yield of £6.5 billion in 2006/07 compared to £625 million in 1996/97. During the 2008/09 recession, no Stamp Duty Tax was levied on residential properties worth up to £175,000 and, just before the 2010 general election, the Chancellor announced that, for two years, first-time buyers would not have to pay Stamp Duty Tax on properties valued at up to £250,000. The 2010 Conservative Party manifesto promised to retain this concession beyond two years.

Rent control

Rent control was perhaps the most effective low-cost homeownership scheme. Between 1915 and 1989, confronted by rent freezes, rent regulation and security of tenure for tenants, many private landlords sold their properties to sitting tenants often at substantial discounts on the market price with vacant possession. Despite its effectiveness in promoting homeownership rent control has disappeared from the Labour Party's agenda although, in response to the Coalition government's proposals to cut Housing Benefit, Ken Livingstone, candidate for Mayor of London, stated he would cap private landlord rents (*Inside Housing*, 2010a).

The Right to Buy (RTB)

The number of dwellings sold under the RTB has fluctuated over time in response to such factors as the pent-up desire to buy unleashed by the 1980 Housing Act (in 1982/83, 170,000 local authority houses were sold in England); variations in house prices (the number of houses sold reached 150,000 in 1988/89 before declining to 33,000 in 1994/95 and then increasing to 70,000 in 2003/04); and discount changes. In 1999 New Labour modified the RTB by introducing regional variations in maximum discounts ranging from £22,000 to £38,000. Later, evidence was uncovered revealing that, in some areas, private companies were using cash incentives to encourage tenants to buy their homes (ODPM, 2003b). In return for a payment, residents were agreeing to move out of their homes so that the company could let them at market rents. Tenants then sold the homes to the company after three years so they could keep their discounts. To maintain the affordable housing pool and curtail the detected abuse, the maximum discount on sales was reduced from £38,000 to £16,000 in specific local authority areas where affordable housing was scarce. Thus, whereas average RTB discounts were 50% in England (London 53%) in 1998/99 they had been reduced to 24% (London 13%) in 2007/08 (King, 2010, p 70). The 2004 Housing Act contained clauses restricting RTB, including the extension of both the initial qualification period and the time after sale when local authorities may require owners to repay some of their initial discount to five years. By 2008/09 only 2880 homes were sold to tenants in England under RTB (DCL, 2010b, Table 648).

The 2001 Housing (Scotland) Act created a uniform RTB for all social-sector tenants with a qualifying period of five years and a maximum discount of £15,000. This scheme did not apply to tenants who were council tenants prior to 2002 – they retained their existing rights. Charitable housing association tenants were exempt and the scheme would not be available to other housing association tenants for a period of 10 years. The 2001 Housing (Scotland) Act also introduced 'pressured area designation' enabling a local authority to submit an application to the Scottish Government which, if approved, suspended the Right to Buy in the designated area for up to five years where the tenancy commenced on or after 30 September 2002. In 2010, a bill was introduced to the Scottish Parliament to end RTB on all new social housing. The impact of RTB is set out in ***Box 6.3***.

Box 6.3: The impact of the Right to Buy

- RTB has had different impacts in different areas. In terms of its impact on homeownership, the biggest difference occurred in Scotland: in 1981, 36% of Scotland's housing stock was owner-occupied, but by 2009 this had increased to 62.2% compared to an increase of 59% to 68% over the same timescale in England.
- Although the good fortune of a council house tenant in Fulham who bought for £50,000 in 2000 under RTB and sold for £900,000 in 2005 was rare, there has been a significant increase in the assets of the overwhelming majority of households who have bought their homes. In the main these households had low levels of wealth.
- On purchase many owners invested in their properties.
- Over 2.5 million council houses have been sold since 1980, but only 750,000 council and housing association homes have been built. Of course, when sitting tenants buy their houses the affordable housing stock available to new tenants is not restricted immediately but, over time, the number of affordable rented properties available to let diminishes (see ***Figure 6.3***). This reduces housing opportunities for people in housing need and, because there has been a tendency for the more desirable properties to be sold, the chances of a council tenant moving to better accommodation in a more attractive locality have diminished. The impact has been particularly severe

in rural areas (Rural Coalition, 2010), and in some London districts the shortage of homes with three bedrooms has led to local authorities buying back homes sold under RTB.

- Although the percentage of flats sold increased in the 2000s, up from 15% in 2000/01 to 34% in 2007/08, proportionately more houses than flats have been purchased.
- According to an HSBC report, summarised by Howker and Malik (2010, p 34), the total value of all RTB sales up to 2010 (without allowing for inflation) was £85.74 billion of which the state received £45.38 billion.
- An unanticipated outcome of RTB has been the interest shown by buy-to-let investors especially in London. As Jones, C (2010, p 66) explains:

RTB resales are attractive to private landlords because they are relatively cheap often selling at a discount relative to comparable properties. In some cases former RTB properties are unattractive or difficult to sell for owner occupation because of weak resale markets in areas where such markets have not been established or sustained. There is, for example, no resale market for flats in multi-storey blocks or for isolated purchases on large estates. This is partly brought about by the lending criteria of major mortgage-providers, who will not fund, for example, the purchase of flats higher than five storeys above ground level. As a consequence many of these dwellings are sold at knock-down prices at auctions.

The extent to which private landlords have bought former council homes is unknown but, in certain areas, such sales have compounded the management problems of council estates especially where flats prevail and, ironically, some local authorities are housing homeless families in expensive private-sector properties formerly owned by the local authority.

- In the first waves of RTB there was a tendency for purchasers to be better-off and with grown-up children and 76% of purchasers were in employment compared to 35% of council tenants overall. More recently, RTB purchasers have become more diverse with, as examples, more families with school-age children, including single parents, and more retired people. Sub-prime mortgages have become more common (Jones, C, 2010, p 63).
- According to Jones and Murie (1998, p 1):

RTB, alongside other policies, has contributed to increased concentration of low-income households in the social rented sector and in particular estates. When resold, former council houses are rarely the cheapest homes on the market and purchasers are often already homeowners. The evidence suggests that open market purchasers often move on after a short period and that the turnover of properties is high.

- The transfer of council houses from needs-based central allocation to the market has allowed more choice in where people live (for those who can afford to buy) and perhaps assisted relatives to reside in closer proximity (Barker, 2009, p 50).

Figure 6.3: Social housing lettings (000s)[1]

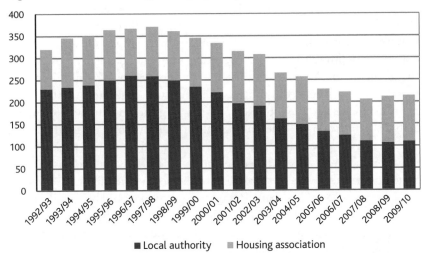

■ Local authority   ■ Housing association

Notes: Although RTB has reduced social housing vacancies, the fall has also been caused by lower 'turnover'. Due to lack of alternatives, for example, more expensive homeownership and higher private-sector rents, fewer tenants are moving from the social sector.
[1] Yearly new lettings minus exchanges and transfers.
Sources: Adapted from DCL (2010b, Table 750) and (Pawson and Wilcox, 2011).

The Right to Acquire and Social Homebuy

The Right to Acquire was introduced in 1996. Its eligibility rules are complicated, but certain tenants of registered social landlords are entitled to purchase their homes at discounts varying from £9000 to £16,000. Social Homebuy offers eligible housing association or council tenants the opportunity to buy a share in the market value of their current home. Under the scheme, tenants can buy a minimum of 25% of a property's value and pay an initial rental charge of not more than 3% of the market value of the remaining equity owned by the landlord. A discount of between £9000 and £16,000 is offered with the amount of discount received in proportion to the share of the property bought. The Right to Acquire and Social Homebuy made a limited impact with less than 3000 homes sold under the Right to Acquire since 2000 and 310 under Social Homebuy.

Protecting homeowners when income is reduced

Until 2009, Income Support paid 'reasonable' mortgage interest – up to 1% above the Bank of England base rate – but never any capital repayments. A claimant's assets had to be less than £8000, there was a mortgage ceiling of £100,000, unchanged since 1995, and assistance became available only after 39 weeks' 'waiting time' from the original Income Support claim. Private mortgage payment protection insurance was available, but the coverage was limited. In early 2009, anticipating a rapid rise in repossessions, the government amended the Income Support rules. 'Waiting time' was reduced to 13 weeks, the mortgage ceiling was raised to £200,000 for many claimants and the interest rate for paying Income Support remained at its 2008 rate of 6.08%, despite significant falls in mortgage interest rates. The Coalition government extended the time span of this package, but the mortgage rate was reduced to 3.63%. New Labour also introduced a mortgage rescue scheme targeted at the most vulnerable households – those on incomes of less than £60,000 a year who would be entitled to be rehoused under homelessness legislation. Households were able to apply to their local authority for two options to help them remain in their homes, depending on their circumstances. They could sell a share of their home to a housing association, enabling their monthly mortgage payments to be reduced, or they could sell the entire home to a housing association and remain in the property as tenants paying a subsidised rent. In addition, a Homeowner Mortgage Support Scheme was announced with lenders allowing households who suffered a sharp income reduction to defer part of their payments for up to two years.

Low-cost homeownership schemes

In the early 1980s, the Conservatives introduced a number of novel but limited low-cost homeownership schemes. Equity-sharing was the most enduring and this idea, together with shared ownership, formed the basis of a variety of constantly changing low-cost homeownership schemes introduced by New Labour. Initially the schemes were aimed mainly at key workers in the public services, but later they were extended to other aspirant homeowners not only to boost owner-occupation, but also to maximise the number of homes produced from a given level of central subsidy. As Monk and Whitehead (2010, p 268) point out:

> The obvious benefit to intermediate housing from the point of view of government is that it requires lower subsidy than social rented housing and it enables the subsidy to be recycled much more quickly than is the case with social housing. Indeed from the government's point of view, shared equity products in a buoyant market may actually pay for themselves in the longer term.

Equity-sharing involves the purchaser buying 100% of the property but obtaining an equity loan to cover a share of the value, whereas shared ownership involves the owner buying a share of the property but renting the rest, usually from a housing association. Low-cost homeownership schemes can enable the occupier to 'staircase' in later years by acquiring more equity. When sold, any increased or decreased value is shared according to equity stakes. Thus, participants in such schemes limit their risk of reduced value in return for forfeiting a share of increased value (see Whitehead, 2010).

Despite being handicapped by frequent changes in the schemes on offer, after 2005, low-cost homeownership formed an increasing share of 'affordable' housing output and, in 2008/09, accounted for about 45% of 'affordable' homes (Shelter, 2010). Grant levels necessary to subsidise such schemes were lower than for social housing and housing associations were able to recycle the purchaser's capital contribution. However, New Labour's schemes were criticised as being responsive to short-term political requirements rather than producing more affordable homes for those in greatest need (House of Commons Public Accounts Committee, 2007; Shelter 2010). The average income of households accessing equity-sharing was £32,000 in 2009 and the schemes were not well-targeted on the people who might, by moving, make a home available in the social sector. Initially, low-cost homeownership was badly affected by the credit crunch, but the schemes – when targeted on new-build – were useful in the government's attempt to 'kick-start' the market in 2009. Scotland, Wales and Northern Ireland have their own versions of low-cost homeownership schemes, for example, Homestake and LIFT.

Planning gain and affordable housing

The 1971 Town and Country Planning Act enhanced the powers of local planning authorities to enter into agreements with developers whereby, in return for planning permission, the developer provided benefits to the local authority. The 'rural exceptions policy', introduced in 1989, allowed exceptional permissions for affordable housing on sites adjacent to rural settlements provided that the dwellings remained available to local, low-income residents.

In the early 1980s, some local authorities started to promote affordable housing through the planning process using section 106 of the 1990 Town and Country Planning Act. Under section 106, developers could be asked to supply low-cost accommodation in return for planning permission and, if this low-cost accommodation was built on the same site as the market-price housing, then more balanced communities might be created (see Chapter Nine). However, despite the rapid increases in land and house prices, creating a favourable climate for acquiring 'betterment gain' for community purposes, the number of affordable homes obtained through the planning process was limited – only 16,380 in 2003/04 – with many also having to rely on Social Housing Grant. The main obstacles to the use of planning gain to secure affordable homes appear to have been:

- the problems involved in producing robust estimates of affordable housing requirements – such estimates are legally necessary for the implementation of a local policy on affordable housing;
- the government's lukewarm attitude to the initiative: its impact has not been regularly monitored and there has been a 'lack of clear instruction offered by government on how the system should be used' (Carmona et al, 2003, p 143);
- the exclusion of small sites, producing the division of larger sites into smaller sites to evade the policy; and
- the protracted negotiations with developers necessary to secure affordable housing (National Audit Office/Audit Commission, 2006).

After 2003/04, the number of affordable homes secured via section 106 agreements increased, but the sharp decline in land prices following the 2008 credit crunch hampered future opportunities to acquire 'betterment gain' for community purposes. Some commentators prefer a transparent development levy to the capture of development gain in specific 'in-kind' deals. The Barker Review (Barker, 2004) recommended that the government should introduce a planning-gain supplement tied to granting planning permission. In April 2010, a version of a planning-gain supplement was introduced as the Community Infrastructure Levy – a charge that local authorities can impose in return for planning permission. Section 106 agreements would be scaled back and only permitted when 'directly related' to new developments. This 'directly related' notion would include affordable housing that would not be eligible for funding from the Community Infrastructure Levy (DCL, 2010f). John Healey, then Housing Minister, justified the new charge on the grounds that only 6% of all planning permissions bring a contribution to supporting infrastructure (Donnelly, 2010). Under the Coalition government's 'localism' agenda a significant proportion of the Community Infrastructure Levy will be earmarked for neighbourhood projects.

Increasing housing supply

Disquiet about affordability in the early 2000s led to the publication of *Sustainable Communities: Building for the Future* (ODPM, 2003a) and the setting up of the Barker Review. Barker maintained that housing supply in the UK was only half as responsive to demand as in France and only one third as responsive as in the US. Reducing the real price trend in England to the European Union average would involve building between 70,000 and 120,000 additional private-sector houses each year. She placed the lion's share of the blame for the poor responsiveness of supply to demand in the UK on the planning system. Amongst her many recommendations was that the government should establish national and regional affordability targets and take steps to increase supply whenever this target was not achieved. The government then commissioned Barker to undertake a specific review of the land-use planning system. This recommended:

- a new system for dealing with major infrastructure projects, based around national statements of strategic objectives with an independent Planning Commission;
- reforming plan-making at the local level so that future development plan documents can be delivered in 18–24 months rather than three or more years; and
- 'ensuring that new development beyond towns and cities occurs in the most sustainable way, by encouraging planning bodies to review their green belt boundaries and take a more positive approach to applications that will enhance the quality of their green belts' (Barker, 2006, p 6).

Barker's reports stimulated the DCL to promote housing supply as a planning objective. *Planning Policy Statement 3 (PPS): Housing* was issued, which included 'market responsiveness' as a planning consideration and required planning authorities to 'maintain a rolling five-year supply of deliverable land for housing, particularly in connection with making planning decisions' (DCL, 2006a, p 5). A National Housing and Planning Advice Unit was set up to provide independent advice on affordability matters to the government and other stakeholders with an interest in the housing market. The Infrastructure Planning Commission was established to make decisions on planning applications for nationally significant infrastructure projects.

The Green Paper *Homes for the Future: More Affordable, More Sustainable* (DCL, 2007a) represented a 'paradigm shift' in housing policy, at least in intent. Rather than rely on market forces, the state would actively promote housing supply. This shift was also marked when Brown, on becoming Prime Minister, elevated housing – alongside health and education – to the list of government priorities. The Green Paper stated that overall housing supply needed to be increased because the latest household projections showed that the number of households was estimated to grow by 223,000 a year until 2026. Housing supply was not keeping pace with household formation with the result that 'house prices have doubled in real terms over the last 10 years' (DCL, 2007a, p 17). The Green Paper also endorsed enhanced social housing construction because the number of households in temporary accommodation was increasing and 'the number of households waiting for social housing has risen from 1 million to 1.6 million over the last ten years, both as the number of households has grown and as more families have found they cannot afford a home' (DCL, 2007a, p 21).

Housing supply was scheduled to increase over time to 240,000 in 2016 then continue at about 240,000 per annum until 2020. Two million additional homes were planned by 2016, 3 million by 2020; and 70,000 affordable homes a year would be provided by 2010/11 with 45,000 of these homes in the social housing sector. New policies would push the overall housing supply to 240,000 by 2016. 'Eco-towns' – with balanced communities and zero carbon emissions – would be created and continuing infrastructure finance to 'growth areas' (with a new one in the North) and the 'growth points' of expanding towns was to be provided. Additional land for housing would come from:

- abolishing Regional Assemblies, which, with their elected councillor representation, had proved troublesome in agreeing house-building targets;
- designating surplus government sites for housing; and
- encouraging local authorities to allocate land by a Planning Delivery Grant and a threat that, if a local authority did not allocate sufficient land for a rolling five-year house-building programme, then developers would find it easy to obtain planning permission.

Social housing would be augmented by additional government finance, encouraging housing associations to use their assets and allowing local government to have a larger role in house-building via local housing companies, Arm's Length Management Organisations (ALMOs) and direct building.

The impact of the credit crunch

The credit crunch had a dramatic impact on new housing construction. As the financial instructions restricted their lending, building workers were withdrawn from sites almost overnight and new housing schemes were suspended. New private-sector housing starts dipped from 155,240 (England) in 2006/07 to 71,160 in 2008/09 and, by July 2008, house prices had entered negative territory – by March 2009 they had declined by 13.6% from their peak. The DCL directed its attention to preventing repossessions and to 'kick-starting' the market by bringing forward resources allocated to future social housing programmes to buy unsold stock from house-builders. This action, plus lower interest rates and bank recapitalisation, helped to pull the housing market out of its nosedive, but, in dealing with the recession, 'much of the impetus appeared to have gone from the [long-term supply] agenda' (Jones and Watkins, 2009, p 138).

Low-income households and homeownership

Homeownership now covers a wide diversity of incomes – in 2004/05, 20% of households in the bottom three deciles of the income distribution had a mortgage (Hills, 2007) – but there is no general system to help low-income homeowners other than Income Support available only to those without full-time work. This absence of general support for low-income homeowners in full-time work, plus the availability of HB for people who rent, tends to push low-income households into the rented sector. It also contributes to inequality. The Gini coefficient in 2007/08 (see Chapter Four) *before* housing costs was 36 but increased to 40 *after* housing costs (DWP, 2010c). Although some of this difference can be attributed to methodological factors, it also reflects the restrictions on state support for low-income homeowners in work. When poverty incidence in the UK is compared before and after housing costs, allowing for various benefits, there is a rise of 5.8% in poverty for mortgaged homeowners (European Commission, 2010, p 27).

The Coalition government and housing supply

The Coalition government immediately abandoned New Labour's regional house-building targets and the apparatus set up to deliver the targets, including not paying the Planning Delivery Grant in 2010/11 that had been worth £148 million in 2009/10. This created a hiatus in the land release process and some authorities reduced their house-building commitments – up to 300,000 in total according to some estimates (*Inside Housing*, 2010b). The Coalition government responded by promising that future incentives for house-building would be backdated, by emphasising that local authorities were still required to identify a five-year land supply and promising to deliver 150,000 new social-sector homes by 2015 (see Chapter Eleven). The abandonment of regional house-building targets, without a replacement system, was later declared illegal by the High Court, but the necessary powers to change the system were incorporated into the 2010 Localism Bill.

Overview

- Until the introduction of a national system of income-related housing benefits in 1972, many households found it difficult to pay for the quality of rented accommodation deemed acceptable at the time.
- In the 1980s and 1990s, there was a marked shift away from 'bricks-and-mortar' subsidies to means-tested consumer subsidies.
- In the past, various forms of subsidies have stimulated homeownership, but today help in becoming a homeowner is limited.
- After 2003, New Labour intervened in the housing market to promote greater supply in the hope of making houses more affordable, but the credit crunch produced a marked slowdown in new housing construction.
- The Coalition government has set a target for social housing construction, but not for overall housing supply.

Questions for discussion

1. What is meant by affordable housing?
2. Assess the merits and limitations of Housing Benefit as a method of subsidising housing costs.
3. How can the planning system promote affordable housing?
4. Assess the impact of the credit crunch on affordable housing supply.

Further reading

The affordability issue is examined in both the interim and final reports of **Kate Barker's** review of housing supply – *Delivering Stability: Securing Our Future Housing Needs; Interim Report* (2003) and *Delivering Stability: Securing Our Future Housing Needs; Final Report, Recommendations* (2004). There is a dearth of analysis on the long-term impact of the Right to Buy, but *The Right to Buy* (2006) by **Colin Jones** and **Alan Murie** is a valuable source. **Peter Kemp** (ed.) (2007) sets Housing Benefit in the UK in a comparative context in *Housing Allowances in Comparative Perspective*.

Website resources

The DCL's website provides statistics on housing prices and supply. Available at: http://www.communities.gov.uk/housing

Statistics on Housing Benefit can be found at the DWP website. Available at: http://www.dwp.gov.uk/research-and-statistics

seven

Homelessness

Summary

- Homelessness is a contested concept with the definitions used in the UK linked to different causal notions and forms of action.
- Several factors interact in the *process* of *becoming* homeless.
- New Labour took steps to reduce the incidence of recorded homelessness in England. In Scotland a different approach was adopted.

What is homelessness?

As Mills (1959) pointed out, numbers can be important in the transformation of a 'personal problem' into a 'public issue'. The meanings attached to the term homelessness influence estimates of the problem's extent and the causal notions ascribed to it.

Three main definitions are current in the UK. Homelessness can be equated with rooflessness, that is, it is claimed that the term homelessness can only be legitimately applied – to quote the definition suggested by the government in 1994 – to 'those who have no accommodation of any sort available for occupation' (DoE, 1994b, p 4). On this definition, homelessness is often interpreted as 'rough sleeping', the homeless count will be low and homelessness may be construed as a 'personal issue' located in an individual's 'lifestyle' rather than as a 'social problem' caused by structural factors. The 1996 Housing Act definition, in current use and still similar to the one in the 1977 Housing (Homeless Persons) Act, is somewhat broader (see *Box 7.1*). It defines homelessness in terms of whether a person has a legal right to occupy a dwelling. Under this definition, despite the obstacles homeless applicants have to overcome before being offered accommodation, there were 51,310 homeless households living in temporary accommodation in

England in 2010. Such a high number makes it difficult to link homelessness to personal 'lifestyle' problems although attempts have been made to establish a connection.

Box 7.1: 1996 Housing Act: Homelessness definition

PART VII HOMELESSNESS
175 Homelessness and threatened homelessness

(1) A person is homeless if he has no accommodation available for his occupation, in the United Kingdom or elsewhere, which he –
   (a) is entitled to occupy by virtue of an interest in it or by virtue of an order of a court,
   (b) has an express or implied licence to occupy, or
   (c) occupies as a residence by virtue of any enactment or rule of law giving him the right to remain in occupation or restricting the right of another person to recover possession.
(2) A person is also homeless if he has accommodation but –
   (a) he cannot secure entry to it, or
   (b) it consists of a moveable structure, vehicle or vessel designed or adapted for human habitation and there is no place where he is entitled or permitted both to place it and to reside in it.
(3) A person shall not be treated as having accommodation unless it is accommodation which it would be reasonable for him to continue to occupy.
(4) A person is threatened with homelessness if it is likely that he will become homeless within 28 days.

176 Meaning of accommodation available for occupation

Accommodation shall be regarded as available for a person's occupation only if it is available for occupation by him together with –
   (a) any other person who normally resides with him as a member of his family, or
   (b) any other person who might reasonably be expected to reside with him.

177 Whether it is reasonable to continue to occupy accommodation

(1) It is not reasonable for a person to continue to occupy accommodation if it is probable that this will lead to domestic violence against him, or against –
   (a) a person who normally resides with him as a member of his family, or

> (b) any other person who might reasonably be expected to reside with him.
>
> For this purpose 'domestic violence', in relation to a person, means violence from a person with whom he is associated, or threats of violence from such a person which are likely to be carried out.
>
> (2) In determining whether it would be, or would have been, reasonable for a person to continue to occupy accommodation, regard may be had to the general circumstances prevailing in relation to housing in the district of the local housing authority to whom he has applied for accommodation or for assistance in obtaining accommodation.

The statutory definition can be labelled 'secondary' homelessness because it includes not only people without shelter ('primary' homelessness), but also people in temporary and insecure accommodation. However, the inclusion of 'home' in the term 'homelessness' suggests a broader definition. 'Home' is an emotional construct so agreement on a 'homelessness' definition is unlikely. Nonetheless, as Waldron (1993) suggests, humans, as social beings, require a private and secure base in which to carry out functions such as washing, sleeping, reproduction socialising and so on, especially if the use of public space for conducting such functions is forbidden. Thus, minimal 'home' requirements might include privacy (thereby including people involuntary sharing accommodation), personal space, sufficient room to store possessions, adequate heating and the security necessary for quiet enjoyment of one's personal life. In the past, Shelter claimed that being homeless, 'in the true sense of the word', means 'living in conditions so bad that a civilised family life is impossible' (Shelter, 1969, p 4). If this definition is adopted then the homeless count soars and would include 'hidden homelessness' such as 'sofa-surfing'; those in night shelters, hostels and Bed and Breakfast accommodation; families living involuntarily with friends and relatives; and severely overcrowded households. Crisis (2010), a housing charity, estimated the number of 'hidden homeless' as 400,000, but on this interpretation the homelessness concept becomes stretched and perhaps loses its meaning.

The causes of homelessness

Becoming homeless is a process involving interaction between several variables. 'Structural' determinants, the housing market, poverty, unemployment and so on, influence the number of people vulnerable to homelessness, but other factors can trigger this vulnerability. The homelessness literature has tended to label these 'triggers' as 'individual', 'pathological' or 'agency', but they can also be divided into categories such as 'individual' and 'interpersonal' (see Fitzpatrick et al, 2009, p 5). However, separating 'causes' is problematic because variables interact over time in the process of *becoming* homeless (see *Figures 7.1* and *7.2*).

Figure 7.1: The process of becoming homeless (family)

2007	2008	2009	2010	2010	2010	2011	2011
Family of two adults with three children buy a house	Spiralling debts re-lated to fa-ther's drink problem force fam-ily to sell and move in with mother's parents			Mother's parents can no longer cope with children Mother approach-es local authority for help	Family placed in Bed and Breakfast accommo-dation and mother becomes depressed due to condi-tions and long wait for offer of better accommo-dation	Family move into private landlord accom-modation leased by the local authority	
	Father loses job in reces-sion		Marital problems related to debt and over-crowding lead to father leaving wife and family				Family allocated a local authority house.

Homelessness: Constructing a social problem

In England, homelessness is officially divided into two categories – 'rough sleeping' and 'statutory homelessness' – a division reflecting a long tradition in attitudes towards homeless people. In the past, people now called 'rough sleepers', mainly men, were regarded as a threat to social order: deemed as *being* a problem they were subject to stern social control. People now referred to as 'the statutory homeless', including a high proportion of people with children, have often been represented as *having* a problem and in need of assistance. Nevertheless, concerns that such aid would lead to

Figure 7.2: *The process of becoming homeless (single person)*

Aged 5	Aged 7	Aged 18	Aged 19	Aged 21	Aged 22	Aged 23
Mother alcoholic Placed on local authority 'at risk' register	Mother dies Spends next 11 years with a variety of relatives	No work since leaving school without qualifications Develops an alcohol problem	Outreach worker helps in finding accommodation in hostel	Alcohol-related be-haviour leads to eviction	Prison sen-tence Housing Benefit stops after 13 weeks	Alcohol problems intensify Joins alcohol treatment programme
1993	**1995**	**2006**	**2007**	**2009**	**2010**	**2011**
	Often excluded from school and spends a lot of time with 'street-mates'	Relatives unwilling to provide accommo-dation Applies as homeless to local authority but deemed not in 'priority need' Sleeps rough	Allocated one-bedroom flat in a housing association property with support Convictions for petty crime	Sleeps rough or, using income from criminal activities, in Bed and Breakfast hotels	Sleeps rough on leaving prison but then accom-modation in hostel supplied Re-establish-es contacts with former 'street-mates'	Finds work and is able to afford a room rented from a private landlord Is helped by the Sup-porting People programme

'jumping the housing queue' and hinder self-help produced low-standard, stigmatised forms of provision.

The Elizabethan Poor Law

The 1601 Act for the Relief of the Poor placed a duty on parish churchwardens to appoint 'overseers of the poor' whose obligations included raising, 'weekly or otherwise (by taxation of every inhabitant ...) convenient stock of flax, hemp, wool, thread, iron, and other ware and stuff, to set the poor on work' (1601 Act for the Relief of the Poor, quoted in Bruce, 1973, p 39). It was the duty of the sovereign, via imposing duties on parishes, to ensure maintenance of the state's human capital – its 'loyal subjects'. By placing an obligation on each parish to set the poor to work, the 1601 Act thereby provided 'loyal subjects' with an income to pay rent. It was aimed at preventing what was then called 'destitution', now subsumed under the term 'homelessness'. Those deemed incapable of work, mainly elderly people, were to be placed in a 'poorhouse' paid for by the parish rate or in an 'almshouse' funded by charitable donations.

Settlement and Removal Laws

The cost of poor relief was met by levying a rate on property in a parish and this raised the issue of the 'rightful place' of any applicant for relief. Which parish had to pay? Various Acts of Settlement and Removal were passed and, by the late 17th century, the basic principles governing parish support obligations had been established. A person acquired a 'settlement' in a particular parish by occupying a property worth more than 10 pounds per year, by serving an apprenticeship in the parish, by marriage or by being hired for more than a year. A 'stranger' could be removed from a parish, without legal procedures, if discovered within 40 days of arrival.

'Rogues, vagabonds and sturdy beggars'

Apportioning the cost of relief was not the only objective of the settlement legislation. Imposing parish obligations to supply a means of subsistence, provided recipients abided in their 'rightful place', also promoted social stability. People who strayed from their 'rightful place' were regarded as a social problem; labelled 'vagrants', they became subject to repressive legislation. In the 16th century, vagrancy laws were directed at the growing number of 'masterless men' who had taken to leaving their parishes of birth in search of work and freedom from feudal ties. These migrants were regarded as a 'new and terrible problem' with the settled population living 'in terror of the tramp' (Humphreys, 1999, p 65). The 1597 Vagrancy Act deemed 'all wandering persons and common Labourers refusing to work for such reasonable wages commonly given in such partes where such persons do or shall happen to dwell or abide' to be 'rogues, vagabondes and sturdy beggars'. They were to be whipped, incarcerated in a 'house of correction' and then removed to their parish of origin.

Homelessness and 'laissez-faire' economics

Adam Smith condemned the settlement laws as a hindrance to liberty and labour mobility, but the growing influence of market theory led only to modest changes to the harshness incorporated in the vagrancy laws. The 1824 Vagrancy Act redefined vagrancy as 'failure to maintain oneself' and vagrants were divided into three groups according to their perceived character: 'idle and disorderly'; 'rogues and vagabonds'; and 'incorrigible rogues'. People 'sleeping out' were classified as 'idle and disorderly' but, following a second offence, they became 'incorrigible rogues' punishable by imprisonment or a public flogging.

Under the 1834 Poor Law Amendment Act unions of parishes were required to build workhouses where inmate conditions were not to be 'really or apparently so eligible as the situation of the independent labourer of the lowest class' (Poor Law Commissioners, 1834, p 228). Workhouses accommodated destitute people with a 'settlement' in the area and also contained 'vagrant' or 'casual' wards, popularly known as 'spikes'. Here, short-term accommodation was available to 'tramps' in return for a work task – usually breaking stones for use on local roads – hence the term 'spike' named after the stone-breaking tool. At the beginning of the 20th century, it was estimated that between 30,000 and 80,000 people used the workhouse casual wards from time to time (Royal Commission on the Poor Laws and Relief of Poverty, 1909). However, rather than rely on the workhouse, many people 'on the tramp' preferred to use Common Lodging Houses. These 'dosshouses' provided accommodation on a nightly basis with the cheapest being the 'halfpenny hang': sleeping hanging over a rope strung across a room. Booth (1902) estimated that there were 165,000 'homeless', people he described as 'loafers, casuals and some criminals', in the UK. During the interwar period, the workhouse casual wards (renamed Public Assistance Institutions in 1929), commercial Common Lodging Houses and provision made by charities such as the Salvation Army were the major sources of accommodation for 'tramps'. People using such accommodation were described as being 'without a settled way of living', a phrase illustrating how single homeless people were regarded as 'rootless' as well as 'homeless': they lacked connections to mainstream society.

The 1948 National Assistance Act

This Act consolidated the distinction between 'single' and 'family' homelessness. Single homelessness was regarded as an employment matter involving 'resettlement' from an 'unsettled way of living', whereas family homelessness was a 'welfare' issue. Under the Act, a National Assistance Board assumed overall responsibility for the workhouse casual wards and hence homeless single people. It had an obligation to 'make provision whereby persons without a settled living may be influenced to lead a more settled life' and a duty 'to provide and maintain centres for the provision of temporary board and lodgings for such persons' (National Assistance Act, 1948 section 16). Local authority public assistance committees, renamed welfare committees, became responsible for various forms of care, including residential provision for homeless people. The National Assistance Act imposed an obligation on local authorities to provide 'temporary accommodation for persons in urgent need thereof, being need arising in circumstances that could not reasonably have been foreseen' (National Assistance Act, 1948 section 21b). This duty was designed for emergencies and was not seen as replacing local authority waiting lists in allocating houses. Homeless people with children could be offered assistance but the help was temporary and provided by a 'social work' authority that, in county areas, was located at a different tier to the housing authority.

The 1977 Housing (Homeless Persons) Act

Local authorities interpreted their duties under the National Assistance Act in a restrictive, some would say mean-spirited, manner. To them, 'circumstances that could not reasonably have been foreseen' meant fire, flood or other natural disaster. Other reasons signalled that the applicant wanted to jump the long housing queue or had a 'feckless' lifestyle. Thus, for example, in Greater London, 75% of all homelessness applications were rejected (Holman et al, 1970) and some local authorities set up rehabilitation units for homeless 'problem families' (Noble, 2009). People without children had little hope of assistance and homeless people with children might be denied help because their 'habitual place of residence' was in another local authority. When local authorities offered a homeless family somewhere to live it was often a caravan or communal accommodation of a very low standard. The system had all the 'less eligibility' characteristics of the Poor Law from which it had descended, indeed, some of the communal accommodation was in former workhouses and many authorities did not allow a man to live with his wife and children. If, after spending time in temporary accommodation, the family could not obtain permanent housing, then the children might be taken into the care of the local authority.

Cathy Come Home, first shown on television in 1966, told the story of how a young couple, Cathy and Reg, became homeless. Having been passed between authorities because of disputes about responsibility for them – echoes of the settlement laws – Cathy and her children had to live in a squalid dormitory to which Reg was not admitted. Eventually their relationship broke down and the local authority took the children into care. *Cathy Come Home* dramatised the experiences of thousands of homeless people in the 1950s and early 1960s and its broadcast converted the condition of family homelessness into a social problem: parliamentary questions were asked, a special cabinet meeting was held and Shelter, the housing charity, sprang to prominence.

The government's immediate response to *Cathy Come Home* was to accelerate the housing programme and it was not until the mid-1970s that specific reform of the housing allocation system to assist homeless families was undertaken. Following a series of circulars urging local authorities to shift responsibility for homelessness from social services departments (the successors of welfare departments) to housing authorities, the government supported a private member's bill. The private member, Stephen Ross, declared that his bill's aim was to introduce 'a new legislative framework to change the outdated concept that homelessness was a social work problem and to place it clearly in the sphere of housing' (Stephen Ross, 1977, quoted in Wilson, 2001, p 9). The 1977 Housing (Homeless Persons) Act still forms the basis of current legislation on homelessness. It defined homelessness in terms similar to the definition used in the 1996 Housing Act.

Had this definition not been qualified by later sections in the Act, local authorities would have had a duty to assist all homeless people. However, as the bill progressed through Parliament, restrictions were placed on local authority obligations. Under the priority need clauses, local authorities would only have a duty to 'secure that accommodation becomes available for his occupation' (1977 Housing [Homeless Persons] Act, Section 4) if:

1
  (a) he has dependent children who are residing with him or who might reasonably be expected to reside with him;
  (b) he is homeless or threatened with homelessness as a result of any emergency such as flood, fire or any other disaster;
  (c) he or any person who resides or might reasonably be expected to reside with him is vulnerable as a result of old age, mental illness or handicap or physical disability or other special reason.
2 For the purposes of this Act a homeless person or a person threatened with homelessness who is a pregnant woman or resides or might reasonably be expected to reside with a pregnant woman has a priority need for accommodation. (1977 Housing [Homeless Persons] Act, Section 2)

Moreover, if a person was in priority need but deemed intentionally homeless then the local authority only had obligations to supply accommodation for a limited period and to offer 'advice and assistance'. Intentionality was defined as 'if he deliberately does or fails to do anything in consequence of which he ceases to occupy accommodation which is available for his occupation and which it would have been reasonable for him to continue to occupy' (1977 Housing [Homeless Persons] Act, Section 17). The third obstacle to homeless people securing accommodation was the 'local connection' clauses that meant a local authority might decide that a homeless applicant did not have a local connection with their area but did have a link elsewhere. However, in contrast to the settlement laws, the obligations of the local authority where the person made the application remained until the 'receiving authority' agreed to the transfer.

'Perverse incentives' and the 1996 Housing Act

By the early 1990s the Conservatives had started to attribute the growth in statutory homelessness to the 'perverse incentives' created by the 1977 Act. It was alleged that the direct route into secure social housing provided by the legislation led many people to engineer their circumstances to conform to its requirements. The Department of the Environment's *Access to Local Authority and Housing Association Tenancies* claimed:

> By giving the local authority a greater responsibility towards those who can demonstrate 'homelessness' than towards anyone else in housing need, the current legislation creates a perverse incentive for people to have themselves accepted by a local authority as homeless. (DoE, 1994b, p 4)

The 'perverse incentives' idea was linked to the notion that the 'traditional family form' was disintegrating. Nicholas Ridley, Secretary of State for the Environment in the late 1980s, commented: 'A young lady with a child is in "priority housing need" – one without is not. It became a way of life for some to have one or more children by unknown men, in order to qualify for a council house' (Ridley, 1991, p 91).

   In an attempt to rectify these 'perverse incentives', the 1996 Housing Act obliged local authorities to provide temporary accommodation for up to two years, but only when satisfied that other suitable accommodation was not available. The aim of this provision was to make clear that local authorities did not have to arrange to supply 'settled' or 'permanent' accommodation to end their obligations under the homelessness legislation. The terms 'settled' and 'permanent' occurred in the Code of Guidance issued under the Act, to which all local authorities had to 'have regard to' in implementing the legislation. Accordingly, most local authorities interpreted their obligations as involving the provision of a local authority or housing association property until, in the case of *R v London Borough of Brent ex parte Awua* (1995), the House of Lords established that this was unnecessary. The 1996 Housing Act reaffirmed this legal interpretation by stating that local authority obligations were discharged when it was satisfied that other suitable accommodation, including a private landlord assured shorthold tenancy, was available in the area. In addition, the duty to provide temporary accommodation for homeless people was separated from allocating local authority dwellings. In allocating tenancies local authorities had to offer 'reasonable preference' only in accordance with guidance incorporated in the Act. In the guidance, homelessness was not included as a need category for which 'reasonable preference' was to be given although homeless people might receive priority under other categories. The Act also stated that a person could not qualify as homeless if he/she had a legal right to occupy accommodation outside the UK.

Lack of empirical evidence makes it difficult to evaluate the 'perverse incentives' thesis. In high-demand areas where the homelessness route was the only realistic track into a 'social housing' property, the temptation to manipulate circumstances to conform to the homelessness legislation must have been strong. Yet the track was not especially fast – the average time spent in Bed and Breakfast accommodation was 22 months – and, at the end of the track, the accommodation offered was often poor. Moreover, the reduction in statutory homelessness started well before the 1996 Housing Act came into force.

The 2002 Homelessness Act

New Labour's 1997 manifesto promised to 'place a new duty on local authorities to protect those who are homeless through no fault of their own and are in priority need' (Labour Party, 1997, p 23). This pledge was partially redeemed in 1997 when 'households who are being accommodated by the main homelessness duty' was added to the need categories list that local authorities were required to give reasonable preference to in allocating dwellings. Significant change to the 1996 Housing Act had to wait until New Labour's second term. The 2002 Homelessness Act imposed a duty on local authorities to develop a homelessness strategy, abolished the two-year limit on the provision of temporary housing and disallowed an offer of an assured shorthold tenancy unless acceptable to the homeless person (a condition that the Coalition government wants to retract – see chapter 11). The 2002 Priority Need Order extended the groups designated as 'in priority need' to cover:

- homeless 16 and 17 year olds;
- care leavers aged 18, 19 and 20;
- those vulnerable as a result of time spent in care, the armed forces, prison or custody; and
- those vulnerable as a result of having to leave home through violence or the threat of violence.

The homelessness definition was changed to include circumstances where it was not reasonable for a person to continue to occupy accommodation if it was probable that this would lead to violence – not just domestic violence as in earlier legislation. In accordance with New Labour's rights/obligations agenda, the 2002 Act included a behaviour condition in the allocation of housing. Section 160A stated:

> A local housing authority may decide that an applicant is to be treated as ineligible for an allocation of housing accommodation by them if they are satisfied that –
>
> a) he, or a member of his household, has been guilty of unacceptable behaviour serious enough to make him unsuitable to be a tenant of the authority; and
> b) in the circumstances at the time his application is considered, he is unsuitable to be a tenant of the authority by reason of that behaviour.

Preventing statutory homelessness

The homelessness legislation generated statistics on homelessness that became media 'headline' figures. Two statistics dominate: 'households accepted as homeless', measuring the 'flow' of people into homelessness, and 'households in temporary accommodation', a snapshot of the number of households who are homeless at a particular point in time (see *Figure 7.3*). Temporary accommodation includes Bed and Breakfast hotels (in 2010 there were 740 households with children in such hotels, greatly reduced from 6970 in 2002); hostels; and leasing, or directly using, private landlord accommodation. Accommodating homeless families in the private landlord sector has increased rapidly from 38% of homeless households in 2002 to 72% in 2010 (DCL, 2010b, Table 775).

In the countdown to the 1997 General Election, New Labour was critical of the Conservatives' homelessness record and its manifesto declared 'Homelessness has more than doubled under the Conservatives. Today more than 40,000 families in England are in expensive temporary accommodation' (Labour Party, 1997, p 10). What the manifesto neglected to say was that, following a large increase in households in temporary accommodation during the late 1980s' house price boom, the number of households in temporary accommodation was on a downward trend – from 63,070 in 1992 to 42,000 in 1996. Embarrassing, then, that under New Labour 101,000 households were in temporary accommodation in 2004/05. Part of this increase could be attributed to the eligibility

***Figure 7.3:** Homeless acceptances and households in temporary accommodation (England)*

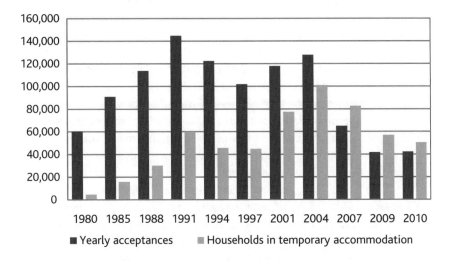

■ Yearly acceptances　　■ Households in temporary accommodation

Sources: Adapted from DCL (2010g) and Wilcox (2009).

liberalisation under the 2002 Act, but the trend had been upward since 1997 and reflected a growing housing shortage.

The Social Exclusion Unit's report on rough sleeping (Social Exclusion Unit, 1998a) had contributed to a shift in the focus on the causes of homelessness amongst single people from the 'structural' to the 'personal', and the extension of the 'priority need' category in 2002 helped to blur the distinction between 'statutory homelessness' (mainly households with children) and single homelessness. When the DCL's Rough Sleeping Unit was merged with the Statutory Homeless Division, attention turned to the possible 'personal' causes of family homelessness. The DCL started to take an interest in 'repeat' statutory homelessness – perhaps under the assumption that 'repeat' homelessness pointed to 'personal' causes – and asked local authorities to record its incidence. It also commissioned research on the aetiology of family homelessness. If the DCL had expected this research to support its new approach related to the personal problems of families experiencing homelessness, it was to be disappointed (see ***Box 7.2***).

Box 7.2: Family homelessness

The DCL-commissioned research demonstrated the following:

- 'Around half (55%) of families applied as homeless from somewhere other than their last settled accommodation. This suggests that many families make short-term accommodation arrangements before applying to a local authority for help' (Pleace et al, 2008, p 7). It also shows that local authority returns on homelessness – giving the 'immediate' reasons for loss of accommodation and indicating that 57% of the reasons involve 'relationship breakdowns' – are misleading because many families, having lost their last settled accommodation, stay with friends and relatives before making a homelessness application.

- 'Only a very small number of adult respondents reported that they had applied as homeless because they perceived this to be the "quickest" or "only" way to gain access to social housing. This evidence, coupled with the fact that the great majority (85%) of adult respondents had made efforts to gain alternative help with their housing problems before approaching the council for assistance (usually by asking to stay with friends or relatives or by trying to acquire a private or social tenancy), weighs against suggestions of widespread "abuse" of the homelessness legislation. For 87% this was their first homelessness application, and the majority (70%) reported at least one concern about making a homelessness application (most commonly that they would have to live in a "rough" area)' (Pleace et al, 2008, p 29).

- 'Adult respondents (usually the mothers) in these families seemed to be a relatively disadvantaged group with respect to their health and access to social support, and many had experienced domestic violence. However, only a minority appeared extremely vulnerable and very few self-reported current drug or alcohol problems. Children in these families were generally happy at home and at school and were reportedly in good health' (Pleace et al, 2008, p 24).

Sustainable Communities: Settled Homes; Changing Lives, a Strategy for Tackling Homelessness (ODPM, 2005c, p 13) affirmed the government's 'new approach to tackling homelessness which focused on people's personal problems rather than just structural bricks and mortar causes'. It continued:

> We recognised that the provision of housing alone cannot solve homelessness. Underlying problems which led to homelessness in the first place have to be addressed in order to provide long–

term solutions. Failure to address these root causes can lead to repeated episodes of homelessness.

It defined homelessness prevention as 'providing people with the ways and means to address their housing and other needs in order to avoid homelessness' and listed three strands in the department's homelessness prevention strategy:

- Encouraging and rewarding the modernisation of services provided by local authorities which offer a wider range of preventative help, support and housing options – so that they reach more people, earlier on.
- Encouraging and supporting stronger partnerships between local authorities, housing associations, private landlords and other statutory and voluntary sector agencies – so that they act in concert to help people avoid homelessness and provide solutions to homelessness.
- Working across Government to achieve wider social policy improvements that help tackle the problems that can cause homelessness or be exacerbated by it – so that people at greatest risk of homelessness are able to access services to enable them to lead healthy, independent lives. (ODPM, 2005c, p 14)

The new prevention emphasis had been heralded by *More Than a Roof* (Casey, 2003) and was in operation before the publication of *Sustainable Communities: Settled Homes; Changing Lives, a Strategy for Tackling Homelessness*. The policy was promoted by a set of 'administrative stratagems' (Pawson, 2009b):

- Setting a target to reduce the use of temporary accommodation by 50% by 2010.
- Issuing revised guidance on interpreting the homelessness legislation Preventing homelessness was the theme of Chapter two of this guidance. It stated that: 'the prevention of homelessness should be a key strategic aim which housing authorities and other partners pursue through the homelessness strategy'. It reminded housing authorities that 'they must not avoid their obligations under Part 7 of the 1996 Act' but stated that 'it is open to them to suggest alternative solutions in cases of potential homelessness where these would be appropriate and acceptable to the applicant' (DCL, 2006b, p 30).
- Offering grants 'to deliver positive outcomes on homelessness and in particular, a step change in the provision and impact of preventative services'. Grants were based, in part, on levels of homelessness but 'also

awarded in recognition of the achievement of clear, positive outcomes on homelessness prevention' (DCL, 2006c, p 6).

- Appointing 'advisors' to spread the ministerial message across the practitioner community (Pawson, 2009b).
- New performance indicators that formed the basis of whether or not a local authority was deemed to be delivering 'best value', for example:

    (1) BV213 counted the number of 'households who considered themselves as homeless, who approached the local authority's housing advice service(s) and for whom housing advice casework intervention resolved their situation'.

    (2) BV225, relating to domestic violence included such criteria as whether a local authority had recently reduced the proportion of homelessness acceptances resulting from domestic violence and whether the local authority made available 'sanctuary' provision to prevent homelessness.

In response to these exhortations, local authorities developed a number of preventative measures, including:

- Interviews, often called 'housing options', prior to a formal homelessness assessment, from which ways of dealing with an accommodation problem other than designation as homeless may emerge, for example, private landlord accommodation;
- rent deposit/bond schemes;
- mediation with landlords/friends and relatives;
- tenancy support; and
- sanctuary schemes.

For the purpose of BV225 the Audit Commission defined a sanctuary scheme as:

> providing security measures to allow the woman to remain in her home where she chooses to do so, where safety can be guaranteed and the violent partner no longer lives within the home.... It must consist of additional security to any main entrance doors to the accommodation and locks to any vulnerable windows. Wherever possible it must provide a safe room in the home secured with a solid core door and additional locks. It is essential that this service is only provided where it is the clear choice of the victim. (Audit Commission, 2006)

Sanctuary schemes prevent the disruption involved in moving home, for example, a possible change of school for the children. Research commissioned by the DCL (2010h) revealed very few breaches of sanctuaries but a dearth of information on the long-term outcomes of such schemes.

Preventing homelessness or preventing politically damaging homelessness statistics?

Applying the 'prevention' strategy to statutory homelessness in England has been very successful (see *Figure 7.3*), especially when it is remembered that historically there has been a link between house prices and homelessness (Barker, 2003) and that house prices increased rapidly between 2003 and 2007. The DCL (2010i) estimated that, in 2009/10, 165,200 cases 'of homelessness prevention or relief' had taken place outside the statutory homeless framework in England ('relief' relating to helping people who were not eligible for direct assistance under the homelessness legislation, eg single 'non-vulnerable' adults). However, the policy has provoked controversy with critics claiming that 'prevention' has been aimed at preventing politically damaging homelessness statistics rather than helping homeless households. A case supporting this allegation would include the following points:

- The 1977 Housing (Homeless Persons) Act and subsequent legislation require local authorities to undertake a formal assessment of a homeless applicant's status under the legislation with a view to applying the law. The housing options interview, now preceding the formal assessment, places a barrier to formal assessment and the 'rights' that flow from it should the homeless person be in priority need and unintentionally homeless. In *Sustainable Communities: Settled Homes; Changing Lives, a Strategy for Tackling Homelessness* (ODPM, 2005c, para 3.15) it was stated that new legislation may be necessary to promote the prevention agenda but, as yet, no legislation has been introduced. The nature of this potential new legislation was not made public, but it was indicated that it would include powers to make the 'housing options' interview and the acceptance of any help to prevent homelessness a condition of being formally accepted as homeless (Housing Quality Network, 2005, p 2).
- A survey of housing officers found that 66% felt under pressure to minimise acceptances and the majority of those responding felt that the pressure was coming from central government (Rashleigh, 2005).
- According to an article in *Inside Housing* (2007b), homeless people were being pushed into the private rented sector in 'housing options'

programmes and, due to a shortfall between the rent demanded and Housing Benefit entitlement, some were being evicted. Eviction for rent arrears could lead to a homeless person being declared intentionally homeless if they reapplied to the local authority.

- The performance indicators used to assess the 'best value' of the preventive strategy did not include indicators of whether or not people presenting themselves as homeless were satisfied with the 'prevention' process. Indeed, there has been a dearth of research commissioned by the DCL on how the prevention emphasis impacts on homeless households. One impact might be that homeless applicants have been diverted from securing a place in social housing. Social-sector accommodation has a dramatic impact on the well-being of former homeless households. Two of the authors of *Statutory Homelessness in England: The Experience of Families and 16–17 Year Olds* (Pleace et al, 2008), in summarising the report's findings, state:

Perhaps the most important overall finding of the English family homelessness survey was that the provision of statutory homelessness assistance seemed to have secured a substantial (net) improvement in families' quality of life. Thus, those parents who reported that life was now better than in their 'last settled accommodation' heavily outnumbered those for whom it was perceived to be worse (57% as compared with 19%). Likewise, they were far likelier to report an improvement (57%) than a decline (12%) in their child(ren)'s overall quality of life. (Fitzpatrick and Pleace, 2009, pp 30–1)

- In 2009, nine 'mystery shoppers', organised by the housing charity Crisis, visited five different local authorities across London, two inner and three outer boroughs, making 45 visits to seek help about homelessness. They 'were frequently deterred from even making a homelessness application, instead being told that they were not in "priority need" or not eligible to apply for an assessment' (Crisis, 2009, p 8).

Rough sleeping

The 1977 Housing (Homeless Persons) Act did not include the majority of the people experiencing the most visible form of homelessness – sleeping rough. Nevertheless, the developing tendency in the 1970s to treat homeless single people as victims of circumstance rather than 'feckless' threats to society (Brennan Committee, 1976) was reflected in changes in the vagrancy laws. Sleeping outdoors was no longer an offence unless it caused a nuisance and begging had to be 'persistent' to be unlawful (Humphreys, 1999).

In the early 1980s, the number of people on the streets appeared to be increasing and they seemed younger than in the past. The Conservatives' response was to stop the payment of Housing Benefit to people under 18 and reduce the amount paid to 18–25 year olds. Margaret Thatcher believed that Housing Benefit availability was encouraging young people to leave home (Thatcher, 1993, p 603). These Housing Benefit restrictions did not have the anticipated impact and, by the late 1980s, considerable media attention had focused on the growth of 'cardboard cities' and begging, especially in central London. Homeless people became regarded as a threat to social order. Margaret Thatcher commented that 'Crowds of drunken, dirty, often abusive and sometimes violent men must not be allowed to turn central areas of the capital into no-go zones for ordinary citizens' (Thatcher, 1995, p 603). A new expression entered the discourse of homelessness – 'rough sleepers' – a term indicating that the sleepers were as coarse as their sleeping conditions. The voluntary sector responded to the young 'rough sleeper' problem by the creation of 'foyers' (see Box 7.3) and, in 1990, a Rough Sleepers Initiative was started. This consisted of a programme, costing £196 million over seven years, to contact rough sleepers in central London, allocate them to emergency hostel places and then offer more permanent, 'move on' accommodation. In addition the police increased their activity with the number of people arrested under the vagrancy legislation increasing from 192 in 1991 to 1445 in 1992 (May et al, 2004). In 1995, the government claimed that the initiative was working and 'the number of people sleeping rough in central London has dropped from over 1000 in 1989 to under 290 in November 1994' (DoE, 1995, p 37).

New Labour's rough sleeping policy – with its emphasis on the personal troubles experienced by people sleeping rough, the 'rough sleeping culture' and persuading people to 'come in from the cold' to receive help – has been described in Chapter Two. According to the official count, the number of people sleeping rough in England on a given night had declined to 440 in 2010. However, counting rough sleepers is difficult, not least because experienced rough sleepers will conceal their whereabouts. New Labour's official counts were questioned because, as examples, a person had to be 'bedded down' to be recorded as a rough sleeper (not sitting or standing near a bed), the counts started at midnight before many rough sleepers had 'bedded down', and not all local authorities compiled figures on rough sleeping. The Coalition government is committed to finding better ways to count rough sleepers and has changed the time when the count is made, stated that those 'sitting or standing near the bedding' should be included and announced that, if they do not make a count, all local authorities must make a robust estimate of the number of people sleeping rough (Shapps,

Box 7.3: Foyers

A programme to link hostel provision for young homeless people to employment and training opportunities was started in 1991. The aim of these 'foyers' was to break the 'no home–no job–no home' cycle for people aged 16 to 25. The idea was imported from France where 500 foyers offered an integrated system enabling young people to move around the country for employment or training with guaranteed accommodation. The foyer idea of linking accommodation, training and employment placement fitted well with New Labour's 'joined-up' mantra and foyers multiplied in the late 1990s. By 2006, there were over 130 foyers helping about 5000 residents in units ranging from converted houses to large purpose-built accommodation. According to the Foyer Federation website (Foyer Federation, 2010):

> the Foyer network has grown rapidly and now operates in over 130 urban and rural communities across the UK, providing safe, quality assured environments, where experts reconnect up to 10,000 vulnerable young people each year with personal development opportunities.

There has been a dearth of up-to-date independent research on the impact of the expanded foyer provision from the user perspective and its success in enabling young people to find work. Lovatt et al (2006, p 161) conclude:

The UK Foyer initiatives remain fundamentally housing based.... In housing terms Foyers are usually seen as being highly successful. Support has been increasingly concentrated on life skills, together with linkages to employment-based initiatives (such as Connexions and New Deal). The changing nature of the client group has meant that the need to provide more resources for accommodation and long-term support is often more pressing than developing education and training services.

2010). The Coalition government estimate that there are 1247 rough sleepers in England.

An alternative to the government figure can be arrived at by looked at the numbers of people recorded as rough sleeping by outreach workers in London over various time periods. This count by outreach workers found more than 3000 rough sleepers in London alone (National Centre for Social Research/Broadway, 2010) with about 26% of new rough sleepers being from countries new to the European Union (mainly from Poland).

The recent focus on rough sleepers has diverted attention from the larger problem of 'single homelessness' from which rough sleeping draws its recruits: people living in squats, staying with friends for short periods or accommodated in night shelters, hostels and Bed and Breakfast hotels. It has been estimated that, in London, 50% of the people sleeping rough are new to the streets. Thus, New Labour's rough sleeping initiative had to contend with a constant throughput: as people were taken in to warmth, others move into the cold.

Asylum, immigration and homelessness

The 1999 Immigration and Asylum Act completed a process, started in 1993, of excluding asylum seekers and other people subject to immigration control from receiving help via the homelessness legislation. With certain exceptions, asylum seekers do not qualify for the housing register and cannot be allocated secure tenancies, or nominated for assured tenancies. The National Asylum Support Service, funded by the Home Office, became responsible for helping asylum seekers to find accommodation. The National Asylum Support Service pursued a dispersal policy, arranging to secure properties through private-sector landlords and local authorities with a 'difficult-to-let' problem. As Hynes and Sales (2010, pp 45–6) comment:

> Dispersal to places where such accommodation was available ensured that asylum seekers were concentrated in areas with high levels of social exclusion. Nearly 80 per cent of the initial dispersal locations in England were in the 88 most deprived districts identified by the Social Exclusion Unit in 2000.

Scotland

Since devolution, the Scottish Government has developed a distinctive approach to homelessness. Labelled 'a rights-based approach' (Anderson, 2009, p 107), it has come to symbolise a distinctive Scottish attitude to social policy and has been referred to as 'the most progressive homelessness legislation in Europe' (Scottish Executive, 2005, p 5).

The 2001 Housing (Scotland) Act required local authorities to house homeless people, whether considered to be in priority need or not, while a homelessness claim was investigated. Moreover, if assessed as non-priority homeless, local authorities had to provide accommodation for a reasonable period. Under the 2003 Homelessness (Scotland) Act, passed by a Labour–Liberal Democrat coalition, the distinction between priority and non-priority need was to be gradually phased out in accordance with local circumstances. By 2012, all unintentionally homeless people would be entitled to a permanent home defined as a 'Scottish secure tenancy' (local authority) or an assured tenancy (usually used by housing associations) *not* an assured shorthold (characteristic of the private landlord sector). Given this broader homelessness interpretation, it is not surprising that the number of applications for assistance assessed as 'in priority need' increased from 20,000 in 2000/01 to 34,940 in 2008/09. Of more concern was the sharp increase in the number of households in temporary accommodation, up from 4060 in 2002 to 10,815 in 2010 (Scottish Government, 2010b), and indicating a dearth of permanent accommodation to meet the new statutory obligations. Some local authorities expressed concern about the consequences of the rights–based approach, with one respondent in a Scottish local authority survey stating:

> The homelessness legislation, when fully in place, will see the end of people in the area being housed from waiting lists. We are already receiving twice the number of homelessness presentations as we get in empty homes each year. As the priority groups extend; we will not be able to cope. (quoted in Anderson, 2009, p 113)

The English 'prevention' strategy was pursued in Scotland, but not with the same forceful central 'administrative stratagems' (Pawson et al, 2007). However, the distinctive Scottish approach is in the process of modification. *Firm Foundations: The Future of Housing in Scotland* (Scottish Government, 2007) maintained that increased use of privately rented housing would help to meet the 2012 target. Moreover, a consultation document (Scottish Government, 2008) suggested that local authorities should be able to discharge their obligations under the homelessness legislation by the offer (and willing acceptance) of a private-sector assured shorthold tenancy (the situation in England). The Scottish Government has also shown an increasing interest in the English 'prevention' strategy. In 2009, new guidance was issued to local authorities on homelessness prevention endorsing the housing options approach and stating that 'The Housing Regulator will refer to this guidance during future inspection activity' (Scottish Government, 2009, p 7).

Wales and Northern Ireland

Given the Welsh Assembly's restricted legislative powers up to 2010 it is not surprising that homelessness policy in Wales has taken the same path as in England. Northern Ireland has also followed the English direction with a time lag. Legislation similar to the 1977 Housing (Homeless Persons)

Act was not applied to Northern Ireland until 1988 and, despite much debate, extension of the priority need categories has not occurred (Gray and Long, 2009).

Overview

- Homelessness has been identified as a social problem because it has been seen as a threat to the social order and as unacceptable in an affluent 'civilised' society.
- Definitions of homelessness are related to notions of causation.
- After an initial rapid increase under New Labour, the 'prevention' strategy reduced the recorded incidence of statutory homelessness in England.

Questions for discussion

1. You have been asked to count the number of rough sleepers in a part of a large city. What problems might you encounter in making the count?
2. Look at Figures 7.1 and 7.2. Identify 'structural', 'personal' and 'interpersonal' factors in the process of becoming homeless.
3. It has been said that defining homelessness is a political act rather than a semantic exercise. What do you think is meant by this statement?

Further reading

Robert Humphreys' (1999) *No Fixed Abode: A History of Responses to the Roofless and Rootless in Britain* is an interesting historical account of responses to homelessness. *Homelessness in the UK: Problems and Solutions* (2009) edited by **Suzanne Fitzpatrick**, **Deborah Quilgars** and **Nicholas Pleace** is a comprehensive review of homelessness.

Websites

Each local authority must publish a Homelessness Strategy. Many of these are available online.

The European Federation of National Organisations Working with the Homeless maintains a web site that contains statistics and information on homelessness in Europe. Available at: http://www.feantsa.org/code/en/hp.asp

Homeless Pages is a useful information source. Available at: http://www.homelesspages. org.uk

eight

Decent and sustainable homes

Summary

- The state has controlled housing standards by building regulations governing new construction, planning controls and enforcing minimum standards on the condition and use of the current housing stock.
- Demolition was the dominant method used to deal with property deemed 'unfit for human habitation' but, from the late 1960s, improvement grants – often distributed on an area basis – gradually replaced clearance.
- Since the 1980s, state aid to the private sector for repair and improvement has been offered on an increasingly selective basis.
- There has been a gradual change in the official benchmarks used to measure housing quality from 19th-century 'sanitary' standards to contemporary 'decent' and 'sustainable' benchmarks.
- In regulating multi-occupied properties governments have attempted to balance enforcing minimum standards with maintaining a stock of cheap accommodation.

The slum

The 1875 Public Health Act, which set out model by-laws for building new homes, plus the subsequent mandatory local authority building regulations, have ensured that new houses have been decent according to the norms of the time. However, because dwellings deteriorate and standards change, successive governments have established minimum housing benchmarks and attempted to ensure that the existing dwelling stock meets these requirements.

In the 19th century, the term 'slum' was applied to an entire area as well as to an individual dwelling deemed 'unfit for human habitation'.

As Mellor (1977, p 67) explains, 'the slum was the locale of vice, crime, delinquency and disease, a disorderly gathering of people beyond society and without community'. Its surrogates were 'plague spot', 'rookery', 'mean streets', 'Abyss' and 'Labyrinth'. From the 1830s, attempts were made to deal with the 'nuisance' caused by individual unfit dwellings and legislation sponsored by authorities in Liverpool and Manchester made it possible to close cellar dwellings. The 1868 Artisans' and Labourers' Dwellings Act, called the 'Torrens Act' after the MP who introduced it into Parliament, allowed local authorities to require owners to demolish unfit houses, but imposed no landlord obligation to rehouse the displaced tenants. Torrens' original bill had included local authority powers to build dwellings but, in its passage through Parliament, the bill was diluted. In its final form, without the new-build provisions, the Act was concerned with health and social order 'externalities' – widening alleys and courts – rather than with the welfare of the people living in the slums. As Rodger (2000, p 233) notes:

> The narrow wynds of pre-modern towns produced a porosity in the urban texture through which people could move easily on foot, but by 1900 many of these pedestrian alleys had been swept away.

Nonetheless, despite the public order dimension to clearance, there was intense hostility to the implementation of the legislation from 'parish vestries, often composed of local property-owners' (Wise, 2008).

The 1875 Artisans' and Labourers' Dwellings Improvement Act

This Act, known as the 'Cross Act', made provision for eradicating slum areas in a planned manner. Its aim was to facilitate, but not compel, the use of public funds to eliminate the threat to public welfare posed by the 'slum'. State expenditure would be minimised by selling the cleared site to philanthropic, 'model dwelling' housing associations and, only if this proved ineffective, could local authorities build houses. Unfortunately, the Act did little to improve the slum dwellers' welfare because demolition costs, with landlord compensation at market value, were far greater than housing associations could pay for the cleared sites and provide adequate accommodation.

The Cross Act placed a duty on local authorities to arrange for new dwellings to be built on or near the cleared site sufficient to rehouse all the displaced persons. However, this provision, even when reduced to 50% in 1882, and like the obligations placed on railway companies to replace the accommodation lost in railway construction, was usually ignored. Joseph

Chamberlain's famous central Birmingham 'grand improvement' scheme, started in 1875 under the Cross Act, led to building Corporation Street and a decline in the death rate from 53.2 to 21.3 per thousand. By 1888, not one new house had been built on the site to replace the slums, prompting a local newspaper to comment:

> New Birmingham recipe for lowering the death rate of an insanitary area. Pull down nearly all the houses and make the inhabitants live somewhere else. 'Tis an excellent plan and I'll tell you for why. Where there's no person living, no person can die. (quoted in Watts, 1992, p 53)

When housing associations did build new properties they had to let them at rents well beyond what former slum inhabitants could afford and many slum inhabitants disliked the numerous rules and regulations applied in the new 'dwelling blocks'. In one London scheme, only 11 of the 5719 slum inhabitants moved to new accommodation (Wise, 2008) and the answer to a query from the Royal Commission on the Housing of the Working Classes on how many people from the slums had benefited from a new home under improvement scheme was 'very few' (Royal Commission on the Housing of the Working Classes, 1885, p 54). Thus, although slum removal helped to achieve the 'sanitary' objective, the last cholera epidemic was in 1867 and the incidence of typhus was reduced, the poor were displaced into adjacent areas of overcrowded housing.

The 1930s' clearance drive

The slum issue was put into abeyance after 1919 whilst efforts were made to rectify the housing shortage caused by the interruption of house-building during the First World War. The 1919 Housing and Town Planning Act established that compensation for an unfit house should be at site value only but, up to 1930, only 11,000 slum houses had been demolished. Local authorities had to meet 50% of the cost and there was strong opposition from tenants 'terrified of having to pay too high rents' (Simon, 1933, p 36).

The 1929–31 minority Labour government started the 1930s' slum clearance drive. The 1930 Housing Act offered additional subsidies to local authorities for demolition and construction and, in 1933, when the Conservatives abolished the subsidy available for 'general needs' housing, almost all local authority building was directed towards clearance. The minister responsible, Hilton-Young, declared that slum clearance was 'a public health problem ... not a first line problem of housing; it is a problem of ridding our social organism of radiating centres of depravity and disease'.

Accordingly, subsidies were 'appropriate in this region as a measure for the protection and preservation of the public health' (Hilton-Young, 1932, quoted in Yelling, 1992, p 134).

During the 1930s, when over 250,000 houses were demolished or closed and over a million people were rehoused, attention focused on the difficulties in rehousing the people affected by the clearance drive. The main concern was former slum inhabitants' inability to pay for their improved living standards. A study of council tenants in Stockton, rehoused from the slums, demonstrated a rise in mortality connected with malnutrition (Ineichen, 1993) and a survey in a Manchester clearance area revealed that only 31% of the people rehoused remained in their new estate three years after the move. Travel-to-work costs from outlying estates were a problem, but Yelling (1992, p 74) maintains that 'the principal cause of this was undoubtedly rent', with local authority rents twice the amount paid in the slum areas. Older property improvement was not totally ignored between the wars. The 1926 Housing (Rural Workers) Act gave local authorities the discretionary power to give improvement grants to private landlords, and the 1930 Housing Act allowed improvement areas to be declared in urban districts with grants available to encourage repair.

The bulldozer returns

Clearance was abandoned in the years immediately after the Second World War as attention focused on making good the housing shortage caused by the five-year cessation of house-building and the large number of dwellings badly damaged or destroyed. Clearance returned to the political agenda in 1954. One million dwellings were demolished in Britain between 1954 and 1975 as part of a large-scale urban renewal exercise. Initially, this clearance drive provoked little controversy – the most significant objection being its limited scale in relationship to the true magnitude of the problem – but in the early 1970s its rationale began to be questioned. The vast majority of the dwellings demolished in the 1950s and early 1960s were grossly unfit and the people living in them, as tenants rather than owners, were excluded from the formal appeal mechanisms against a clearance decision. However, by the late 1960s, local authorities were beginning to deal with a different type of area in which not all the dwellings were seriously unfit and where there were more owner-occupiers, former tenants who had purchased their houses from their landlords. Objections to compulsory purchase orders became more frequent and community activists started to assist local people to devise rehabilitation schemes as alternatives to clearance. Social research began to reveal insensitive 'top-down' approaches to clearance (Dennis, 1972; Gower Davies, 1974). The loss of community spirit when people were rehoused to different areas was highlighted and attention was drawn to the increased living costs in the new estates, both in terms of rent – few authorities operated a rent rebate scheme – and the increased travel-to-work costs from new periphery estates.

Clearance or improvement?

The 1949 Housing Act allowed local authorities to offer improvement grants of 50% of rehabilitation costs up to a specified limit, but only 7000 grants were issued between 1949 and 1953 mainly because local authorities did not inform the public of their availability. The value of improvement grants was increased by the 1954 Housing Repairs and Rents Act, and the 1959 House Purchase and Housing Act made it mandatory for local authorities to pay 'standard' grants for installing basic amenities such as a bath and an internal water closet. Additional discretionary grants were available to assist owners to improve their dwellings to a standard necessary for a 30-year life. A dual strategy, unfit property clearance and improvement for 'substandard' dwellings, was promoted in the late 1950s and 1960s. However, Labour's enthusiasm for demolition was beginning to ebb with Richard Crossman (1977, p 177), Housing Minister at the time, declaring 'it was really a pleasure to see how happy old people are when their traditional old houses are transformed by being given a bathroom and a skylight in the attic and proper dry roofing and modern kitchens'. Against a background of financial constraint, the Labour government announced that 'within a total of public investment at about the level it has now reached, a greater share should go to the improvement of older houses' (MHLG, 1968, p 4).

The 1969 Housing Act increased grant payments, introduced a special grant for the basic amenity provision in multi-occupied dwellings, and made grants available for environmental measures in 'General Improvement Areas' (GIAs). Great reliance was placed on the 'halo' impact of area selectivity:

> The effort and resources devoted to improvement provides a much better return when directed to the up-grading of whole areas – the houses and the environment. People are more likely to find it worth their while to co-operate and to maintain their houses after improvement. (MHLG, 1969, p 3)

In the early 1970s, higher grant rates were offered in certain regions and the number of grants approved soared as Edward Heath's government attempted to inject demand into the economy and use home improvement to limit the requirement for new council housing. Improvement grants helped to upgrade the private-sector housing stock but many people with low incomes left their homes as landlords encouraged tenants to move to enable sales to homeowners – a process to become known as 'gentrification'. The White Paper *Better Homes: The Next Priorities* (MHLG, 1973) heralded rationing by more specific area selectivity. Its principles were adopted by the Labour Party and the 1974 Housing Act introduced the Housing Action Area (HAA) idea to complement existing GIAs. HAAs were to be areas of housing and social stress exhibiting a combination of problems such as a high proportion of unfit houses, furnished tenancies and shared accommodation. In HAAs, local authorities had powers to pay more generous grants, to compel private landlords to refurbish their properties and to acquire rented properties by compulsory purchase. In the 1950s, the Labour Party committed itself to 'socialising' the private landlord sector and compulsory purchase of private landlord accommodation, perhaps to pass on to a housing association, marked a step in this direction. However, funding restraints limited the initiative's impact.

Income selectivity and home improvement

Margaret Thatcher's first government (1979–83) displayed a strong commitment to private-sector housing rehabilitation. In the 1970s, clearance was automatically associated with council housing and hence private-sector improvement was a mechanism to prevent more local authority building. This rehabilitation commitment was accompanied by a shift in policy towards extending improvement grant availability regardless of location. However, following the 1983 general election, improvement grants were badly affected by public spending cuts. *Home Improvement: A New Approach* (DoE, 1985) revealed government thinking on unfit and substandard housing. It proposed to switch responsibility for the older private stock from the government to the owner stating that 'home ownership offers opportunities for individuals to alter and improve their homes as they wish; they must carry the primary responsibility for keeping their property in good repair' (DoE, 1985, p 7). In future, improvement grant eligibility would be determined by two criteria: property fitness and the occupier's income. New Right distaste for relativity in defining minimum yardsticks was revealed when, in relationship to the fitness standard, the Green Paper declared that 'a policy of raising the minimum standard to match rising social expectations would be inappropriate' (DoE, 1985, p 10). The owner-occupier of any dwelling deemed unfit according to an unchanging standard would be eligible for an improvement grant only if household income was below a specified level. This income-testing was justified by citing evidence that a significant proportion of the grants available had been claimed by more affluent groups. The new grant would cover only the cost of making a dwelling fit; additional expenditure to give a house a 30-year life would be covered by an equity-sharing loan whereby the local authority would acquire a share in the value of the property.

No action was taken on the principles outlined in the 1985 Green Paper until the 1989 Local Government and Housing Act, and, in the interim, the idea of equity-sharing loans was abandoned. Under the Act a new benchmark for assessing unfitness was introduced, which became the basis for the award of means-tested renovation grants. Declarations of HAAs and GIAs were abolished but local authorities were allowed to undertake group repair schemes, for example, 'enveloping', which involved making sure an entire street of terraced housing was sound, and to designate renewal areas. Clearance area declaration was permitted only when a local authority had carried out a detailed cost–benefit appraisal of the options for the area.

The new urban renewal regime produced disappointing results mainly because insufficient resources were available to enable the system to operate effectively. The notion of a mandatory grant to households with a low income living in unfit property implied that such households had a right to the grant, but central government failed to make the finance available to meet the demand especially in neighbourhoods where low income and a major unfitness problem coincided. Local authorities responsible for such areas had to remain silent on the mandatory grant entitlement and to delay the payments to those who had applied, thus creating uncertainty and frustration among applicants. Selectivity had, yet again, been accompanied by resource constraints. The 1996 Housing Grants, Construction and Regeneration Act made all grants discretionary, except for the disabled facilities grant (see Chapter Ten).

New Labour and decent homes

The private sector

The 1996 English House Condition Survey exposed a disconcerting level of unfitness and disrepair in the private rented sector: 19.3% of the stock was unfit and 28.9% of private tenants lived in 'poor' housing. In the homeownership sector, 10.9% lived in 'poor' housing and 6% of the stock was unfit. Despite the problem, New Labour retained the discretionary nature of private-sector improvement grants established by the Conservatives and state expenditure on private-sector improvement declined. Nevertheless, the 2001 English House Condition Survey revealed that the number of unfit private-sector dwellings had fallen between 1996 and 2001, a testimony to the impact of rising house prices on equity availability for home improvement and on homeowners' willingness to invest in their properties at a time of house price inflation.

The 2001 English House Condition Survey contained a new benchmark for accessing housing stock condition – the decent homes standard (see **Box 8.1**). The decent homes standard was an aspirational threshold, to be achieved in the private sector at some unspecified future date, whereas the fitness standard became a minimum standard that could trigger specific action to rectify the unfitness. In 2006, under the 2004 Housing Act, the fitness standard was replaced by the Housing Health and Safety Rating System (HHSRS) (see **Box 8.2**).

Box 8.1: A decent home

The decent homes standard was changed in 2006, which makes it difficult to assess the progress made in reducing the number of non-decent homes. Under the 2006 benchmark, to be defined as decent a home must meet each of the following criteria (DCL, 2006d):

- It is above the current statutory minimum housing standard, that is, it fails to meet one or more of the hazards assessed as serious (category 1) under HHSRS.
- It is in a reasonable state of repair. Dwellings failing on this point will be those where either:
  - one or more key building components are old and need replacing or major repair; or
  - two or more of the other building components are old and need replacing or major repair.
- It has reasonably modern facilities and services. Dwellings failing on this point are those that lack three or more of the following:
  - a reasonably modern kitchen (20 years old or less);
  - a kitchen with adequate space and layout;
  - a reasonably modern bathroom (30 years old or less);
  - an appropriately located bathroom and WC;
  - adequate insulation against external noise (where external noise is a problem);
  - adequate size and layout of common areas for blocks of flats.
- It provides a reasonable degree of thermal comfort.

Scotland, Wales and Northern Ireland have their own housing quality benchmarks. In Scotland, for example, the Scottish Tolerable Standard is used to measure and promote action to tackle the lowest-quality homes whereas the Scottish Housing Quality Standard (SHQS), higher than the English decent home benchmark, is the aspirational standard. In 2008 about 64% of dwellings in Scotland failed the SHQS (Scottish Government, 2010c).

Box 8.2: Housing Health and Safety Rating System (HHSRS)

Under this system, property 'hazards' are assessed and given a score by a local authority environmental health officer. Assessment is a two-stage process based on the likelihood of an occurrence and the probable harm to the most vulnerable potential occupant that would result from the occurrence. If the assessment produces a high score, labelled category 1, then the local authority has a duty to take action. Action can take the form of hazard awareness advice, improvement notices requiring repair and/or improvement, making a demolition order, declaring a clearance area or issuing a prohibition notice that prohibits the use of all or part of the dwelling to all occupants or to members of a vulnerable group. A lower assessment score, category 2, gives local authorities the power, but not the duty, to take action. HHSRS can be regarded as a minimum standard – contravention can involve legal action – whereas the decent homes standard is an aspirational benchmark. Roys et al (2010) calculated that it would cost in excess of £17.6 billion to remove all category 1 hazards.

Initially the target for decent homes applied only to social housing and it appeared that New Labour had stepped away from private-sector involvement. A consultation document stated: 'it is only right that the responsibility for maintaining privately owned homes, which for many people is their most valuable asset, should rest first and foremost with the owner' (DETR, 2001, paras 3.1–3.2).

The consultation document proposed that the detailed provisions governing the way local authorities facilitated private-sector improvement should be removed and replaced with a broad power to provide assistance for home repair and improvement. Local authorities were encouraged to develop private-sector housing renewal strategies with loan schemes forming a major element in such strategies. Given that renovation grants had already been made discretionary in 1996, these proposals to abolish statutory requirements on the types of assistance offered by local authorities made sense. However, the changes meant that housing renovation would be competing for resources from the 'single capital pot' with other local capital expenditure proposals. The lack of a specified national grant entitlement structure, plus the tone of the government's statements on personal responsibility for home improvement and the use of loans, created concern that the new regime's likely impact would be to reduce the help available to low-income households in the private sector.

Targeting vulnerable households

The suggestions in the 2001 consultation document were implemented by the 2002 Regulatory Reform (Housing Assistance) (England and Wales) Order. However, perhaps in recognition of concerns about possible reductions in the share of the local authority 'capital pot' spent on private-sector home improvements, the decent homes target was extended to cover privately owned homes occupied by 'vulnerable' families. The target was for 70% of vulnerable households living in private-sector housing to have a decent home by 2010, but, later, this target was downgraded to 'dormant status' (House of Commons Communities and Local Government Committee, 2010).

The ODPM had identified 'vulnerable' households as 'those who are in receipt of certain means tested or disability related benefits' (House of Commons Office of the Deputy Prime Minister Select Committee, 2004, para 2.7). In 2001, there were 1,151,000 (42.7%) such vulnerable households in non-decent homes potentially eligible for help from local authorities. Government-sponsored home improvement agencies, often called 'staying put' or 'care and repair', assisted vulnerable people to access financial sources such as local authority grants and equity loans and provided support in finding a reliable builder. Between 2001 and 2006, the percentage of private-sector vulnerable households occupying non-decent homes declined to 32.3% on the old decent definition but, on the upgraded yardstick, it was 39% in 2007 (National Audit Office, 2010a).

In 2010 the House of Commons Communities and Local Government Committee concluded:

> We consider it a huge missed opportunity that the considerable political will demonstrated by the Government in raising social sector housing to the decent homes standard has not been matched by similar energies with respect to the private sector; and that the policy in the private sector appears to have failed. The downgrading of the target for decency in the private sector has weakened local authorities' already patchy engagement with their responsibilities towards private sector housing. (House of Commons Communities and Local Government Committee, 2010, p 95).

The social sector

The Conservatives limited the resources available for the upkeep of local authority-sector dwellings and, in 1997, New Labour inherited a repairs backlog costing an estimated £19 billion. In 2000, a target to ensure that all social housing met the decent homes standard by 2010 was set. Four resource channels were available to local government to facilitate the achievement of this target:

- Mainstream Housing Revenue Account resources supplemented by 'prudential borrowing' backed by income streams but not asset values.
- Stock transfer to a registered social landlord thereby providing access to private finance not subject to Treasury constraints aimed at keeping the Public Sector Borrowing Requirement at a 'prudent' level (see Chapter Two). This channel was centrally supported via debt write-off and 'gap funding' when there was negative value on transfer.
- The Housing Private Finance Initiative, which, while retaining ownership of dwellings by the local authority, tapped private finance (see Chapter Four). Although this route attracted government assistance it 'suffered significant cost increases and delays' (National Audit Office, 2010b, p 7) with only 12,343 homes brought up to the decent homes standard by 2009 and another 15,000 properties in the pipeline.
- Under the Arm's Length Management Organisation (ALMO) Initiative local authorities could access additional central resources if their housing service received a two- or three-star rating from the Audit Commission and housing management was delivered through an arm's-length organisation. An ALMO is a not-for-profit organisation run by an unpaid board of directors that includes councillors and tenant representatives but with no group having a controlling majority. The council continues to own the homes and determines allocation policy but the ALMO is responsible for stock management. By 2010, despite the queuing process for ALMO status introduced by the DCL, there were 70 ALMOs managing more than a million council homes. In 2008, as part of its rediscovered confidence in council housing, New Labour allowed certain ALMOs to bid for Social Housing Grant but the future of ALMOs remains uncertain. They hold only short-term contracts and the extra subsidy they receive ends when the decent homes standard has been achieved. Some are in the process of becoming 'independent' housing associations whilst others are being merged back into their local authorities. However, the majority have retained their existing status, and their tenant involvement plus specific geographical boundaries may appeal to the Coalition government's 'localism' agenda.

The 2006 change in the decent homes definition and the time delay in issuing statistics based on housing condition surveys make it difficult to assess New Labour's impact in upgrading the existing stock, especially as landlords are 'running to stand still'. As stock is made decent, others deteriorate. In 2009/10, 53,331 local authority houses became non-decent (DCL, 2010j).

Sustainable homes

Table 8.1: Non-decent homes, 2008, 2007, 2006 and 1996 (%)

	2008	2007[1]	2006[2]	1996
Owner-occupied	32.3	34.1	34.6 (24.0)	42.0
Private rented	44.0	45.4	46.8 (40.4)	63.2
Local authority	31.5	32.8	32.4 (33.3)	55.4
Registered social landlord	22.8	25.5	25.2 (23.6)	37.5
All social sector	27.2	29.2	29.0	n/a
All tenures	33.1	34.6	35.0	40.1

Notes: These figures are based on the English House Condition Survey. This was the database initially used by the DCL to measure progress towards its targets but, in 2008, it was replaced by landlord returns. These returns were regarded as more up to date and allowed authorities to include as decent a property where the tenant has been offered but has refused improvement work and non-decent homes scheduled for demolition. The English House Condition Survey has consistently found more houses to be non-decent than landlord returns, for example, 27.2% in 2008 in the social housing sector compared to 21.8% for landlord returns.

[1] The decent home definition was updated in 2006 and thus the figures are not comparable with 1996.

[2] For 2006, figures based on the old definition (comparable with 1996) are given in brackets.

Sources: Adapted from National Audit Office (2010a) and (DCL, 2010k).

When applied to housing the term 'sustainable' includes both a social dimension relating to community cohesion, affordability and social exclusion (see Chapters Six and Ten) plus an ecological aspect related to *a built environment 'which meets the needs of the present without compromising the ability of future generations to meet their own needs'* (World Commission on the Environment and Development, 1988). Carbon dioxide emissions from the domestic housing sector supply around 24% of all UK CO^2 output and homes use about two thirds of the water supply plus 30% of UK energy.

Constructing homes at higher densities on brownfield sites has contributed to environmental sustainability by concentrating activity and thereby reducing residents' overall ecological footprint. *The Code for*

Sustainable Homes (DCL, 2006e) set six levels of sustainability ranging from one (above existing building regulations) to six – a zero-carbon home. Compliance with the Code at level 3 became mandatory for housing built with Social Housing Grant, but voluntary for the private sector. All new-build had to have a rating in 2008 with the Code intended to act as an incentive to private-sector builders to start improving the energy efficiency of new homes in anticipation of future statutory standards.

The Green Paper *Homes for the Future: More Affordable, More Sustainable* (DCL, 2007a) proposed a phased enhancement of the building regulations so that, by 2016, all new homes would be 'zero-carbon', defined as 'over a year, the net carbon emissions from all energy use in the home would be zero' (2007a, p 4). To promote this policy objective it was announced that new zero-carbon homes valued at up to £500,000 would be exempt from Stamp Duty Tax and five eco-towns would be created. Eco-towns – reminiscent of old Labour's new towns – were an attempt to combine the social and environment dimensions of sustainability. They would be new small towns with at least 5000–20,000 homes that would have a mixed community consisting of a variety of tenures and house sizes. They would be 'places with a separate identity but with good links to surrounding towns and cities in terms of jobs, transport and services and 'the development as a whole will achieve zero carbon' and 'be an exemplar in at least one area of environmental technology' (DCL, 2007a, p 4). Eco-towns met with resistance in many areas and the initial list of places where eco-towns might be established produced four firm proposals. In 2009, New Labour announced a second wave of eco-towns and new planning guidance was issued that included measures such as power points in all new developments to charge electric vehicles.

New Labour's commitment to ensuring that, by 2016, all new homes would be 'zero carbon' created concern in the construction industry and a report, commissioned by the Coalition government, concluded that New Labour's 2016 target 'would significantly constrain the range of house types (and designs) which could be built' (Zero Carbon Hub, 2010 p 2). In response, the Housing Minister, Grant Shapps (2010) announced that there would be 'greater flexibility' in meeting the 2016 objective with contributions from developers to the Community Energy Fund counting towards carbon reduction compliance.

At current levels new home construction adds less than 1% to the housing stock each year. Thus, if the housing sector is to make a significant contribution to the government's legally binding target, set out in the 2008 Climate Change Act, to cut greenhouse gas emissions by 80% by 2050, existing homes will need to be retrofitted. The decent home standard, applied to the social sector, includes a thermal comfort criterion that contributes to energy efficiency and, in the private sector, energy efficiency reports help to raise awareness about energy consumption. Such reports were phased in after 2007 as part of Home Information Packs and were retained by the Coalition government when other elements in the packs (eg house condition reports and searches) were abolished. Grants to owners for micro-energy generation such as wind turbines and solar energy plus assistance to low-income households via the Warm Front (Warm Deal in Scotland) programmes also encourage efficient energy consumption. In 2008, The Carbon Emissions Reduction Target (CERT) came into effect, obliging electricity and gas suppliers in Great Britain to help reduce CO^2 emissions from homes under the Community Energy Savings Programme, especially in deprived areas. In 2009, New Labour published an updated green agenda. *Warm Homes, Greener Homes: A Strategy for Household Energy Management* (DCL and Department of Energy and Climate Change, 2010) declared a commitment to a 29% cut in CO^2 emissions from homes by 2020 via initiatives such as a new Warm Homes standard for social housing, enhanced regulation of the rented sector and 'Invest to Save', including 'pay as you save' financing, supplied by energy companies, to provide people with eco-retrofits without upfront costs. New Labour expected energy companies to finance 66% of the cost with the threat of fines of up to 10% of their global turnover for non-compliance. It also suggested that eligibility for Housing Benefit might be related to 'certain defined standards in terms of quality, energy efficiency and carbon footprint' (DWP, 2009, p 62) and, in 2010, it was announced that new properties, extensions and conversions will be required to meet higher standards of energy efficiency under Part L of the building regulations. This included using more energy-efficient boilers and windows.

Progress in energy efficiency is measured by the Standard Assessment Procedure (SAP) that rates a home on a 0–100 scale with 100 as highly efficient and 0 as totally inefficient. Between 1996 and 2007, the average score increased from 42 to 50 with the housing association sector outperforming other tenures with a 60 rating (Housing Finance Group, 2010). The Coalition government endorsed the Conservatives' manifesto commitment to the 'Green Deal' – supplying loans of £6500 per home for energy-saving improvements, to be paid back via reduced energy bills – and later announced that, after 2015, both tenants and local authorities would have powers to force landlords to carry out reasonable energy-efficiency improvements. Given the dearth of simple energy-saving measures in UK homes – 8.6 million dwellings in England would benefit from better loft insulation (DCL, 2010l, p 118) – the 'Green Deal' has the potential to make a significant contribution to carbon reduction, but it has been estimated that the cost of a full retrofit varies from £6000 to £40,000 per home (Housing Finance Group, 2010). The 2010 Spending Review (HM Treasury, 2010b, p 62) announced that, in addition to the 'Green Deal', 'extra support to reduce energy bills and help improve heating and insulation will be provided by energy companies to combat fuel poverty. This will allow the Warm Front public spending programme to be phased out over time, saving £345 million by 2013–14'.

Overcrowding

Whereas homelessness is a visible housing shortage symptom, overcrowding is a concealed response. This invisibility and the lack of a single, authoritative and up-to-date definition have combined to make overcrowding a neglected issue in contemporary housing policy.

Overcrowding externalities

Overcrowding was recognised as a social problem in the mid-19th century because of its association with disease, depravity and anarchy. Edwin Chadwick, a firm believer that disease spreads by breathing foul air – the 'miasmic' theory – regarded densely populated areas and crammed buildings as major causes of illness because they produced concentrations of putrefying waste. However, Chadwick ignored evidence that overcrowded dwellings had a direct connection to health independent of its influence via creating sewage disposal problems (Wohl, 1977). He was more concerned about how 'the want of separate apartments' influenced the 'morals of the population' (Chadwick, 1842, p 190). Numerous witnesses to his sanitary investigation testified to 'young men and women promiscuously sleeping in the same apartment' (Chadwick, 1842, p 191). This worry about the immorality linked to overcrowding was an enduring concern in the 19th century. Lord Shaftesbury, in his evidence to the 1885 Royal Commission on Housing, claimed that a family sharing a room often meant a family sharing a bed. He went on to comment:

> a friend of mine … going down one of the back courts, saw on the pavement two children of tender years, of 10 or 11 years old, endeavouring to have sexual connection on the pathway. He ran and seized the lad, and pulled him off, and the only remark of the lad was, 'Why do you take hold of me? There are a dozen of them at it down there'. You must perceive that that could not arise from sexual tendencies, and that it must have been bred by imitation of what they saw. (Lord Shaftesbury, 1885, quoted in Jones, 1976, p 224)

Despite this anxiety about how overcrowding impacted on the nation's physical and moral fibre, robust action would have interfered with property rights and, without specific action to rehouse the overcrowded inhabitants, exacerbated the destitution problem. Accordingly, local authority powers to control overcrowding were minimal and, until the 1875 Public Health Act, did not apply to dwellings occupied by a single family. Intervention was applied sparingly except to Common Lodging Houses and, in Scotland, to tenements where 'block living' was seen as an extra threat to public order. The model by-laws issued by the Local Government Board specifying thresholds at which local authorities might take action were expressed in terms of cubic feet of air per person. Adults were allowed 300 cubic feet in a sleeping room and children 150 cubic feet, compared to the 600 cubic feet allowed in army barracks. In some areas the by-laws were enforced by night visits from police officers and sanitary inspectors to check that the number of people living in a dwelling conformed to the statutory requirements as set out on a plaque fixed to the building.

The 1935 Housing Act

Towards the end of the 19th century, pressure from the labour movement concerning a 'housing famine' prompted more robust attempts to measure the extent of overcrowding. The 1891 Census contained questions about the number of rooms in a dwelling and the number of inhabitants. On an overcrowding definition as more than two people per room, but excluding people living in houses with more than four rooms and with a somewhat vague room definition, 11.2% of the population was overcrowded. This declined to 8.2% in 1911, but the national average in England concealed a range from 36% in Jarrow to 0.5% in Bedford. The increase in house construction and the lower birth rates in the 1920s helped to alleviate the problem but, in the 1930s, serious overcrowding remained. The 1931 Census recorded 7 million people living at densities of more than 1.5 persons per room and 397,000 households at more than two persons per room. The findings of the Moyne Report (Moyne Committee, 1933) convinced officials that overcrowding was a more serious menace to health than unfitness, but overcrowding presented a troublesome issue to the Conservatives because the magnitude of the problem indicated that mass housing might be required in the suburbs. Hilton-Young, the responsible minister, argued that overcrowding could be dealt with by 'rehousing on the overcrowded and slum sites in flats' (quoted in Yelling, 1992, p 105) thereby presenting overcrowding as an inner-city redevelopment matter rather than a general housing problem that might interfere with the operations of private enterprise in the suburbs.

The 1935 Housing Act set out a framework for tackling overcrowding. A duty was imposed on local authorities to survey the houses in their districts to ascertain the extent of overcrowding according to a statutory definition (see ***Box 8.3***) and assess how many new dwellings were necessary to overcome the problem. When satisfied that the new dwellings would be forthcoming, the minister could trigger legislation permitting local authorities to make overcrowding illegal and allowing any landlord to regain possession if a property became overcrowded (thereby portraying overcrowding as created by the tenants rather than the landlord). The Act offered subsidies to assist new building, but they were limited to flats in central areas. The major attack on overcrowding was scheduled to follow the completion of the slum clearance task, but the outbreak of the Second World War prevented significant action.

After the Second World War, there was no specific initiative directed towards reducing overcrowding; the problem was regarded as a dimension of an overall housing shortage to be overcome by building more homes. Section 113 of the 1957 Housing Act, in establishing the duties of local authorities when allocating council houses, stated that they should give reasonable preference to 'persons who are occupying insanitary or overcrowded houses, have large families or are living under unsatisfactory housing conditions'. The overcrowding definition in the 1957 Act was identical to that in the 1935 Housing Act and 'was, even in 1935, a very limited one' (Cullingworth, 1969, p 7). Indeed, the term 'overcrowding' suggested that 'crowding' was normal.

The extent of overcrowding

Overcrowding estimates are related to the criteria used to measure its incidence. A number of measures are available, but all are subject to under-reporting. Illegal migrants are more likely to live in overcrowded dwellings and, because statutory overcrowding may lead to eviction, many people living in overcrowded conditions will not want to draw attention to their circumstances. The paucity of evidence on overcrowding amongst migrant workers was revealed in the report on private landlordism commissioned by the Department for Communities and Local Government (DCL). It was only possible to state that 'there is anecdotal evidence on bed sharing amongst shift workers' (Rugg and Rhodes, 2008, p 102).

Box 8.3: Overcrowding: 1935 Housing Act definition

The definition of overcrowding in the 1935 Housing Act was designed to ensure that any overcrowding identified by local authorities could be dealt with in a reasonable timescale and in central areas. Two standards were specified. The first standard related to 'sexual overcrowding' and was contravened when:

the number of persons sleeping in a dwelling and the number of rooms available as sleeping accommodation is such that two persons of opposite sexes who are not living together as husband and wife must sleep in the same room. For this purpose:

(a) children under the age of ten shall be left out of account; and
(b) a room is available as sleeping accommodation if it is of a type normally used in the locality either as a bedroom or as a living room [this meant that kitchens could be included as living and sleeping rooms].

Table 8.2: The number of rooms to people permitted under the second overcrowding standard

Number of rooms	Maximum number of persons
1	2
2	3
3	5
4	7.5
5	10

The second standard compared the number of rooms and the floor area of these rooms with the number of persons permitted to live in the accommodation.

An additional two persons were permitted for every room in excess of five and the numbers permitted were scaled down if any room was less than 110 square feet. No account was taken of children under one and a child under 10 was reckoned as one half of a person.

On this definition it was estimated that 341,000 people were living in overcrowded conditions, but a slightly less austere definition – excluding living rooms and kitchens as sleeping accommodation – increased the number to 853,119 (Bowley, 1945).

The statutory standard

This standard is identical to the one in the 1935 Housing Act. Many local authorities use it to assess rehousing priorities and to gauge whether the housing conditions of a family applying for accommodation under the homelessness legislation are bad enough for the household to be designated as homeless. Few local authorities use the 1935 Act to reduce overcrowding directly because evicting overcrowded families creates rehousing obligations in areas where social housing is scarce.

The statutory standard is very low: as Ormandy (1991, p 9) has observed, 'the average two storeyed, terraced house (with three bedrooms, two living rooms and a kitchen) could be occupied by the equivalent of 10 persons without being overcrowded – and that could mean six adults and eight children aged between one year and 10 years'. The parliamentary committee that oversees the DCL recommended that the statutory standard should be upgraded, but this was rejected on the argument that such a change would lead to 'increased demand for housing, to the detriment of other people whose living conditions may be worse; and would make it more difficult for authorities to juggle their priorities' (ODPM, 2003c). However, the 2004 Housing Act allowed local authorities, should they choose to do so, to take action if overcrowding produced a health and safety hazard, and contained provisions to amend the overcrowded definition through secondary legislation. In 2007, an action plan was published involving piloting a new statutory standard based on the bedroom definition in 38 local authorities. This was accompanied by extra resources for the authorities with the most acute problems to extend and convert stock and use cash incentives to make large houses available. In early 2010, New Labour rejected a petition, organised by Shelter, calling for a revision of the standard to reflect modern expectations of space and privacy.

The bedroom standard

This occupation density indicator was developed by the Government Social Survey in the 1960s for use in social surveys. A standard number of bedrooms required is calculated for each household in accordance with its age/sex/marital status composition and the relationship of household members to one another. A separate bedroom is required for each married or cohabiting couple, for any other person aged 21 or over, for each pair of adolescents aged 10 to 20 of the same sex, and for each pair of children under 10. Any unpaired person aged 10 to 20 is paired, if possible, with a child under 10 of the same sex, or, if that is not possible, he or she is counted as requiring a separate bedroom, as is any unpaired child under

10. This standard is then compared with the actual number of bedrooms (including bedsits) available for the sole use of the household. If a household has fewer bedrooms than implied by the standard then it is deemed to be overcrowded and a shortfall of more than two rooms is described as 'severe' overcrowding. Shelter has adopted the bedroom standard as the norm for assessing overcrowding on the grounds that the statutory standard is too stringent and the 'occupancy rating' is too generous. In 2008/09, there were 1.1 million children (11.6%) living in overcrowded homes: 5.8% of children in owner-occupied houses were overcrowded, 27.7% in social housing and 15.2% in the private landlord sector (DCL, 2010l). According to the National Housing Federation (2010a, p 1):

> The problem of overcrowding is particularly acute for larger families of five or more people – with 25% currently living in overcrowded properties. But ... that figure is expected to increase sharply over the next three years, with over 28% of larger families predicted to be living in unsuitable homes by 2013.

The problem is particularly serious in London with 207,000 of London's households overcrowded and the number of overcrowded households in the private rented sector increasing rapidly (Mayor of London, 2010).

2001 Census standards

The 2001 Census used what is called the 'occupancy rating' to measure the extent of overcrowding. It was more generous than the 'bedroom standard' because all households were assumed to require two common rooms (excluding bathrooms) plus a specified number of bedrooms calculated from the number and ages of the household members and the relationships between them. Any person over 16 was deemed to require a separate bedroom if not part of a couple. Thus, for example, a family of four (two parents and two children aged 10 and 17) with two bedrooms and two common rooms would have an occupancy rating of −1 and be classified as 'overcrowded'. Unfortunately, 'occupancy ratings' are available only for the 2001 Census. The 'room' standard is also used. This simply divides the number of people in the household by the number of rooms (excluding bathrooms, lavatories, halls, landings and storage spaces). More than one person per room is deemed overcrowded whereas more than 1.5 persons per room is considered as severely overcrowded. **Box 8.4** provides statistics on overcrowding according to the different definitions.

Box 8.4: Overcrowding statistics

Statutory standard

No attempt has been made to make a robust assessment of the number of statutory overcrowded households despite local authorities having powers under the 1985 Housing Act to prepare and submit a report on the extent of overcrowding in their areas. An estimate in 2005 put the number at 20,000 households in England (ODPM, 2005d).

Occupancy standard

Table 8.3: Overcrowding (the bedroom standard): England, 1971– 2008/9 (%)

	1971	1981	1991	2001	2008/09
1 or more below standard	7	5	3	2	3

Source: Adapted from Wilson (2010a).

Table 8.4: Overcrowding (the bedroom standard) by tenure and ethnicity: England and London, 2008/09 (%)

	England	London	England (BME)[1]	London (BME)[1]
Social	6.8	13.5	15.1	18.3
Private landlord	5.4	10.1	11.5	15.3
Owner-occupied	1.6	3.0	7.5	6.8

Notes: Overcrowding in the social and private rented sectors increased sharply from 1995/96 to 2008/09 from 5.1% to 6.8% in the social sector and 4.2% to 5.4% in the private rented sector. The acceleration was rapid after 2003/04.
[1] 2003/04–2005/06 (average over three years)
Source: Adapted from Wilson (2010a) and DCL (2010k, 2010l).

Bedroom standard

Table 8.5: Overcrowding: Households with one or more rooms below the 'occupancy' standard, 2001 (%)

England and Wales	7.4
London	10.8
Tower Hamlets	27.6
Most overcrowded ward in Tower Hamlets	38.7
North West	5.4
Oldham	7.3
Most overcrowded ward in Oldham	23.3

Source: Adapted from ODPM (2005d).

Overcrowding: Its impact

The lack of a contemporary, authoritative threshold by which to measure overcrowding means that it is difficult to draw robust conclusions on its impact because the benchmark used varies between studies. There are also forms of 'selection effects' that should be taken into account when examining the relationship between overcrowding and health: people with poor health, for example, may be forced to live in overcrowded houses, so overcrowding may not be the cause of their poor health. Moreover, it is difficult to disentangle the effects of overcrowding from other housing conditions such as dampness and lack of basic amenities.

A literature review on the impact of overcrowding (ODPM, 2004a) concluded the following:

- Overall there was a weak relationship between overcrowding and aspects of health of both children and adults but a robust relationship between meningitis, tuberculosis and overcrowding.
- Overcrowding in childhood affects adult health.
- There is mixed evidence on the relationship between overcrowding and mental health.
- There is limited evidence on overcrowding, childhood development, growth and education.
- No studies were found that specifically drew out the differential effects of overcrowding on the education of people from different minority ethnic backgrounds.
- There is little in the way of evidence to conclusively demonstrate an impact of overcrowding.

This literature review was more a condemnation of the limitations of existing research than a testimony to the weakness of the relationship between overcrowding and health and education. As the review stated, 'the kind of evidence required to demonstrate that 'A causes B' is not necessarily available. To do this would require a large-scale longitudinal study that compared two groups of households – one group where overcrowding has been alleviated with a group where overcrowding remained' (ODPM, 2004a, p 7).

The number of children living in overcrowded homes increased rapidly in the 2000s, reaching over a million in 2008 (DCL, 2010l). Shelter's survey of 505 overcrowded households with children (Shelter, 2005) found that:

- at least one child shared a bedroom with their parent(s) in 74% of overcrowded families;

- children slept in rooms other than designated bedrooms in 27% of overcrowded families;
- in 10% of overcrowded families, teenagers of opposite sexes shared the same bedroom;
- nine out of 10 families also reported that:
  - overcrowding made it more difficult for their children to study;
  - overcrowding harmed the health of their children; and
  - being overcrowded caused depression, anxiety or stress in the home.

Houses in multiple occupation (HMOs)

Local authority powers to regulate HMOs evolved from the 1851 Act for the Regulation and Inspection of Common Lodging Houses. In the early part of the 19th century, Common Lodging Houses provided cheap accommodation, usually in the form of straw mattresses, rented on a nightly basis, in a communal room. These 'doss-houses' were regarded as breeding grounds for crime and immorality. Overcrowding occurred on a massive scale. In 1851, the Police Commissioner for Leeds found 'in one small area 222 lodging houses in which lived 2,500 people, averaging two and a half persons per bed' (quoted in Hodgkinson, 1980, p 10). Although Lord Shaftesbury recognised the connection between regulating overcrowding and the need to build new dwellings – his Act for the Regulation and Inspection of Common Lodging Houses was accompanied by his 1851 Labouring Classes Lodging Houses Act – this was not the dominant view. Many believed that the poor caused overcrowding because they preferred to spend their incomes on drink rather than on more spacious accommodation. Thus action taken to overcome the problem consisted of regulations issued under the 1851 Act allowing the police and sanitary authorities to set standards and control the number of people occupying a dwelling. Although largely ignored in the growing Northern industrial towns, the Act was enforced in London where, to discourage prostitution, women were not allowed to use Common Lodging Houses. Dickens (1888, p 24) commented:

> Every establishment of this kind throughout the metropolis is now under direct and continual police supervision; every room being inspected and measured before occupation, a placard being hung up in each stating the number of beds for which it is licensed, calculated upon the basis of a minimum allowance of space for each person.

Over time, Common Lodging Houses evolved into what are known today as boarding houses and the lower end of the Bed and Breakfast (B&B) sector. By the 1990s, B&B hotels had an important housing role. Local authorities used them to house people classified as homeless under the 1977 Housing (Homeless Persons) Act and the payment of 'board and lodgings' allowances led many people without permanent accommodation to use such hotels. Carter (1997) studied the extent and nature of this 'self-placement' and found that people with drug, alcohol or mental health problems, ex-prisoners, care leavers, young people, and refugees were over-represented in London B&B hotels.

Letting rooms in a single dwelling to separate households without supplying food (multiple occupation) was linked to the externalities generated by population density and, before the 2004 Housing Act became law, local authorities had acquired powers to regulate the fit between the premises and the number of occupants, to introduce registration schemes and to require the person managing an HMO to observe specified management standards. The 1997 Housing (Fire Safety in Houses in Multiple Occupation) Order placed a duty on local authorities to ensure that fire safety measures were adequate in all HMOs of three storeys or above.

Who lives in houses in multiple occupation?

The legal definition of an HMO is complicated (see Wilson, 2010b), but the basic idea relates to a dwelling being occupied by persons who do not form a single household and the related sharing of bathrooms, toilets and kitchens. Today bedsits form a large percentage of HMOs and their concentration in 'student areas' caused concern due to the alleged problems that accompany such concentrations. In early 2010, New Labour made planning permission mandatory for houses to be converted to multi-occupation, but the Coalition government required planning permission only in areas where multi-occupation was a particular problem.

HMOs provide affordable housing options for some of the most vulnerable groups including social security claimants, those on low earned incomes, students, asylum seekers and migrant workers. However, despite HMOs offering the highest yields to private landlords (Lowe, 2007, p 10), standards are often poor. In justifying the compulsory licensing of certain houses in multiple occupation, the DCL (2005a, p 1) maintained:

> it is possible to find the very worst housing standards in HMOs and these tenants are most at risk from poor management. The most common problems associated with multiple occupancy

relate to poor fire safety standards, overcrowding, inadequate facilities and poor or unscrupulous management....

[In] all houses converted into bedsits, the annual risk of death per person is 1 in 50,000 (six times higher than in comparable single occupancy houses). In the case of bedsit houses comprising three or more storeys the risk is 1 in 18,600 (sixteen times higher).

The 2004 Housing Act

Although local authorities had powers to introduce licensing schemes for HMOs, they were permissive, not mandatory. New Labour's 1997 manifesto promised to introduce a compulsory licensing scheme for HMOs. This pledge was redeemed in Scotland in 2000 and the 2004 Housing Act placed a duty on local authorities in England and Wales – to be implemented through regulations – to ensure that prescribed HMOs in their areas were licensed. As Kemp (2004) has observed, the 2004 Housing Act represented a trade-off between property condition, affordability and homelessness: if local authorities enforced higher standards then rents might increase making accommodation less affordable and more people vulnerable to homelessness.

HMOs prescribed for compulsory licensing under the 2004 Housing Act were those of three storeys and above in which at least five people live. In granting a licence, local authorities have to consider if:

• the property is reasonably suitable for occupation by the number of persons or households specified in the application;
• the proposed licence-holder or manager is a 'fit and proper' person; and
• the proposed management arrangements are satisfactory.

Landlords letting property breaching the licensing provisions would commit an offence punishable by a fine of up to £20,000 and were liable to the recovery of Housing Benefit payments. Local authorities could also introduce an additional licensing scheme for multi-occupied houses not covered by the mandatory scheme provided that they supplied evidence on the need for such a scheme

In addition to licensing, the 2006 Management of Houses in Multiple Occupation Regulations applied to almost all HMOs. These regulations imposed a series of obligations on the person managing an HMO including the duty to take safety measures, to maintain water and drainage, to supply and maintain gas and electricity, and to maintain living accommodation in good repair. Duties were also imposed on tenants such as the prohibition of conduct likely to hinder or frustrate the manager in the performance of his duties. The penalty for breaching these regulations was a fine (maximum £5000).

The DCL commissioned the Building Research Establishment (BRE) to evaluate the impact of the 2004 licensing regime. It estimated that there were between 236,000 and 379,000 HMOs in England of which 56,000 were eligible for mandatory licensing, but there were still 23,000 outstanding licences indicating that local government has not been proactive in implementing the 2004 regime. Discretionary licensing schemes were rare, with local authorities stating that the main barriers to applying for permission to run such schemes were that 'the criteria are too narrow and tightly specified; lack of resources to research and compile the evidence; and uncertainty about whether problems will be deemed to be severe enough' (DCL, 2010m, p 8). The private landlordism review by Rugg and Rhodes (2008, p 104) stated: 'The Audit Commission inspection regime has recently found that local authorities do not score well with regard to their responsibilities relating to the sector compared with its other housing services'. Local authority neglect of private landlord regulation is revealed in the limited number of sentences made for breaches of the 2004 Housing Act – 175 between 2006 and 2008 (House of Commons, 2010).

Overview

- In the past, slum clearance was directed towards the removal of 'rookeries' and 'plague spots', regarded as a threat to the nation's moral and physical health.
- Demolition of unfit property was virtually abandoned in the late 1970s, but, in the 2000s, clearance returned as part of the Housing Market Renewal Initiative (see Chapter Nine).
- From the 1980s, both the Conservatives and Labour regarded private-sector maintenance and improvement as the owners' responsibility and state assistance for improvements has been targeted and reduced.
- New Labour concentrated on delivering the decent home standard in the social housing sector.
- Overcrowding is a neglected problem and the statutory definition of the problem remains limited.
- Multi-occupied dwellings are an important source of accommodation for low-income households and government regulation is aimed at enforcing minimum standards whilst retaining a supply of low-priced accommodation.

Questions for discussion

1. What problems did slum clearance create for the people who lived in the slums?
2. How did New Labour justify stock transfer from local authorities to registered social landlords?
3. What is meant by 'sustainable' housing?
4. Is the definition of overcrowding in the 1935 Housing Act an adequate basis for tackling the overcrowding problem today?

Further reading

Jones (1976) in *Outcast London* provides an interesting account of the impact of slum clearance in London in the 19th century. *Housing, the Environment and Our Changing Climate* (2008) edited by **Tony Juniper**, **Christoph Simm** and **John Perry** is a useful guide to sustainable housing.

Website resources

Overcrowded Housing (2010a) written by **Wendy Wilson** is a good overview of New Labour's policies on overcrowding. It is available at: http://www.parliament. uk/briefingpapers/commons/lib/research/briefings/snsp-01013.pdf

Sustainable Homes (available at: http://www.sustainablehomes.co.uk) provides information on green housing issues.

nine

Low demand and neighbourhood deprivation

Summary

- Low demand was recognised in the late 1970s as a 'difficult-to-let' local authority housing estate problem to be tackled by tenant involvement in neighbourhood housing management and design improvements.
- New Labour identified an 'unpopular housing' issue across all tenures. Initially it concentrated on improving 'human' and 'social' capital as solutions to the problems in 'deprived neighbourhoods'.
- The Housing Market Renewal Fund, set up in 2002, marked an acknowledgement that 'low demand' was related to housing market drivers as well as to neighbourhood deficits in 'human' and 'social' capital.
- Creating 'balanced communities' has come to be recognised as a potential solution to the 'unpopular places' problem.

Priority estates

Diminishing demand first received central attention in 1974 when a national survey identified 62,000 council properties in low demand; a surprising finding given the notion, current at the time, that there was a national housing shortage. In 1981, when an investigation of 'difficult-to-let' estates was published (DoE, 1981), Glennerster and Turner (1993, p 3) commented:

> the team concluded that the 'hard to let' label was a misnomer. What they were really observing was merely the most

unattractive end of the public housing market. They were the tip of a much larger problem of poor housing management.

In response to these perceived management problems, the DoE set up the Priority Estates Project (PEP). At first, PEP focused on centralised, fragmented administration as the most important cause of 'problem estates' with local estate management promoted as the solution. Existing housing administrative structures meant that 'estates deteriorated rapidly as a consequence of the remote, town–hall–based administrative system and the low level of direct services' (Power, 1993, p 202). Later, PEP coupled management decentralisation to tenant participation by promoting Estate Management Boards to engage tenants. PEP evaluation demonstrated modest achievement. Decentralised management systems were more expensive, but the opportunities for tenant involvement offered by such arrangements plus 'on–the–spot' housing managers produced improvements in some outcome indicators (Glennerster and Turner, 1993). Nevertheless, despite associated investment in physical improvements, the projects were 'swimming against the tide', their impact thwarted by the 'growing social disadvantages' that created 'intense management pressures' (Power and Tunstall, 1995, p 6).

Architectural determinism

In contrast to Anne Power's management/participatory approach, Alice Coleman emphasised bad design. Adopting Oscar Newman's 'defensible space' idea – characterised by a dearth of surveillance and numerous escape routes (Newman, 1973) – Coleman claimed that many problems in unpopular estates could be eradicated by design improvements. Her argument was grounded in a study of 4099 blocks of flats containing 106,520 dwellings and 4172 houses. Five social malaise indicators – litter, graffiti, urine and faeces, vandalism, and children in care – were correlated with 15 design features and significant relationships were identified. Dwellings per entrance, dwellings per block, storeys per block, overhead walkways and spatial organisation registered the highest relationships to social malaise. Coleman linked such design faults to the ideas of Ebenezer Howard and Le Corbusier. Such 'utopian planners' had failed to recognise the 'territorial imperative', inbuilt through human evolution, which 'has led us to produce a shelter with its adjoining piece of territory and to impress it with distinctive marks of identity' (Coleman, 1985, p 18).

The Estate Action Initiative and the Design Improvement Controlled Experiment

The Estate Action Initiative (EA) introduced in 1986 provided funds according to a central assessment of proposed local authority action. Management decentralisation was an essential ingredient for a successful EA bid and an element of stock transfer to homeownership was important. Compliance with central demands produced substantial central capital resources for estate refurbishment. An evaluation of six early EA schemes concluded that 'all the EAs were effective in achieving regeneration' but 'there was little evidence of estate-based financial management', 'little success in involving residents in estate management with residents often expressing only limited interest' and 'only minimal reductions in crime and incivilities' (DoE, 1996, p 1).

In addition to EA, £50 million was set aside for the Design Improvement Controlled Experiment (DICE) through which the number of flats with a common entrance was reduced, walkways were demolished and cul-de-sacs were converted into roads. Despite its methodological flaws, in particular her 'desultory' attempt to test for social factors (Hillier, 1986, p 39), Alice Coleman's work had impressed Margaret Thatcher. 'I went further', she said, 'than the DoE in believing that the design of estates was crucial to their success and to reducing the amount of crime. I was a great admirer of the work of Professor Alice Coleman and I had made her an adviser to the DoE, to their dismay' (Thatcher, 1993, p 605). A DICE evaluation (DoE, 1997, p 1) noted that all the individual schemes achieved some benefits, but that 'compared to the early EA schemes (the most relevant policy alternative) the evaluation suggests that DICE was not a more successful regeneration initiative (nor, at best, does it appear to be less successful)'.

During the late 1980s, there were signs that DoE officials were beginning to recognise an economic dimension to 'problem' estates. Guidance on EA bids started to emphasise the inclusion of job-creation measures and, via City Challenge and the Single Regeneration Budget, created in 1994, the specific measures targeted at council estates had to form part of a comprehensive and integrated package aimed at the economic and social revitalisation of the area.

Unpopular housing

The idea that 'problem estates' were caused by utopian planning and bureaucratic incompetence fitted well with New Right ideology, but this causal notion received a setback when Page (1993) identified similar problems in the housing association sector – chosen by the Conservatives to inherit local authority housing in part because of its alleged superior management ability. Page noted that, as housing associations became the major new social housing providers, they were under pressure to house homeless people and to produce more dwellings from each pound of government subsidy. They reacted by building larger estates, often through housing association consortia formed to take advantage of the economies of scale available from volume builders. He identified 'social malaise' on these estates and a developing 'difficult-to-let' problem. A later study of larger estates built by housing association consortia in the early 1990s confirmed Page's predictions. They were encountering difficult management problems and the percentage of people feeling unsafe on the street was 45% compared to the national figure of 24% (Manzi and Smith Bowers, 2004). Some housing associations were finding their estates 'difficult to let'. Media interest focused on the issue, with Dr Henry Russell Court, a 50-dwelling development in Newcastle-upon-Tyne, attracting particular attention. Built in 1996 at a cost of £2 million, it was demolished three years later due to low demand.

New Labour and unpopular housing

New Labour adopted the notion that 'unpopular' housing was not just a local authority estate issue. *Bringing Britain Together: A National Strategy for Neighbourhood Renewal* (Social Exclusion Unit, 1998b, para 1.2) stated: 'Poor neighbourhoods are not a pure housing problem. They are not all the same kind of design, they don't all consist of rented or council housing, and they are not all in towns and cities'. The report was an assessment of 'unpopular' housing across all tenures set in a neighbourhood deprivation context. It identified 1370 deprived neighbourhoods ranging from 50 to 5000 households with 44 local authorities having the highest deprivation intensities. In the absence of robust neighbourhood statistics, the characteristics of these 44 local authorities were compared to the rest of England, the limitations of previous policies were identified and principles for future policy were set out (see **Box 9.1**).

Box 9.1: *Bringing Britain Together: A National Strategy for Neighbourhood Renewal* (Social Exclusion Unit, 1998b): Summary

A comparison of the 44 authorities with the highest concentrations of deprivation with the rest of England

In making this comparison the report included indicators of deficient 'human' capital alongside income measures. Thus, as examples, the 44 deprived authorities had:

- almost one-and-a-half times the proportion of lone-parent households;
- one-and-a-half times the underage pregnancy rate;
- 37% of 16 year olds without a single GCSE at grades A–C (against 30% for the rest of England; and
- a quarter more adults with poor literacy or numeracy.

The limitations of previous initiatives to overcome deprivation

- There had been too many initiatives governed by too many centrally imposed rules on the distribution of the resources.
- Programmes had not been 'joined up' and there had been a lack of local cooperation.
- Insufficient consideration had been given to links beyond the neighbourhood.
- Community commitment had not been harnessed.
- What works had been neglected.

Future policy: Guiding principles

- Investing in people, not just buildings.
- Involving communities, not parachuting in solutions.
- Developing integrated approaches with clear leadership.
- Ensuring mainstream policies really work for the poorest neighbourhoods.
- Making a long-term commitment with sustained political priority.

New Labour declared 'no-one should be seriously disadvantaged by where they live' (Social Exclusion Unit, 2001) and that its aim was to 'narrow the gap between the most deprived areas and the rest of the country' (HM Treasury, 2000, p 1). Its 'gap' diagnosis placed emphasis on deficits in 'human' and 'social' capital (see *Box 9.2*). Deficiencies in 'human' capital would be rectified by area-based initiatives such as Sure Start – started in 1998 and aimed at pre-school children and their parents living in deprived areas – plus other 'action zones' covering health, education and employment.

'Social' capital would be augmented by a new initiative, the New Deal for Communities.

> ## Box 9.2: Human and social capital
>
> Human capital refers to the education, skills, health status and social competence an individual possesses that can be utilised to provide a future income and contribute to the public interest. In *Bowling Alone: The Collapse and Revival of American Community* (2001) Putnam defined *social* capital in terms of the collective value of all social networks and the inclinations that arise from these networks to do things for each other. The World Bank (2000) made a distinction between 'bonding' social capital, 'bridging' social capital and 'linking' social capital. 'Bonding' social capital relates to the ties connecting family members, neighbours, close friends and business associates. 'Bridging' social capital concerns the weaker horizontal bonds between people with different ethnic and occupational backgrounds, whereas **'linking' social capital consists of vertical tie**s between people and organisations such as banks, local government and employers. The different forms of social capital may be contradictory, for example, enhancing 'bonding' capital may limit 'bridging' capital.

The New Deal for Communities (NDC)

The New Deal for Communities was launched in 1998 and, by 2000, 39 'pathfinder partnerships' had been identified, each to benefit from £50 million invested over 10 years. Emphasis was placed on community involvement in diagnosing problems and promoting local solutions in the hope that such involvement would enhance community cohesion. Lupton and Fuller (2009, p 1016) contrast 'improvement' and 'transformation' approaches to neighbourhood deprivation stating that 'Transformation was not the original goal of NDC. In fact, the initial remit of the programme did not include housing, which was a later addition'.

At first, the extensive community involvement at the heart of the initiative seems to have produced delay and disillusionment in some areas. The first official programme evaluation identified concerns such as community engagement costs in terms of 'burn-out of key local community players; intra-community tensions; the demands placed on the time and resources of NDC employees and agencies'; and a dearth of links between 'needs and aspirations' and 'appropriate projects and outcomes' (ODPM, 2003d, p 1). The projects encountered the reality of 'community': young people resistant to more police, older people welcoming them; those in favour of housing regeneration, those against; 'insiders' of established residents against 'outsiders' – students and asylum seekers (Wallace, 2010).

As the 'pathfinders' matured, more positive impacts emerged from the national evaluation commissioned by the DCL. Coordinated by the Centre for Regional Economic and Social Research (CRESR) at Sheffield Hallam University, this evaluation was a sophisticated analysis producing many reports recording complex outcomes. A distinction was made between 'people-based' (educational underachievement, worklessness and poor health) and 'place-based' (high levels of crime, inadequate housing and a poor physical environment) initiatives. With regard to 'people-based' schemes the evaluation concluded:

> For only three people-related indicators is change in NDC between 2002 and 2008 greater than that which has also been observed in similarly deprived comparator areas: having a high score on the SF36 mental health index; having taken part in education or training in the past year; and thinking that health is worse than one year ago. (CRESR, 2010a, p 92)

On place-based initiatives the conclusion was:

> NDC areas have also improved relative to similarly deprived areas, particularly in relation to indicators for crime, dereliction and area satisfaction. And there has been a greater proportional change in the numbers of NDC residents thinking that their area has improved and expressing satisfaction with their area as a place to live, than has been the case nationally. But there has been less absolute and relative change in some outcomes, particularly those relating to community and social capital indicators, and there has been no change overall in the numbers of NDC residents who wish to move. (CRESR, 2010b, pp 83–4)

On 'social' capital the verdict was:

> While there has been a significant increase in the numbers of NDC residents feeling that they are part of the local community, other social capital indicators have improved only marginally. Across all community indicators, changes in NDC areas were similar to those in comparator areas; however, people in NDC areas remained less likely to feel part of the community, think local people friendly, look out for each other and to know most/

many people locally than counterparts in the comparator areas. (CRESR, 2010b, p 8)

Wales had its version of NDC launched as Communities First in 2001. It was evaluated by Hincks and Robson (2010) through a comparison of the extent to which first-generation Communities First neighbourhoods had improved between 2001 and 2008 relative to other deprived neighbourhoods. The evaluation mainly used economic indicators and found that, although house price differences in Communities First neighbourhoods and comparator areas had converged, the number of Jobseeker's Allowance claimants was significantly higher for Communities First neighbourhoods and, in terms of general economic inactivity, both Communities First neighbourhoods and comparator areas had improved to the same degree. Disappointing, perhaps, to the advocates of the NDC approach, but in both England and Wales the comparator areas were also subject to various special initiatives outside the NDC and Communities First programmes.

The Neighbourhood Renewal Fund

In 2002, the NDC was supplemented by a Neighbourhood Renewal Fund (NRF) targeted on the 88 most deprived local authorities and available for use by local 'pathfinders' in promoting 'joined-up' action by *mainstream* services whose earlier attempts to improve deprived neighbourhoods had been perceived as a 'fragmented effort' (ODPM, 2005e, para 4.97). Various local interventions would be synchronised by Local Strategic Partnerships (LSPs) and day-to-day service provision would be coordinated by neighbourhood managers, an extension of the local housing management idea. The aim was to 'bend' mainstream provision to achieve 'floor' (absolute) and 'convergence' (relative) targets by 'joined-up' thinking from mainstream services. Targets included increases in employment rates, reductions in burglaries and a reduction of the gap in life expectancy between the national average and the fifth of areas with the lowest life expectancy.

Up to 2007/08, the NRF spent £2925 million on crime and community safety projects, education, health, housing, and work-promotion schemes, but an evaluation commissioned by the DCL concluded:

> Hard, attributable evidence of outcomes and impact of NRF on service delivery, mainstreaming or contribution to floor targets at an area level is very limited, and will remain so until further work relating to evidence collection and impact evaluation is embedded within LSPs. (Cowen et al, 2008, p 6)

This evaluation criticised the programme because 'it could, and has in some places, become a process in "spending the cash" resulting in disparate and incoherent interventions, with poor strategic fit, that does not maximise the effectiveness or value of the Fund' (Cowen, 2008, p 73). A later report, including data up to 2006/07, was more upbeat. It concluded:

> change, as measured by indicators in the four domains of worklessness, education, health and crime, suggests a broadly positive, though mixed, picture in terms of narrowing the gap … but even where there has been greatest positive change … the most deprived neighbourhoods are still a long way behind. (Amion Consulting, 2010, p 40)

However, given the limited hard evidence of neighbourhood change attributable to the £2.9 billion spent and a widening worklessness gap, it was not surprising that, in 2008, as part of Brown's emphasis on 'economics first' (Houghton, 2010), the Neighbourhood Renewal Fund's name was changed to the Working Neighbourhood Fund and resources were targeted on improving employment in the 88 local authorities with the highest deprivation scores. The Coalition government abolished the Working Neighbourhood Fund.

Neighbourhood management

Neighbourhood management was trialled through a special initiative. The Neighbourhood Management Pathfinder Programme funded 35 schemes with most adopting a model of a professional team led by a Neighbourhood Manager accountable to a multi-service partnership including local residents. An evaluation of the initiative noted:

> Not all service providers have been equally involved, with some difficult to engage and resistant to influence. The Police and Environmental Services have been the strongest and most active partners, and consistently so. The next most engaged group of services include schools, Primary Care Trusts, local authority housing services, local authority youth and leisure services and Registered Social Landlords (RSLs)/Housing Associations. (SWQ Consulting, 2008, p 6)

Nonetheless, the evidence indicated that neighbourhood management was having an impact in making the areas cleaner and safer, and residents' satisfaction with the area had increased faster than comparator areas.

Moreover, it was exerting positive influences on a wider range of services and this 'is providing benefits in Pathfinder areas, even if the scale of change is insufficient to measure at a neighbourhood level' (SWQ Consulting, 2008, p 8).

Low demand

Just as the Conservatives had shifted focus from the specific pathologies of 'problem estates' to broader economic and spatial perspectives, New Labour's initial concentration on the dearth of 'joined-up' managerial thinking and deficiencies in 'social' and 'human' capital was also modified. The *Report by the Unpopular Housing Action Team* (DETR, 1999c) identified 928,000 dwellings as 'unpopular'. Amongst the reasons given for 'unpopular', low-demand housing were the relative economic decline and out-migration from certain regions and the fact that first-time buyers were bypassing particular areas. Although specific local drivers could influence demand, the risk of low demand was significantly higher in the Northern industrial conurbations. Nevin et al's (2001) influential study located a particular demand deficit along the 'M62 corridor'.

The Housing Market Renewal Fund

New Labour introduced a number of specific policies to tackle the problem of low demand:

- Having identified that new building in the North was exceeding new household formation the government started to reduce the release of greenfield housing sites in the North West and the North East to limit new supply in areas close to low-demand districts. According to Lupton and Power (2002), this would reduce the social segregation caused by people with choice leaving inner cities.
- The resources available for new social housing in regions experiencing low demand were reduced.
- The 2004 Housing Act allowed local authorities to license private landlords in selected areas.

The flagship initiative – the Housing Market Renewal Fund (HMRF) – was based on the premise that there was a housing oversupply, or at least a surfeit of specific housing types, such as older terraced houses, in certain areas. Its introduction marked a 'rescaling' in perceptions of what drives low demand: a shift in state concern 'from housing as an inherently local problem to housing as a sub-regional asset within the wider economy ...

linked to place – towns and neighbourhoods – which could determine access to wider social opportunities' (Ferrari and Lee, 2010, p 5).

Initially, nine 'pathfinder' agencies had access to the HMRF and, in 2005, three new 'pathfinders' were added. The 'pathfinders' covered about 60% of the identified low-demand stock and were set the task of closing by a third the gap between the level of vacancies and house values in 'pathfinder' areas compared to regional averages. The areas selected were large in relationship to other area-based initiatives with populations between 150,000 and 300,000, and they cut across local authority boundaries. The 'pathfinders' were expected to establish partnerships involving 'stakeholders' and develop strategic plans for whole housing markets based on detailed local studies that would reconnect 'pathfinder' areas with nearby functioning housing markets.

At first the emphasis was on demolition and subsequent new-build with a prediction that 400,000 dwellings might need to be flattened (Mathiason, 2004). This clearance emphasis provoked opposition on the grounds that improvement was far cheaper, communities would be uprooted and that part of English heritage would be lost (even Ringo Starr's childhood house was scheduled for demolition!). Moreover, almost at the time the 'pathfinders' started their work, house prices in low-demand areas started to increase – an outcome of accelerating national house prices linked to credit expansion and buy-to-let investors moving into the market. Rising house prices fuelled resistance from some communities affected by demolition: 'Why is demolition necessary?' they asked, and 'How will we find a better house with our compensation when prices are rising fast?' Some academics posed questions such as whether the initiative was an example of what Naomi Klein (2007) has called 'disaster capitalism' – the use of a crisis to promote profit – with, in the case of 'low demand', the crisis being manufactured (Glynn, 2009). Others regarded the 'pathfinders' as an assault on working-class values – appreciation of community and family and a house as an end in itself – by middle-class housing 'experts' concerned with housing as an identity statement and investment good (Allen, 2008). The term 'gentrification' – the transformation of a working-class area into a middle-class residential district – was applied to the market renewal process with Lees and Leys (2008, p 2381) claiming that it was 'state-led gentrification ... promoted in the name of community regeneration'.

In response to this antagonism and increased acquisition costs at a time of rising house prices, the 'pathfinders' backed away from demolition and 'by the end of 2008, the housing market renewal programme had refurbished and improved around 40,000 homes, built 1,100 new properties and demolished just under 10,000 properties' (Homes and Communities Agency, 2009, p 1). Thus, up to 2008, the impact of the HMRF was to reduce supply, especially in the social housing sector where much of the demolition was concentrated.

Given that housing market renewal is a long-term initiative and the 'pathfinders' started to intervene significantly only in 2004, the project is a 'work in progress' and evaluation is premature. Nonetheless, in the absence of a dedicated funding source (under Coalition government proposals 'pathfinders' will have to apply, in competition to 'economic' projects, to the Regional Growth Fund), it is likely that they will be rapidly terminated.

Up to 2006, house price growth was faster in the 'pathfinders' than in the northern regions (Ferrari, 2007). The proportion of difficult-to-let social housing was down in all the 'pathfinder' areas except one. In 2002, 28% of properties in all 'pathfinder' areas were classed as in low demand, but this had dropped to 6.3% by 2008 (DCL, 2009g, p 19). However, because evaluations have not used comparator areas, it is not possible to access the share of the improvement generated by the 'pathfinders' in relationship to the influence of the wider housing market and there has been a dearth of information on displacement of people from the 'pathfinder' areas.

Balanced communities

Over the last 50 years there has been a marked change in the social composition of local authority tenants: local authority housing has increasingly become the tenure of younger and older people, single people, single-parent families, low-income households, and households without paid work (see Table 9.1 and Monk, 2009). In discussing Bevan's mission to create mixed communities in council estates, Kynaston (2007, p 598) comments that 'this was not quite such a fanciful aspiration as it would come to seem, given that it has been estimated that in 1953 the average income of council tenants was virtually the same as the overall average income'. By 1972, the average income of household heads living in council housing was 56.4% of those buying with a mortgage, in 2008/09 it was 31% (DCL, 2010l). This change, often called 'residualisation', has also been reflected, but to a lesser extent, in the composition of the registered social landlord sector. Had social housing been dispersed throughout the community then this 'residualisation' may not have been problematical. However, concentration of social housing in particular localities has produced difficulties. Hills (2007, p 5) points out:

> Two-thirds of social housing is still located within areas originally built as council estates. These originally housed those with a range of incomes, but now the income polarisation between tenures also shows up as polarisation between areas.

Nearly half of all social housing is now located in the most deprived fifth of neighbourhoods, and this concentration appears to have increased since 1971.

Table 9.1: Social housing: Residents' economic circumstances

	Social tenants	Private tenants	Buying with mortgage
In full-time employment (men) %	38	58	70
In full-time employment (women) %	21	40	45
Hourly wage rate (men) £s	7.7	9.2	12.6
Hourly wage rate (women) £s	6.6	8	9.8
Equivalent net weekly income £s	205	250	390
Total wealth £s (median)	17,500	24,600	269,700

Source: Hills (2010)

Moreover, local authority housing is not a uniformly desirable commodity and numerous studies have documented how the formal and informal procedures for allocating council housing have led to those people with the most pressing housing needs and the lowest incomes receiving the least-desirable properties. Jones (1988, p 96) summarises the process:

> The result of this process of complex bargaining is to establish a clear hierarchy wherein offers of good quality property are most often made to those most able to 'operate' the system whether by political influence, by possessing a bargaining counter, or by articulacy and social acceptability. Conversely, property perceived by the allocations staff as poor quality will be offered to those least able to refuse, least articulate and least able to enlist effective support.

The mechanism by which low-income households have become spatially concentrated within the owner-occupied sector is straightforward. In the virtual absence of specific state assistance to working low-income homeowners, the market, strongly influenced by 'location, location and location', dictates that the least-desirable homes will be occupied by those with the lowest incomes.

The spatial concentration of people with low incomes: Why it matters

- Marked residential segregation by income is a convincing manifestation of social exclusion per se. It is simply wrong for people with low incomes to be concentrated in certain areas. They can become ghettos.
- If it is policy to concentrate on the *combined* impact of health, education, housing and employment opportunities through area-based strategies, then it is logical to try to mitigate the amalgam's impact by attempting to reduce the opportunities for such factors to compound at the neighbourhood level.
- Although one should be aware of the 'ecological fallacy', committed when area characteristics are held to convey information about individuals in these areas (an area with a high incidence of crime and poverty does not necessarily mean that the poor people in the area are the criminals), there is some evidence that it is worse to be poor in a poor area than in one that is socially mixed. Isolating neighbourhood impacts is difficult, not least because people bring characteristics to an area (Goering et al, 2003), and the British evidence on the impact of poverty concentration is sparse and inconsistent. Experiments in selling each alternative vacant house on estates have produced increases in property values, higher demand and more tenant satisfaction plus reductions in stigma, turnover and voids (Watkinson, 2004). Atkinson and Kintrea found the biggest 'area effect' was an area's reputation. On the basis of interviews with residents of 'mixed' and 'poor' neighbourhoods and with professionals working in deprived areas, they concluded that 'overall the research demonstrates that area effects are a daily reality constituted of norms and stories about what the people from an area can aspire to achieve' (Atkinson and Kintrea, 2004, p 453). However, Bolster et al (2004), using longitudinal data from the British Household Panel Survey to examine the impact of neighbourhood on adult income, found 'no evidence of a negative relationship between neighbourhood and subsequent income growth. This is true for one-year, five-year and ten-year changes' (Bolster et al, 2004, p 2). An evaluation of a number of reviews of balanced community initiatives reported mixed evidence on their impact on resident attitudes, outsider's views, crime and anti-social behaviour, positive effects on physical characteristics and residential sustainability but:

> The evidence reported by the reviewers indicated there was either no effect or negative effects of mixed tenure on social cohesion and that therefore tenure mix did not have any effect on social capital ....According to the reviews, mixed tenure did not produce change in income mix and inequalities, in job opportunities or

employment rates for social tenants (Bond, Sautkina and Kearns, 2011, pp.13–14)

Blair's Prime Minister's Strategy Unit (2005) itemised some 'area effects' in the UK (see ***Box 9.3***), but the most comprehensive evidence on neighbourhood impacts comes from the USA, albeit that its relevance to the UK may be limited because 'in the USA deprivation and poverty are more substantial; there is still racial isolation' (Katz, 2006 quoted in Tunstall and Lupton, 2010, p 27). (see ***Box 9.4***).

Box 9.3: Area effects

- People living in deprived areas are less likely to exit poverty than those living away from concentrations of deprivation.
- Living in deprived areas can help perpetuate worklessness as there are fewer employed contacts through which individuals can find work. Finding work through personal contacts is the most common route into employment.
- Educational attainment is affected by neighbourhood characteristics. Concentrations of deprivation in an area affect the mix of children in a school; children from low socio-economic groups tend to benefit from a more mixed school intake.
- The likelihood of using drugs is raised by living in an area where they are more readily available. Of heroin users, 65% say that their friends are all users.
- Furthermore, 48% of offences are 'peer-induced' (Prime Minister's Strategy Unit, 2005, p 35).

Box 9.4: The impact of concentrated poverty: Evidence from the USA

- Under the HOPE VI programme in the USA, public housing estates have been replaced by mixed-tenure and mixed-income communities. Studies of the impact of HOPE VI have demonstrated that the initiative has at least stabilised the areas and, in some cases, achieved considerable gains. Zielenbach's (2005) study, for example, found that unemployment dropped by 8.4% compared to no change in the city average, crime fell by 21% more than the city average and concentrated poverty declined significantly. Other research found an increase in business confidence and a positive impact on surrounding areas (Popkin, 2007). However, these gains were mainly achieved by changing neighbourhoods' socio-economic composition; only 19% of the original residents remained (Popkin et al, 2004). Better evidence on area effects comes from studies of those who moved out of concentrated poverty areas.

- Under the Gautreaux programme, established in Chicago in 1976 following lawsuits filed against the US Department of Housing and Urban Development, alleging deliberate segregation of African-American families via selection policies, families were allowed to move to a home in the suburbs or remain in situ. Rubinowitz and Rosenbaum (2001) examined the fortunes of the suburban movers compared to those who stayed in the city. Of the suburban movers, 75% were working compared to 41% of those who stayed in the city and 40% of the movers' children past the age of 17 were enrolled in college compared to 24% of the city children.
- A survey of residents in five HOPE VI sites indicated that the outcomes for residents moving into other neighbourhoods with the aid of vouchers tended to be good 'with improved quality of life, increased safety and less stress' (DCL, 2009h, p 26). The impact on children was significant with Popkin et al (2009, p 491) reporting that 'children in voucher households were more likely than children in other public housing to exhibit five out of six positive behaviours 62 versus 43 per cent'. However, there were no differences in employment rates, a finding that Popkin et al (2009) attributed to health problems related to mobility, although it must be remembered that many of the 'voucher households' relocated to areas where employment prospects were not much better than in their original public housing projects.

Creating balanced communities

Under New Labour there were four initiatives aimed at producing more balanced communities. Each of these is described in the following.

'Choice-based' lettings (CBL)

Creating balanced communities is a potential by-product of this scheme, which is mainly directed at changing the image of local authority housing by rebranding social housing applicants as active 'consumers' with more choice. Possible gains from CBL include higher satisfaction and lower tenant turnover and the prospect that new groups of 'customers', who might not have considered social housing as an option due to its association with 'need', will be identified.

Whereas an early evaluation of CBL discovered an increase in demand in almost all the pilot areas and an increase in interest from working households in several pilots (ODPM, 2004b), as yet, there is limited evidence of a positive impact in creating more balanced communities. Indeed, Barnard and Pettigrew (2004, p 6) noted that 'the introduction of choice-based letting systems has not led applicants to be more willing to move to areas they considered "rough" or unsafe'. Later research found that although in some areas CBL had increased the number of people from ethnic minorities applying for social housing, 'In general there would appear to be no strong evidence that CBL has had an independent impact on the share of social landlord lets to minority ethnic households' (Pawson et al, 2006, p 13). Nonetheless:

> There is no evidence that CBL has resulted in more ethnically polarized patterns of lettings than those arising from previous lettings systems where decisions on which properties to offer to which applicants were largely in the hands of landlord staff.... On the contrary most of the areas examined here have seen some diffusion of minority ethnic settlement away from existing areas of concentration and towards 'non-traditional areas'. (Pawson et al, 2006, p 13)

Housing Market Renewal Fund

This fund enables local authorities to upgrade existing properties, demolish others and replace them with new dwellings in the hope that a more balanced community may emerge. However, despite extensive research into the fund's effect, no robust evidence is available on its impact on the displacement of established residents into other areas.

New balanced communities

Section 106 of the 1990 Town and Country Planning Act allows local authorities to insist that a proportion of affordable homes be supplied in any new development thereby, as a planning approval condition, pushing developers into partnerships with housing associations to create 'balanced communities'. If implemented with enthusiasm then, over time, areas will become more balanced in their social composition and possible reductions in social housing availability to low-income households, caused by creating mixed communities in existing deprived neighbourhoods, will be mitigated. However, the supply of affordable homes via the Section 106 mechanism has been restricted (see Chapter Six) and its impact on 'balanced communities' has been modified by permission to provide the affordable housing 'off-site' (Monk et al, 2005).

Some research evidence indicates that engineered attempts to promote balanced communities have achieved only modest success, with little interaction between the 'market price' inhabitants and the 'affordable' housing inhabitants (Jupp, 1999; Ruming et al, 2004). Atkinson and Kintrea (2000) found that social renters and owners living on the same estates in Scotland had different levels of interaction in their locality, mainly because work and car-ownership meant that homeowners could interact with others outside the neighbourhood; renters conducted 60% of their daily activities within the neighbourhood, but owners conducted 75% of their activities outside the neighbourhood. However, the 'balanced' estates scrutinised had little time to develop community spirit – the evaluation of the Gautreaux programme in the United States revealed initial tensions that settled down over time. Moreover, in many neighbourhoods, the affordable housing was concentrated in particular parts of the development – as Gregory (2009, p 59) states 'the public housing component of a development is often in the darker recesses, overlooking the bins, in the least desirable part of the estate' – rather than intermingled with the 'market price' housing. It also needs to be remembered that there may be very little interaction between people on exclusively 'market price' estates and that benefits may accrue from better performance in primary schools, the availability of amenities prompted by the general affluence in an area and by a reduction in stigma. The Scottish experience of 'gro grants', available to developers in the 1990s to supply quality homes in low-cost areas, indicates positive gains from more balanced communities such as the absence of 'postcode' discrimination (Minton, 2002). Some support for the 'mixed communities' idea came from the evaluation of the impact of Communities First in Wales. In their evaluation, Hincks and Robson (2010) divided neighbourhoods into four types: 'Transit' (in which most in-movers come from less deprived areas and most out-movers go to less deprived areas); 'Escalator' (in-movers come from areas equally or more deprived but out-movers go to less deprived areas); 'Isolate' (neighbourhoods in which households come and go from equally or more deprived areas); and 'Gentrifer' (most in-movers come from less deprived areas). 'Gentrifer' and 'Transit' areas outperformed both 'Escalator' and 'Isolate' neighbourhoods in measures of improvement.

The Mixed Communities Demonstration Initiative (MCDI)

In 2005, Gordon Brown, then Chancellor of the Exchequer, announced a new initiative aimed specifically at creating balanced communities in existing council estates. He declared that 'overcoming ... "area" effects will require the transformation of neighbourhoods from mono-tenure social housing estates into communities containing a much broader socio-economic mix of households' (HM Treasury, 2005, p 147). The Mixed Communities Demonstration Initiative was described as a new and more comprehensive approach to tackling area disadvantage, bringing together 'housing and neighbourhood renewal strategies to reduce concentrations of deprivation, stimulate economic development and improve public services'. Its aim was 'to go "further and faster" than previous regeneration schemes by altering population and housing mix as well as making physical, environmental and service improvements' (DCL, 2009h, p 1). Lupton and Fuller (2009) placed MCDI in the 'transformation' category of approaches to neighbourhood change with poverty concentration identified as the problem and de-concentration the solution. Twelve demonstration projects were established in different locations and in different types of housing market. No specific public funding was allocated to the initiative and, in 2009, 'the demonstration projects were at different stages, but mostly at the masterplanning stage' (DCL, 2009h, p 12).

Crime and anti-social behaviour

The distinction between crime and anti-social behaviour is opaque. The DCL has claimed that:

> Anti-social behaviour includes a wide range of problems – and includes behaviour that is capable of causing nuisance or annoyance to an individual/s or the wider community.... This type of behaviour can include:
>
> - harassment and intimidating behaviour;
> - hate crime, for example racist or homophobic abuse;
> - behaviour that creates alarm and fear;
> - noisy neighbours and loud parties;
> - problems associated with people dealing or using drugs;
> - people being drunk or rowdy;
> - vandalism, graffiti and other deliberate damage to property;
> - rubbish or litter lying around, abandoned cars etc.
>
> These types of behaviour need not involve serious criminal activity but sometimes do, for example drug dealing or racially motivated abuse. (DCL, 2010n, p 1)

Tenure-related action

Surveys of housing managers and tenants on what makes certain estates 'difficult to let' and 'difficult to live in' have demonstrated a consensus on an important factor – the presence of crime and anti-social behaviour in the area. In 1974, a Housing Development Directorate survey showed that what is now called 'anti-social behaviour' was cited by managers and tenants as a cause of houses being 'difficult to let' more often than any other reason, and a 2002 review of the research evidence by the Social Exclusion Unit concluded:

> Anti-social behaviour destroys quality of life and contributes to fear of crime. It can result in people not going out or stopping their children playing outside. For black and ethnic minority groups the impact of racially motivated attacks can be seen as an attack on the whole community.... The impact on deprived neighbourhoods is particularly profound, as anti-social behaviour can rapidly tip struggling neighbourhoods into decline. (Social Exclusion Unit, 2002)

The incidence of crime is unevenly distributed between different types of area, with people living in low-income areas most likely to identify crime and disruptive behaviour as a serious problem (see *Tables 9.2* and *9.3*).

Local authorities have long held the power to evict a tenant involved in anti-social behaviour, but such action required the victims to give evidence in court and judges were reluctant to grant the necessary possession orders.

Table 9.2: Perceptions of Crime: 2001/2 and 2006/7

Crime a serious problem	2001/02	2006/07
In 10% most-deprived areas	31	28
Not in 10% most-deprived areas	12	8

Source: Adapted from DCL (2009i).

Table 9.3: Perception of anti-social behaviour by Scottish Index of Multiple Deprivation (% saying each is very or fairly common), 2009

	10% most deprived	Scotland
Noisy neighbours/loud parties	20	10
Vandalism/graffiti/damage to property	35	14
Rubbish or litter lying around	48	26
Neighbour disputes	14	6
Groups or individuals harassing others	28	10
Drug misuse or dealing	32	12
Rowdy behaviour	37	16
Abandoned or burnt-out vehicles	5	1

Source: Scottish Government (2010d).

The 1996 Housing Act extended the grounds for possession for nuisance or annoyance, stating that the perpetrator of the behaviour could be a visitor to a household and established that it could be in a locality as well as directed to a specific household. It allowed evidence from observers not targeted by the perpetrator to supply the evidence for a possession application and created 'introductory' tenancies for council house tenants and 'starter' tenancies (assured shorthold tenancies) in the housing association sector. If a local authority decided to operate introductory tenancies, then any subsequent tenancy did not become 'permanent' until 12 months after it started. If the tenant misbehaved at any time before this period ended, the local authority could evict the tenant via simpler procedures than possible under a 'secure' tenancy. The 1996 Housing Act also enhanced social landlord powers to use injunctions against anti-social tenants. A court injunction prohibits specified forms of behaviour and may be accompanied by arrest powers if the injunction is breached.

Anti-social behaviour orders

The 1998 Crime and Disorder Act introduced the Anti-Social Behaviour Order (ASBO) allowing the police or the local authority to seek *civil* court orders to control the anti-social behaviour of anyone aged 10 or over if actual or threatened violence was involved. An ASBO prohibited action likely to lead to a criminal act and enforcement was to be by prosecution for the *criminal* offence of failure to comply with the order. Acceptable Behaviour Contracts were also introduced. These were voluntary agreements made between people involved in anti-social behaviour and the local police, the housing department, the registered social landlord or the wrongdoer's school. The 2003 Anti-Social Behaviour Act strengthened the power of the police and local authorities to combat anti-social behaviour by removing the violence requirement and permitting 'dispersal areas' where 'dispersal orders' could be made to move on, or remove back home, two or more people under 16 hanging around without supervision. It also gave registered social landlords the same powers as local authorities to prohibit anti-social behaviour and all social landlords obtained the power to 'demote' tenancies providing less security and removing the Right to Buy. Initially, it was proposed that the 2003 Anti-Social Behaviour Act should include a clause to withdraw Housing Benefit from anti-social tenants, but this was not included in the legislation. However, the 2007 Welfare Reform Act included provisions for the establishment of pilot schemes to test applying Housing Benefit restrictions to families who, having been evicted for anti-social behaviour, refused to participate in a rehabilitation scheme. Such pilots became operational in eight local authority areas in 2007. ASBOs and behaviour-related changes in tenancy conditions were derived from the 'zero-tolerance' idea popular in the United States and appear to have been an attempt to forestall the potential cumulative impact of 'incivilities' by circumventing the often protracted criminal justice process. On relaunching ASBOs in 2006, as part of the 'Respect' agenda, Blair (2006a) said:

> spitting at an old lady on her way to the shops is and has always been a crime; graffiti is a crime and always has been….In theory, in each case the police charge, the prosecutor prosecutes and the court decides. In theory there is no need therefore to change these criminal law processes. Except that, in practice, it's not what happens. In practice, the person who spits at the old lady is not prosecuted because to do so takes many police hours, much resources and if all of that is overcome, the outcome is a fine. The result is the police do not think it worth it; and so it doesn't happen.

At first ASBOs were used sparingly, but their use accelerated reaching a highpoint in 2005 when the use of ASBOs started to decrease. According to some commentators, ASBO use has meant the bypassing of the criminal justice system and 'social landlords have become behaviour managers as much as property managers' (Burney, 2009, p 194). Between 1999 and 2008, 16,999 ASBOs were issued, of which 55% were breached once and 40% more than once and, if an ASBO was breached, it was breached an average of 4.2 times. Of the ASBOs breached at least once, 53% were given an immediate custodial sentence and a further 26% a community sentence (Home Office, 2010).

Conclusion

Low demand has many causes and, under New Labour, a remedy was put in place for almost every potential cause. Surestart, Health Action Zones, Excellence in Cities and so on were aimed at developing 'human' capital; the New Deal for Communities would foster 'human' and 'social' capital and improve 'place'; the Market Renewal Fund would build up physical capital; anti-social behaviour initiatives would promote social order; and the Neighbourhood Renewal Fund was aimed at coordinating these initiatives, and others, at local level.

In combination, these programmes were aimed at reducing the gap between deprived neighbourhoods and the rest of England, so that 'by 2021 no one should be seriously disadvantaged by where they live' (Prime Minister, 2001). Although evaluations of specific interventions covering different time spans are available, there is a dearth of up-to-date information on which to assess progress in narrowing the gap between deprived neighbourhoods and the rest of England. In order to improve the neighbourhood information base, the Office for National Statistics divided England into 'Super Output Areas' with the 32,482 'Lower Level Super Output Areas' having a minimum population size of 1000 and an average of 1500. An Index of Multiple Deprivation is available at 'Lower Level Super Output Area' level that combines a number of indicators relating to 'Income', 'Employment', 'Health Deprivation and Disability', 'Education, Skills and Training Deprivation', 'Barriers to Housing and Services', 'Living Environment Deprivation', and 'Crime' into a single deprivation score. This allows each 'Lower Level Super Output Area' to be ranked relative to one another according to their level of deprivation. The overall index and its constituent parts supply data on which trends in neighbourhood deprivation can be monitored. However, directly comparable figures are available only for 2004 and 2007. No official attempt to combine this data with earlier and later information to generate an assessment of the impact of New Labour's policies has been published. Indeed, perhaps in anticipation of failure, the 'narrowing the gap objective' was replaced by 'tackling deprivation' in the 2007 Spending Review (Houghton, 2010).

According to the Young Foundation (2009, p 5), 'the government's unpublished analysis of the Index of Multi Deprivation (IMD) still shows that "patterns of concentrated deprivation have remained largely the same for the past 25 years"'. This finding was reinforced in *Tackling Economic Deprivation in New Deal for Communities Areas* (Wilkinson and Noble, 2010), a study of the impact of the New Deal for Communities (NDC) on economic deprivation between 1999 and 2005. It concluded that, although absolute rates of deprivation had fallen quite significantly, 'at the Programme-wide level there is little change in the relative levels of economic deprivation in the NDC or comparator areas' (Wilkinson and Noble, 2010, p 5). In other words, if NDC and their comparator areas are taken as representative of deprived neighbourhoods, New Labour was failing to close the gap between deprived neighbourhoods and the rest of England. Data beyond 2005 is available on concentrations of worklessness, and one of the more disappointing outcomes of New Labour's area-based initiatives has been its failure to make an impact on this:

> in terms of both numbers of claimants and its geographic concentration, the situation in February 2009 was similar to the situation in February 2001. In this sense at least, the policies of the last decade have not in general succeeded in reducing the gap between the most deprived areas of the country and the rest. (Poverty Site, 2009)

Life expectancy is a sensitive indicator of relative deprivation. In 2010, the National Audit Office (2010c) examined New Labour's 2002 commitment to narrow the health gap between the most deprived areas and the rest of the country by 10% by 2010 as measured by life expectancy at birth and infant mortality. It compared the 70 most deprived areas with the rest of England and concluded that the gap has widened by 7% for males and 14% for females between 1995–97 and 2006–08.

Overview

- The labels attached to the problem now called 'low demand' have changed since the 1970s, as the focus in causal explanation has shifted from poor management, poor design and lack of tenant involvement in council estates towards a shortage of 'human' and 'social' capital in deprived neighbourhoods and then to housing market 'drivers' and 'unbalanced' communities.
- New Labour's initiatives, aimed at enhancing 'human' and 'social' capital, produced disappointing outcomes.

Questions for discussion

1. How have different social constructions of the problem of 'low demand' influenced policy initiatives?
2. What evidence is there to support the idea that it is worse to be poor in a poor area than in one that is socially mixed?
3. Compare and contrast the Estate Action Initiative and New Deal for Communities.

Further reading

Evaluation of the Mixed Communities Demonstration Projects: Baseline and Early Process Issues published by the **DCL** (2009h) includes a discussion of the possible impact of mixed communities.

Websites

The New Deal for Communities National Evaluation has produced many reports on the programme's outcome. They are available at: http://extra.shu.ac.uk/ndc/ndc_reports_02.htm

The Joseph Rowntree website (http://www.jrf.org.uk/publications) contains the findings from research projects on unpopular housing.

ten

Housing and social justice

Summary

- Social justice and social exclusion differ in that social exclusion refers to deficits in the human and social capital necessary to compete within the structure of a particular society whereas social justice focuses on embedded structural unfairness.
- There are entrenched class relationships, mediated via tenure, built into current housing pathways through the housing system.
- In the past, various types of discrimination, with contemporary resonances, have influenced the access of minority ethnic groups to good-quality housing.
- Gender differences in housing consumption have reflected a dominant patriarchal family model.
- People with disabilities have encountered barriers to independent living in integrated communities.

What is social justice?

Social justice is what philosophers call a 'contested' concept because there is no agreement about its meaning. At a basic level, social justice is concerned with fair processes in the distribution of goods and services. There are two broad approaches to assessing process outcomes. Current time–slice theorists view the existing social product as a collectively produced cake to be divided according to impartial principles. In *A Theory of Justice*, John Rawls (1971) maintains that rational people, behind a 'veil of ignorance' about their future life chances, will agree to join a particular society so arranged that social and economic inequalities are permitted only if they are 'to the greatest benefit of the least advantaged' (Rawls, 1971, p 102).

Thus, for Rawls, inequalities are just if they lead to improving the position of the 'least advantaged' to a situation better than that they would have obtained from an equal resource division. Equality is Rawls' starting point – inequalities require specific justifications. In contrast, entitlement theorists examine the historical processes by which a particular social distribution has occurred. Robert Nozick, for example, argued that a social distribution is just if fashioned through fair procedures, that is, by creating an object, barter between free agents or as a gift. If people attain resources by these legitimate means they are entitled to keep them but, if resources have not been so acquired, reparations are necessary (Nozick, 1974).

Social justice and social exclusion

The Commission on Social Justice, set up by John Smith when Labour Party leader, conceptualised social justice in terms of a four-idea hierarchy:

> First, the belief that the foundation of a free society is the equal worth of all citizens, expressed most basically in political and civil liberties, equal rights before the law, and so on. Second, the argument that everyone is entitled, as a right of citizenship, to be able to meet their basic needs for income, shelter and other necessities.... Third, self-respect and equal citizenship demand more than the meeting of basic needs: they demand opportunities and life chances.... Finally, to achieve the first three conditions of justice, we must recognise that although not all inequalities are unjust (a qualified doctor should be paid more than a medical student), unjust inequalities should be reduced and where possible eliminated. (Commission on Social Justice, 1994, pp 17–18)

The second and third social justice dimensions identified by the Commission relate to what has come to be known as social exclusion. They are concerned with the human and social capital necessary to meet basic needs and facilitate equal opportunities to become unequal. The resources to promote social inclusion can be supplied through collective assets without necessarily requiring the specific causal agents of an unequal society to make reparations for their past and current contributions to the exclusionary process. In contrast, social justice is about structured inequalities. As the report of the National Equality Panel (Hills, 2010, p 2) stated:

Most people and all the main political parties in Britain subscribe to the ideal of 'equality of opportunity'. The systematic nature of many of the differentials we present, and the ways in which advantages and disadvantages are reinforced across the life cycle make it hard, however, to sustain an argument that what we show is the result of personal choices against a background of equality of opportunity, however defined.

Why is social justice in housing important?

When the social justice idea is used to identify what is problematic, differences in housing conditions and housing wealth, if unfairly structured, become matters of concern. Moreover, such inequalities expose some people to greater hardship than others and, through the ways that poor housing conditions impact on health and education, impair capacities to compete in a market economy, thereby restricting equality of opportunity. In 2008, nearly 2 million children in England were living in poor housing conditions – overcrowded, in temporary accommodation or below the decent homes standard (DCL, 2010b, Table 813). Friedman reviewed the evidence on the interactions between health, education and life chances and, by connecting established relationships between poor housing and educational achievement with qualifications and lifetime earnings, he calculated that 'the bill amounts to £14.8 billion pounds in lost earnings forecast for this generation in poor housing' (Friedman, 2010, p 1). There is also evidence that it is not just the excluded poor who suffer in an unequal society, but the mass of a nation's population. Wilkinson and Pickett (2009, p 31) argue that 'inequality gets under the skin'. Self-esteem is linked to inequality and anxiety up the income scale so:

> If the social hierarchy is seen – as it often is – as if it were a ranking of the human race by ability, then the outward signs of success or failure (the better jobs, higher incomes, education, housing, car and clothes) all make a difference. (Wilkinson and Pickett, 2009, p 40)

The visibility of housing consumption, with is long associations with status (see Chapter One), is likely to be especially salient.

Social class

Examining the relationship between social class and housing is complicated by different interpretations of what class means. Marx thought in terms of a two-class model – a bourgeoisie owning the means of production and a proletariat without access to capital. In contrast, Max Weber (1864–1920) claimed that class refers to a market situation, with a class existing when a number of people share a specific causal component of their life chances represented exclusively by economic interests in the possession of goods and opportunities for income (Weber, 1924). In not designating capital-ownership as the decisive factor in social stratification, Weber opened the way to identifying a more differentiated stratification system. Weber's class notion was widely adopted in the 1960s and became the basis for compiling official statistics on the subject. Classification into five or six categories based on occupation became the norm and it was commonplace to find tables in housing textbooks linking housing conditions to class accompanied by commentaries based on the assumption that, because class was a determining force, *any* link between housing standards and class is unjustified. However, it is not sufficient to assume that the capitalist system, mediated by the state, is unfair. Such unfairness has to be established by exploring, on a historical basis, the ways in which housing market operations have perpetuated unjustifiable inequalities. Thus, this chapter is grounded in Nozick's notion of justice – it examines whether or not current housing outcomes have been created by *historically fair* procedures.

Tenure

The evidence (Daunton, 1983; Dennis, 1984) indicates that by the end of the 19th century homeownership varied from 60% in parts of South Wales to 5.9% in York, indicating that tenure did not totally replicate social class divisions. Tenure differences between the artisan elite and the middle class were, in part, a response to individual choice and local factors – support for self-help movements and an area's industrial prosperity – as well as a reflection of differences in social class position.

By the late 1930s, tenure had acquired an identifiable class relationship. Suburban homeownership was led by social classes I and II and the estates constructed by local authorities 'for the working class' became residential areas mainly for social classes III and IV, although a significant section of the skilled working class were becoming homeowners. A metamorphosis in the class composition of housing tenures began in the late 1950s, gathered momentum throughout the 1970s and snowballed from the 1980s. The owner-occupied sector diversified through the inclusion of more people from classes III and IV, whereas local authority estates increasingly became the territory of classes V and VI and the economically inactive. Until its revival from the late 1990s, private renting continued to decline, becoming the tenure of young, geographically mobile groups and older people who continued to live in the house where they had first settled.

Tenure and social justice

Between 1959 and 2007 the average house price increased by 273% in real terms. As Aldred (2010, p 2) comments, 'This is a huge increase – if the price of eggs had risen at the same rate, a dozen would now cost over £18'. In 2007, housing wealth was 42% of total wealth (Pensions Policy Institute, 2009), an increase of 20% since 1971. Hills (2010) estimated 'personal worth' in 2006–08 according to tenure. Households owning their home outright had median non-housing wealth of £75,000, rising to £285,000 including housing and £411,000 including private pension rights. Those buying with a mortgage loan had about £260,000 in total wealth compared to £18,000 for social tenants.

Homeownership involves a number of possible sacrifices. Many people with mortgages have been obliged to make a down payment on their homes involving reductions in living standards while the deposit is saved; in the early years, mortgage repayments are high relative to earnings and the mortgagee is responsible for maintenance. Homeowners are more prone to risk than in the past. Any sustained downturn in house prices or upturn in interest rates can have a marked impact on a homeowner's finances and, outside a national 'credit crunch' crisis, there has been little state protection against income reduction. Homeowner wealth has been modified by taxes such as Inheritance Tax and Stamp Duty Tax and the use of capital tests to determine eligibility for social care (the value of a house is taken into account in assessing residential and nursing home charges and this can result in rapid housing wealth erosion). Nevertheless, the historic gains from homeownership have been considerable and, in part, it was the state rather than the market that created the yield. The state planning system has restricted new house-building, thereby forcing up the price of existing dwellings, and, in the past, tax relief on mortgage interest provided high subsidies to homeowners who have also enjoyed exemption from taxation on capital gains.

It can be argued that the positive equity arising from real increases in house prices is illusionary: the capital gains made from house price increases above general inflation cannot be spent because, when a house is sold, the owner must buy a replacement property at the new, higher price levels. Nonetheless, homeowners can benefit from house price inflation in a number of ways:

- using enhanced housing equity to raise income often via equity-release products supplied by financial institutions – in the first quarter of 2007, for example, 6.3% of post-tax income resulted from housing equity withdrawal (Bank of England, 2007);
- house sale, then renting for the remainder of a life span;
- moving 'downmarket' as an owner-occupier – easier for those already 'upmarket';
- inheritance – providing the beneficiary with a home or a capital sum raised from sale.

The potential to use housing assets to reduce the requirement for state welfare such as pensions formed part of the rationale of New Labour's 'aspiration', declared in 2005, to increase the homeownership rate to 75% (HM Treasury and ODPM, 2005). Long-term tenants cannot benefit from positive equity and hence selling council houses with discounts based on length of tenancy has a historical justice rationale.

The injustice of positive equity is not confined to tenure divisions. The diversity *within* homeownership means that the capital gains it produces depend on a number of variables such as when the house was purchased, its location and its quality. Thus, the wealth of households owning a property outright – median £411,000 – included a tenth with more than £1.23 million (Hills, 2010). Wealth distribution is much more unequal than income distribution having a Gini coefficient of 67 in 2003 (the latest available estimate) compared to 34 for disposable income. In contemplating the viability of equity release to boost the incomes of future pensioners, the Pensions Policy Institute (2009) estimated the housing wealth of people over 50: 62% of the wealth was held by the richest 30%, only 3% by the poorest 30%. There is also a 'positional' element in housing consumption, with value relational to other people's consumption. Thomas and Dorling (2004, p 12) calculated that, between 1983 and 2003, house prices increased twentyfold in the most expensive areas whereas prices doubled in the least expensive areas. The potential restrictions on where people can live associated with such differential price hikes has implications for the self-esteem arguments advanced by Wilkinson and Pickett (2009).

Following the 'credit crunch', the spectre of negative equity reappeared. At the end of 2008, after house prices had fallen nationally by about 18% from their peak a year previously, it was estimated that 900,000 households were in negative equity (Council of Mortgage Lenders, 2009), but the 2009/10 recovery in house prices reduced the problem.

Land

The 1945 Labour Party manifesto stated that 'Labour believes in land nationalisation and will work towards it', but, in power, Labour concentrated on taxing the development gain arising from planning permission. 'Old' Labour attempted to tax 'betterment' value – the difference between the land value with an existing use and its value with planning permission – in each of its periods of office. In 1967 it set up a Land Commission with powers to acquire land and collect a Betterment Levy – initially 40% of development value. The 1976 Development Land Tax imposed an 80% tax on development gain after the first £160,000. Subsequent Conservative governments repealed each Labour measure and so the community received meagre benefit from the substantial increases in land values arising from planning permission.

The landownership pattern in the UK is opaque, but Cahill's extensive investigation into landownership has cast some light on the issue (Cahill, 2001). About 6000 landowners, mainly aristocrats, but including some large institutions and the Crown, own about two thirds of the land and, according to Cahill, a high proportion of the land available for residential development is almost wholly owned by aristocrats who make substantial gains from land sales. As Ferdinand Mount (2004, p 290), former policy advisor to Margaret Thatcher, has commented, land release 'is strongly reminiscent of the way De Beers keeps up the price of diamonds, by controlling the supply and releasing gems onto the market in carefully calculated batches so that the price is never in danger of collapse'. Landowner constraints on land release have been compounded by the planning system, which allows established local residents, assisted by national lobby groups such as the Campaign to Protect Rural England, to resist new developments (Satsangi et al, 2010).

Figures on residential land values are set out in ***Table 10.1***. Viewed in relationship to houses built per hectare they reveal that, in early 2008, land cost per dwelling in England was £90,772, but, had the lower densities in the late 1990s been applied producing more family homes with gardens, the land cost per dwelling would have been £159,759.

Gender

Promoting gender equality was the remit of the Equal Opportunities Commission until 2007 when this commission, with the Disability Rights Commission and the Commission for Racial Equality (CRE), were merged to form the Equality and Human Rights Commission (EHRC) with responsibility to 'protect, enforce and promote equality across the seven "protected" characteristics – age, disability, gender, race, religion

Table 10.1: Residential land prices, 1994–2010

	Weighted average valuation per hectare (£s), England	Mean density: units/ hectare, England	Weighted average valuation per hectare (£s), London	Mean density: units/hectare, London
1994	731,168	24	1,912,127	44
1995	812,328	24	2,107,732	48
1996	816,828	25	2,104,519	56
1997	921,268	25	2,486,641	51
1998	1,098,965	25	3,059,363	53
1999	1,223,258	25	3,484,825	56
2000	1,514,824	25	4,244,864	56
2001	1,851,505	25	5,410,990	48
2002	2,208,962	27	6,827,319	59
2003	2,609,072	34	7,820,462	85
2004	3,114,430	39	8,138,131	98
2005	3,242,182	40	8,351,342	106
2006	3,503,514	41	9,122,050	95
2007	3,741,677	44	9,322,052	76
2008	3,993,961	44	10,497,978	122
2009	2,688,326	45	7,014,038	120
2010	2,360,338	n/a	6,283,593	n/a

Source: DCL (2010o).

and belief, sexual orientation and gender reassignment' (EHRC, 2009). The 2010 Equality Act was an attempt to synchronise and strengthen discrimination law and promote progress on equality. Existing law on discrimination was consolidated, strengthened and extended to the seven 'protected' characteristics covered by the EHRC. Section 149 of the 2010 Equality Act contained clauses requiring a 'public authority' not only to 'eliminate discrimination', but also to 'advance equality of opportunity between persons who share a relevant protected characteristic and persons who do not share it' and to 'remove or minimise disadvantages suffered by persons who share a relevant protected characteristic'. It also contained a clause requiring public authorities to have due regard to the desirability of reducing socio-economic disadvantage, in line with ministerial guidance. Thus, although the Coalition government has concerns about the socio-economic disadvantage clause, in theory, all inequality dimensions – with 'socio-economic disadvantage' perhaps a surrogate for class – have been incorporated into a harmonised public authority duty that, in future, may lead to a more comprehensive consideration of how different dimensions of inequality interact.

Gender inequality in housing now forms part of the political and academic agenda, but in the early 1960s, almost all housing discourses assumed that policy should be focused on the 'patriarchal family'. The term 'patriarchal family' was devised by a section of the feminism movement to conceptualise the relationships involved in the ideal family form, promoted in the 19th and 20th centuries as the 'natural' household structure (see Chapter One). Some feminists argued that, rather than accepting this family form as society's basic building block, it is necessary to disaggregate its structure to assess its impact on women's life chances. Such disaggregation is a difficult task. In the past, data compilation seldom incorporated a gender dimension and, even today, the family is regarded as a private area in which relationships are negotiated on a voluntary basis. Thus, gender divisions in housing consumption, such as a study or workroom for many men but for few women, have received scant attention in the housing literature.

One way into the gender and housing issue is to consider the position of women who form separate households. As Morris and Winn (1990, p 180) argue:

> Most women will go through stages in their lives when they either wish to, or are forced to, be part of a household where there is not a man present – such as younger single women, women experiencing relationship breakdown, and older women. The opportunities and constraints for all women are therefore indicated by the housing experiences of the 25% of households which, at any one point in time, are headed by a woman.

Single women

The 1975 Sex Discrimination Act made it illegal to discriminate against a person, directly and indirectly, on grounds of their sex. This Act helped to reduce such practices as refusing to accept a woman's salary for a mortgage because of insecurity due to possible pregnancy – direct discrimination – and mortgage providers insisting that only people who worked full time could be given a mortgage – indirect discrimination because it is more likely to have an adverse effect on women. In 2006, although the gender gap was closing, fewer single women than single men – 42% compared to 51% – were owner-occupiers, mainly because women receive lower pay. Moreover, as Gilroy and Woods (1994, p 34) have pointed out, 'the British form of home ownership with mortgages which bear down heavily in the early years, favours high or dual earners and therefore generally not women'.

Single women appear to have a lower homelessness risk than single men. A 1993 survey of single homeless people found that 'the great majority of single homeless people interviewed were men ... 23% of people in hostels and Bed and Breakfasts were women as were only 7% in day centres and 13% on soup runs' (Anderson et al, 1993, p ix). However, Watson and Austerberry (1986) have argued that female homelessness is not less common than male homelessness, it is simply less conspicuous. Women are more likely to experience homelessness in private – sleeping on a friend's floor for example – than in public. They will strive to avoid becoming street homeless due to the attendant risks of rape, harassment and violence.

Lone parents

In 2008, 22% of children lived in a one-parent family and a woman headed nine out of 10 lone-parent households. The housing circumstances of lone parents are set out in **Table 10.2**. The high proportion of lone mothers living in the social housing sector is the outcome of a number of factors. A job is a route from restricted housing choices, but, in 2009, only 56.7% of lone parents were in work – a consequence, in part, of the spatial segregation of lone parenthood in metropolitan areas where good jobs are relatively scarce, lone parents' relative lack of marketable skills, and affordable childcare shortages. Even when in work, lone mothers are likely to have a low income, which, in part, explains the low economic inactivity rate of lone parents. In 2009, there was a gender gap of 12.2% between the hourly pay rates of men and women working full time, rising from 5% for those under 30 to 27% when workers are aged 40 (EHRC, 2010). Clapham et al (1990) showed that, following separation and divorce, men were more likely to be in owner-occupation than women, and Feijten and van Ham (2010) have demonstrated that the adverse impacts of divorce and separation on 'housing careers' are long-lasting. In 2001, 42% of lone fathers compared to 25% of lone mothers were buying a home with a mortgage.

Losing a home because of domestic violence is a further reason why lone parents are more likely to be found in the social housing sector. There are a number of procedures available to enable a victim of domestic violence to remain in their home and to remove the perpetrator, but these can be difficult to enforce. Thus, the most viable option for many women needing to escape from domestic violence is to seek temporary accommodation through the homelessness legislation with a view to securing permanent housing in the social housing sector.

Table 10.2: *Lone-parent families: Housing profile*

	Lone-parent families (%)	Other families (%)
Tenure		
Owner-occupied	35	77
'Social' housing	44	12
Private rented	21	11
Accommodation		
Detached house	8	28
Semi-detached house	30	37
Terraced house	40	28
Flat or maisonette	22	7
One or more rooms below the bedroom standard	9	4
With non-decent homes	33	31
Serious disrepair	17	13[1]
% of homelessness applications	49	20
'Worst' neighbourhoods	20	12[1]

Notes: In 2007, 15% of lone parents living in England were dissatisfied with the area in which they lived compared to 8% of couples with children, and, in Scotland, 54% of lone parents with children aged around 10 months lived in areas of high deprivation compared to 18% of couples.

[1] All households with children.

Sources: DCL (2009i, 2010k), Office for National Statistics (2009) and Growing Up in Scotland (2009).

Women, housing design and planning

Some feminists have explored the implications of male dominance in architecture and planning for the everyday lives of women. Roberts (1991) notes the low level of female representation on the committees that determined the design of working-class housing (Tudor Walters Committee, 1918; Central Housing Advisory Committee, 1944), and the ways that patriarchal family forms have been reflected in housing layouts such as the absence of adequate space in which children can play and the reluctance to include labour-saving amenities in working-class housing. However, attempts to change basic domestic living patterns have been unsuccessful. Colonies, established by Robert Owen between 1821 and 1845, based on cooking rotas and communal nurseries, were short-lived, although this may have been due to domestic labour being collectivised but not divided equally between men and women. Unwin and Parker, two pioneers of the Garden City, included communal kitchens in two areas of Letchworth, but proposals to include such facilities in working-class estates, when investigated in 1919 by the Women's Sub-Committee of the Tudor Walters Committee, found limited support from women. Burgess (2008, p 12) notes that 'planning policy has tended to ignore the fact that women and men use public space differently and have different concerns about how it meets their needs', citing as examples more complex journeys with 'trip chains' to childcare, schools, work and shops, plus after-dark safety concerns.

Ethnicity

Ethnicity refers to the characteristics that connect a particular group or groups of people to each other. It is self-perceived and people can belong to more than one ethnic group. Thus, an ethnic group is a social group whose members have the following characteristics:

- they share a sense of common origins;
- they identify with a common and distinctive history and destiny; and
- they feel a sense of unique collective solidarity.

Although 'race' is often used as a surrogate for ethnicity, it is usually used to refer to people who are believed to belong to the same genetic stock. However, since most biologists doubt that there are important genetic differences between 'races' of human beings, in this chapter 'race' will be interpreted as a socially constructed term. A note of caution also needs to be attached to the ethnicity idea. In completing questions related to ethnicity, people have to assign themselves to a category – despite 'other' appearing in the list. Thus, the ethnicity category may not conform to personal perceptions and ethnicity is likely to be far more diverse than officially recorded.

Differences in housing outcomes

Box 10.1 examines the relationship between ethnicity and homelessness. **Table 10.3** sets out the statistical evidence on differences in housing outcomes according to ethnicity.

Box 10.1: Ethnicity and homelessness

The relationship between ethnicity and homelessness illustrates the multiple, interacting factors involved in producing housing outcomes. People with minority ethnic backgrounds are about three times more likely to become statutory homeless than the white majority (Gervais and Rehman, 2005), although this disparity may be an underestimate because there is evidence to suggest that minority ethnic groups may be less likely to contact their local authority for help. Although part of the recorded difference is explainable by settlement patterns – proportionately more people from minority ethnic groups live in London where homelessness is higher – in all regions minority ethnic groups are more likely to become homeless.

Factors such as pregnancy involving family disputes, relationship breakdown sometimes connected to domestic violence, overcrowding and having to leave private rented accommodation, common 'trigger' causes of homelessness across all ethnicities, affect the array of ethnic communities in different ways. With regard to South Asian and Black Caribbean communities, Gervais and Rehman (2005, p 6) summarise these differences as:

- Among South Asians, domestic violence, forced marriages and family disputes were the main causes of homelessness among single female-headed households. The most common cause of homelessness amongst South Asian couples with children was being forced by private landlords to leave their accommodation. Overcrowding was a common housing need; many South Asian households lived in large three-generational households before becoming homeless.
- Among Black Caribbeans, many young, single women became homeless when pregnancy led to family disputes, overcrowding, and family and friends no longer able to accommodate them. Homelessness due to multiple and complex problems related to child abuse, time in care, drug abuse, school exclusion, crime and mental health problems was also present. Other less common causes included being forced to leave private rented accommodation, domestic violence and financial difficulties leading to rent arrears.

In explaining these outcomes some commentators have used the concept of 'racist discrimination', defined by the United Nations as:

Table 10.3: *Ethnicity and housing outcomes*

	White British	African Caribbean	Indian	Bangladeshi	Pakistani	Black African[1]
% of total population (2007)	79	1.2	2.4	0.65	1.7	1.35
Tenure						
Owner-occupier	70	43	68	38	65	22
Renting from private landlord	8	7	21	20	20	27
Social rented	17	50	11	49	17	50
Overcrowded by bedroom standard (2007)	2	7	7	27	18	15
Below 'decent' standard (2006)[2]	25	29	29	29	29	29
Without central heating (children) (2001)	5.6	4.6	4.4	8.7	18.5	n/a
Flat or maisonette (2001)	12	48	14	38	36	n/a
Statutory homeless (% of total, 2009)[3]	69	14	6	6	6	14
Dissatisfied with area (2009)	17	18	16	16	20	22
Troublesome teenagers a problem (2008/09)	8.5	15	13.7	18	18	11.7
General level of crime a problem (2008/09)	5.9	16	13.9	13.8	13.8	12.9
Racial or religious harassment a problem (2008/09)	1.1	3.1	1.8	2.7	2.7	3.2
Dissatisfied with accommodation (2007)	6	14	9	25	9	32

Notes: All figures relate to England. Where the figure given for Bangladeshi, Indian and Pakistani households is the same it is because separate figures are not available for each community.
[1] The category 'Black African' includes people with origins in over 50 countries including Ghana, Nigeria, Somalia, Angola and Zaire.
[2] The figure given for each ethnic minority is the average for all ethnic minorities.
[3] Homeless statistics identify only 'White', 'Black or Black British' and 'Asian or Asian British'

Sources: Adapted from DCL (2009j, 2009k, 2010l, 2010p).

any distinction, exclusion, restriction or preference based on race, colour, descent, or national or ethnic origin which has the purpose or effect of nullifying or impairing the recognition, enjoyment or exercise, on an equal footing, of human rights and fundamental freedoms in the political, economic, social, cultural or any other field of public life. (Office of the High Commissioner for Human Rights, 1989, Part 1, Article 1)

Ginsburg (1992), although careful to point out the interactions between the categories, makes a useful distinction between subjective racism, institutional racism and structural racism. The salience of these forms of racism in determining housing outcomes may be diminishing but, because housing circumstances change slowly, past discrimination affects current outcomes.

Subjective racism

Applied to housing, subjective racism refers to overt racial prejudice and discrimination by individual landlords, estate agents, homeowners and tenants. It can take a variety of forms such as racially motivated attacks, harassment, the steering of minorities to certain geographical areas and the refusal to sell or rent a property to a member of a particular ethnic group. Subjective racism by landlords and estate agents was investigated by Daniel (1968) who arranged for three testers, one English, one West Indian and one Hungarian, to apply for rented accommodation or to buy a house. Discrimination was found in 60% of the tests, a finding that was influential in the passing of the 1968 Race Relations Act outlawing discrimination in employment and housing. A test replication in 1973 found that discrimination had been reduced to 12% in the sales sector and to 27% in the private landlord sector (Riach and Rich, 2002). There was some use discrimination tests in the late 1980s as part of formal investigations by the CRE. Evidence of 'steering' – estate agents directing minority ethnic groups to particular areas, a practice common in the 1970s – was identified. In 1990, the CRE examined the practices of accommodation agencies, landlords and landladies, small hotels and guesthouses. Testers differing only in their ethnic origin visited agencies asking for details of accommodation, and testers with pronounced African Caribbean or Asian accents telephoned to request details of a property and, if told none was available, a white tester telephoned 10 minutes later. They found that 20.5% of accommodation agencies, 5.5% of landlords and 5% of small hotels and guest-houses discriminated against minority ethnic groups (CRE, 1990). In 2008/09, a DCL citizenship survey (DCL, 2010q) found that 6% of Indian people, 8% of Pakistani and Bangladeshi people, 14% of Black African people and 15% of Black Caribbean people expected to be treated worse than other races by a council housing department or housing association compared to 25% of white people (see Chapter Six). The figures for private landlords were 8% of Indian people, 8% of Pakistani people 11% of Black African people and 14% of Black Caribbean people compared to 4% for white people.

Racially motivated harassment is an important factor in restricting housing opportunities because apprehension about harassment restricts the choices available in where people live. The DCL citizenship survey (DCL, 2009l) found that 6% of white households thought that racial or religious harassment was a very or fairly big problem in the local area compared to 16% for Indian, 18% for Pakistani, 14% for Bangladeshi and 10% for Black Caribbean households. Women were particularly concerned.

Institutional racism

Institutional racism was defined by the Stephen Lawrence Inquiry (Macpherson, 1999, para 6.34) as:

> The collective failure of an organisation to provide an appropriate and professional service to people because of their colour, culture or ethnic origin. It can be seen or detected in processes, attitudes and behaviour which amount to discrimination through unwitting prejudice, ignorance, thoughtlessness and racist stereotyping which disadvantage Black and Minority Ethnic people.

The 1976 Race Relations Act extended the anti-discrimination legislation of the 1960s. Under the Act it became unlawful to discriminate, both directly and indirectly, on racial grounds. Direct discrimination was defined as treating a person less favourably than another on the grounds of race, and included segregation on racial grounds. Indirect racial discrimination was defined as applying a condition such that the proportion of persons of the victim's racial group who could comply with it was considerably smaller than the proportion of persons not of that group who could comply. The condition had to be to the detriment of the victim, and the discriminator had to fail to demonstrate that the practice was justifiable irrespective of race, colour, nationality or the ethnic or national origins of the person to whom it applied. Individuals who believed they were victims of discrimination could bring civil proceedings against the alleged discriminator through the courts. In addition, the CRE acquired the power to instigate a formal investigation into an organisation of which it had a reasonable belief that discriminatory procedures were being practised. When the formal investigation was complete, the CRE was obliged to prepare a report on its findings and, if it concluded that an act of unlawful discrimination had been committed, it could issue a non–discrimination notice. This notice could require the organisation to change its practices and gave the CRE the power to monitor these changes. If an organisation did not comply with the terms of a confirmed notice then the CRE could start proceedings to obtain an injunction prohibiting the respondent from continuing to breach the terms of the notice.

The indirect discrimination idea, incorporated into the 1976 Race Relations Act, prompted academic studies and CRE investigations into the practices of social landlords. The main findings of these investigations were that the formal and, more significantly, the informal processes involved in council house allocation and the activities of estate agents discriminated against minority ethnic groups. Under the 2010 Equality Act all forms of discrimination were brought together under a single code and the EHRC can conduct an inquiry into any matter that relates to sections 8, 9 or 10 of the 2010 Equality Act, namely equality and diversity, human rights or good relations between groups, without need to suspect that there has been a breach of equality or human rights. With regard to the specific duties of public authorities, the EHRC can conduct an assessment to test compliance.

Structural racism

This refers to the overall context of housing policy set by the government that results in racial inequality. Although academics and the CRE concentrated their attention on local authorities, 'national legislation has been influential in determining the location and quality of black peoples' housing opportunities' (Smith, 1989, p 49). Thus, for example, the Right to Buy has resulted in many of the most desirable council homes being sold on those estates 'populated mostly by white working–class households who benefited from the racialised allocation policies of previous decades' (Ginsburg, 1992, p 121).

Housing and the labour market

Examination of the relationship between ethnicity and housing outcomes shows considerable diversity between different minority groups. This diversity has led some authors to conclude that:

the operation of racism, elaborated in its subjective, institutional and structural forms, provides an 'easy' explanation for the development and persistence of racial inequality. The development of a more complex and holistic account of racial inequalities in the housing market must also address a range of other factors. (Law et al, 1999, p 42)

In the 1960s and 1970s, when the state had a major role in housing, it was reasonable to concentrate on state housing activity when considering housing outcomes. However, in 2010, 80% of the UK housing stock was distributed by market forces, that is, according to the ability to pay. Thus, explaining diversity in housing outcomes involves examining the market position of minority ethnic groups. *Table 10.4* sets out some of the economic and related educational variables that may influence the housing circumstances of minority ethnic groups.

The initial settlement patterns of minority ethnic groups were influenced by job and accommodation availability, and their homes became concentrated in the inner areas of towns and cities in London, the Midlands, the North West and parts of Yorkshire. Inner area economic decline had started before the newcomers arrived (which partially accounts for the pattern of initial settlement), but structural change in the economy accelerated this decline during the 1970s, 1980s and 1990s. Since 1977, these inner areas have been subject to a large variety of social and economic initiatives, but such policies have had only a marginal impact on the economic and the associated housing problems of inner areas. Thus, although there are variations in the unemployment and wage rates of different minority ethnic groups according to locality, a disproportionate number of people from minority ethnic groups remain in areas with limited employment opportunities and where pay rates are low. Moreover, a significant percentage of the people who have managed to become homeowners have only modest levels of equity in their property, which places constraints on their ability to move within the owner-occupied sector (Smith, 1989).

Sleepwalking to segregation?

In 2005, Trevor Phillips, then Chair of the Commission for Racial Equality, claimed that the United Kingdom was 'sleepwalking to segregation'. He defined an integrated society as involving equality, participation and interaction with no one 'trapped within their own community' (Phillips, 2005). He went on to say:

Table 10.4: *Ethnicity: Social and economic circumstances*

	White British	African Caribbean	Indian	Bangladeshi	Pakistani	Black African
% of children living on a low income (60% of median) after housing costs (2005) (UK)	25	37	32	73	57	54
Proportion living in most deprived areas compared to white = 100 (2001)	100	230	110	410	390	220
Free school meal eligibility (primary) (2005)	15.1	34.7	11.5	53.2	35.9	46.2
Economic inactivity rate GB (men) (2006)	16	20	17	28	27	18
Economic inactivity rate GB (women) (2006)	24	28	33	65	66	36
Median Wealth (GB) 2006–08 £s	220,700	75,500	203,300	15,000	96,900	20,600
% of pupils achieving 5+ GCSE grades A* to C with maths and English (2009) England	50	42	68	48	42	48
% of employees with gross pay less than 60% of hourly median (GB) 2006–09	13	12	12	26	25	14

Note: Figures relate to England unless specified otherwise.

Sources: Adapted from the Poverty Site (2009), Department for Education and Skills (2006), Tinsley and Jacobs (2006), Hills (2010), Office for National Statistics (2010c), EHRC (2010) and Platt (2007).

Residentially, some districts are on their way to becoming fully fledged ghettoes – black holes into which no-one goes without fear and trepidation, and from which no-one ever escapes undamaged.... Residential isolation is increasing for many minority groups, especially South Asians. Some minorities are moving into middle class, less ethnically concentrated areas, what is left behind is hardening in its separateness. The number of people of Pakistani heritage in what are technically called 'ghetto' communities trebled during 1991–2001; 13% in Leicester live in such communities (the figure was 10.8% in 1991); 13.3% in Bradford (it was 4.3% in 1991).

Phillips' speech sparked a controversy encapsulated in 'Sleepwalking to Segregation'? Challenging Myths about Race and Migration (Finney and Simpson, 2009) in which the authors questioned the facts on segregation, the causative notions attached to division and the significance assigned to separation. They claimed that 'sleepwalking to segregation' was a myth, basing their argument on local and national statistics:

- Evidence from Bradford demonstrating:
  Only 3 of the 30 wards in the district of Bradford have 50% or more of their population from ethnic groups other than White (Bradford Moor, University, Toller) and each of these has more than 25% White population. These are mixed areas rather than ghettos of single origin.... The number of mixed wards (which are conceptually opposite to ghettos) in Bradford increased from 12 in 1991 to 15 in 2001.... There is considerable movement of people from minority ethnic groups out of the minority ethnic areas of Bradford, such as University ward to elsewhere in the UK.... There is a movement of White populations on balance into the diverse areas of Bradford. In 2000–01, 185 more White residents moved to University ward from other parts of the UK than left it. (Finney and Simpson, 2009, pp 186–7)
- National figures showing:
  the spread of the population of each minority ethnic group has become more even and less clustered over time. This is true at each geographical scale: local authority districts, electoral wards and street-level census areas. This is indicated by the Index of Dissimilarity which for the minority ethnic population taken as a whole has decreased from 61.4 in 1991 to 58.8 in 2001. (Finney and Simpson, 2009, p 187)

Finney and Simpson also disputed the notion that ethnic minority separation was self-segregation, which was alleged to be implicit in Phillips' speech and contained in earlier reports relating the 2001 riots in Bradford, Burnley and Oldham (Cantle, 2001; Ouseley, 2001). In contrast, they pointed to the continuing socio-economic obstacles faced by minority ethnic groups wanting to move out of their traditional settlement areas, stating: 'Barriers to minorities achieving their preferred housing include racism, lack of affordable housing and housing market structures that may steer people of different ethnicities to live in particular areas' (Finney and Simpson, 2009, p 186).

Finally, they asked the question of why residential separation is not regarded as problematic when applied to the majority community but becomes a problem when applied to ethnic minorities? Is it because of the suspicion that residential clusters of ethnic minorities are 'dangerous places'? Was New Labour's concern about self-segregation and its abandonment of multiculturalism in favour of community cohesion a reaction to a potential vote loss in white working–class areas?

The Phillips versus Simpson/Finney debate illustrates the complexities, uncertainties and politics surrounding the segregation issue. Segregation is an ambiguous concept and its measurement is fraught with difficulties. Thus, for example, the Index of Dissimilarity used by Finney and Simpson is a measure that identifies the average situation without any intimation of variation about that figure, and it therefore conceals considerable disparities (see Poulsen et al, 2009). Then there is the vexed causation issue. Finney and Simpson (2009, p 118) make a distinction between voluntary, 'good' separation and enforced, 'bad' segregation. However, 'agency', 'choice' and 'structure', as influences on residential patterns, are difficult to disconnect. The current specific settlement patterns of minority ethnic groups are the product of historical factors such as employment opportunities, income, various forms of racism and the choices made by members of minority ethnic communities. Initial migration was influenced by the community networks in the country of origin, with kinship and local affiliations affecting the places where people settled in the UK. Thus, for example, the 1962 'voucher system', whereby employers in the UK could apply for vouchers to admit workers for specific jobs, gave the opportunity for those who were already in Britain to arrange jobs and vouchers for their relatives and friends. Over time, the pull of identity and the push of constraints created areas where many members of minority ethnic groups felt secure, at ease, at home and, hence, reluctant to leave. The 2008/09 citizen survey (DCL, 2009l) found that 85% of people from the Pakistani community, 82% from the Indian community, 78% of Afro-Caribbeans and 83% of Bangladeshis strongly felt they belonged to their neighbourhoods compared to 77% of whites. A study by Phillips et al (2008, p 94), based on interviews in Oldham and Rochdale, concluded: 'Our research indicates that many white and Asian young adults still identify and favour areas partly in terms of their ethnic composition in ways that might encourage clustering'.

Nonetheless, attitudes were changing, epitomised by the comment of a young Pakistani woman:

> I would look for different things than my mum and dad would look for....We want a nice area. My mum and dad, they want an Asian community. I would want nice scenery, a nice spacious garden or something like that. (quoted in Phillips et al, 2008, p 89)

The debate on ethnicity and housing has tended to be polarised between those who emphasise 'constraint', 'discrimination' and 'structure' and those who concentrate on 'agency', 'choice' and self-segregation, but the issue has always been more complicated and is becoming more intricate. 'Structure' and 'agency' interact and there are gender, class, generational and specific spatial dimensions to housing outcomes (Housing Corporation, 2008; Markkanen, 2009; Radcliffe, 2009).

Disability

In the 1970s, a social justice paradigm, linked to the idea of social constructionism (see Chapter One), began to emerge that stressed 'identity' politics. It argued that social justice is not just a matter of command over resources, it is related to 'disrespect' towards a person's authenticity. It emphasised the importance of including marginalised groups in decision-making processes in order to strengthen 'identity recognition' (Young, 1990). Although 'identity politics' is pertinent to ethnicity and gender, in this chapter it will be elaborated with reference to disability.

What is disability?

Historically disability has been equated with impairment, that is, the condition of being unable to perform specified tasks due to physical or mental unfitness. This definition is related to the medical model of disability characterised by:

- a focus on the individual, specifically on the body;
- reliance on a strong notion of normality as being able-bodied;
- an emphasis on rehabilitation to ensure the disabled person is as 'normal' as possible; and

- the medical profession as the 'expert' on impairment and hence on disability.

In the 1970s, a different definition of disability emerged, which made a distinction between 'impairment' and 'disability', with disability meaning 'the disadvantage or restriction caused by contemporary social organisation which takes no or little account of people who have physical impairments and thus excludes them from the mainstream of social activities' (Union of the Physically Impaired against Segregation, quoted in Oliver and Barnes, 1998, p 17). This notion of disability as the consequence of a disabling process was embodied in a 'social' model that regarded disability as a set of challenges faced by people whose requirements have not been accommodated by the dominant culture. The social model generated two approaches to the disability and housing issue. 'Independent living' tended to stress the availability of cash benefits to enable disabled people to make choices about where they lived and the nature of their personal assistance, whereas 'integrated living' emphasised the collective involvement of disabled people in making choices about the overall pattern of accommodation. Section 6.1 of the 2010 Equality Act defines a disabled person as 'a person with a disability. A person has a disability ... if he or she has a physical or mental impairment and the impairment has a substantial and long-term adverse effect on his or her ability to carry out normal day-to-day activities'.

The pattern of housing provision for disabled people

For most of the 20th century, housing provision for disabled people was influenced by the medical model and the idea that disability was a personal tragedy to be mitigated by raising money to reduce the 'suffering' of 'the disabled'. Disabled people were hidden at home or lodged in state or voluntary-sector institutions. The advent of a community care policy in the 1960s started to shift this residence pattern, but, under the tutelage of the medical model, the accommodation was often supplied in 'clustered' or 'group' units. This spatial exclusion of disabled people was compounded by the tendency to provide adapted property on council estates. From the 1970s, the accommodation deemed necessary for 'community care' evolved under a number of different capital and revenue funding streams involving social services departments, health authorities, housing departments and housing associations. These income sources were often supplemented by Housing Benefit being used to meet the revenue costs involved in providing housing-related support. In 2003, an attempt was made to bring some order to the haphazard sources of finance for supported accommodation. The 2010 system is outlined in ***Box 10.2***.

Box 10.2: Housing and disabled people

Lifetime homes

In the early 1990s, the Joseph Rowntree Foundation developed the lifetime homes idea, with 16 design features chosen to ensure that a new house will meet lifetime needs. If all new homes were built to this standard then, over time, disabled people would not have to move to secure suitable accommodation and they would find it easier to visit friends and relatives. A few of the lifetime homes design features were incorporated into Part M of the England & Wales Building Regulations in 1999 and the concept was widely used by housing associations when commissioning new dwellings. In 2008, as part of its review of the implications for social policy of an ageing population, New Labour announced that by 2011 the lifetime homes standard would be mandatory for public-sector housing and that it was an aspiration that by 2013 all new homes would be built to this standard (DCL, Department of Health and Department for Work and Pensions, 2008).

Disabled Facilities Grants (DFGs)

This grant must be awarded if the relevant criteria of being 'necessary', 'appropriate', 'reasonable' and 'practicable' are met. It is provided for essential adaptations to be made that allow disabled people better freedom of movement into and around their homes and access to the essential facilities within it. It is means-tested but, in 2005, this was abolished for families with children under 19. The grant now forms part of the income streams that, in pilot areas, can be pooled to give disabled people more control over the support available to them. In 2009, the maximum grant that a council was required to pay was £25,000 in Northern Ireland, £30,000 in England and £36,000 in Wales per application, but, if the cost of the eligible works was more, the council could use discretionary powers to increase the amount. A different system operates in Scotland.

Supporting People

Over the years, social housing providers identified a requirement to provide support to some of their tenants in addition to the normal landlord role of repair and rent collection – help from wardens in sheltered accommodation is an example. Funding for housing-related support evolved piecemeal in the 1980s and, by 1998, the nine different funding streams available had produced a pattern of service provision that was 'seen to be uncoordinated, unrelated to local priorities and frequently provider and funding driven' (Foord and Simic, 2005, p 7). In 1998, the government announced that the existing funding schemes for housing-related support would be amalgamated into a single stream, to be known as Supporting People, and would be allocated to local authorities for distribution to a range of housing-related support providers mainly in the voluntary, 'third arm' sector. Supporting People would cover a range of circumstances including physical and sensory disability, homelessness, domestic violence, HIV and AIDS, alcohol and drug dependency, mental illness, learning disability, and old age.

Supporting People is distributed to local government according to a needs-based formula. The assistance has the advantage that, in the form of 'floating support', help can be detached from tenure and concentrations of dwellings for people with 'special needs' in particular locations. A downside to the programme has been a tendency for commissioners to purchase large-scale, generic floating support services that are not geared to the needs of any particular specialist group, and there is controversy about the loss of wardens in sheltered housing for elderly people (House of Commons Communities and Local Government Committee, 2009).

Given that the distinction between 'care' and 'support' is somewhat artificial New Labour's decision to end the 'ring-fencing' of Supporting People resources in 2009 may facilitate more pertinent 'care and support' packages and offers an opportunity to integrate housing support into the 'right to control' agenda – with its 'self-directed support' and 'personal budgets' – being developed within the health and personal social services domains. The idea of 'personal budgets' has been applied on an experimental basis to rough sleepers and, at a low cost (£794 per person in the first year), was successful in helping established rough sleepers to obtain and retain accommodation (Hough and Rice, 2010). The Coalition government reduced the resources allocated to Supporting People by 11.5%, but endorsed the idea of 'personal budgets'.

Despite the extra resources for DFGs, and the progress in providing more integrated housing for disabled people with the extra support 'floating' to the person rather than the person being moved to the available support, a number of problems remain. There are no routine procedures in place for assessing disabled people's requirements that can be matched against the suitability of existing provision to identify unmet needs and plan future supply. The limited available evidence indicates shortfalls in supply:

- In 2007/08, there were 1.5 million households in England with a medical condition or disability who required specifically adapted housing, with 20% considering their existing accommodation to be unsuitable (DCL, 2009m). The figures do not include those people living in institutions who could leave such care if appropriate accommodation was available. Thus, although New Labour tripled the cash available for DFGs, the waiting list for adaptations is long and, given an ageing population, is likely to increase – more than 70% of DFGs go to people over 60. The

Coalition government limited future resources for DFGs to inflation-level increases, effectively a cut in relationship to rising demand.

- Disabled people are twice as likely to be social housing tenants, less likely to own their own homes and more likely to live in 'non-decent' homes (Cambridgeshire County Council, 2009).
- 'There is a grave shortage of housing stock suitable for re-housing.... For families a wait of three years or more would be likely in 70% of all authorities' (Heywood et al, 2005, p 6).
- Access to the private landlord sector has been restricted by the limited space standards allowed in calculating the Local Rental Allowance (House of Commons Work and Pensions Committee, 2010a). However, in the June 2010 Budget, the Chancellor announced that disabled people would be allowed an extra room.
- Just over half of all homes met at least six of the 11 criteria for an 'accessible and adaptable' home, but only 110,000 (0.5%) of homes met all the criteria and the four features regarded as most important for accessibilty – level access to main entrance; flush threshold to main entrance; width of internal doors; and WC at entrance level – were present in only 3% of homes (DCL, 2009m).
- About 4.5 million households (21%) include one or more people with a reported mobility problem, the majority aged 60 years or more. Of 'vulnerable' private tenants (those with a low income or disability), 52% were living in non-decent accommodation compared to 35% of 'vulnerable' homeowners and 28% of 'vulnerable' social tenants (DCL, 2009m).
- Of families with a disabled child, 54% are homeowners compared to 69% of families with non-disabled children.
- Families with a disabled child are 50% more likely than other families to live in overcrowded accommodation, to think that their home is in a poor state of repair and to report problems with wiring, draughts and damp in the child's bedroom.
- Compared to other groups of disabled people, disabled children requiring specifically adapted homes are the least likely to be living in suitable accommodation and the majority of families with disabled children report that their homes are unsuitable for their child's needs and the associated needs of other family members. Often the home is inappropriate in a number of ways. (All figures and comment on disabled children and housing are taken from Joseph Rowntree Foundation [2008].)

Overview

- Social justice is about fairness in the distribution of goods and services. The idea has also been linked to the 'respect' given to different members of the community.
- Class inequality has been partially reflected in tenure divisions.
- Gender differences in housing outcomes have been influenced by the dominance of the patriarchal family form.
- Discrimination in the housing system, choice, location factors and economic variables have influenced ethnic variations in housing outcomes.
- The housing choices available to disabled people have been affected by the dominance of the medical model of disability.

Questions for discussion

1. What is the difference between social justice and social exclusion?
2. Distinguish between subjective, institutional and structural racism and give examples of their operation.
3. What have been the major objections of the disabled persons' movement to the dominant form and location of the housing available to disabled people?
4. What evidence is there to support the contention that gender inequality is reflected in access to good-quality accommodation?

Further reading

The relationships of class, gender and disability to housing outcomes are explained in *Housing and Social Inequality* (1990) by **Jenny Morris** and **Martin Winn**. *Race and Ethnicity in the 21st Century* (2010), edited by **Alice Bloch** and **John Solomos**, contains chapters on housing and policies relating to asylum seekers.

Website resources

A number of research findings relating to housing, disability and ethnicity can be found at the website of the Joseph Rowntree Foundation. Available at: www.jrf.org.uk

Social Policy Digest has sections on: housing; disability; gender and sex equality; poverty, inequality and social security. Available at: http://journals.cambridge.org/spd/action/topic?type=new&category=Social%20policy%20themes

eleven

Conclusion: housing policy – past and future

In 1944, Lord Woolton, Chair of the wartime coalition government's reconstruction committee, declared that he had reached the conclusion that 'the key to the housing problem is to build more houses' (quoted in Lyttelton, 1962, p 101). Until well into its second term, New Labour had equal difficulty in spotting the obvious and, overall, its house-building record was disappointingly poor. There was a four million increase in population between 1997/98 and 2009/10 with a 3.4 million rise in households (DCL, 2010b, Table 401). Until the 'credit crunch', loans at modest interest rates were abundant yet, under New Labour, UK house construction averaged only 187,000 houses per annum compared to a 206,000 average over the previous 13 years and a 270,000 post-war mean. When conversions minus demolitions are taken into account the record improves but, as Bramley (2009, pp 161–2) has commented, 'planning policy for new housing was, in retrospect, perhaps the most significant failure of housing policy in that period [early 2000s]' and, since 2004, 'one can see much evidence of good intentions by government but the evidence of achievement on the ground is disappointing'. It has been estimated that 'if current homes typically last 100 years then to replace the existing stock ... needs 266,000 [houses] per year' (Goodier and Pan, 2010 p 42). In addition, the DCL (2010r, p 1) declared 'around 252,000 new households could form each year between now and 2031 ...134,000 above current build levels'.

New Labour's housing dearth, when added to the slowdown in construction since the early 1980s, had weighty consequences. Had housing supply between 1997 and 2007 matched the EU average – the UK was building fewer new houses per head than every EU-15 country except Italy (Ministry of Infrastructure, Italian Republic, 2007) – house price inflation might have abated. A DCL study (2005b) indicated that an extra 100,000 houses per year would reduce prices by 12–14% over

10 years. However, supply constraints only partially explain the 1997 to 2007 house price boom. Although new construction makes a significant contribution to supply coming onto the housing market in a given year (about 11% in 2007/08) the market is 'made' by houses put up for sale from the existing stock relative to the demand made possible by credit availability. Charged by New Labour with controlling inflation according to the Consumer Price Index (which excluded housing costs) rather than a Retail Price Index, the Bank of England kept interest rates low. Between 1997 and 2007, mortgage debt increased from £419 billion to £1,131 billion (Grant Thornton, 2009). Enhanced credit availability plus low supply had a predictable outcome: the average house price increased from £60,754 in 1997 to £184,131 in 2007 (Nationwide, 2010) and median-priced homes were over seven times average incomes in 2007 compared to 3.5 times a decade earlier. This price rise had knock-on effects. Housing became more of an investment than consumption good, with the popular phrase 'getting onto the housing ladder' – only upwards – epitomising the mood. New Labour promoted homeownership as 'asset-based' welfare, with the notion that 'when individuals own homes they can get by on smaller pensions' (Castles, 1998, p 13). As the housing boom gained momentum, the Treasury (HM Treasury, 2004, p 96) declared:

> Traditional methods of aggregate saving, such as the saving ratio, often fail to reflect this variety [of asset-building activities] and to highlight the positive impact asset growth has had on households' balance sheets in recent years. Broader measures, for example, including capital growth, indicate that saving behaviour has been more robust in recent years than is often appreciated.

Private landlordism was revived, with the new landlords using rent as an income stream and capital accumulation as a wealth store. In 2007, the sector accounted for 18% of all house purchase loans (Housing Finance Group, 2010), about the same share as loans to first-time buyers, and households renting from private landlords increased by over a million between 2001 and 2010. High house prices also brought soaring land costs generating a hefty increase in what Crosland (1962, p 193) once described as 'the most undeserved of all undeserved wealth'. Increased equity in house-ownership affected housing politics. As demonstrated in Chapter Ten, rising house prices benefit only a proportion of the supposed beneficiaries, but this is not the electorate's perception: voters with paper housing wealth react badly to the notion that their asset is declining in value. Accordingly, New Labour's 1997 election campaign focused on the Conservatives' housing market management and promised to 'reject the boom and bust policies which caused the collapse of the housing market' (Labour Party, 1997, p 27). When New Labour's housing bubble burst, measures were taken to halt the price decline (see Chapter Three). Although mortgage repossessions increased they were well below the level of the early 1990s (DCL, 2010b, Table 1300). As a consequence, 'forced' sales, which depress house prices, were low and people with 'tracker' mortgages, based on the Bank of England's base rate, made lower repayments. The result was a return to house price inflation in the second half of 2009 that continued until mid-2010 when prices became more volatile. According to *The Economist* (2010), of 22 countries examined over the period 1997–2010, only Australia, South Africa and Ireland had higher house price inflation than Britain.

Laissez-faire

The conduct of the financial institutions, especially those located in the USA, in generating the 'sub-prime' mortgage expansion that precipitated the 'credit crunch' offers cold comfort to 'laissez-faire' advocates. Even Alan Greenspan, a firm believer in Adam Smith's theory of a self-regulating market throughout his Chairmanship of the Federal Reserve of the United States from 1987 to 2006, had to admit:

> I made a mistake in presuming that the self-interest of organisations, specifically banks and others, were such that they were best capable of protecting their own shareholders and their equity in the firms.... The problem here is something that looked a very solid edifice, and, indeed, a critical pillar of market competition and free markets, did break down. (Greenspan, 2008, quoted in Cassidy, 2009, p 5)

There was no rational supply–demand calculus driving the credit explosion that produced the banking crisis: it was the outcome of the fees to be garnered from each stage of the 'securitisation' process and complex financial models that confused risk, which can be measured, with uncertainty, which cannot (Hutton, 2010). Although the credit crunch in the UK was, in part, a consequence of events in the USA, UK-based financial institutions cannot escape culpability. The Financial Services Authority (2010, p 5) claimed that, before the 'credit crunch':

> Circumstances led lenders to feel insulated from losses arising from poor lending, largely as a result of being able to pass risks onto others (e.g. by securitisation) and also by the widely held

expectations of continuing growth in property values. This resulted in relaxed lending criteria and increased risk taking, and increased competition pushed lending further along the risk curve with a rash of new market entrants (often non-deposit taking lenders) adding to this.

Social reformism

If the laissez-faire perspective has been dented by recent housing market experience, then what of social reformism? Social reformism's guiding maxim is that housing markets function inefficiently and produce unjustifiable inequalities, and, hence, strong state corrective action is necessary. Many social reformists would argue that New Labour was sluggish in applying this maxim. Apart from modest gains from Section 106 agreements, 'betterment' was ignored and financial sector regulation was, as the Financial Services Authority (2010) later confessed, featherweight. Blair, with his area-based programmes – following a long-established conservative tradition that focused on limited intervention to mitigate housing market 'externalities' – concentrated on the social impact of neighbourhood deprivation. New social housing construction for rent declined to a very low level – 16,600 in 2002/03 compared to 43,460 in 1995/96 (DCL, 2010b, Table 1000). From 2003, 'rival narratives' can be detected in New Labour's housing policies, with Blair still concentrating on mitigating market-generated 'externalities' and Brown favouring state action to promote supply. When Brown gained ascendancy in housing policy, new social housing completions for rent started to increase reaching 27,220 in 2009/10, but still well below average annual output under the Major government.

New Labour's record in maintaining and improving the housing stock was better than its performance in stimulating new house construction. Despite its association with stock transfer – ironically much of the 'private' borrowing undertaken by stock transfer associations became part of the Public Sector Borrowing Requirement created as part of the 2007/08 measures to stabilise the banking sector – the decent homes programme in the social sector had a significant impact. At a cost of £37 billion, social landlord returns suggested that, in 2010, almost 95% of housing association property was decent (TSA, 2010), as was 83.8% in the council house sector. Less progress was made in the non-social sector but, before it lost office, New Labour was on track to meet its limited target of increasing the percentage of private-sector vulnerable households in decent homes to 70% by 2010. In its 2010 Spending Review (HM Treasury, 2010b, p 48) the Coalition government declared that 'investment via the Decent

Homes programme will continue to improve the existing social housing stock'. Two billion pounds was allocated over the review period compared to the estimated £3.2 billion needed to complete the programme and authorities with less than 10% non-decent homes would be expected to fund renovation from their own resources.

Marxist political economy

Marxist political economy gathered oxygen from the role played by global capital in creating the credit crunch and the subsequent worldwide recession. Bellamy and Magdoff (2009), for example, argue that the crisis was precipitated by capital's capacity to generate a vast surplus by keeping wages down but, in order to continue accumulation, it required the working class to consume. The answer was debt and, in promoting 'privatised Keynesianism' (Crouch, 2009), the 'financialisation' of capital created new and increasingly intricate opportunities for profit. The eventual inability of the working class to pay this debt produced the financial crisis. However, Marxists have always predicted that each successive capitalist crisis must be more severe than the previous one leading to capitalism's inevitable collapse. Yet capitalism did not disintegrate during the 2008/09 financial crisis: states, 'as lenders of last resort', stepped in to stabilise the system. Moreover, despite the virtues of Marxist political economy as an explanatory theory, its normative dimension remains undeveloped. What is the alternative to market capitalism? The record of monopoly state housing is drab and, without specifics for its vision, Marxist political economy is 'an intellectual toy rather than a serious political project' (Gray, 2009, p 19).

The behavioural approach

Neighbourhood approaches

Between 1997 and 2003, it appeared that Blair had subsumed housing policy under his social exclusion agenda. In his first speech as Prime Minister, delivered at the Aylesbury Estate in Southwark, he said:

> There is a case not just in moral terms but in enlightened self interest to act, to tackle what we all know exists – an underclass of people cut off from society's mainstream, without any sense of shared purpose. (Blair, 1997a)

The phrase 'in enlightened self interest' echoed a long-established justification for state action in the housing domain: excluded neighbourhoods are 'dangerous places' due to their impact on social order and the nation's moral fabric. New Labour's 'special measures' applied to deprived neighbourhoods were the flip side to containing suburban and rural development. 'Middle England' was to be protected from violation by the urban working class that was to be helped, in their place, by a raft of measures to encourage community cohesion, coordinate service delivery and control anti-social behaviour (see Chapter Nine). Blair's area-based programmes, with their rhetorical stress on upgrading 'human' and 'social' capital, carried connotations that the residents in deprived neighbourhoods were responsible for their dispossession.

Large parts of the Aylesbury Estate, a site for many of Blair's 'special measures', were demolished in 2010, but the jury is still out on the outcomes of New Labour's glut of area initiatives. Although variable in robustness, useful information is available on the outcomes of specific programmes, but their *overall* impact is difficult to assess. As 19th-century experience demonstrates (see Chapter Three), targeted intervention may displace problems elsewhere. A robust assessment of New Labour's area-based initiatives in 'narrowing the gap' between deprived neighbourhoods and the rest of England would require comparisons between the 10% most deprived neighbourhoods in 1997 and the 10% most deprived neighbourhoods in 2010 in relationship to national averages. No such comprehensive assessment has been published and, hence, the extent of any displacement impact is unknown. Hutton's overall assessment of New Labour's area-based initiatives was that they 'at best achieved small gains and held the line; at worst were overwhelmed by the way the economy has developed' (Hutton, 2010, p 10). Nonetheless, a message emerged from New Labour's area-based initiatives: it is easier to improve run-down areas than enhance the 'human' and 'social' capital of the people living in the targeted neighbourhood. The New Deal for Communities (NDC) produced better 'place-based' than 'people-based' outcomes, with property-based crime reduction the most notable success. Lawless (2010, p 27), director of the NDC evaluation, concluded that 'there is an argument for area regeneration' because 'they achieve change in relation to place', but 'people-based change is best left largely to existing agencies'.

With some area-based initiatives coming to the end of their allotted time span, New Labour's 2010 manifesto (Labour Party, 2010, para 2.6) announced 'We will make savings in regeneration funding and focus on tackling worklessness, transforming the prospects of those areas most disconnected from the wider economy'. This emphasis on worklessness was reflected in Conservative Party proposals, some of which were adopted by the Coalition government. *Universal Credit: Welfare That Works* (DWP, 2010b) set out proposals on how work incentives would be promoted.

Noting that 'the simultaneous withdrawal of different benefits at different taper rates creates uncertainty as it produces variable, unpredictable and often very high Marginal Deduction Rates, depending on how much the individual earns' (2010b, p 8), the White Paper committed the government to introducing a universal credit to replace a range of benefits including Housing Benefit. It would be administered by HM Revenue & Customs as part of the Pay As You Earn tax system with a 65% taper as income increased – equivalent to the current rate for Housing Benefit and far higher than the 55% proposed in Iain Duncan Smith's 2009 plan (Centre for Social Justice, 2009). Phased in over a number of years the Universal Credit would eventually incorporate mortgage interest payments to those claiming Income Support. Many social housing providers had been concerned that the new credit would involve direct cash payments to social tenants for rent payments, but the White Paper stated:

> There are advantages in paying the housing component to individuals, rather than the current system of payments direct to landlords. This would encourage people to manage their own budget in the same way as other households. However, we also recognise the importance of stable rental income for social landlords to support the delivery of new homes and will develop Universal Credit in a way that protects their financial position. Options for achieving this could include some ongoing use of direct payments to landlords, use of direct debits, and a protection mechanism which safeguards landlords' income. (2010b, p 20)

Absent from Coalition government policy was any specific commitment to transforming the prospects of those areas most disconnected from the wider economy. The NDC reached the end of its 10-year time span in 2010 and the 2010 Spending Review announced the demise of the Working Neighbourhoods Fund. Funding for the Market Renewal Initiative reached a zenith in 2007/08 (£405 million), but declined to £311 million in 2010/11 and, given that projects will have to apply to the Regional Growth Fund, in competition with economic initiatives for the limited £1.4 billion pot, their future is bleak. As the Institute for Public Policy North (2010, p 5) predicted 'large scale area based initiatives will not continue' with the prospect that many inhabitants of deprived neighbourhoods will be forced to live in blighted areas.

Neighbourhoods, families and 'the social tenant'

Blair applied the behavioural approach to deprived neighbourhoods, but, towards the end of his term in office, his focus turned to deprived families:

> My thesis today is straightforward: some aspects of social exclusion are deeply intractable. The most socially excluded are very hard to reach. Their problems are multiple, entrenched and often passed down the generations.... About 2.5 per cent of every generation seem to be stuck in a life-time of disadvantage and amongst them are the excluded of the excluded, the deeply excluded.... Their poverty is, not just about poverty of income, but poverty of aspiration, of opportunity, of prospects of advancement. (Blair, 2006b)

Three years later, in his speech to the Labour Party Conference, Brown adopted Blair's premise and promised 'Starting now and right across the next Parliament every one of the 50,000 most chaotic families will be part of a family intervention project – with clear rules, and clear punishments if they don't stick to them' (Brown, 2009).

The Blair/Brown spotlight on families rather than neighbourhoods echoed an emerging policy orientation in Cameron's Conservative Party. Under the 'Broken Britain' slogan the Social Justice Policy Group, set up by Cameron with Iain Duncan Smith as its chair, identified 'five pathways to poverty' – 'family breakdown, educational failure, economic dependence, indebtedness and addiction' – which were 'all interrelated' (Centre for Social Justice, 2006, p 15). This emphasis on families rather than areas was reflected in the Coalition government's announcement that 15 hours per week of free early education and care would be made available to all disadvantaged two year olds, and a 'school premium' would be provided to promote the educational development of disadvantaged pupils. In addition the Department for Communities and Local Governments (DCL, 2010s, p 1) announced pilot schemes in 16 areas to merge various funding streams in a concerted effort to tackle 'social problems around families with complex needs ... so that families are given the chance to turn their lives around'.

Although the focus on deprived areas was downplayed by the Coalition government, the economic dependence limelight was directed at the 'social tenant'. The Conservatives' *Breakthrough Britain: Housing Poverty* declared that 'the level of dependency among social housing renters is quite staggering' and 'this is not a situation that will resolve itself. How can we expect different from people who never see anything different?' (Centre for Social Justice, 2008, p 5). It went on to say that 'with the right support and help, many of the young and not so young people moving into social housing can be helped to build successful lives' (2008, p 55). It recommended:

> Housing Managers should be actively involved in the improvement of service delivery, becoming specialists in meeting people's support needs and acting as advocates for social and economic mobility; enabling people to realise their aspirations. (2008, p 110)

To counter the 'the chronic lack of turnover in the social sector', which meant that 'whole generations are growing up, living and dying in the estates where they were born' (Conservative Party, 2009, p 6), the Conservatives proposed a 'right to move' allowing 'good social tenants to demand their social landlord sell their current property and use the proceeds ... to buy ... another property of their choice – anywhere in England' (Conservative Party, 2009, p 6). 'Good social tenants' were also promised equity stakes (Conservative Party, 2010, p 75).

In the event, the Coalition government encouraged mobility by 'right to move' pilot schemes in two authorities; by a new National Affordable Home Swap Scheme – a national scheme existed before this announcement but was underused relative to demand (Gulliver, 2010) – and by proposals to end 'tenancy for life' for new local authority tenants. In a consultation document, *Local Decisions: A Fairer Future for Social Housing* (DCL, 2010t), it was announced that the Coalition government would allow local authorities to offer 'flexible tenancies' with a statutory minimum of two years, but with the discretion to extend this statutory minimum or offer existing forms of agreements, for example, secure and starter tenancies. At the end of the 'flexible tenure' local authorities would discuss options with the tenant under threat of eviction. The rationale of this change was 'localism', but it was also argued that 'the security and subsidised rent that social housing provides do not appear to help tenants to independence and self-sufficiency' (DCL, 2010t, p 12). Moreover, it was claimed that 'need' at the time of allocation should not mean a tenancy for life and, as existing tenants moved on as their circumstances changed, more homes would become available for those in need. *Local Decisions: A Fairer Future for Social Housing* (DCL, 2010t) contained other proposals to reduce the waiting list for social housing. Rather than being required to operate so-called 'open' lists, local authorities would have the discretion to decide which categories of applicant should qualify to join the waiting list (although the 'reasonable preference' framework for allocations would remain); existing social tenants seeking a move would be removed from waiting lists; and local authorities would no longer have to secure the consent of the applicant before discharging its duty under homelessness legislation by offering a private landlord tenancy with a shorthold of at least one year.

Although presented as part of the 'localism' agenda, *Local Decisions: A Fairer Future for Social Housing* contained central control stratagems. A centrally determined Tenancy Standard would set out principles to be applied locally and it was proposed that local authorities would have a new duty to publish a strategic policy on tenancies and be required to 'explain how they propose to take advantage of the new flexible tenancies' (DCL, 2010t, p 27), thereby opening up the possibility of financial penalties should the explanation not be acceptable to central government.

Since 1989, registered social landlords – usually housing associations – have been subject to the same legislative framework on security of tenure as private landlords but, under the rules of their regulator, they have been required to offer longer security. *Local Decisions: A Fairer Future for Social Housing* stated that, in future, an 'affordable rent' tenancy would be available on a fixed term of at least two years with safeguards around termination. The 'affordable rent' tenancy, set at 80% of the Local Housing Allowance (LHA) rate, will not be available to local authorities. New Labour attempted to blur the distinction between local authority and housing association tenancies, categorising both as 'social housing'. The Coalition government appears to be in a process of re-establishing the division, with housing associations letting to those on higher incomes ('intermediate' tenancies) and the council sector, shorn of 'open' waiting lists, becoming a 'last resort' tenancy for people with low incomes. New building by local authorities, to be boosted by New Labour, will be restricted by the Coalition government, with the reform of the Housing Revenue Account to exclude enhanced use of Right to Buy receipts for a number of years and directed to ensuring that 'rents are kept and used locally to *maintain* homes for current and future tenants' (DCL, 2010t, p 50, emphasis added).

However, more radical ideas were in vogue in right-wing circles. The Policy Exchange, appalled by the level of dependency in social housing, put forward a scheme to end allocation according to need, extend the Right to Buy and put vacant and new non-profit housing into a 'Pathway to Ownership' scheme (Morton, 2010).

Social constructionism

Social constructionism made a valuable contribution to housing studies by debunking the allegedly 'rational' approach to housing policy with its assumption that housing problems could be treated by 'top-down' directives based on 'expert' knowledge. In addition, through a reminder that what is socially constructed can be changed, it created an intellectual framework from which 'identity politics' could emerge. Yet, at the heart of social constructionism is a languid, 'nothing is real'/'nothing to get hung about' mantra that, whilst helpful in demonstrating a social construction process, is not sufficient. If the paradigm is to cultivate accomplishment, a more determined attempt will need to be made to distinguish plausible from implausible constructions. Thus, for example, the shameless construction of *the* 'social' tenant as a 'work-unready' dependant who is deficient in 'human' and 'social' capital requires interrogation. Longitudinal research by Lupton and Tunstall (2009a) showed negative adult outcomes for children who grew up in social housing in the 1960s, 1970s and 1980s, but not for the immediate post-war generation. However, such research demonstrates the impact of deprived families concentrated in particular areas rather than an independent impact of living in social housing. As Lupton and Tunstall (2009b) have pointed out, 'it is deprivation that does the most harm' and, as Monk et al (2010, p 13) claim, 'these people are not disadvantaged because they live in the social sector; they are in the social sector because of their multiple disadvantages'.

To label all 'social' tenants as part of a dependent, self-perpetuating cultural 'underclass' is misleading. Nationally, the Treasury makes a surplus from council housing and there are 2.6 million local authority tenants plus 2.3 million living in housing association properties, many former council tenants. Of working-age social tenants, 14% have a disability compared to 3% of homeowners, and work participation varies from 33% in Northern Ireland to 56% in South East England (Greater London Authority, 2007, pp 19, 36). According to some commentators (Hills, 2007; Morton, 2010), even when differences such as the incidence of disability and lone parenthood are taken into account, there is an 'unexplained gap' in work participation rates between social housing tenants and those in other tenures, but one does not have to postulate a 'social housing culture' to account for any gap. Postcode discrimination features strongly in social tenants' accounts of their difficulties in finding work (DWP, 2008), and there are rational disincentives to finding work such as the obstacles to improving your housing circumstances when the next step is high-priced private landlord accommodation or expensive homeownership.

In contrast to the dominant discourse on the 'social tenant', the construction of '*the* person sleeping rough' has greater credibility. Although 'rough sleeping' should not be used as a proxy for the single homelessness problem, the evidence suggests that tackling rough sleeping requires 'more than a roof' because the majority of rough sleepers have personal problems that compound their housing needs.

'The Big Society'

As Prime Minister, Cameron announced that the 'Big Society' involves giving 'professionals much more freedom' and opening up 'public services to new providers like charities, social enterprises and private companies so we get more innovation, diversity and responsiveness to public need' (Cameron, 2010). On this portrayal, the 'Big Society' involves strengthening 'exit' politics with consumers choosing between an assortment of providers – for-profit, non-profit, cooperatives, charities and so on – that flourish or fail by their ability to satisfy consumer preferences. Nonetheless, the 'Big Society' with its emphasis on neighbourhood groups, 'the "little platoons" of civil society' (Conservative Party, 2010, p 38), offers enhanced opportunities to diversify the ethos of housing service providers in the form of cooperatives, tenant management organisations and social enterprises (to deliver gardening, cleaning and caretaking). Initial funding might come from the 'Big Society Bank' that will acquire its resources from dormant bank accounts. Other elements in 'the Big Society' include the appointment of more community development workers, especially in deprived areas, plus the establishment of Local Housing Trusts through which local people could promote new house construction without planning permission with the enhanced land value remaining in the trust. Under the 'Big Society' umbrella, housing associations might move into the territory vacated by the spending squeeze on local authorities by offering services and charging through rents.

The 'jilted generation'

A generational dimension to housing outcomes emerged over the last 20 years. Willetts (2010, p xv) presents an argument that 'the boomers, roughly those born between 1945 and 1965, have done and continue to do some great things but now the bills are coming in; and it is the younger generation who will pay them', and Howker and Malik (2010) refer to those born after 1979 as 'the jilted generation'. Part of the case against the 'baby boomers' relates to the generational gap in housing wealth: in 2009, half of all homeownership wealth belonged to the 'baby boomers' whereas only 15% belonged to those aged under 44 (Willetts, 2010).

Of course, there are ethnic, gender and class dimensions to housing wealth (see Chapter Ten), but the generational gap is also reflected in other facets of the housing issue. The remorseless post-war growth in homeownership started to stall in 2004 and, by 2009, there were 370,000 fewer homeowners than in 2001. The credit crunch had a disproportionate impact on potential first-time buyers. The down payment required increased: in 2009, only

28,000 mortgages were made to first-time buyers who did not have a 10% deposit compared to 245,000 in 2006 (Genworth Financial, 2010). The average deposit of first-time buyers increased from £13,000 in 2007 to £33,000 in 2010, with the best interest rates reserved for those who could offer a 25–35% deposit. The result was that 'it is thought that around 80% of first-time buyers are now dependent on parental contributions' (Housing Finance Group, 2010, p 8). This reflects the class dimension of the 'generation gap': the 'Bank of Mum and Dad' is only available if Mum and Dad have a bank!

There has been a marked shift in the type, location and quality of the new construction available to the under-40s. Between 1997/98 and 2008/09, less land was used for development in England (Housing Finance Group, 2010), the proportion of houses built declined from 84% to 50% and homes with three or more bedrooms (flats or houses) dropped from 66% to 41% (DCL, 2010b, Table 254). Dwellings built on 'brownfield', mainly urban, sites increased from 56% in 1997 to 77% in 2007, accompanied by density soaring from 25 to 44 per hectare over the same period. Space standards declined and the term 'hobbit houses' began to be used to describe new developments. As Sir Bob Kerslake, remarked 'it's no secret that the UK has held the dubious honour of building the smallest average rooms and new homes in Europe' (Kerslake, 2010b): they were 25% smaller than the EU average and 40% smaller than in Germany or the Netherlands (Aldred, 2010).

People who bought new homes were disappointed: a survey of households living in new dwellings built in Greater London and the South East (Drury, 2009) revealed widespread dissatisfaction about space standards, especially with regard to space for furniture layout and storage in the kitchen. Later research compared the space available in new flats in Greater London and the South East with the minimum 'safety-net' standards set by the Greater London Council and 'good-practice' benchmarks such as those set by Parker-Morris in 1961. It concluded:

> Overall, most dwelling types fall short, on average, of both good-practice and safety-net standards.… If dwellings provide inadequate space for people to be able to be reasonably comfortable these dwellings may not function effectively as homes, making them less useful and popular over the long term. This has implications for their longevity and consequently for future costs of early redevelopment, which will be payable in both monetary and environmental currencies, such as CO_2. (Drury and Somers, 2010, p 42)

When the housing market faltered in 2007 it was apartment developments, built on 'brownfield' sites in cities such as Birmingham, Manchester and Leeds, that experienced the largest fall in prices – down by up to 60% from their peak. The emphasis on smaller, high-density development on 'brownfield' sites was justified, in part, by projections of growth in one-person households, but such projections are now in danger of becoming a self-fulfilling prophecy. According to a survey commissioned by the National Housing Federation, four out of 10 young adults were delaying starting a family until they could afford to buy a new home (National Housing Federation, 2010b).

Minding the gaps

Narrowing the generational gap, reducing unjustifiable ethnic, gender and class differences in access to quality housing, and making an impact on homelessness and overcrowding depends on reducing occupancy costs and this objective is related to a constant, high-level supply of quality homes (quality in terms of size, amenities and energy efficiency). A report, commissioned by the DCL and based on data including the differential impact of planning permission refusal rates, was emphatic on the nature and causes of the problem. It declared:

> On the basis of this rich dataset, this report provides unambiguous *causal* evidence demonstrating that regulatory supply constraints and, to a lesser extent, physical supply constraints have had a serious negative long-run impact on housing affordability and have increased house price volatility. (Hibler and Vermeulen, 2010, p 7, emphasis original)

The report made a number of estimates of the impact of the planning system on house prices concluding, for instance, that if the most restrictive region (the South East) had the same planning regime as the least restrictive region (the North East) then, in 2008, house prices in the South East would be between £35,000 and £69,000 lower.

New Labour's 2007 housing Green Paper (DCL, 2007a) had promised a 'step change' in housing production to 240,000 per annum, but limited progress was made in removing the long-term barriers to extra construction identified in the Barker Report. In 2010, for example, of the 132 out of 337 authorities where information was available, 38.6% had yet to identify sufficient sites to supply the housing required for the next five years (DCL, 2010s). Thus, even without the 'credit crunch', the prospect of New Labour achieving its target was remote. In July 2010, Eric Pickles, Secretary of State for Communities and Local Government, announced that New Labour 'soviet-style' regional planning (Pickles, 2010, quoted in Johnstone, 2010) would be axed and replaced by incentives to deliver homes. A consultation document issued in November 2010 (DCL, 2010r) set out the details of the New Homes Bonus:

- It would be equal to the national average for the council tax band and paid for six years, for example, £1439 per annum for a property in band D and £1759 per annum for a property in band E.
- There would be an enhancement of £350 per annum for each affordable home.
- Bringing empty property into use could qualify for the bonus.

The impact of the New Homes Bonus, financed by the abolition of New Labour's Planning and Delivery Grant plus reductions in other central grants to local government, will depend on how local authorities react to the incentives of extra resources at a time when mainstream income will be restricted. The prognosis is uncertain because the predicted additional income is limited – £946 million between 2011 and 2015 (HM Treasury, 2010b) – and, according to Aldred (2010), the extra resources to an average-sized local authority building 1000 homes would be only £8 per year per person. There is also the problem of whether a particular local authority will be willing to build homes to contribute to meeting regional and national requirements if its 'local' need is limited. Moreover, as Morton (2010) points out, NIMBY politics in local government is very important. Satsangi et al (2010, p 109) reinforce the point in relationship to rural housing:

> There is then a high degree of consistency in studies of housing land provision in rural Britain … attempts to secure more housing are commonly hindered by well-organised local elites.… This bottom-up pressure on supply finds some agreement with national policies that, irrespective of rhetoric, are keen to place strict limits on development in smaller village locations.

The Coalition government proposal, first put forward by the Conservative Party (2010b) and contained in the Localism Bill, to allow neighbourhoods to compile a local plan, which if endorsed by 50% of the local electorate, must be adopted by the local authority, offers further opportunities for NIMBY politics. The editor of Planning has commented:

> We may be about to enter a period in which planning discourse is dominated by sharp-elbowed, well-resourced, well-healed busybodies with time on their hands and whose concept of local need is constrained to a few hundred metres from their house (quoted in Wilson, 2011, pp 28-29).

Thus, because resistance to new development is deep and vociferous it may not respond to extra resources (however high) channelled at local government level and a neighbourhood share of a tariff on developers. The Local Housing Trust idea offers the opportunity for locally generated housing schemes, but the idea has been in circulation for several years in the form of Community Land Trusts and finding suitable land at a reasonable price has stalled their development. Moreover, under the proposal, presented as the 'Community Right to Build', local community expansion is limited to 10% and 90% of local people must vote in favour of a scheme. Even the Rural Coalition (2010), which includes the Council for the Protection of Rural England, found these conditions too restrictive and the 90% was later reduced to 50%.

Limiting demand

In addition to the land supply issue, there are serious concerns about the capacity to build more homes. As the Housing Finance Group (2010, p 4) commented: 'Whilst the patient has moved out of intensive care, the period of recuperation now appears long and uncertain'. In 2008/09, 111,420 houses were started in the UK with 120,749 in 2009/10 (DCL, 2010b, Table 211), but only by the central government pump-priming the market with resources brought forward from future spending commitments. Social housing contributed almost a quarter to these new starts. The 2010 Spending Review reduced central contributions for new social housing construction to £4.4 billion over the four years from 2011/12 to 2014/15 (HM Treasury, 2010b), down from £8.4bn over the previous three-year period. However, the remaining central contribution plus the extra resources deemed to become available via the new 'affordable' tenure was expected to contribute 150,000 new affordable homes over the period 2011/12–2014/15.

Given the projected 3.1 million additional households between 2011 and 2021 (DCL, 2010b, Table 401) and overall housing construction likely to be well below New Labour's 240,000 per annum target, attention can be expected to focus on constraining demand and making more efficient use of the existing housing stock. In 1996, the Conservative government published *Household Growth: Where Shall We Live?* (Secretary of State for the Environment, 1996). This explicitly ruled out meeting housing demand in the areas where demand was highest because such a policy was 'environmentally unsustainable'. In addition to proposing an increase in the use of 'brownfield' sites, the 1996 paper contained proposals on how household formation might be restrained. Encouraging more students to remain at home; persuading more elderly people to live with their children; measures to reduce the incidence of divorce and separation; and 'taking action to ensure that benefits do not encourage household formation unnecessarily' (1996, p 16) were included. The Coalition government has emphasised efficiency in the use of the social housing stock and the proposals, contained in the 2010 Budget, to limit Housing Benefit for working-age social tenants to a specified household size act as an incentive for tenants to move to smaller properties. In addition, new social tenancies at higher rents and with less security will probably affect the demand for social housing as reflected in the 'headline' figures produced by waiting lists.

Immigration curbs were considered in the 1996 paper, but it concluded:

> Given EU and international law, and the stringency of UK law on immigration and asylum, it is unlikely that there is a great deal of scope for reducing this component of household growth. (Secretary of State for the Environment, 1996, p 17)

However, net immigration is now projected to account for 33% of future housing demand (House of Lords, 2010). Housing was not a major issue in the 2010 general election campaigns – although immigration was, and the Coalition government promised a cap on the number of non-EU economic migrants allowed to live in the UK.

Increasing supply

A number of proposals are in circulation on how the supply of new homes might be increased, as follows.

Redefining public borrowing

It has been suggested (Chartered Institute of Housing, Scotland, 2009) that, because housing investment by local authorities produces real assets, it should not count as part of the Public Sector Borrowing Requirement – now known as Public Sector Net Cash Requirement. Many European countries do not count investment in social housing as part of the public debt, but redefining the UK's public deficit might be construed as 'creative accounting' and reduce the confidence of the financial institutions in the willingness of the UK government to reduce its Public Sector Net Cash Requirement.

Asset realisation

The 2008 Housing Regeneration Act allowed 'for-profit' bodies to become registered social housing providers. Its relevant provisions came into force in April 2010. Elphicke (2010), a finance lawyer, has recommended that housing associations, with assets worth £205 billion at current market values and with a £1.6 billion surplus in 2009 (now used for direct investment in housing), should become 'social enterprise' organisations seeking equity investment and paying dividends to shareholders. Even with no change in the rights of existing tenants, she suggests that equity finance sufficient to build 100,000 new 'social' homes per annum could be attracted to the sector. Given that 'social enterprise' organisations such as the employee stakeholder model of the John Lewis Partnership are unlikely to be able to raise even a fraction of the equity necessary to deliver 100,000 'social' homes per annum Elphicke's scheme is pure privatisation. However, because the 'social' nature of housing associations has been diluted, they are vulnerable to such privatisation.

Filtering and consumption to production incentives

As Ball (2010b), the economist commissioned by New Labour to examine ways to promote recovery in housing supply, has pointed out, subsidies to consumers of existing houses push prices upwards. Thus, all existing *consumption* subsidies such as Stamp Duty Tax relief, Capital Gains Tax exemptions, Right to Buy discounts and allowing private landlords to offset rent against mortgage payments might be abolished to free resources for new-build *production* incentives. This new-build fund might be enhanced by a property tax similar to the 'mansion tax', included in the Liberal Democrat's 2010 manifesto but abandoned when the Coalition was formed. The LHA has also contributed to rent inflation in areas where its recipients dominate the market. In evidence given to the House of Commons Work and Pensions Committee (2010b, p 1), Lord Freud, Minister for Welfare Reform, stated:

> The total market for private rentals is around 3.6 million currently. So you can see we are looking at a position where the Government represent 40% of the market. Now, that varies depending on the market: some places it is 20%; some places it is 70%, obviously. Now, what our data are showing is that the

> rents that we are paying – what benefit recipients are paying – are rising faster than the market.... For instance, figures for 2006/2007 show an overall private rental market gain of around 15% in real terms; our rents are going up 25%.

Thus, the Coalition government's restrictions on LHA payments may make a modest contribution to reducing private-sector rents in certain areas, albeit that rent regulation of existing properties would, of course, have a bigger impact. Housing associations could be encouraged to use their considerable asset base to raise loans for market rent accommodation and to produce more investment capital by selling vacant properties (London and Quadrant, 2010). In relation to housing associations, *Local Decisions: A Fairer Future for Social Housing* (DCL, 2010t, p 56) anticipated early sales of vacant property and stated 'In line with the "something for something" approach ... we will also be expecting enhanced contribution to development from providers'.

Filtering theory indicates that such production subsidies should not be concentrated on people with low incomes. Rather, their purpose should be to enhance overall production and, if targeted, the target should be people on the margins of affordability, thereby minimising public subsidy per unit produced. Low-income households would benefit by 'filtering up' into the dwellings left vacant by the inhabitants of the new houses. This use of filtering theory underlies the Coalition government's proposals on new social homes to be let at 80% of LHA rates, producing, so it is claimed, more homes for each £1 of public subsidy. Its impact will depend on lettings policy. If the new homes are allocated to people with low incomes, then the Housing Benefit outlay will increase and more people will be caught in the unemployment and poverty traps, but, as seems likely, if higher-income groups are chosen, they will pay a large part of the cost.

Bringing empty homes into use

It has been estimated that, in 2009, over 650,000 houses have been empty for six months or more (Empty Homes Agency, 2010). These empty homes are not only a waste of housing, they also contribute to an atmosphere of neighbourhood dereliction. The New Homes Bonus and the £100 million pounds allocated to the utilisation of empty homes in the 2010 Spending Review may alleviate the problem and assist in bringing houses blighted by stalled regeneration projects back into use.

Land

New Labour attempted to improve land supply by injecting 'economics' into the planning system with new targets, based on affordability indicators, cascading from the centre and requirements for the identification of five-year land supply banks. The Coalition government is relying not on top-down targets, but financial incentives. Nonetheless, the DCL's Business Plan contains 'impact indicators' – similar to New Labour's national targets – including the 'total number of housing starts and completions' and 'number of affordable starts and completions', which may influence central views of local authority performance (DCL, 2010u, p 38). Combining New Labour's 'sticks' (the enforcement of a five-year rolling land supply – perhaps extended to 10 years – by allowing automatic planning permission where no required supply exists) with the Conservatives' 'carrots' (enhanced by higher payments financed by reductions in other central grants) should boost land supply. In addition, incentives paid to *individuals* affected by developments (not neighbourhoods) to accept new housing, paid for by developers, could be introduced (Morton, 2010).

Green Belts

It is worth rehearsing Green Belt history. It was a social reformist idea aimed at preventing conurbation sprawl, providing a 'green lung' for urbanite recreation and promoting new town development. The 1938 Green Belt (London and Home Counties) Act empowered local authorities to buy land and keep it as Green Belt, and for landowners to enter into covenants with local government to keep their land 'green'.

After 1957, Green Belts became a Conservative mechanism for protecting counties from the growth of large cities. In the 1980s, the new town idea, which was to complement the containment of urban growth by Green Belts, was abandoned and even an attempt by a consortium of major developers, encouraged by Margaret Thatcher's free-market rhetoric, to build 15 'private enterprise' new country towns around London was thwarted by virulent opposition from the 'Conservative grassroots of England's outer south-east' (Ward, 2005, pp 352–3).

Green Belts are now close to the hearts of environmentalists and 'middle England'. They have strong public support, albeit based on some misconceptions. Although 54% of the public believe that around half of England is developed and 10% think that more than 75% is developed (Barker, 2006), less than 10% of all land in England is classified as 'built up' (including gardens): 72.3% is agricultural with over a third of agricultural land consisting of 'grasses and rough grazing' (Aldred, 2010, p 9). Land in designated Green Belts has not been eroded in the last 10 years – in England it has increased (Barclay, 2010) – and 13% of England's land area is Green Belt.

The Ipsos/Mori poll carried out for Barker's (2006) *Review of Land Use Planning* found that 60% of respondents thought that Green Belts protected wildlife and 46% believed that they preserved areas of natural beauty, yet wildlife flourishes in suburban gardens and 'areas of outstanding natural beauty' are protected by other policies. Green Belts are mainly about preventing 'urban sprawl' and contain swathes of scrubland on the edge of cities – only 17% of the Ipsos/Mori respondents thought that 'edge of city land' was the most important to protect against development and even the Campaign to Protect Rural England classifies 18% of Green Belt land as 'neglected' (CPRE, 2010). Moreover, as Champion (2010, viii) points out:

> more affluent households have 'leapfrogged' the Green Belt into the smaller towns and villages beyond. Not only has this had with implications for commuter journeys, congestion and pollution but the galloping "residential gentrification" of much of Britain and a virtual embargo on new business enterprise ... represents a double whammy as far as the continued presence of less well-off families in the countryside is concerned.

Green Belt designation is a local government prerogative and enhanced payments for extra houses – accompanied by restrictions on other revenue flows and penalties for failure to produce a five-year rolling programme of land release – may be sufficient to persuade local authorities to review their Green Belts. Other ideas are in circulation. Land auctions are one idea (Aldred, 2010; Leunig, 2010). Leunig, for example, suggests a system whereby:

1. A council asks local landowners if they want to sell land for development, and the price at which they would sell (price '1').
2. Setting a price gives the council the right to buy the land at that price for 18 months.
3. The council decide what land can be given planning permission.
4. The council auctions off the right to buy the selected land from the original landowner, at price '2' and keeps the difference.

Such a scheme allows local authorities to benefit from all the 'betterment gain' involved in granting planning permission and encourages Green Belt release.

Paternalism and class containment

Looking back over 150 years of housing policy reveals dominant and related themes. There has been an entrenched tendency to 'lump' the urban working class as incapable of determining the form and nature of their accommodation. As Shapely (2008, p 1) comments:

> One of the underlying problems which led to some of the mistakes, especially after the Second World War, was the failure to ask tenants themselves about fundamental issues such as the design and location of new homes. Choice was never on the agenda.

The paternalism persists in the contemporary construction of the 'social' tenant – still subject to the 'social engineering' that would be regarded as an affront to civil liberty if applied to homeowners. Why is it that only 'social' tenants have been the 'subjects' of proposals such as work contracts as a tenancy condition, enforced ending of 'under-occupancy' (i.e. no spare bedroom), rewards for good behaviour and, under the Coalition governments' proposals on flexible tenure, lifestyle reviews aimed at social betterment every two years? Lack of respect is a recurring theme amongst housing association and council house tenants with a recent survey stating that 'many residents felt regarded "as the lowest of the low"' (Joseph Rowntree Foundation, 2010). Such disrespect has consequences. As Blokland (2008, p 31) concludes from a study of 'place-making' with its associated behaviour controls (see Chapter Five) in an American housing project:

> In contrast to what urban policy-makers might like to see, residents refuse to engage with their neighbourhood, as attaching themselves through neighbourhood action to 'the community' would imply a recognition that they are in fact the type of person the projects are 'meant' for in the dominant discourse of subsidized housing: losers with whom no-one wants to identify or be identified.

Containing the 'urban' working class has been a related and enduring policy objective. During the 19th century this was accomplished by the refusal to grant even temporary subsidies to reduce urban overcrowding. Between the 1930s and the early 1970s, state housing became the containment vehicle. At first, suburban development for the middle and 'respectable' working class was accompanied by municipal, low-rise flats for people housed from the overcrowded slums. From the mid–1950s, Conservative concern about the plans of the major cities to expand into county areas (Hall et al, 1973) and a determination to contain inner London (Young and Kramer, 1978) led to Green Belt restrictions on urban expansion and high–rise developments in urban areas. New Labour's 'brownfield' policies also protected suburban and rural Britain at the cost of high-density building in cities and towns.

The 2010 Conservative Party manifesto (2010, p 132) praised the suburbs as playing:

> a vital role in the success of Britain's cities, providing housing and green spaces for millions of families. Suburbs are places where a sense of community can flourish, and where people raise their children and play an active part in neighbourhood groups.

Perhaps, in time, this reaffirmation of suburban virtues will produce a renaissance of the idea that building eco-friendly houses in garden suburbs, villages and new towns has considerable individual and 'public good' impacts.

References

Addison, P. (2010) *No Turning Back: The Peacetime Revolutions of Post-War Britain*, Oxford: Oxford University Press.

Aldred, T. (2010) *Arrested Development: Are We Building Houses in the Right Places?* London: Centre for Cities.

Allen, C. (2008) *Housing Market Renewal and Social Class*, London: Routledge.

Allen, J., Barlow, J., Leal, J., Maloutas, T. and Padovani, L. (2004) *Housing and Welfare in Southern Europe*, London: Blackwell.

AMION Consulting (2010) *Evaluation of the National Strategy for Neighbourhood Renewal: Final Report*, London: DCL.

Anderson, E. (1992) *Streetwise: Race, Class and Change in an Urban Community*, Chicago, IL: University of Chicago Press.

Anderson, I. (2009) 'Homelessness Policy in Scotland: A Complete State Safety Net by 2012?', in S. Fitzpatrick, D. Quilgars and N. Pleace (eds) *Homelessness in the UK: Problems and Solutions*, London: Chartered Institute of Housing, pp 107–22.

Anderson, I., Kemp, P. and Quilgars, D. (1993) *Single Homeless People*, London: HMSO.

Angotti, T. (2006) 'Apocalyptic Anti-Urbanism: Mike Davis and His Planet of Slums', *International Journal of Urban and Regional Research*, vol 30, no 4 pp 961–7.

Atkinson, R. and Kintrea, K. (2000) 'Owner-Occupation, Social Mix and Neighbourhood Impacts', *Policy & Politics*, vol 28, no 1, pp 93–108.

Atkinson, R. and Kintrea, K. (2004) '"Opportunities and Despair, It's All in There": Practitioner Experiences and Explanations of Area Effects and Life Chances', *Sociology*, vol 38, no 3, pp 437–53.

Audit Commission (2004) *Housing: Improving Services through Resident Involvement*, London: Audit Commission.

Audit Commission (2006) *Best Value Performance Indicators*, London: Audit Commission.

Bachrach, P. and Baratz, M. (1962) 'Two Faces of Power', *American Political Science Review*, vol 56, pp 947–52.

Ball, M. (2009) *European Housing Review 2009*, RICS, www.rics.org/site/scripts/download_info.aspx?fileID=2150&categoryID=450

Ball, M. (2010a) *European Housing Review 2010*, RICS, www.rics.org/site/scripts/download_info.aspx?downloadID=4853

Ball, M. (2010b) *The Housebuilding Industry: Promoting Recovery in Housing Supply*, London: DCL.

Bank of England (2007) *Equity Withdrawal*, www.bankofengland.co.uk/statistics/hew/2007/dec/tablea.pdf

Barbour, A. (2008) *Housing Benefit in 2008: Issues, Examples and Recommendations, Communitylinks Evidence Paper No. 11*, London: Communitylinks.

Barclay, C. (2010) *Green Belt: Standard Note SN/SC/934*, www.parliament.uk/briefingpapers/commons/lib/research/briefings/snsc-00934.pdf

Barker, J.E. (1909) 'The Land, the Landlords and the People', *Nineteenth Century*, vol 66, pp 550–66.

Barker, K. (2003) *Delivering Stability: Securing Our Future Housing Needs; Interim Report*, London: HM Treasury.

Barker, K. (2004) *Delivering Stability: Securing Our Future Housing Needs; Final Report, Recommendations*. Available at: http://webarchive.nationalarchives.gov.uk/+/www.hm-treasury.gov.uk/consult_barker_index.htm

Barker, K. (2006) *Review of Land Use Planning*, www.communities.gov.uk/documents/planningandbuilding/pdf/154265.pdf

Barker, P. (2009) *The Freedoms of Suburbia*, London: Frances Lincoln.

Barnard, H. and Pettigrew, N. (2004) *Applicants' Perspectives on Choice-Based Lettings*, London: Office of the Deputy Prime Minister.

BBC News (2010) 'Goldman Sachs Agrees Record $550m Fine', 16 July, www.bbc.co.uk/news/business-10656699

Bellamy, J. and Magdoff, F. (2009) *The Great Financial Crisis: Causes and Consequences*, New York: Monthly Review Press.

Best, R. (Lord) (2010) *Report of the Independent Commission on the Future for Housing in Northern Ireland*, www.cih.org/northernireland/housingcommission

Birrell, D. (2009) *The Impact of Devolution on Social Policy*, Bristol: Policy Press.

Blair, T. (1997a) Speech by Prime Minister, Aylesbury Estate, 2 June.

Blair, T. (1997b) 'Next on the List: Clean Up the Councils', *The Guardian*, 3 November.

Blair, T. (1998) *Leading the Way: A New Vision for Local Government*, London: Institute for Public Policy Research.

Blair, T. (2006a) *Respect Action Plan Speech*, 10 January. Available at: http://news.bbc.co.uk/1/hi/uk_politics/4600156.stm

Blair, T. (2006b) 'Our Nation's Future – Social Exclusion', Speech, 5 September. Available at: *video.twofour.co.uk/play/video.asp?videoID=1933*

Bloch, A. and Solomos, J. (eds) (2010) *Race and Ethnicity in the 21st Century*, Basingstoke: Palgrave Macmillan.

Blokland, T. (2008) '"You Got to Remember You Live in Public Housing": Place-Making in an American Housing Project', *Housing Theory and Society*, vol 25, no 1, pp 31–46.

Blond, P. (2010) *Red Tory: How the Left and Right Have Broken Britain and How We Can Fix It*, London: Faber and Faber.

Boddy, M. (1980) *The Building Societies*, London: Macmillan.

Boddy, M. and Gray, F. (1979) 'Filtering Theory: Housing Policy and the Legitimation of Inequality', *Policy & Politics*, vol 7, no 1, pp 39–54.

Bolster, A., Burgess, S., Johnstone, R., Jones, K., Propper, C. and Sarker, R. (2004) *Neighbourhoods, Households and Income Dynamics: A Semi-Parametric Investigation of Neighbourhood Effects*, Bristol: University of Bristol.

Bond, L., Sautkina, E. and Kearns, A. (2011) 'Mixed Messages about Mixed Tenure: Do Reviews tell the Real Story?' *Housing Studies*, vol 26, no 1, pp 69-94.

Booth, C. (1902) *The Life and Labour of the People of London*, London: Macmillan.

Bosanquet, H. (1906) *The Family*, London: Macmillan and Co.

Bovenkirk, K. (1984) 'The Rehabilitation of the Rabble: How and Why Marx and Engels Wrongly Depicted the Lumpen-Proletariat as a Reactionary Force', *The Netherlands Journal of Sociology*, vol 20, no 1, pp 13–42.

Bowley, M. (1945) *Housing and the State 1919–1944*, London: George Allen and Unwin.

Bradshaw, J. and Finch, N. (2004) 'Housing Benefit in 22 Countries', *Benefits*, vol 12, no 2, pp 87–94.

Bradshaw, J., Chzhen, Y. and Stephens, M. (2008) 'Housing: The Saving Grace in the British Welfare State?' in S. Fitzpatrick and M. Stephens (eds) *The Future of Social Housing*, London: Shelter, pp 7–26.

Bramley, G (2009) 'Meeting Demand', in P. Malpass and R. Rowlands (eds) *Housing, Markets and Public Policy*, Abingdon: Routledge, pp 161–4.

Branson, N. and Heinemann, M. (1973) *Britain in the Nineteen Thirties*, St Albans: Panther.

Brennan, A.J.E. (1976) *Vagrancy and Street Offences*, London, HMSO.

Brown, G. (2009) 'Speech to 2009 Labour Party Conference', www.guardian.co.uk/politics/2009/sep/29/gordon-brown-labour-conference-speech-in-full

Bruce, M. (1973) *The Rise of the Welfare State: English Social Policy 1601–1971*, London: Weidenfeld and Nicolson.

Brummer, A. (2008) *The Crunch: The Scandal of Northern Rock and the Escalating Credit Crisis*, London: Random House Business.

Build.co.uk (2009) '"Millions of Pounds Wasted on Housing Benefit Reforms", says NLA', www.build.co.uk/national_news.asp?newsid=99243

Burgess, G. (2008) 'Planning and the Gender Equality Duty – why does gender matter?' *People, Place and Policy Online*, vol 2, no 3, pp 112–21.

Burnett, J. (1986) *A Social History of Housing*, London: Routledge.

Burney, E. (2009) *Making People Behave: Anti-Social Behaviour, Politics and Policy*, Devon: Willan Publishing.

Cabinet Office (2006) *The UK Government's Approach to Public Service Reform*, London: Cabinet Office.

Cabinet Office (2010) *About the Cabinet Office*, http://webarchive.nationalarchives.gov.uk/20070402090534/http://cabinetoffice.gov.uk/about_the_cabinet_office/

Cahill, K. (2001) *Who Owns Britain: The Hidden Facts behind Landownership in the UK and Ireland*, Edinburgh: Canongate Books.

Callcutt, J. (2007) *The Callcutt Review of Housebuilding Delivery*, London: Stationery Office.

Cambridgeshire County Council (2009) *Disability and Housing Issues*, www.cambridgeshirehorizons.co.uk/documents/shma/ch_35_disability_and_housing_issues.pdf

Cameron, D. (2006) 'We'll Build More Homes. and They Will Be Beautiful: People Must Be Given a Bigger Say. The Current System Is Bananas', *Independent*, 26 March.

Cameron, D. (2010) *Big Society Speech, Prime Minister's Office*, www.number10.gov.uk/news/speeches–and–transcripts/2010/07/big–society–speech–53572

Cameron, Lord (1969) *Disturbances in Northern Ireland: Report of the Commission under the Chairmanship of Lord Cameron*, Cmd 532, Belfast: HMSO.

Campaign to Protect Rural England (2010) *Green Belts: A Greener Future*, www.cpre.org.uk/filegrab/FullGreenBeltreport.pdf?ref=4118

Cantle, T. (2001) *Community Cohesion: A Report of the Independent Review Team*, London: Home Office.

Carmona, M., Carmona, S. and Gallent, N. (2003) *Delivering Homes: Processes, Planners and Providers*, London: Routledge.

Carter, M. (1997) *The Last Resort: Living in Bed and Breakfast in the 1990s*, London: Shelter.

Casey, L. (2003) *More Than a Roof*, www.communities.gov.uk/documents/housing/pdf/156600.pdf

Cassidy, J. (2009) *How Markets Fail: The Logic of Economic Calamities*, London: Allen Lane.

Castles, F. (1998) 'The Really Big Trade-Off: Home Ownership and the Welfare State in the New World and the Old', *Acta Politica*, vol 33, no 1, pp 5–19.

Cave, M. (2007) *Report of the Independent Review of Social Housing Led by Professor Martin Cave*, London: Stationery Office.

Centre for Social Justice (2006) *Interim Report on the State of the Nation*, London: Centre for Social Justice.

Centre for Social Justice (2008) *Breakthrough Britain: Housing Poverty, from Social Breakdown to Social Mobility*, London: Centre for Social Justice.

Centre for Social Justice (2009) *Dynamic Benefits: Towards Welfare That Works*, London: Centre for Social Justice.

Chadwick, E. (1842) *Report on the Sanitary Condition of the Labouring Population of Great Britain*, London: HMSO.

Champion, T. (2010) 'Foreword', in M. Satsangi, N. Gallent and M. Bevan (eds) *The Rural Housing Question*, Bristol: Policy Press.

Chancellor of the Exchequer (2010) *Spending Review Statement*, www.hm-treasury.gov.uk/spend_sr2010_speech.htm

Chartered Institute of Housing, Scotland (2009) *Investing in Affordable Housing – A Radical Rethink?* Edinburgh: Chartered Institute of Housing.

Checkland, S.G. and Checkland, E.O. (eds) (1974) *The Poor Law Report of 1834*, Harmondsworth: Penguin.

Churchill, W. (1909) Speech delivered at King's Theatre, Edinburgh, 17 July, www.cooperativeindividualism.org/churchill_monopolyspeech.html

Clapham, D., Kemp, P. and Smith, S. (1990) *Housing and Social Policy*, London: Palgrave.

Coleman, A. (1985) *Utopia on Trial*, London: Hilary Shipman.

Collison, P. (1963) *The Cutteslowe Walls: A Study in Social Class*, London: Faber and Faber.

Commission on Social Justice (1994) *Social Justice: Strategies for National Renewal*, London: Vintage.

Conservative Party (1951) *Conservative Party Manifesto 1951*, London: Conservative Party.

Conservative Party (2009) *Strong Foundations, Building Homes and Communities: Nurturing Responsibility, Policy Green Paper No. 10*, London: Conservative Party.

Conservative Party (2010a) *Invitation to Join the Government of Britain*, London: Conservative Party.

Conservative Party (2010b) *Open Resource Planning: Green Paper 14*, London: Conservative Party.

Cooper, G. (2008) *The Origins of the Financial Crisis: Central Banks, Credit Bubbles and the Efficient Market Fallacy*, Petersfield: Harrison House Ltd.

CORE (2010) *Factsheet Presenting Key Results from Housing Association Lettings and Sales That Have Taken Place during the 08/09 Reporting Year.* Available at: https://core.tenantservicesauthority.org/AnalyseData/ASDPublication.aspx?TypeOfDocumentId=2&TypeOfDocument=Annual%20C

Council of Mortgage Lenders (2009) 'Homeowner Housing Equity through the Downturn', *Housing Finance*, issue 1.

Cowan, D. and McDermont, M. (2006) *Regulating Social Housing: Governing Decline*, Abingdon: Routledge.

Cowen, G., Wilton, M., Russell, G. and Stowe, P. (2008) *Impacts and Outcomes of the Neighbourhood Renewal Fund*, London: DCL.

CRE (Commission for Racial Equality) (1990) *Sorry, It's Gone: Testing for Racial Discrimination in the Private Sector*, London: Commission for Racial Equality.

CRESR (Centre for Regional Economic and Social Research, Sheffield Hallam University) (2010a) *Making Deprived Areas Better Places to Live: Evidence from the New Deal for Communities Programme. The New Deal for Communities National Evaluation: Final Report – Volume 4*, London: DCL.

CRESR (2010b) *Making Deprived Areas Better Places to Live: Evidence from the New Deal for Communities Programme. The New Deal for Communities National Evaluation: Final Report – Volume 3*, London: DCL.

Crisis (2009) *No One's Priority: The Treatment of Single Homeless People by Local Authority Homelessness Services*, www.crisis.org.uk/publications-search.php?fullitem=254

Crisis (2010) *Hidden Homelessness*, www.crisis.org.uk/pages/about-hidden-homelessness.html

Crook, T. and Kemp, P.A. (2010) *Transforming Private Landlords: Housing, Markets and Public Policy*, Chichester: Wiley-Blackwell.

Crosland, A. (1962) *The Conservative Enemy: A Programme of Radical Reform for the 1960s*, London: Jonathan Cape.

Crossman, R. (1977) *The Diaries of a Cabinet Minister: Minister of Housing, 1964–66*, London: Hamish Hamilton.

Crouch, C. (2009) 'Privatised Keynesianism: An Unacknowledged Policy Regime', *British Journal of Politics and International Relations*, vol 11, no 3, pp 382–99.

Cullingworth, J.B. (1969) *Council Housing: Purposes, Procedures and Priorities*, London: Ministry of Housing and Local Government/Welsh Office.

Dahl, R.A. (1961) *Who Governs?* New Haven: Yale University Press.

Daily Mail (2010) 'Housing Benefit Cap Will Lead to "Kosovo-Style" Cleansing of London: Cameron and Boris at War Over Eviction Jibe', 29 October, www.dailymail.co.uk/news/article-1324514/Boris-Johnson-slams-David-Cameron-housing-benefit-cuts.html#ixzz142NtambT

Daily Mirror (1945) 14th June 1945.

Daily Telegraph (2010) 'Former Asylum Seeker on Benefits Given £2 million house', www.telegraph.co.uk/news/uknews/7883944/Former-asylum-seeker-on-benefits-given-2-million-house.html

Daniel, W.W. (1968) *Racial Discrimination in Britain*, London: Penguin.

Daunton, M.J. (1983) *House and Home in the Victorian City: Working Class Housing 1850–1914*, London: Edward Arnold.

Davies, A. and Lupton, M. (2010) *Future Directions in Intermediate Rented Housing: A Discussion Paper*, London: Chartered Institute of Housing.

DCL (Department for Communities and Local Government) (2005a) *Why Is HMO Licensing Being Introduced?* Available at: http://webarchive.nationalarchives.gov.uk/+/www.communities.gov.uk/housing/rentingandletting/privaterenting/housesmultiple/hmofaq/landlords/hmolicensing1/?id=668225

DCL (2005b) *Affordability Targets: Implications for Housing Supply*, London: DCL.

DCL (2006a) *Planning Policy Statement 3 (PPS): Housing*, www.communities.gov.uk/documents/planningandbuilding/pdf/planningpolicystatement3.pdf

DCL (2006b) *Homelessness Code of Guidance for Local Authorities: July 2006*, www.communities.gov.uk/publications/housing/homelessnesscode

DCL (2006c) *Homelessness Statistics December 2006 and the Homeless Funding Allocation for Local Authorities – Policy Briefing 17*, www.communities.gov.uk/publications/housing/homelessnessstatisticsdecember2

DCL (2006d) *A Decent Home: Definition and Guidance for Implementation*, www.communities.gov.uk/publications/housing/decenthome

DCL (2006e) *Code for Sustainable Homes: A Step-Change in Sustainable Home Building Practice*, London: DCL.

DCL (2007a) *Homes for the Future: More Affordable, More Sustainable*, cm7191, www.communities.gov.uk/documents/housing/pdf/439986.pdf

DCL (2007b) *Tenant Empowerment: A Consultation Paper*, www.communities.gov.uk/archived/publications/housing/tenantempowerment

DCL (2008a) *No One Left Out: Communities Ending Rough Sleeping*, www.communities.gov.uk/publications/housing/roughsleepingstrategy

DCL (2008b) *Creating Strong, Safe and Prosperous Communities*, www.communities.gov.uk/publications/localgovernment/strongsafeprosperous

DCL (2008c) *Communities in Control: Real People, Real Power*, www.communities.gov.uk/publications/communities/communitiesincontrol

DCL (2009a) *Homes and Communities Agency*, London: DCL.

DCL (2009b) *Local Strategic Partnerships*, London: DCL.

DCL (2009c) *Citizens of Equal Worth: The Project Groups Proposals for the National Tenant Voice*, www.communities.gov.uk/publications/housing/equalworthreport

DCL (2009d) *The Private Rented Sector – Professionalism and Quality: The Government Response to the Rugg Review Consultation*, www.communities.gov.uk/documents/housing/pdf/1229922.pdf

DCL (2009e) *Review of Council House Finance, Analysis of Rents*, www.communities.gov.uk/publications/housing/rentspolicyanalysis

DCL (2009f) *Fair and Flexible: Statutory Guidance on Social Housing Allocations for Local Authorities in England*, www.communities.gov.uk/documents/housing/pdf/1403131.pdf

DCL (2009g) *Key Messages and Evidence on the Housing Market Renewal Pathfinder Programme 2003–2009*, London: DCL.

DCL (2009h) *Evaluation of the Mixed Communities Demonstration Projects: Baseline and Early Process Issues*, www.communities.gov.uk/documents/housing/pdf/1185667.pdf

DCL (2009i) *Survey of English Housing*, www.communities.gov.uk/documents/housing/xls/140372.xls

DCL (2009j) *Improving Opportunity, Strengthening Society: A Third Progress Report on the Government's Strategy for Race Equality and Community Cohesion, Volume 2, Race Equality in Public Services: Statistical Report*, www.communities.gov.uk/publications/communities/raceequalitythirdreport

DCL (2009k) *Housing in England 2007–08: A Report Principally from the 2007–08 Survey of English Housing, Carried Out by the National Centre for Social Research on Behalf of Communities and Local Government*, www.ignite-ne.com/ignite/Documents-hvstr.nsf/0/C1D176169B02D4458025765D004E4A71/$file/HousingEngland200708.pdf

DCL (2009l) *2007–08 Citizenship Survey: Community Cohesion Topic Report*, www.communities.gov.uk/publications/corporate/statistics/citizenshipsurvey200708cohesion

DCL (2009m) *English House Condition Survey 2007: Decent Homes and Decent Places*, http://www.communities.gov.uk/documents/statistics/pdf/1133548.pdf

DCL (2010a) *About Housing*, www.communities.gov.uk/housing/about

DCL (2010b) *Housing: Live Tables*, www.communities.gov.uk/housing/housingresearch/housingstatistics/livetables

DCL (2010c) *Review of Social Housing Regulation*, www.communities.gov.uk/documents/housing/pdf/1742903.pdf

DCL (2010d) *Choice Based Lettings*. Available at: http://webarchive.nationalarchives.gov.uk/+/communities.gov.uk/housing/housingmanagementcare/choicebasedlettings/

DCL (2010e) *Views of Choice When Allocated Current Home,* , www. communities.gov.uk/documents/housing/xls/139925.xls

DCL (2010f) *New Policy Document for Planning Obligations Consultation,* www. communities.gov.uk/documents/planningandbuilding/pdf/1518602.pdf

DCL (2010g) *Statutory Homelessness, 2nd Quarter,* www.communities.gov. uk/publications/corporate/statistics/homelessnessq22010

DCL (2010h) *The Effectiveness of Schemes to Enable Households at Risk of Domestic Violence to Remain in Their Own Homes,* www.communities.gov. uk/documents/housing/pdf/1697788.pdf

DCL (2010i) *Homelessness Prevention and Relief: England 2009/10 Experimental Statistics,* www.communities.gov.uk/publications/corporate/ statistics/homelessnessprevention200910

DCL (2010j) *Local Authority Non-Decent Homes: Provisional Estimates 2009/10,* www.communities.gov.uk/publications/corporate/statistics/ bpsanondecenthomes0910

DCL (2010k) *English Housing Survey 2008: Housing Stock Report,* www.communities.gov.uk/publications/corporate/statistics/ ehs2008stockreport

DCL (2010l) *English Housing Survey 2008–09: Household Report,* www.communities.gov.uk/publications/corporate/statistics/ ehs200809householdreport

DCL (2010m) *Evaluation of the Impact of HMO Licensing and Selective Licensing,* www.communities.gov.uk/publications/housing/hmoimpactevaluation

DCL (2010n) *Anti-Social Behaviour in Social Housing,* www.communities. gov.uk/documents/housing/pdf/157179.pdf

DCL (2010o) *Average Valuations of Residential Building Land with Outline Planning Permission,* www.communities.gov.uk/documents/housing/ xls/141389.xls

DCL (2010p) *Citizenship Survey April–September 2009,* www.communities. gov.uk/documents/statistics/pdf/1448135.pdf

DCL (2010q) *2008/9 Citizenship Survey: Race, Religion and Equalities Report,* www.communities.gov.uk/publications/corporate/statistics/ citizenshipsurvey200809equality

DCL (2010r) *New Homes Bonus: Consultation,* http://www.communities. gov.uk/publications/housing/newhomesbonusconsult

DCL (2010s) '16 Areas Get "Community Budgets" to Help the Vulnerable', www.communities.gov.uk/news/corporate/1748111

DCL (2010t) *Five-Year Housing Land Supply Coverage in England,* www. communities.gov.uk/publications/planningandbuilding/fiveyearhousing

DCL (2010u) 'Business Plan 2011–2014', www.number10.gov.uk/wp- content/uploads/CLG_FINAL-2.pdf

DCL (2011) *Implementing Self-Financing for Council Housing*, www. communities.gov.uk/publications/housing/implementingselffinancing

DCL and Department of Energy and Climate Change (2010) *Warm Homes, Greener Homes: A Strategy for Household Energy Management*, www.decc. gov.uk/en/content/cms/what_we_do/consumers/saving_energy/hem/ hem.aspx

DCL, Department of Health and Department for Work and Pensions (2008) *Lifetime Homes, Lifetime Neighbourhoods: A National Strategy for Housing in an Ageing Society*, www.communities.gov.uk/publications/housing/ lifetimehomesneighbourhoods

Dennis, N. (1972) *People and Planning: The Sociology of Housing in Sunderland*, London: Faber and Faber.

Dennis, R. (1984) *English Industrial Cities of the Nineteenth Century: A Social Geography*, Cambridge: Cambridge University Press.

Department for Education and Skills (2006) *Ethnicity and Education: The Evidence on Minority Ethnic Pupils Aged 5–16*, www.dcsf.gov.uk/rsgateway/ DB/RRP/u014955/index.shtml

Department for Social Development (2010) *Building Sound Foundations: A Strategy for the Private Rented Sector*, www.dsdni.gov.uk/index/ consultations/archived-consultations/consultations-building-sound-foundations.htm

Department of the Environment and Welsh Office (1995) *Our Future Homes: Opportunity, Choice, Responsibility: The Government's Housing Policies for England and Wales*, cm 2901, London: HMSO.

Depastino, T. (2003) *Citizen Hobo: How a Century of Homelessness Shaped America*, Chicago, IL: University of Chicago Press.

DETR (Department of the Environment, Transport and the Regions) (1999a) *Rough Sleeping: The Government's Strategy: Coming in Out of the Cold*, London: DETR.

DETR (1999b) *National Framework for Tenant Participation Compacts*, London: DETR.

DETR (1999c) *Report by the Unpopular Housing Action Team*, London: DETR.

DETR (2000a) *Quality and Choice: A Decent Home For All: The Housing Green Paper*, London: DETR.

DETR (2001) *Private Sector Renewal: A Consultation Paper*, London: DETR.

Dickens, C. (1888) *Dickens's Directory of London*, London: Macmillan.

Dickens, C. (1953 [1846–8]) *Dombey and Son*, London: Collins.

Directgov (2010) 'The Government, Prime Minister and the Cabinet'. Available at: http://direct.gov.uk/en/Governmentcitizensandrights/ UKgovernment/Centralgovernmentandthemonarchy/DG_073444

Disraeli, B. (1867) 'Speech to the House of Commons', Hansard (CLXXXVIII [3d Ser.], 1599–1614 [15 July]).

DoE (Department of the Environment) (1971) *Fair Deal for Housing*, Cmnd 4728, London: HMSO.

DoE (1973) *Better Homes:The Next Priorities*, Cmnd 5339, London: HMSO.

DoE (1977) *Housing Policy:A Consultative Document*, Cmnd 6851, London: HMSO.

DoE (1981) *An Investigation into Hard to Let Housing*, London: HMSO.

DoE (1985) *Home Improvement: A New Approach*, Cmnd 9513, London: HMSO.

DoE (1987) *Housing:The Government's Proposals*, London: HMSO.

DoE (1994a) *Housing and Construction Statistics 1983–1993*, London: HMSO.

DoE (1994b) *Access to Local Authority and Housing Association Tenancies*, London: DoE.

DoE (1995) *The Rough Sleepers Initiative: Future Plans*, London: HMSO.

DoE (1996) *An Evaluation of Six Early Estate Action Schemes, Urban Research Summary No 5*, London: DoE.

DoE (1997) *An Evaluation of DICE (Design Improved Controlled Experiment) Schemes, Regeneration Research Summary No 11*, London: DoE.

Doling, J. (1997) *Comparative Housing Policy: Government and Housing in Advanced Industrialized Countries*, Basingstoke: Macmillan.

Doling, J. (2006) 'A European Housing Policy?', *European Journal of Housing Policy*, vol 6, no 3, pp 335–49.

Donnelly, M. (2010) 'CIL Regulations Published', *PlanningResource*, 11 February.

Donnison, D. (1967) *The Government of Housing*, Harmondsworth: Penguin.

Drury, A. (2009) *Resident Satisfaction with Space in the Home*, London: HATC Limited and CABE.

Drury, A. and Somers, E. (2010) *Room to Swing a Cat? A Survey of Dwelling Sizes in London and the South East*, London: HATC Limited.

Dunleavy, P. (1981) *The Politics of Mass Housing in Britain:A Study of Corporate Power and Professional Influence in the Welfare State*, Oxford: Clarendon Press.

DWP (Department for Work and Pensions) (2007) *Local Housing Allowance*, www.dwp.gov.uk/local-authority-staff/housing-benefit/claims-processing/local-housing-allowance/background

DWP (2008) *Social Housing and Worklessness: Qualitative Research Findings, Research Report No 521*, London: DWP.

DWP (2009) *Supporting People into Work:The Next Stage of Housing Benefit Reform – Public Consultation*, www.dwp.gov.uk/consultations/2009/supportingpeopleintowork.shtml

DWP (2010a) *Expenditure Tables*. Available at: http://research.dwp.gov.uk/asd/asd4/index.php?page=medium_term

DWP (2010b) *Universal Credit: Welfare That Works*, Cm 7957, www.dwp.gov.uk/docs/universal-credit-full-document.pdf

DWP (2010c) *Households Below Average Income*. Available at: http://research.dwp.gov.uk/asd/hbai/hbai2008/excel_files/chapters/chapter_2ts_hbai09.xls

Economic and Social Research Council (2009) *Making a Difference: Risk, Trust and Betrayal: A Social Housing Case Study*, www.esrc.ac.uk/ESRCInfoCentre/Images/RESEARCH%20GRANT%20-%20COWAN%20web_tcm6-31858.pdf

Egan, J. (1998) *Rethinking Construction: The Report of the Construction Task Force on the Scope for Improving Quality and Efficiency in UK Construction*, London: DETR.

EHRC (Equality and Human Rights Commission) (2009) *Our Job*, www.equalityhumanrights.com/our-job

EHRC (2010) *How Fair is Britain? Equality, Human Rights and Good Relations in 2010: The First Triennial Review*, London: Equality and Human Rights Commission.

Elphicke, N. (2010) *Housing People; Financing Housing*, London: Policy Exchange.

Elson, M.J. (1986) *Green Belts: Conflict Mediation in the Urban Fringe*, London: Heinemann.

Empty Homes Agency (2010) *2009 Strategy Statistical Appendix*, www.emptyhomes.com/usefulresources/stats/2009breakdown.htm

Engels, F. (1845) 'Irish Immigration', in *The Condition of the Working Class in Britain*, www.marxists.org/archive/marx/works/1845/condition-working-class/ch06.htm

Engels, F. (1872) *The Housing Question Part Two: How the Bourgeoisie Solves the Housing Question*, www.marxists.org/archive/marx/works/1872/housing-question/

Esping-Andersen, G. (1990) *The Three Worlds of Welfare Capitalism*, Cambridge: Polity Press.

Esping-Andersen, G. (1999) *Social Foundations of Postindustrial Economics*, Oxford: Oxford University Press.

Etzioni, A. (1993) *The Spirit of Community: Rights, Responsibilities, and the Communitarian Agenda*, London: Crown Publications.

European Commission (2010) *Housing Exclusion: Welfare Policies Housing Provision and Labour Markets*, www.york.ac.uk/inst/chp/publications/PDF/EUExclusion/English%20Executive%20Summary.pdf

Eurostat (2010) *Housing Statistics*. Available at: http://epp.eurostat.ec.europa.eu/statistics_explained/index.php/Housing_statistics#Housing_quality

Evans, A. (1988) *No Room! No Room! The Costs of the British Town and Country Planning System*, London: Institute of Economic Affairs.

Feijten, P. and van Ham, M. (2010) 'The Impact of Splitting Up and Divorce on Housing Careers in the UK', *Housing Studies*, vol 25, no 4, pp 483–507.

Ferrari, E. (2007) 'Housing Market Renewal in an Era of New Housing Supply', *People, Place & Policy Online*, vol 1, no 3, pp 124–35.

Ferrari, E. and Lee, P. (2010) *Building Sustainable Housing Markets: Lessons from a Decade of Changing Demand and Housing Market Renewal*, London: Chartered Institute of Housing.

Ferrera, M. (1996) 'The "Southern Model" of Welfare in Social Europe', *Journal of European Social Policy*, vol 6, no 1, pp 17–37.

Financial Services Authority (2010) *Mortgage Market Review: Responsible Lending*, www.fsa.gov.uk/pages/Library/Policy/CP/2010/10_16.shtml

Finney, N. and Simpson, L. (2009) *'Sleepwalking to Segregation'? Challenging Myths about Race and Migration*, Bristol: Policy Press.

Fitzpatrick, S. and Pleace, N. (2009) 'Family Homelessness', in S. Fitzpatrick, D. Quilgars and N. Pleace (eds) *Homelessness in the UK: Problems and Solutions*, London: Chartered Institute of Housing, pp 19–33.

Fitzpatrick, S., Quilgars, D. and Pleace, N. (eds) (2009) *Homelessness in the UK: Problems and Solutions*, London: Chartered Institute of Housing.

Foord, M. and Simic, P. (eds) (2005) *Housing, Community Care and Supported Housing: Resolving Contradictions*, London: Chartered Institute of Housing.

Foot, M. (1975) *Aneurin Bevan: 1945–60, Volume 2*, London: Paladin.

Foucault, M. (1991) 'Governmentality', in G. Burchell, C. Gordon and P. Miller (eds) *The Foucault Effect: Studies in Governmentality*, Hemel Hempstead: Harvester Wheatsheaf, pp 87–104.

Foyer Federation (2010) *Our History*, www.foyer.net/level2.asp?level2id=2

Friedman, D. (2010) *Social Impact of Poor Housing*, London: Ecotec.

Gardiner, J. (2010) *The Thirties: An Intimate History*, London: Harper Press.

Genworth Financial (2010) *Financial Barriers to Home Ownership*, www.genworth.co.uk/content/genworth/uk/en/About_Us/research/First_Time_Buyer_Study.html

George, H. (1979 [1879]) *Progress and Poverty*, London: Hogarth Press.

Gervais, M. and Rehman, H. (2005) *Causes of Homelessness Amongst Ethnic Minority Populations: Research*, London: ODPM.

Giddens, A. (1998) *The Third Way: Renewal of Social Democracy*, Cambridge: Polity Press.

Giles, J. (2004) *The Parlour and the Suburb: Domestic Identities, Class, Femininity and Modernity*, Oxford: Berg.

Gilmour, I. (1992) *Dancing with Dogma: Britain Under Thatcher*, London: Simon and Schuster.

Gilroy, R. and Woods, R. (eds) (1994) *Housing Women*, London: Routledge.

Ginsburg, N. (1992) 'Racism and Housing: Concepts and Reality', in P. Braham, A. Rattans and R. Skellington (eds) *Racism and Antiracism*, London: Sage Publications, pp 109–33.

Glendinning, M. and Mulhesius, S. (1994) *Tower Block: Modern Public Housing in England, Scotland, Wales and Northern Ireland*, New Haven: Yale University Press.

Glennerster, H. (2009) *Understanding the Finance of Welfare*, 2nd edn, Bristol: Policy Press.

Glennerster, H. and Turner, T. (1993) *Estate Based Housing Management: An Evaluation*, London: Department of the Environment.

Glynn, S. (ed) (2009) *Where the Other Half Lives: Lower Income Housing in a Neoliberal World*, London: Pluto Press.

Goering, J., Fiens, J.D. and Richardson, T.M. (2003) 'What Have We Learned about Housing Mobility and Poverty Deconcentration', in J. Goering and J.D. Feins (eds) *Choosing a Better Life: Evaluating the Moving to Opportunity Experiment*, Washington, DC: The Urban Institute Press.

Goodier, C. and Pan, W. (2010) *The Future of UK Housebuilding*, http://www.rics.org/ukhousebuilding

Gower Davies, J. (1974) *The Evangelistic Bureaucrat: Study of a Planning Exercise in Newcastle-upon-Tyne*, London: Tavistock.

Grant Thornton (2009) 'Amount of UK Consumer Debt Exceeds UK GDP as Country Struggles to Pay Off Personal Debt', www.grant-thornton.co.uk/press_room/amount_of_uk_consumer_debt_exc.aspx

Gray, J. (2009) 'What Price True Happiness', *Observer*, 13 December.

Gray, P. and Long, G. (2009) 'Homelessness Policy in Northern Ireland: Is Devolution Making a Difference?', in S. Fitzpatrick, D. Quilgars and N. Pleace (eds) *Homelessness in the UK: Problems and Solutions*, London: Chartered Institute of Housing, pp 141–57.

Greater London Authority (2007) *A Profile of Londoners by Housing Tenure*. Available at: http://legacy.london.gov.uk/gla/publications/factsandfigures/dmag-briefing-2007-17.pdf

Gregory, J. (2009) *In the Mix: Narrowing the Gap between Public and Private Housing*, London: Fabian Society/Webb Memorial Trust.

Griffiths, J.A.G. (1966) *Central Departments and Local Authorities*, London: George Allen and Unwin.

Growing Up in Scotland (2009) *Lone Parent Families with Young Children: Findings from the Growing Up Scotland Study*, www.crfr.ac.uk/gus/Lone%20parents.pdf

Gulliver, K. (2010) *Counting Costs: The Economic and Social Impact of Reduced Mobility in Social Housing*, Human City Institute: Birmingham.

Gulliver, K. and Morris, J. (2009) *Exceeding Expectations: The Nature and Extent of Resident and Community Controlled Housing in the UK*, Human City Institute: Birmingham.

Haffner, M., Hoekstra, J., Oxley, M. and Van Der Heiden (2009) *Bridging the gap between social and market rented housing in six European countries*, Delft: IOS Press.

Haines, J. (1977) *The Politics of Power*, London: Jonathan Cape.

Hall, P.A. (1993) 'Policy Paradigms, Social Learning, and the State: The Case of Economic Policymaking in Britain', *Comparative Politics*, vol 25, no 3, pp 275–96.

Hall, P., Gracey, H., Drewett, R. and Thomas, R. (1973) *The Containment of Urban England, Volume One: Urban and Metropolitan Growth Processes or Megalopolis Denied*, London: George Allen and Unwin.

Hamlin, C. (1998) *Public Health and Social Justice in the Age of Chadwick: Britain, 1800–54*, Cambridge: Cambridge University Press.

Hanley, L. (2007) *Estates: An Intimate History*, London: Granta.

Harloe, M. (1995) *The People's Home: Social Rented Housing in Europe and America*, Oxford: Blackwell.

Harriott, S. and Matthews, L. (2009) *Introducing Affordable Housing*, London: Chartered Institute of Housing.

Harrison, B. (2010) *Finding a Role? The United Kingdom 1970–1990*, Oxford: Clarendon Press.

Hay, J.R. (1983) *The Origins of the Liberal Reforms 1906–1914*, Basingstoke: Macmillan.

Hayek, F.V. (1960) *The Constitution of Liberty*, London: Routledge.

Healey, J. (2009) 'Foreword', in *Fair and Flexible: Statutory Guidance on Social Housing Allocations for Local Authorities in England*, www.communities.gov.uk/documents/housing/pdf/1403131.pdf

Heywood, F., Gangoli, G., Hamilton, J., Hodges, M., Langan, J., March, A., Moyers, S., Smith, R. and Sutton, E. (2005) *Reviewing the Disabled Facilities Grant Programme*, London: ODPM.

Hibler, C. and Vermeulen, W. (2010) *The Impact of Restricting Housing Supply on House Prices and Affordability: Final Report*, London: DCL.

Hill, A. (2003) 'Council Estate Decline Spawns New Underclass', *The Observer*, 30 November.

Hillier, B. (1986) 'City of Alice's Dreams', *The Architects Journal*, 9 July.

Hills, J. (ed) (1990) *The State of Welfare: The Welfare State in Britain since 1974*, Oxford: Clarendon.

Hills, J. (1998) 'Housing: A Decent Home Within the Reach of Every Family', in N.A. Barr, H. Glennerster and J. Hills (eds) *The State of Welfare: The Economics of Social Spending*, Oxford: Oxford University Press, pp 122–88.

Hills, J. (2004) *Inequality and the State*, Oxford: Oxford University Press.

Hills, J. (2007) *Ends and Means: The Future Roles of Social Housing in England*, London: CASE/London School of Economics.

Hills, J. (2010) (Chair) *An Anatomy of Economic Inequality in the UK: Report of the National Equality Panel*, London: CASE/London School of Economics.

Hilton, B. (2006) *A Mad, Bad and Dangerous People: England 1783–1846*, Oxford: Clarendon Press.

Hincks, S. and Robson, B. (2010) *Regenerating Communities: First Neighbourhoods in Wales*, York: Joseph Rowntree Foundation.

HM Government (2010) *The Coalition: Our Programme for Government*, London: Stationery Office.

HM Treasury (2000) *2000 Spending Review: Prudent for a Purpose: Building Opportunity and Security for All*, London: HM Treasury.

HM Treasury (2003) *Housing, Consumption and EMU*. Available at: http:// news.bbc.co.uk/1/shared/spl/hi/europe/03/euro/pdf/4.pdf

HM Treasury (2004) *Pre-Budget Report*, Cm 6408, London: Stationery Office.

HM Treasury (2005) *Britain Meeting the Global Challenge: Enterprise, Fairness and Responsibility, Pre-Budget Report, December 2005*, London: HM Treasury.

HM Treasury (2010a) *Budget 2010*, www.hm-treasury.gov.uk/2010_june_budget.htm

HM Treasury (2010b) *Spending Review, 2010*. Available at: http://cdn.hm-treasury.gov.uk/sr2010_completereport.pdf

HM Treasury (2010c) *Investment in the UK Private Rented Sector*, www.hm-treasury.gov.uk/consult_investment_private_rented_sector.htm

HM Treasury and ODPM (2005) *The Government's Response to Kate Barker's Review of Housing Supply*, London: Stationery Office.

Hodgkinson, R. (1980) *Science and the Rise of Technology since 1800*, Block V, Unit 10, Milton Keynes: Open University.

Hollow, M. (2010) 'Governmentality on Park Hill Estate: The Rationality of Public Housing', *Urban History*, vol 37, no 1, pp 117–35.

Holman, R., Lafitte, F., Spencer, F. and Wilson, H. (1970) *Socially Deprived Families in Britain*, London: Bedford Square Press.

Holmans, A.E. (1987) *Housing Policy in Britain: A History*, London: Croom Helm.

Holmans, A.E. (2008) *Historical Statistics of Housing in Britain*, Cambridge: University of Cambridge.

Holmans, A.E., Monk, S. and Whitehead, C. (2004) *Building for the Future*, London: Shelter.

Home Office (2010) *Moving Beyond the ASBO*, www.homeoffice.gov.uk/media-centre/news/moving-beyond-asbos

Homes and Communities Agency (2009) *Housing Market Renewal*, www. homesandcommunities.co.uk/housing_market_renewal

Hough, J. and Rice, B. (2010) *Providing Personalised Support to Rough Sleepers: An Evaluation of the City of London Pilot,* York: Joseph Rowntree Foundation.

Houghton, J. (2010) 'A Job Half Done and Half Abandoned: New Labour's National Strategy for Neighbourhood Renewal 1999–2009', *The International Journal of Neighbourhood Renewal*, vol 2, no 2, pp 1–13.

House of Commons (2010) *Written Answers*, 7 September, col 512W, London: House of Commons.

House of Commons Business and Enterprise Committee (2008) *Construction Matters: Ninth Report of Session 2007–8*, London: Stationery Office.

House of Commons Communities and Local Government Committee (2009) *The Supporting People Programme: Thirteenth Report of Session 2008–9, Volume 1*, London: House of Commons.

House of Commons Communities and Local Government Committee (2010) Beyond *Decent Homes: Fourth Report of Session 2009–10, Volume 1*, London: House of Commons.

House of Commons Office of the Deputy Prime Minister Select Committee (2004) *Decent Homes*, London: House of Commons.

House of Commons Office of the Deputy Prime Minister Select Committee (2006) *Affordability and the Supply of Housing, Third Report of Session 2005–6, vol 1: Report and Minutes*, London: The Stationery Office.

House of Commons Public Accounts Committee (2007) *A Foot on the Ladder: Low Cost Home Ownership Assistance: Nineteenth Report of Session 2006–07*, London: House of Commons.

House of Commons Work and Pensions Committee (2010a) *Local Housing Allowance: Fifth Report of Session 2009–10*, London: House of Commons.

House of Commons Work and Pensions Committee (2010b) *Uncorrected Evidence to Be Published as HC 469ii*, www.publications.parliament.uk/pa/cm201011/cmselect/cmworpen/uc469-ii/469ii.htm

House of Lords (2010) *Economic Affairs – First Report*, www.publications. parliament.uk/pa/ld200708/ldselect/ldeconaf/82/8202.htm

Housing Corporation (1989) *Rent Policy and Principles*, London: Housing Corporation.

Housing Corporation (2008) *Planning for the Future: Housing Needs and Aspirations of Ethnic Minority Communities*, London: Housing Corporation.

Housing Finance Group (2010) *Meeting the Challenge: Market Analysis*, London: Homes and Communities Agency.

Housing Quality Network (2005) *Homelessness: What's New*, London: Housing Quality Network.

Howard, E. (1902) *Garden Cities of Tomorrow*, London: Faber.

Howker, E. and Malik, S. (2010) *Jilted Generation: How Britain Has Bankrupted Its Youth*, London: Icon Books.

Huckshorn, R. (1984) *Political Parties in America*, Monterey, California: Brooks/Cole.

Hudson, J. and Lowe, S. (2009) *Understanding the Policy Process: Analysing Welfare Policy and Practice*, Bristol: Policy Press.

Humphreys, R. (1999) *No Fixed Abode: A History of Responses to the Roofless and Rootless in Britain*, Basingstoke: Macmillan.

Hutton, W. (2010) *Them and Us: Changing Britain – Why We Need a Fair Society*, London: Little, Brown.

Hynes, P. and Sales, R. (2010) 'New Communities: Asylum Seekers and Dispersal', in A. Bloch and J. Solomos (eds) *Race and Ethnicity in the 21st Century*, Basingstoke: Palgrave Macmillan, pp 39–62.

Independent Commission for Co-operative and Mutual Housing (2009a) *Housing Needs, Mutual Solutions*, www.ccmh.coop

Independent Commission for Co-operative and Mutual Housing (2009b) *Bringing Democracy Back Home*, www.ccmh.coop/sites/default/files/Commission%20Report.pdf

Ineichen, B. (1993) *Homes and Health: How Housing and Health Interact*, London: E. and F.N. Spon.

Inside Housing (2007a) 'Gove: Higher Housing Targets under Tory Government', 25 June.

Inside Housing (2007b) 'Homeless Pushed into Private Rented Sector', 1 February.

Inside Housing (2010a) 'Livingstone: I'll Cap Private Rents', 1 October.

Inside Housing (2010b) 'Planning Shakeup Sees 300,000 Homes Axed', 4 October.

Institute for Public Policy Research North (2010) *Rebalancing Local Economies: Widening Economic Opportunities for People in Deprived Communities*, www.ippr.org.uk/ipprnorth/publicationsandreports/publication.asp?id=779

Jacobs, K., Kemeny, J. and Manzi, T. (2003a) 'Power, Discursive Space and Institutional Practices in the Construction of Housing Problems', *Housing Studies*, vol 18, no 4, pp 429–46.

Jacobs, K., Kemeny, J. and Manzi, T. (2003b) 'Privileged or Exploited Council Tenants? The Discursive Change in Conservative Housing Policy from 1972–1980', *Policy and Politics*, vol 31, no 3, pp 307–20.

Johnson, P.B. (1968) *Land Fit for Heroes*, Chicago, IL: University of Chicago Press.

Johnstone, N. (2010) 'Pickles Officially Axes "Soviet-Style" Regional Planning', *Public Property UK*, www.publicpropertyuk.com/2010/07/06/pickles-officially-axes-soviet-style-regional-planning

Jones, B. (2010) 'Slum Clearance, Privatization and Residualisation: The Practices and Politics of Council Housing in Mid-Twentieth Century England', *Twentieth Century British History*. Available at: http://tcbh. oxfordjournals.org/content/early/2010/07/13/tcbh.hwq025.full. pdf+html

Jones, C. (2010) 'The Right to Buy', in P. Malpass and R. Rowlands (eds) *Housing, Markets and Policy*, London: Routledge, pp 59–75.

Jones, C. and Murie, A. (1998) *Reviewing the Right to Buy*, York: Joseph Rowntree Foundation.

Jones, C. and Murie, A. (2006) *The Right to Buy*, London: Wiley-Blackwell

Jones, C. and Watkins, C. (2009) *Housing Markets and Planning Policy*, Chichester: Wiley-Blackwell.

Jones, G.S. (1976) *Outcast London: Study in the Relationship between Classes in Victorian Society*, Harmondsworth: Penguin.

Jones, M. (1988) 'Utopia and Reality: The Utopia of Public Housing and Its Reality at Broadwater Farm', in M. Teymur, T. Marcus and T. Woolley (eds) *Rehumanizing Housing*, London: Butterworths, pp 89–101.

Jones, N. (2002) *Control Freaks: How New Labour Gets Its Own Way*, London: Portico's Publishing.

Joseph Rowntree Foundation (2008) Housing and Disabled Children, York: Joseph Rowntree Foundation

Joseph Rowntree Foundation (2010) Participation and Community on Bradford's Traditionally White Estates, www.jrf.org.uk/sites/files/jrf/Bradford-participation-community-summary.pdf

Joyce, P. (1980) *Work, Society and Politics. The Culture of the Factory in Later Victorian England*, Brighton: Harvester Press.

Juniper, T., Simm, C. and Perry, J. (eds) (2008) *Housing, the Environment and Our Changing Climate*, London: Chartered Institute of Housing.

Jupp, B. (1999) *Living Together: Community Life on Mixed Estates*, London: Demos.

Katz, B. (2010) 'Obama's Metro Presidency', *City and Community*, vol 9, no 1, pp 23–31.

Kemeny, J. (1994) *From Public Housing to the Social Market*, London: Taylor and Francis.

Kemp, P. (1999) 'Housing Policy Under New Labour', in M. Powell (ed) *New Labour, New Welfare State: The 'Third Way' in British Social Policy*, Bristol: Policy Press, pp 123–45.

Kemp, P. (2004) *Private Renting in Transition*, London: Chartered Institute of Housing.

Kemp, P. (ed) (2007) *Housing Allowances in Comparative Perspective*, Bristol: Policy Press.

Kemp, P. (2008) 'Housing Benefit and Social Housing in England', in S. Fitzpatrick and M. Stephens (eds) *The Future of Social Housing*, London: Shelter, pp 53–68.

Kerslake, B. (2010a) 'Department for Communities and Local Government Announces New Top Structure', www.communities.gov.uk/news/corporate/1748492

Kerslake, B. (2010b) 'Spaced Out', *Inside Housing*, 29 January.

Kilminster, R. (1998) *The Sociological Revolution: From Enlightenment to the Global Age*, London: Routledge.

King, P. (2010) *Housing Policy Transformed: The Right to Buy and the Desire to Own*, Bristol: Policy Press.

Kirchner, J. (2007) 'The Declining Social Rental Sector in Germany', *European Journal of Housing Policy*, vol 7, no 1, pp 85–101.

Klein, N. (2007) *The Shock Doctrine: The Rise of Disaster Capitalism*, London: Penguin.

Kynaston, D. (2007) *Austerity Britain 1945–1951*, London: Bloomsbury.

Kynaston, D. (2009) *Family Britain 1951–1957*, London: Bloomsbury.

Labour Party (1951) *Labour Party Manifesto*, London: Labour Party.

Labour Party (1997) *New Labour Because Britain Deserves Better*, London: Labour Party.

Labour Party (2010) *A Future Fair for All*, London: Labour Party.

Lanchester, J. (2010) *Whoops! Why Everyone Owes Everyone and No One Can Pay*, London: Allen Lane.

Lasswell, H.D. (1951) 'The Policy Orientation', in D. Lerner and H.D. Lasswell (eds) *The Policy Sciences: Recent Developments in Scope and Method*, Stanford: Stanford University Press.

Latham, M. (1994) *Constructing the Team: Final Report of the Government/Industry Review of the Procurement and Contractual Arrangements in the UK Construction Industry*, London: HMSO.

Law, I., Davies, J., Lyle, S. and Deacon, A. (1999) 'Race, Ethnicity and Youth Homelessness', in F.E. Spiers (ed) *Housing and Social Exclusion*, London: Jessica Kingsley Publications, pp 141–62.

Lawless, P. (2010) 'Urban Regeneration: Is There a Future?' *People, Place and Policy Online*, vol 4, no 1, pp 24–8.

Lawson, N. (2010) *Memoirs of a Tory Radical*, London: Biteback.

Le Corbusier (1927) *Towards a New Architecture*, London: Architectural Press.

Lees, L. and Leys, P. (2008) 'Introduction to the Special Issue "Gentrification as Public Policy"', *Urban Studies*, vol 45, no 12, pp 2379–84.

Le Grand, J. (2001) *The Quasi-Market Experiments in Public Service Delivery: Did They Work?*, paper for presentation at the Pontigano Conference 2001, London: Department of Social Policy, London School of Economics and Political Science.

Le Grand, J. (2003) *Motivation, Agency and Public Policy: Of Knights and Knaves, Pawns and Queens*, Oxford: Oxford University Press.

Lelkes, O. and Zólyomi, E. (2010) *Housing Quality Deficiencies and the Link to Income in the EU*, www.euro.centre.org/data/1270820381_27296.pdf

Leunig, T. (2010) *A Housing Agenda That Will Make a Difference?* Housing Studies Association, www.york.ac.uk/inst/chp/hsa/spring10/papers.htm

Liberal Democrats (2010) *Liberal Democrat Manifesto 2010: Change That Works for You*, London: Liberal Democrats.

Lindblom, C.E. (1959) 'The Science Of "Muddling Through"', *Public Administration Review*, vol 19, pp 79–88.

Lister, R. (2010) *Understanding Theories and Concepts in Social Policy*, Bristol: Policy Press.

Lloyd, A.H. (1901) *Dynamic Idealism: An Elementary Course in the Metaphysics of Psychology*, Chicago: McClurg.

Local Government Association (2008) *My Rent Went to Whitehall*, www.lga.gov.uk/lga/aio/772277

London and Quadrant (2010) *Hard Times, New Choices: A New Deal for Housing Associations*, London: London and Quadrant.

Lovatt, R., Whitehead, C. and Levy-Vroelant, C. (2006) 'Foyers in the UK and France – Comparisons and Contrasts', *European Journal of Housing Policy*, vol 6, no 2, pp 151–66.

Lowe, S. (2007) 'The New Private Rented Sector – Regulation in a Deregulated Market', in D. Hughes and S. Lowe (eds) *The Private Rented Housing Market*, Aldershot: Ashgate, pp 1–13.

Lund, B. (2008) 'Major, Blair and the Third Way in Social Policy', *Social Policy and Administration*, vol 42, no 1, pp 43–58.

Lupton, R. and Fuller, C. (2009) 'Mixed Communities: A New Approach to Spatially Concentrated Poverty in England', *International Journal of Urban and Regional Research*, vol 33, no 4, pp 1014–28.

Lupton, R. and Power, A. (2002) 'Social Exclusion and Neighbourhoods', in J. Hills, J. Le Grand and D. Piachaud (eds) *Understanding Social Exclusion*, Oxford: Oxford University Press, pp 118–40.

Lupton, R. and Tunstall, R. (2009a) *Growing Up in Social Housing in Britain: A Profile of Four Generations, 1946 to the Present Day*, York: Joseph Rowntree Foundation.

Lupton, R. and Tunstall, R. (2009b) 'It's Easy to Blame Social Housing', *Inside Housing*, 21 August.

Lux, M. (2009) *Housing Policy and Housing Finance in the Czech Republic during Transition: An Example of the Schism between the Still-Living Past and the Need for Reform*, Delft: Delft University Press.

Lux, M. and Sunega, P. (2007) 'Housing Allowances in the Czech Republic in Comparative Perspective', in P. Kemp (ed) (2007) *Housing Allowances in Comparative Perspective*, Bristol: Policy Press, pp 239–64.

Lyttelton, O. (1962) *The Memoirs of Lord Chandos*, London: Bodley Head.

Macmillan, H. (2004) *The Macmillan Diaries: The Cabinet Years 1950–1957*, London: Pan Macmillan.

Macpherson, W. (1999) *The Stephen Lawrence Inquiry*, Cm 4262, London: The Stationery Office.

Maile, S. and Hoggett, P. (2004) 'Best Value and the Politics of Pragmatism', *Policy & Politics*, vol 29, no 4, pp 509–16.

Malpass, P. (2000) *Housing Associations and Housing Policy: A Historical Perspective*, Basingstoke: Macmillan.

Malthus, T.R. (1803) *An Essay on the Principle of Population*, Cambridge: Cambridge University Press.

Manzi, T. and Smith Bowers, B. (2004) 'So Many Managers, So Little Vision: Registered Social Landlords and Consortium Schemes in the UK', *European Journal of Housing Policy*, vol 4, no 1, pp 57–75.

Markkanen, S. (2009) 'Looking to the Future: Changing Black and Minority Ethnic Housing Needs and Aspirations', *Better Housing Briefing 11*, London: Race Equality Foundation.

Marquand, D. (2008) *Britain since 1918: The Strange Career of British Democracy*, London: Weidenfeld and Nicolson.

Marsh, D. and Stoker, G. (2002) *Theory and Methods in Political Science*, London: Palgrave Macmillan

Marx, K. (1859) *A Contribution to the Critique of Political Economy*, www.marxists.org/archive/marx/works/1859/critique-pol-economy/preface-abs.htm

Marx, K. and Engels, F. (1848) *The Communist Manifesto*, www.marxists.org/archive/marx/works/1848/communist-manifesto/ch01.htm

Mathiason, N. (2004) 'Prescott to Raze 400,000 Homes', *Observer*, 22 August.

Matthews, P. (2010) 'Mind the Gap? The Persistence of Pathological Discourses in Urban Regeneration Policy', *Housing Theory and Society*, vol 27, no 3, pp 221–40.

May, J., Cloke, P. and Johnsen, S. (2004) *Re-phasing Neo-liberalism: From Governance to 'Governmentality': New Labour and Britain's Crisis of Street Homelessness*, www.geog.qmul.ac.uk/homeless/homelessplaces/re-phasingneo-liberalism.pdf

Mayor of London (2010) *Overcrowding in Social Housing: A London Action Plan*, London: Mayor of London.

McDermont, M. (2010) *Governing Independence and Expertise: The Business of Housing Associations*, Oregon: Oxford and Portland.

McKenna, M. (1991) 'The Suburbanisation of the Working-Class Population of Liverpool between the Wars', *Social History*, vol 16, no 2, pp 173–89.

Mellor, J.R. (1977) *Urban Sociology in an Urbanised Society*, London: Routledge and Kegan Paul.

Merrett, S. (1979) *State Housing in Britain*, London: Routledge and Kegan Paul.

Merrett, S. (with Gray, F.) (1982) *Owner Occupation in Britain*, London: Routledge and Kegan Paul.

Merton, R.K. (1949) *Social Theory and Social Structure*, New York: Free Press.

MHLG (Ministry of Housing and Local Government) (1953) *Housing: The Next Step*, Cmd 8996, London: HMSO.

MHLG (1963) *Housing: Government Proposals for Expanding the Provision of Homes*, Cmnd 2050, London: HMSO.

MHLG (1968) *Old Houses into New Homes*, Cmnd 3602, London: HMSO.

MHLG (1969) *Circular 65/69*, London: HMSO.

MHLG (1973) *Better Homes: The Next Priorities*, Cmnd 5339, London: HMSO.

Mills, C.W. (1959) *The Sociological Imagination*, London: Oxford University Press.

Milner Holland, E. (Chair) (1965) *Report of the Committee on Housing in Greater London*, Cmnd 2605, London: HMSO.

Ministry of Infrastructure, Italian Republic (2007) *Housing Statistics in the European Union, 2005/6*, www.federcasa.it/news/housing_statistics/Report_housing_statistics_2005_2006.pdf

Ministry of Regional Development of the Czech Republic (2005) *Housing Statistics in the European Union 2004*, www.iut.nu/EU/HousingStatistics2004.pdf

Minton, A. (2002) 'Utopia Street', *The Guardian*, 27 March.

Mitchell, L. (2007) *The Whig World 1760–1837*, London: Hambleton Continuum.

Monk, S. (2009) 'Understanding the Demand for Social Housing: Some Implications for Policy', *International Journal of Housing Markets and Analysis*, vol 2, no 1, pp 21–38.

Monk, S. and Whitehead, C. (2010) 'Conclusions', in S. Monk and C. Whitehead (eds) *Making Housing More Affordable: The Role of Intermediate Housing*, Chichester: Wiley-Blackwell.

Monk, S., Crook, T., Lister, D., Rowley, S., Short, C. and Whitehead, C. (2005) *Land and Finance for Affordable Housing*, York: Joseph Rowntree Foundation.

Monk, S., Tang, C. and Whitehead, C. (2010) *What Does the Literature Tell Us about the Social and Economic Impact of Housing?* Report to the Scottish Government: Communities Analytical Services, www.scotland.gov.uk/Resource/Doc/313646/0099448.pdf

Moran, M., Rein, M. and Goodin, R.E. (2008) *The Oxford Handbook of Public Policy*, Oxford: Oxford University Press.

Morgan, N. (1993) *Deadly Dwellings: The Shocking Story of Housing and Health in a Lancashire Cotton Town*, Preston: Mullion Books.

Morris, J. and Winn, M. (1990) *Housing and Social Inequality*, London: Hilary Shipman.

Morton, A. (2010) *Making Housing Affordable: A New Vision of Housing Policy*, London: Policy Exchange.

Morton, J. (1991) *'Cheaper than Peabody': Local Authority Housing from 1890 to 1914*, York: Joseph Rowntree Foundation.

Mount, F. (2004) *Mind the Gap: The New Class Divide in Britain*, London: Short Books.

Moyne Committee (1933) *Report of the Departmental Committee on Housing*, cmd 4397, London: HMSO.

Mullins, D. and Murie, A. (2006) *Housing Policy in the UK*, Basingstoke: PalgraveMacmillan.

Murie, A. and Nevin, B. (2001) 'New Labour Transfers', in D. Cowan and A. Marsh (eds) *Two Steps Forward: Housing Policy in the New Millennium*, Bristol: The Policy Press, pp 29–46.

Murray, C. (1984) *Losing Ground*, New York, NY: Basic Books.

Murray, C. (1992) *The Emerging British Underclass*, London: Institute of Economic Affairs.

National Assistance Act (1948) http://www.legislation.gov.uk/ukpga/1948/29/pdfs/ukpga_19480029_en.pdf

National Audit Office (2010a) *The Decent Homes Programme*, www.nao.org.uk/publications/0910/the_decent_homes_programme.aspx

National Audit Office (2010b) *PFI in Housing*, www.nao.org.uk/publications/1011/pfi_in_housing.aspx

National Audit Office (2010c) *Tackling Inequalities in Life Expectancy in Areas with the Worst Health and Deprivation*, www.nao.org.uk/publications/1011/health_inequalities.aspx

National Audit Office and Audit Commission (2006) *Building More Affordable Homes: Improving the Delivery of Affordable Housing in Areas of High Demand*, London: National Audit Office/Audit Commission.

National Centre for Social Research/Broadway (2010) *Profiling London's Rough Sleepers: A Longitudinal Analysis of Chain Data*, London: National Centre for Social Research/Broadway.

National Federation of Housing Associations (1995) *Core Lettings Bulletin*, London: National Federation of Housing Associations.

National Housing Federation (2010a) 'Three Million People to Be Stuck in Overcrowded Housing by 2013', 27 April, www.housing.org.uk/default. aspx?tabid=212&mid=828&ctl=Details&ArticleID=2904

National Housing Federation (2010b) 'Young Adults Delaying Getting Married and Starting a Family Due to Affordable Housing Drought', www.housing.org.uk/default.aspx?tabid=212&mid=828&ctl=Details& ArticleID=2835

Nationwide (2010) *House Prices*, www.nationwide.co.uk/hpi/historical.htm

Nevin, B., Lee, P., Goodson, L., Murie, A. and Phillimore, J. (2001) *Changing Housing Markets and Urban Regeneration in the M62 Corridor*, Birmingham: Centre for Urban and Regional Studies, University of Birmingham.

Newman, O. (1973) *Defensible Space*, London: Architectural Press.

NHPAU (National Housing and Planning Advice Unit) (2010) *Housing Affordability: A Fuller Picture*, http://webarchive.nationalarchives.gov. uk/+/http://www.communities.gov.uk/nhpau/keypublications/ research/housingaffordabilityfuller/

Niskanen, W.A. (1973) *Bureaucracy: Servant or Master?* London: Institute of Economic Affairs.

Noble, V.A. (2009) *Inside the Welfare State: Foundations of Policy and Practice in Post-War Britain*, Abingdon: Routledge.

Norman, J. (2010) *The Big Society: The Anatomy of the New Politics*, Buckingham: University of Buckingham Press.

Nozick, R. (1974) *Anarchy, State and Utopia*, Oxford: Blackwell.

Nozick, R. (2001) *Invariance: The Structure of the Objective World*, Cambridge, MA: Belnap/Harvard University Press.

O'Brien, M. and Penna, S. (1998) *Theorising Welfare: Enlightenment and Modern Society*, London: Sage Publications.

ODPM (Office of the Deputy Prime Minister) (2003a) *Sustainable Communities: Building for the Future*, www.communities.gov.uk/ publications/communities/sustainablecommunitiesbuilding

ODPM (2003b) *Exploitation of the Right to Buy Scheme by Companies*, London: ODPM.

ODPM (2003c) *The Draft Housing Bill – Government Response Paper*, Cm 2000, London: ODPM.

ODPM (2003d) *New Deal for Communities: Annual Review 2001/2*, London: ODPM.

ODPM (2004a) *The Impact of Overcrowding on Health and Education: A Review of Evidence and Literature*, London: ODPM.

ODPM (2004b) *Piloting Choice Based Lettings: An Evaluation*, London: ODPM.

ODPM (2005a) *Evaluation of English Housing Policy 1975–2000 Theme 2: Finance and Affordability*, London: ODPM.

ODPM (2005b) *Sustainable Communities: Homes for All*, www.communities.gov.uk/archived/publications/corporate/homesforall

ODPM (2005c) *Sustainable Communities: Settled Homes; Changing Lives. A Strategy for Tackling Homelessness*, London: ODPM.

ODPM (2005d) *Overcrowding in England: The National and Regional Picture: Statistics*, www.communities.gov.uk/documents/housing/pdf/157920.pdf

ODPM (2005e) *Making it Happen in Neighbourhoods: The National Strategy for Neighbourhood Renewal – Four Years On*, London: ODPM.

Office for National Statistics (2009) *Social Trends 2008*, www.statistics.gov.uk/socialtrends38/

Office for National Statistics (2010a) *Public Sector*, www.statistics.gov.uk/cci/nugget.asp?id=206

Office for National Statistics (2010b) *Housing Tenure*, www.statistics.gov.uk/cci/nugget.asp?id=1105

Office for National Statistics (2010c) *Work and Worklessness among Households*, www.statistics.gov.uk/pdfdir/work0910.pdf

Office of the High Commissioner for Human Rights (1989) *International Convention on the Elimination of All Forms of Racial Discrimination*, www.unhchr.ch/tbs/doc.nsf/0/3888b0541f8501c9c12563ed004b8d0e?Opendocument

Olecnowicz, A. (1997) *Working-Class Housing in England between the Wars: The Becontree Estate*, Oxford: Clarendon Press.

Oliver, M. and Barnes, C. (1998) *Disabled People and Social Policy*, Harlow: Longman.

Ormandy, D. (1991) 'Overcrowding', *Roof*, March/April, pp 9–11.

Orwell, G. (1937) *The Road to Wigan Pier*, London: Left Book Club.

Osborne, P. (2005) *The Rise of Political Lying*, London: Free Press.

Ouseley, H. (2001) *Community Pride Not Prejudice, Making Diversity Work in Bradford*, Bradford: Bradford Vision.

Oxley, M., Lishman, R., Brown, T., Haffner, M. and Hoekstra, J. (2010) *Promoting Investment in Private Renting Supply: International Policy Comparisons*, London: DCL.

Packer, I. (2001) *Lloyd George, Liberalism and the Land: The Land Issue and Party Politics in England, 1906–1914*, Suffolk: Boydell Press.

Page, D. (1993) *Building for Communities: A Study of New Housing Association Estates*, York: Joseph Rowntree Foundation.

Pawson, H. (2009a) 'Two Decades of Council Stock Transfers: Contrasts and Commonalities in Organisational and Financial Models Across Britain', in S. Wilcox (ed) *UK Housing Review 2009/10*, London: Chartered Institute of Housing/Council of Mortgage Lenders, pp 23–31.

Pawson, H. (2009b) 'Homelessness Policy in England: Promoting "Gatekeeping" or Effective Prevention?', in S. Fitzpatrick, D. Quilgars and N. Pleace (eds) *Homelessness in the UK: Problems and Solutions*, London: Chartered Institute of Housing, pp 90–104.

Pawson, H. and Jacobs, K. (2010) 'Policy Intervention and Its Impact: Analysing New Labour's Public Service Reform Model as Applied to Local Authority Housing in England', *Housing, Theory and Society*, vol 27, no 1, pp 76–94.

Pawson, H. and Wilcox, S. (2011) *UK Housing Review 2010/11*, London: Chartered Institute of Housing.

Pawson, H. and Mullins, D. (with Gilmour, T.) (2010) *After Council Housing: Britain's New Social Landlords*, Basingstoke: PalgraveMacmillan.

Pawson, H., Jones, C., Donohoe, T., Netto, G. and Fancy, C. (2006) *Monitoring the Longer Term Impact of Choice Based Lettings*, London: DCL.

Pawson, H., Davidson, E. and Netto, G. (2007) *Evaluation of Homelessness Prevention Activities in Scotland*, Edinburgh: Scottish Executive Development Department.

Pensions Policy Institute (2009) *Retirement Income and Assets: How Housing Can Support Retirement*, www.*pensionspolicyinstitute.org.uk/default. asp?p=12&publication=246*

Phillips, D., Simpson, L. and Ahmed, S. (2008) 'Shifting Geographies of Minority Ethnic Settlement: Remaking Communities in Oldham and Rochdale', in J. Flint and D. Robinson (eds) *Community Cohesion in Crisis: New Dimensions of Diversity and Difference*, Bristol: Policy Press.

Phillips, T. (2005) 'After 7/7: Sleepwalking to Segregation', speech to the Manchester Council for Community Relations, 22 September, www. humanities.manchester.ac.uk/socialchange/research/social-change/ summer-workshops/documents/sleepwalking.pdf

Platt, L. (2007) *Poverty and Ethnicity in the UK*, York: Joseph Rowntree Foundation.

Pleace, N., Fitzpatrick, S., Johnsen, S., Quilgars, D. and Sanderson, D. (2008) *Statutory Homelessness in England: The Experience of Families and 16–17 Year Olds for Housing Policy*, York: University of York.

Poor Law Commissioners (1834) *Poor Law Commissioners' Report of 1834*, London: HMSO.

Poovey, M. (1995) *Making a Social Body: British Cultural Formation 1830–1864*, Chicago: University of Chicago Press.

Popkin, S. (2007) 'Has HOPE VI Transformed Residents' Lives? New Findings from the HOPE VI Panel Study', presentation to the Department of Communities and Local Government, 6 July.

Popkin, S.J., Katz, B., Cunningham, M.K., Brown, K.D., Gustafson, J. and Turner, MA.. (2004) *A Decade of HOPE VI: Research Findings and Policy Challenges*, Washington: Urban Institute.

Popkin, S., Levy, D. and Buron, L. (2009) 'Has Hope V1 Transformed Residents' Lives? New Evidence From The Hope V1 Panel Study', *Housing Studies*, vol 24, no 4, pp 477–502.

Poulsen, M., Johnston, R. and Forrest, J. (2009) *Using Local Statistics to Portray Ethnic Residential Segregation in London*, Bristol: Centre for Market and Public Organisation.

Poverty Site (2009) *Concentrations of Worklessness*, www.poverty.org.uk/43/index.shtml

Powell, J. (2010) *The New Machiavelli: How to Wield Power in the Modern World*, London: Bodley Head.

Power, A. (1993) *Hovels to High Rise: State Housing in Europe since 1850*, London: Routledge.

Power, A. and Tunstall, R. (1995) *Swimming against the Tide: Polarisation or Progress on 20 Unpopular Council Estates, 1980–1995*, York: Joseph Rowntree Foundation.

Price Waterhouse (1995) *Tenants in Control: An Evaluation of Tenant-Led Housing Management Organisations*, London: Department of the Environment.

Prime Minister (2001) Foreword to Social Exclusion Unit (2001) *A New Commitment to Neighbourhood Renewal: National Strategy Action Plan*, London: Cabinet Office.

Prime Minister's Strategy Unit (2005) *Improving the Prospects of People Living in Areas of Multiple Deprivation in England*, London: Cabinet Office.

Prokhovnik, R. (ed) (2005) *Making Policy, Shaping Lives*, Edinburgh: Edinburgh University Press.

Purkis, A. (2010) *Housing Associations in England and the Future of Voluntary Associations*, London: Baring Foundation.

Putnam, R. (2001) *Bowling Alone: The Collapse and Revival of American Community*, New York, NY: Simon and Schuster.

Radcliffe, P. (2009) 'Re-evaluating the Links between "Race" and Residence', *Housing Studies*, vol 24, no 4, pp 433–50.

Ranelagh, J. (1991) *Thatcher's People*, London: Fontana.

Rashleigh, B. (2005) 'Keeping the Numbers Down', *Roof*, January/February, pp 18–21.

Ravetz, A. (2001) *Council Housing and Culture: The History of a Social Experiment*, London: Routledge.

Ravetz, A. and Turkington, R. (1995) *The Place of Home*, London: Spon and Co.

Rawls, J. (1971) *A Theory of Justice*, Oxford: Oxford University Press.

Rawnsley, A. (2010) *The End of the Party: The Rise and Fall of New Labour*, Viking: London.

Readman, P. (2010) 'The Edwardian Land Question', in M. Cragoe and P. Readman (eds) (2010) *The Land Question in Britain 1750–1950*, Basingstoke: Palgrave Macmillan, pp 181–200.

Rhodes, R.A.W (1994) 'The Hollowing Out of the State', *Political Quarterly*, no 65, pp 138–51.

Riach, P.A. and Rich, J. (2002) 'Field Experiments of Discrimination in the Marketplace', *The Economic Journal*, vol 112, no 483, pp 480–18.

Ridley, N. (1986) 'The Local Right: Enabling Not Providing', speech by the Secretary of State for the Environment, 7 October.

Ridley, N. (1991) *'My Style of Government': The Thatcher Years*, London: Hutchinson.

Roberts, M. (1991) *Living in a Man-made World*, London: Routledge.

Rodger, R. (2000) 'Slums and Suburbs: The Persistence of Residential Apartheid', in P. Waller (ed) *The English Urban Landscape*, Oxford: Oxford University Press.

Rogaly, B. and Taylor, B. (2009) *Moving Histories of Class and Community: Identity, Place and Belonging in Contemporary England*, Basingstoke: Palgrave Macmillan.

Ronald, R. (2008) *The Ideology of Home Ownership: Homeowner Societies and the Role of Housing*, Basingstoke: Palgrave Macmillan.

Rose, N. and Miller, P. (2008) *Governing the Present: Administering Economic, Social and Personal Life*, Cambridge: Polity Press.

Royal Commission on the Housing of the Working Classes (1885) *Reports, with Minutes of Evidence*, London: HMSO.

Royal Commission on the Poor Laws and Relief of Poverty (1909) *Minority Report of the Royal Commission on the Poor Laws and Relief of Distress*, Cd 4499, HMSO: London.

Roys, M., Davidson, M. and Monk, S. (2010) *The Real Cost of Poor Housing*, Bracknell: BRE Press.

Rubinowitz, L. and Rosenbaum, J. (2001) *Crossing the Class and Color Lines: From Public Housing to White Suburbia*, Chicago, IL: University of Chicago Press.

Rugg, J. and Rhodes, D. (2008) *Review of Private Sector Rented Housing*, York: University of York, Centre for Housing Policy.

Ruming, K. J., Mee, K. J. and McGuirk, P. M. (2004) *Questioning the rhetoric of social mix: courteous community or hidden hostility?*, Australian Geographical Studies, vol 42, no 3, pp. 234–248.

Rural Coalition (2010) *The Rural Challenge: Achieving Sustainable Rural Communities for the 21st Century*. Available at: http://ruralcommunities. gov.uk/wp-content/uploads/2010/08/RuralCoalitionWEB_MH.pdf

Rutter, J. and Latorre, M. (2009) *Social Housing Allocation and Immigrant Communities*, www.equalityhumanrights.com/uploaded_files/4_social_housing_allocation_and_immigrant_communities.pdf

Saraga, E. (1998) *Embodying the Social: Constructions of Difference*, London: Routledge.

Satsangi, M., Gallent, N. and Bevan, M. (2010) *The Rural Housing Question*, Bristol: Policy Press.

Saunders, P. (1990) *A Nation of Home Owners*, London: Routledge.

Scanlon, K. and Whitehead, C. (2004) 'Housing Tenure and Mortgage Systems: How the UK Compares', *Housing Finance*, no 60, pp 41–51.

Schmidt, S. (1989) 'Convergence Theory, Labour Movements and Corporatism: The Case of Housing', *Scandinavian Housing and Planning Research*, vol 6, pp 83–101.

Schwartz, A.F. (2010) *Housing Policy in the United States*, London: Routledge.

Schwartz, H.M. and Seabrooke, L. (2009) *The Politics of Housing Booms and Busts*, Basingstoke: Palgrave Macmillan.

Scott, P. (2003) 'Selling Owner Occupation to the Working Classes in 1930s Britain'. Available at: http://ideas.repec.org/p/rdg/emxxdp/em-dp2004-23.html

Scottish Executive (2005) *Homes for Scotland's People: A Scottish Housing Policy Statement*, Edinburgh: Scottish Executive.

Scottish Federation of Housing Associations (2010) *Fresh Thinking: New Ideas: A Response*, www.sfha.co.uk/index.php?pg=84&doc_id=2130

Scottish Government (2007) *Firm Foundations: The Future of Housing in Scotland. A Discussion Document*, Edinburgh: Scottish Government.

Scottish Government (2008) *Consultation on Regulations Made Under Section 32a of the Housing (Scotland) Act 1987*, Edinburgh: Scottish Government.

Scottish Government (2009) *Prevention of Homelessness Guidance*, www.scotland.gov.uk/Publications/2009/06/08140713/0

Scottish Government (2010a) *Housing: Fresh Thinking, New Ideas*. Available at: http://housingdiscussion.scotland.gov.uk/media/2597/Housing_Debate_Green_Paper.pdf

Scottish Government (2010b) *Operation of the Homeless Persons Legislation in Scotland 2009/10*, www.scotland.gov.uk/Publications/2010/08/31093245/26

Scottish Government (2010c) *Scottish House Condition Survey: Key Findings for 2008*, www.scotland.gov.uk/Publications/2009/11/23090958/5

Scottish Government (2010d) *Scotland's People Annual Report 2009*, www.scotland.gov.uk/Publications/2010/08/25092046/5

Secretary of State for the Environment (1996) *Household Growth: Where Shall We Live?* , Cm 3271, London: Stationery Office.

Seldon, A. (1981) *Churchill's Indian Summer: The Conservative Government 1951–1955*, London: Hodder & Stoughton.

Shapely, P. (2007) *The Politics of Housing: Power, Consumers and Urban Culture*, Manchester: Manchester University Press.

Shapely, P. (2008) 'Social Housing and Tenant Participation', *History and Policy*, www.historyandpolicy.org/papers/policy-paper-71.html

Shapps, G. (2010) 'Local Experts to Map the Scale of Rough Sleeping', www.communities.gov.uk/news/corporate/1714203

Shapps, G. (2010) *Next steps on the road to zero carbon*, http://www.communities.gov.uk/news/housing/1804027

Shelter (1969) *Face the Facts*, London: Shelter.

Shelter (2005) *Full House*, London: Shelter.

Shelter (2010) 'London Neighbourhoods That Are Affordable to Those on Housing Benefit to Halve by 2010'. Available at: http://media.shelter.org.uk/Press-releases/London-neighbourhoods-that-are-affordable-to-those-on-housing-benefit-to-halve-by-2016-35c.aspx

Simon, E.D. (1933) *The Anti-Slum Campaign*, London: Longman.

Skelton, N. (1924) *Constructive Conservatism*, London: Blackwood.

Smiles, S. (1859) *Self-Help*, London: John Murray.

Smiles, S. (1871) *Character*, London: John Murray.

Smith, A. (1970 [1776]) *An Inquiry into the Nature and Causes of the Wealth of Nations*, Harmondsworth: Penguin.

Smith, S. (1989) *The Politics of 'Race' and Residence*, London: Polity Press.

Smith, S.J., Searle, A. and Powells, G.D. (2010) 'Introduction', in S.J. Smith and A. Searle (eds) *The Economics of Housing: The Housing Wealth of Nations*, Chichester: Wiley-Blackwell, pp 1–29.

Social Exclusion Unit (1998a) *Rough Sleeping*, Cm 4008, London: The Stationery Office.

Social Exclusion Unit (1998b) *Bringing Britain Together: A National Strategy for Neighbourhood Renewal*, London: Cabinet Office.

Social Exclusion Unit (2001) *A New Commitment to Neighbourhood Renewal: National Strategy Action Plan*, London: Cabinet Office.

Social Exclusion Unit (2002) *National Strategy for Neighbourhood Renewal: Report of Action Team 8: Anti-Social Behaviour*, London: SEU.

Springler, E. and Wagner, K. (2010) 'Determinants of Homeownership Rates: Housing Finance and the Role of the State', in P. Arestis, P. Mooslechner and K. Wagner (eds) *Housing Market Challenges in Europe and the United States*, Basingstoke: Palgrave Macmillan, pp 60–85.

Squires, G.D. (2010) 'Foreclosures – Yesterday, Today and Tomorrow', *City and Community*, vol 9, no 1, pp 50–60.

Statistics Bundesamt, Deutschland (2010) *Housing Situation*, www.destatis.de/jetspeed/portal/cms/Sites/destatis/Internet/EN/Content/Statistics/BauenWohnen/Wohnsituation/Tabellen/Content75/EntwicklungEigent_C3_BCmerquote,templateId=renderPrint.psml

Stephens, M. (2005) 'Lessons from the Past, Challenges for the Future', paper to the Housing Studies Association Conference, York.

Stone, E.M. (2006) 'What Is Housing Affordability? the Case for the Residual Income Approach', *Housing Policy Debate*, vol 17, no 1, pp 151–84.

Stone, M. (2009) *How Not to Beat the BNP: A Critique of the EHRC Report on Social Housing Allocation*, London: Civitas, www.civitas.org.uk/pdf/Stone_EHRCSocialHousing2009.pdf

Swenarton, M. (2009) *Building the New Jerusalem: Architecture, Housing and Politics 1900–1930*, Bracknell: Bre Press.

SWQ Consulting (2008) *Neighbourhood Management Pathfinders: Final Evaluation Report, People, Places, Public Services: Making the Connections*, London: DCL.

Tang, C.P.Y (2010) *Trends in Housing Association Stock in 2009*, Cambridge Centre for Housing and Planning Research, www.dataspring.org.uk/projects/detail.asp?ProjectID=77

Thatcher, M (1979) Letter to a council tenant, *The Times*, 9 April.

Thatcher, M. (1993) *The Downing Street Years*, London: HarperCollins.

Thatcher, M. (1995) *The Path to Power*, London: HarperCollins.

The Economist (2010) 'Global House Prices: Froth and Stagnation', 8 July.

The Lancet (1858), 12th February.

Thomas, B. and Dorling, D. (2004) *Know Your Place: Housing Wealth and Inequality in Great Britain 1980–2003 and Beyond*. Available at: http://england.shelter.org.uk/professional_resources/policy_library/policy_library_folder/know_your_place_-_housing_wealth_and_inequality_in_great_britain_1980-2003_and_beyond

Tinsley, J. and Jacobs, M. (2006) *Deprivation and Ethnicity in England: A Regional Perspective. An Analysis of Ethnicity and Levels of Deprivation in Different Local Areas, Within English Regions*, www.statistics.gov.uk/CCI/article.asp?ID=1560

Torgersen, U. (1987) 'Housing: The Wobbly Pillar Under the Welfare State', in B. Turner, J. Kemeny and L. Lundqvist (eds) *Between State and Market: Housing in the Post-Industrial Era*, Stockholm: Almqvist and Wiksell, pp 116–26.

TSA (Tenants Services Authority) (2010) *Regulatory and Statistical Return 2010*, www.tenantservicesauthority.org/upload/pdf/RSR2010_Statistical_Release.pdf

Tudor Walters, J. (1918) *Building Construction in Connection with the Provision of Dwellings for the Working Classes*, Cmd 9191, London: HMSO.

Tullock, G. (1976) *The Vote Motive*, London: Institute of Economic Affairs.

Tunstall, R. and Lupton, R. (2010) *Mixed Communities: Evidence Review*, London: DCL.

UN-HABITAT (2003) *The Challenge of Slums: Global Report On Human Settlements*, London, Earthscan Ltd.

UN-HABITAT (2007a) *Slums – Some Definitions*, www.unhabitat. org/downloads/docs/4625_1459_GC%2021%20Slums%20some%20 definitions.pdf

UN-HABITAT (2007b) 'Slum Dwellers to Double by 2030', www. unhabitat.org/downloads/docs/4631_46759_GC%2021%20Slum%20 dwellers%20to%20double.pdf

Voigtländer, M. (2009) 'Why Is the German Homeownership Rate So Low?' *Housing Studies*, vol 24, no 3, pp 355–72.

Waldron, J. (1993) 'Homelessness and the Issue of Freedom', in J. Waldron (ed) *Liberal Rights: Collected Papers 1981–91*, Cambridge: Cambridge University Press, pp 309–38.

Walker, B. and Niner, P. (2010) *Low Income Working Households in the Private Rented Sector*, London: Department for Work and Pensions.

Walker, P. (1977) *The Ascent of Britain*, London: Sidgwick and Jackson.

Wallace, A. (2010) *Remaking Community? New Labour and the Governance of Poor Neighbourhoods*, Farnham: Ashgate.

Ward, S.W. (2005) 'Consortium Developments Ltd and the Failure of "New Country Towns" in Mrs Thatcher's Britain', *Planning Perspectives*, vol 20, pp 329–59.

Watkinson, J. (2004) *Rebalancing Communities: Introducing Mixed Incomes into Existing Housing Estates*, London: Chartered Institute of Housing.

Watson, S. (with Austerberry, H.) (1986) *Housing and Homelessness: A Feminist Perspective*, London: Routledge.

Watts, D. (1992) *Joseph Chamberlain and the Challenge of Radicalism*, London: Hodder and Stoughton.

Webb, B. (1948) *Our Partnership*, London: Longman, Green and Co.

Webb, S. (1890) *Socialism in England*, London: Swan Soonenchien.

Webb, S. (1908) *The Basis & Policy of Socialism, Fabian Socialist Series No. 4*, London: Fabian Society.

Webb, S. and Webb, B. (1913) 'What is Socialism?', *New Statesman*, 10 May.

Weber, M. (1948 [1924]) 'Class, Status and Party', in H. Gerth and C.W. Mills (eds) *Essays from Max Weber*, London: Routledge and Kegan Paul, pp 180–95.

Weiler, P. (2003) 'The Conservatives' Search for a Middle Way in Housing, 1951–64', *Twentieth Century British History*, vol 14, no 4, pp 260–390.

Weiss, L. (1998) *The Myth of the Powerless State: Governing the Economy in a Global Era*, Cambridge: Polity Press.

Wells, H.G. (1905) *A Modern Utopia*, www.marxists.org/reference/archive/hgwells/1905/modern-utopia/ch02.htm

Whitehead, C. (2010) *Shared Ownership and Shared Equity: Reducing the Risks of Home-Ownership*, York: Joseph Rowntree Foundation.

Wilcox, S. (2009a) 'Devolution and Housing', in S. Wilcox (ed) *UK Housing Review 2009/10*, London: Chartered Institute of Housing/Council of Mortgage Lenders, pp 13–22.

Wilcox, S. (2009b) *UK Housing Review 2009/10*, London: Chartered Institute of Housing/Council of Mortgage Lenders.

Wilcox, S. (2011) 'Constraining choices: the housing benefit reforms' in H. Pawson, and S. Wilcox, *UK Housing Review 2010/11*, London: Chartered Institute of Housing , pp 32-40.

Wilkinson, K. and Noble, N. (2010) *Tackling Economic Deprivation in New Deal for Communities Areas*, London: DCL, www.communities.gov.uk/publications/communities/trackingeconomicdeprivation

Wilkinson, R. and Pickett, K. (2009) *The Spirit Level: Why More Equal Societies Almost Always Do Better*, London: Allen Lane.

Willetts, D. (2010) *The Pinch: How the Baby Boomers Took Their Children's Future – and Why They Should Give It Back*, Atlantic Books: London.

Wilson, W. (2001) *The Homelessness Bill*, House of Commons Research Paper 01/58, London: House of Commons.

Wilson, W. (2006) *Affordable Housing in England*, House of Commons Research Paper 06/41, London: House of Commons.

*Wilson, W. (2009) Overcrowded Housing, Standard Note SN/SP/101, London: House of Commons, www.*parliament.uk/commons/lib/research/briefings/snsp-01013.pdf

Wilson, W. (2010) *Houses in Multiple Occupation (HMOS) Standard Note SN/SP/708*, London: House of Commons.

Wilson, W. (2010a) *Overcrowded Housing*, Standard Note SN/SP/1013, London: House of Commons.

Wilson, W. (2010b) *Houses in multiple occupation* (HMOs) Standard Note SN/SP/708, London: House of Commons.

Wilson, W. (2011) *Localism Bill: Planning and Housing*, Research Paper 11/03, London: House of Commons.

Zero Carbon Hub (2010) *Carbon Compliance: What is the appropriate level for 2016? Interim Report*

http://www.zerocarbonhub.org/resourcefiles/Carbon_Compliance_Interim_Report_16_12_10.

Wilson, W. and Cracknell, R. (2010) *Housing Benefit: Implications of the June 2010 Budget, Standard Note SN/SP 5638*, www.parliament.uk/briefingpapers/commons/lib/research/briefings/snsp-05638.pdf

Wintour, P. (2008) 'Labour: If You Want a Council House, Find a Job', *Guardian*, 5 February.

Wise, S. (2008) *The Blackest Streets: The Life and Death of a Victorian Slum*, London: Vintage Books.

Wohl, A.S. (1977) *The Eternal Slum: Housing and Social Policy in Victorian London*, London: Edward Arnold.

Wohl, A.S. (1983) *Endangered Lives: Public Health in Victorian Britain*, London: Methuen.

Wordnet (2004). Available at: http://wordnet.princeton.edu/

World Bank (2000) *World Development Report 2000–2001*, Washington, DC: World Bank.

World Commission on the Environment and Development (1988) *Our Common Future*, London: Oxford University Press.

Wyly, E.K. (2010) 'The Subprime State of Race', in S.J. Smith and B.E. Searle (eds) *The Economics of Housing: The Housing Wealth of Nations*, Chichester: Wiley-Blackwell, pp 381–413.

Yelling, J.A. (1992) *Slums and Redevelopment: Policy and Practice in England, 1918–45, with Particular Reference to London*, London: UCL Press.

Young, I. (1990) *Justice and the Politics of Difference*, Princeton, NJ: Princeton University Press.

Young, K. and Kramer, J. (1978) *Strategy and Conflict in Metropolitan Housing: Suburbia versus the Greater London Council 1965–75*, London: Heinemann.

Young Foundation (2009) *Solutions for Entrenched Deprivation on Small Estates: Scoping Paper January 2009*, www.youngfoundation.org/files/images/Small_estates_scoping_paper_WEB_VERSION.pdf

Zielenbach, S. (2005) *The Economic Impact of HOPE VI on Neighbourhoods*, Washington: Housing Research Foundation.

Index

Note: The letter f following a page number indicates a figure, n a footnote and t a table

A

Acceptable Behaviour Contracts 225
Access to Local Authority and Housing Association Tenancies (DoE) 162
Acts
  Act for the Regulation and Inspection of Common Lodging Houses (1851) 199
  Act for the Relief of the Poor (1601) 157–8
  American Dream Downpayment Act (2003) 109
  American Recovery and Reinvestment Act (2009) 110
  Anti-Social Behaviour Act (2003) 225
  Artisans' and Labourers' Dwellings Act (1868) 178
  Artisans' and Labourers' Dwellings Improvement Act (1875) 178–9
  Building Societies Act (1986) 63, 89
  Cheap Trains Act (1883) 47
  Climate Change Act (2008) 189
  Crime and Disorder Act (1998) 225
  Cross Act *see* Artisans' and Labourers' Dwellings Improvement Act
  Equality Act (2010) 236, 245, 251
  Government of Wales Act (2006) 96
  Green Belt (London and Home Counties) Act (1938) 276
  Homelessness Act (2002) 81, 163–4
  House Purchase and Housing Act (1959) 181
  Housing Act (1923) 50
  Housing Act (1925) 51
  Housing Act (1930) 50, 131, 179, 180
  Housing Act (1935) 50, 192–3
  Housing Act (1949) 181
  Housing Act (1957) 193
  Housing Act (1969) 181
  Housing Act (1974) 182
  Housing Act (1980) 63, 140
  Housing Act (1985) 197
  Housing Act (1988) 36, 64, 65, 66
  Housing Act (1996) 36, 153–5, 162–3
  Housing Act (2004) 93, 141, 184, 195, 201–2, 214, 225
  Housing (Additional Powers) Act (1919) 51
  Housing and Planning Act (1909) 48

  Housing and Town Planning Act (1919) 49, 50, 130, 179
  Housing Executive (Northern Ireland) Act (1971) 78
  Housing Finance Act (1972) 60, 61, 122, 131–2
  Housing (Financial Provisions) Act (1924) 50
  Housing (Financial Provisions) Act (1933) 49, 50
  Housing Grants, Construction and Regeneration Act (1996) 183
  Housing (Homeless Persons) Act (1977) 160–1, 169, 170, 174–5, 200
  Housing Regeneration Act (2008) 274
  Housing Repairs and Rents Act (1954) 181
  Housing (Rural Workers) Act (1926) 180
  Housing (Scotland) Act (2001) 141, 173
  Housing (Scotland) Act (2003) 173–4
  Housing (Scotland) Act (2006) 95
  Immigration and Asylum Act (1999) 173
  Labouring Classes Lodging Houses Act (1851) 130, 199
  Local Government Act (1999) 81
  Local Government and Housing Act (1989) 183
  National Assistance Act (1948) 159–60
  New Towns Act (1946) 54
  Planning and Compulsory Purchase Act (2004) 77
  Poor Law Amendment Act (1834) 159
  Public Health Act (1848) 45
  Public Health Act (1875) 46, 177, 192
  Quality Housing and Work Responsibility Act (1998) (USA) 110
  Race Relations Act (1968) 243
  Race Relations Act (1976) 244, 245
  Reform Act (1832) 17
  Reform Act (1884) 18
  Rent Act (1957) 57
  Restriction of Ribbon Development Act (1935) 52
  Sex Discrimination Act (1975) 237
  Small Dwellings Acquisitions Act (1899) 51
  Torrens Act *see* Artisans' and Labourers' Dwellings Act

317

Dunleavy, P. 34–5, 58–9
Durkheim, Emile 32

E

EA *see* Estate Action Initiative
EHRC *see* Equality and Human Rights
  Commission
eco-towns 148, 189
Economist (journal) 259
education 219, 264
elderly people 253
elections, general 23–4 *see also* vote: right
  to; voters
Elphicke, N. 83, 274
emissions 90, 188, 189, 190
employment
  lone parents 237
  tenants 219, 267
  voucher system 249
energy 25, 190
Engels, Friedrich 9, 19
English House Condition Survey 183–4,
  188
English Partnerships 75
Englishness 18
enveloping 183
Equal Opportunities Commission
  see Equality and Human Rights
  Commission
equality 31, 229–30, 231
Equality and Human Rights Commission
  (EHRC) 138, 235–6
equity-sharing 144
Esping-Andersen, G. 105
An Essay on the Principle of Population
  (Malthus) 10
essentialism 12
Estate Action Initiative (EA) 207
estate agents: racial discrimination by 243,
  245
Estate Management Boards 87, 206
estates
  design 32
  Liverpool 131
  Mixed Community Demonstration
    Initiative 222–3
  priority 205–6
  problem 207–8
  and redevelopment 35
  and social class 232
  see also council housing; Design
    Improvement Controlled Experiment
Estates: An Intimate History (Hanley) 41
ethnic minorities 221, 224 *see also* Asians;
  Black Caribbeans; immigrants
ethnicity

definition of 240
and homelessness 241
and housing 240–3, 245–6
and labour market 245–6
and racism 243–5
and segregation 246, 248–50
social and economic circumstances of
  247t
Etzioni, A. 29
European Commission
  and energy efficiency 105
  *Housing Exclusion: Welfare Policies Housing
    Provision and the Labour Markets* 105
European Union 104–5
Eurostat 127
exclusion *see* discrimination; othering;
  social exclusion
experts 31–2, 44

F

Fabian socialism 7, 8–9, 11, 15, 32, 34
Fabian Society 49
Fair Deal for Housing (DoE) 60–1
A Fairer Future for Social Housing (DCL)
  265–6
families
  concepts of 237
  deprived 264, 267
  and homelessness 155, 156f, 159, 160–1,
    164–5, 170
  and overcrowding 191
The Family (Bosanquet) 18
Feijten, P. 237
feminists 237, 239
filtering theory 5, 130, 275
financial institutions 69 *see also* Bank of
  England; banks; building societies
Financial Services Authority 259–60
Finch, N. 103, 104
Finney, N.: *'Sleepwalking to Segregation'?
  Challenging Myths about Race and
  Migration* 248–9
fire safety 200
*Firm Foundations: The Future of Housing in
  Scotland* (Scottish Government) 174
fitness standard 184
Fitzpatrick, S. 170
flats 59–60
  prefabricated (Czech Republic) 118
  Right to Buy 142
  safety-net standards 269
  subsidies 50, 193
  see also Design Improvement Controlled
    Experiment; Estate Action Initiative;
    housing: high-rise; tower blocks
Flint, Caroline 41